Encounters with Loneliness: Only the Lonely

Edited by Arlene Kramer Richards,
Lucille Spira and
Arthur A. Lynch

IPBOOKS
International Psychoanalytic Books

Contents

Acknowledgments

It took a village to grow from experiences with lonely patients to an idea about the usefulness of focusing on loneliness in treatment, to a study group on the topic, to a symposium on the topic, to an idea for a book on loneliness and now to the manuscript we have assembled here. This anthology was a communal effort. As the editors, we thank the authors for generously sharing their ideas, and describing their feelings about working with the lonely patient. We especially treasure their sharing of moments of their own loneliness with patients and in their lives as these impacted on their treatment.

Tamar Schwartz and Lawrence L. Schwartz of IPBooks were instrumental in coordinating this project., designing covers, doing publicity, and spending many hours helping to format this document for print publication. Matthew Bach, our diplomatic line editor, was there to suggest revisions and fine-tune wherever it was needed. Arnold Richards, our publisher, gave us his full enthusiasm and support. Elizabeth Ronis and the members of the Symposium on Loneliness Committee, who developed and coordinated the March 2012 symposium, deserve acknowledgment for their contribution. Richard Gottlieb merits special recognition for undertaking the task of pulling the red thread through each author's paper to form a conclusion. A thank you goes to Dr. Harold P. Blum. We are honored that he undertook to write the Foreword for our book.

—The Editors

Arlene Kramer Richards:

Having had the support and advice of so many friends and family that I hardly know where to begin, I have to thank my parents for giving me the first-rate education neither of them had for themselves; my teachers and fellow students at the University of Chicago, for honing my mind and helping me to respect my intellect, the architects of that Great Books program; the friends and colleagues at IPTAR and the Contemporary Freudian Society, who entrusted me with referrals for clinical work; Dr. George Gross, who read the Standard Edition of Freud with a group of psychologists interested in learning psychoanalysis; Martin Bergmann, who insisted on continuing our seminar on psychoanalytic technique for so many years, the other members of that group; John DeCecco and Irene Willis, the co-authors who taught me how to write, and all the patients who taught me how to help them.

I have had the good fortune to become the proud colleague of two former students, Lucille Spira and Arthur Lynch, who have inspired, collaborated on, and made this book happen.

Most of all I want to thank my children, Stephen Richards, Rebecca Richards and Tamar Schwartz, for putting up with my focus on school and career during their growing up years and cheering me on when I needed it; and my husband Arnold Richards, for supporting me through graduate school and into the early years of my practice and from whom I continue to learn every day.

Lucille Spira:

While loneliness has been, from my earliest memories, a persistent presence and force in my life, so many deserve thanks for helping me to attenuate and weather its sting. For their support and love, I thank Bill Spira and my family. My good fortune is to have Carol Munter as my "go-to" friend; she generously brings her clarity and creativity to all my endeavors. Other friends and colleagues, among them, Lillian Berman, Barbara Rauch, Lynne Herbst, Linda Halperin, Laura Melano Flanagan, Paul Mulinski, and the late Eda Goldstein, each in their unique way have made my world warmer and wider.

My patients, for sharing their narratives, experiences and encounters with loneliness, deserve recognition for all that they teach me. My professional education at Smith College School for Social Work and New York University School of Social Work provided a solid foundation for my becoming a psychotherapist. My studies at the Institute for the Study of Psychotherapy, my attendance at the Wednesday Martin Bergmann Seminar, and my affiliation with the New York School of Psychoanalytic Psychotherapy and Psychoanalysis, enriched my professional and personal life immeasurably.

This project, and the others on loneliness where I participated, would not have happened without the interest and generosity shown by Arlene Kramer Richards. Her graciously sharing her wealth of experience, intellectual and clinical knowledge, over years, affirms for me why she is esteemed in her profession and so valued by all of us who know her. Arthur Lynch's willingness to take on any task that was needed, coupled with his good humor and repertoire of talents, contributed to making this project a pleasure. For being there and making our encounters stimulating and fun, I thank you both.

Arthur Lynch:

There should always be too many people to thank when one completes a project. So, thank you to my friends, colleagues and candidates who have welcomed me for over a decade at the American Institute for Psychoanalysis of the Karen Horney Center. Thank you all for providing the potential space to grow with you. To the many patients who have allowed me to enter their lives with the hopes of something better, thank you for showing me how to be helpful.

Specifically, I want to thank Dr. Arnold Richards, who led our Freud Study Group for 10 years. Here my fellow Freudian compatriots and I learned Freud's work page by page, bit by bit. Arnie treated the Freudian corpus like a dream, readily tying the concepts of each specific work to the residue of the day. The study group also became a launching pad for many creative projects.

Walking into Arlene Kramer Richards' class was a life-changing event that took years to grasp. My gratitude for her influence is profound. I am also grateful for having been so warmly welcomed by her and Lucille Spira to participate in this project.

My deepest appreciation goes to my family to my mother, now deceased and my father, still a role model for generativity, who taught me empathy and care for those who suffer; to my wife Lourdes Rigual-Lynch, who is the source of my love and my closest friend for the last 40 years—words are not enough; to my daughter Megan, whose accomplishments and courage often astound me.

Preface: *Encounters with Loneliness: Only the Lonely*

> Loneliness expresses the pain of being alone and
> solitude expresses the glory of being alone.
> —Paul Tillich

Almost ten years ago, Arlene Kramer Richards and Lucille Spira began a discussion group—Towards an Understanding of Loneliness and Aloneness in Women (now, Towards an Understanding of Loneliness and Aloneness)—at the American Psychoanalytic Association meetings in New York City. The enthusiasm generated there for exploring loneliness in all its manifestations spurred us to delve more deeply into the dynamics of loneliness. We continued this group where we and our guests presented cases in which loneliness and or social isolation were major themes.

Our thanks go to those who shared their experiences in working with what we believe is a highly challenging group of patients: Jerome S. Blackman, Nancy Cromer Grayson, Jane Kupersmidt, Annette Leavy, Arthur A. Lynch, Eric K. Milliner, Carol Munter, Sidney Phillips, Lisa Piazza, Arlene Kramer Richards, George Sagi, Lucille Spira, Jeffrey Stern, Matthew von Unwerth, Urban Vestin, Martin Widzer, Brent Willock, Sara Zarem, and literary scholar Victor Brombert.

Exposure to these narratives of clinical situations, coupled with reading the relevant psychoanalytic literature, enlarged what we learned from the narratives of our own patients and our own experiences. All of these sources informed our understanding of the variables that drive painful loneliness. Later we included contributions from social science theory, literary works, and other art forms in order to enrich our understanding of what we see as a ubiquitous human experience. As we became more sensitive to the role loneliness plays in our own lives and in the lives of our patients, we had more questions than answers. What drives loneliness? Who or what are the lonely longing for? Who is vulnerable to the more painful forms of loneliness? What is the inner experience of the lonely person? How can loneliness be resolved? *Encounters with Loneliness: Only the Lonely* addresses some of these questions through the unfolding of ideas and experiences of psychoanalytically oriented clinicians, a number of whom presented on this topic at the symposium On Loneliness that met in New York City in March of 2012, chaired by Arthur Lynch.

Encounters with Lonelines: Only the Lonely demonstrates the ways in which psychotherapy, psychoanalysis, and artistic productions, are used to mitigate a person's loneliness and alienation by strengthening the connection to self and other. We hope that the contributions here will help to illuminate the dimensions of loneliness so that we can better enable our patients to find their own unique solutions to their loneliness.

Foreword to Loneliness
By Harold P. Blum[1]

This remarkable anthology of fascinating papers on loneliness is unique in the psychoanalytic literature. Although loneliness is a universal ubiquitous experience, it has not previously been discussed in the rich variety of its sources and manifestations. There have been scattered valuable papers on loneliness in the past, but never before brought together in a kaleidoscopic collection allowing a survey of different definitions, approaches, perspectives, and conclusions. This anthology includes different avenues of investigation, varied approaches, multiple dimensions, clarifications, and understandings, as well as questions and controversies about loneliness. The four sections of the book: Loneliness, Creativity and Artists; Clinical Dimensions of Loneliness; Loneliness/Solitude in the Psychoanalytic Training Process; Loneliness and Life Events testify to the encompassing scope of the inquiry into this relatively neglected, yet very important subject. A great many otherwise lonely ideas resonate with each other, enhancing our understanding of the breadth of this topic. This book is so wide ranging that it is not possible in a brief foreword to cite specific authors' formulations and propositions. I will include some of my own thoughts.

Though a universal emotional experience, loneliness was not well-defined in the past. In this book loneliness is considered to be a painful longing for the missing absent love object. Loneliness is experienced as unpleasure on a spectrum from frustrating and disappointing to unbearable torment. Loneliness may imply secure rather than avoidant or disorganized attachment. For the analytic patient, the analyst's vacation frequently is associated with loneliness and both overt and unconscious separation reactions. One can be lonely in a crowd, desirous of the specific object and an intimate relationship; loneliness can also be elicited in a crowd by seeing people apparently pleasurably attached to each other. Though loneliness is usually regarded as a feeling state to be avoided, it may be consciously or unconsciously sought, paradoxically for creative, as well as narcissistic and masochistic motives.

Loneliness overlaps with, but is distinguished from solitude. Solitude may be sought and may be pleasurable. Loneliness is usually experienced as unpleasant and troublesome. Loneliness may be transformed into solitude. Solitude may be actively chosen, whereas loneliness is hardly chosen, but endured. Contrary to the absence of the love object, solitude may represent self-

---

[1] Dr. Harold P. Blum is Executive Director, Sigmund Freud Archives; Training and Supervising Analyst, Institute for Psychoanalytic Education, Affiliated with New York University School of Medicine; Past Editor in Chief, *Journal of the American Psychoanalytic Association* and Past Vice President, International Psychoanalytical Association.

possession or omnipotent control of the ambivalently loved object. The absent object may be displaced onto a representation of the object, a part object, a project, a work of art, etc. Drugs may be used to relieve loneliness, based on pharmacological effects as well as the drug unconsciously representing a comforting or consoling object. The drug may also be regarded as the dangerous split off object who may punish or retaliate against the self. Drugs may alleviate loneliness or paradoxically foster loneliness consequent to impairment of relatedness and social activity.

Solitude may also serve the reality principle, avoiding distraction, unwanted intrusion and safeguarding attention to the task at hand. The section of the book "Loneliness and Creativity" provides original stimulating discourse on the lonely artist and scientist, and on the person who is creative and highly original while working alone. Unconscious fantasy is yet an ever present influence in the most solitary reality oriented activity. Some states of mind, such as meditation or novel affective and cognitive hypnoid states clearly require the interaction of fantasy and reality though flights of imagination or realistic judgment may be dominant at any time. Meditation may permit fantasy contact with absent spirit objects, e.g. ancestors, in an imaginary ambivalent world at a protective distance from reality. Separation, abandonment anxieties associated with loneliness or solitude may be compensated by fantasies of fusion, togetherness, or rebirth and final reunion. The creative personality may have special access to regressive fantasies of separation and merger.

Companionship is aptly discussed as the compensation for loneliness. Eve was created from Adam's rib to provide a companion for lonely Adam. When Adam and Eve are exiled from the Garden of Eden, they leave the paradise of blissful union with the divine. They undergo the process of separation-individuation, struggling toward independent existence, on the road toward object and self constancy. With the absent love object securely internalized and consolidated in object and self representations, the lonely exile can tolerate "paradise lost". Lonely independence may be a stimulus or goad toward creativity. Gepetto creates Pinocchio from wood to substitute for his absent wife. Imaginary companions of childhood have appeared as characters in the creative productions of authors who have experienced childhood object loss. Persons exposed to extreme prolonged isolation as in isolation chamber experiments will often hallucinate voices and images of their self and object relationships. In the imperfect narcissistic withdrawal of sleep and dream, the dreamer is not alone; the dream invokes past and present self and object relationships. The person to whom the dream is reported will characteristically represent a disguised object of both past and present wishes and conflicts. In the myth of Pygmalion and Galatea, Pygmalion's love for the beautiful Galatea sculpture he created proves to be highly ambivalent. Pygmalion's wife has left him, and Galatea's magical becoming alive engenders the danger of conflict between reality and fantasy, as well as the dangers of separation and merger. As development proceeds from infancy to childhood, Oedipus travels the lonely road in search of his biological parents and the answer to the riddle of where babies come from. His reunion with his mother in incest union is universally both desired and condemned, fated and tragic. Deprived adolescent girls who have babies frequently view the infant as compensation for loneliness and unconsciously fantasy a restoration of their own mother-child relationship. Some deprived mothers yearning and lonely for their mothers may enjoy the intimacy with their infant, only to be threatened when the infant develops toward greater independence. Narcissistic individuals may display a detached pseudo-independence, while attempting omnipotent control of their affects, impulses and their self-centered self-object world.

Since loneliness is consequent to separation and loss, a number of authors address mourning. To mourn acknowledges loss of the object or a valued aspect of the self, the ideal self, or part of the self. The person in mourning longs for the absent object and may utilize both realistic and pathogenic forms of adaptation to the loss. Phantom limb is a form of imaginary substitution for the amputated part, with a neurobiological foundation for the fantasy. Painful mourning generally coalesces with the torment of loneliness. The availability of other caring objects, the capacity to be alone and the capacity to sublimate and to eventually replace the lost object with an appropriate new object varies with the individual's age, personality and life circumstances. Prolonged or delayed mourning may be an attempt to avoid loneliness by preserving the lost object; on the other hand it may prolong loneliness by precluding the investment in other relationships. Working through mourning and depressive affect leads to new integration and internalization of what was lost and greater capacity to enjoy both solitude and social contact.

Is there an age or gender relationship to loneliness? Those in advanced age are more likely to be lonely, enduring loss of family and friends who have died earlier. Object loss, narcissistic regression, and physical decline limit relationships, intensifying loneliness. Loneliness merges with tragedy in the desolate figure of King Lear. The architect of his own undoing, remorseless, yet filled with rage and guilt, Lear is mournful, doleful, and pitiful in his solitary grandeur. Alone, facing catastrophic loss with new fortitude and insight, he is so sadly wise only after he is old. Lonely Lear becomes the paradox of the hero and anti-hero with whom we can empathically identify.

Aged, lonely therapists may be reluctant to terminate patients, facing their own professional retirement, loss of professional identity, diminished self esteem, and the last years of life before final separation. A lonely therapist may arrange to see patients on vacations, weekends, or holidays, not only to benefit a needy patient, but to avoid their own disappointing isolation. Analyst and patient may jointly avoid separation. That the last papers of some prominent analysts were on the topic of loneliness is not surprising, given an inevitable autobiographical perspective to their farewell contributions. The candidate analyst may also feel lonely in the maelstrom of his/her own analysis and doing analytic work with patients.

The candidate is in a two person analytic situation, subject to the unfamiliar exigencies of transference and counter-transference pressures. The candidate tyro may feel lonely in the novel experience of analytic intimacy, in the context of maintaining an analytic attitude and framework, and the uncertain choices of silence, non interpretative intervention, and interpretation.

Those relatively scarce papers on loneliness will no longer be lonely in the analytic literature. They are now joined by their thought provoking multi-focal companions in this original, extraordinary anthology, so poignantly pertinent to the human condition.

Introduction
Arthur A. Lynch

Loneliness is perhaps one of the most painful affective states a person can experience. Fromm-Reichmann (1959) noted that it is something we usually try to avoid at all costs. It is a subjective experience that most of us have had to some degree, at some point in our lives, and we have usually experienced it in many ways. Loneliness can be experienced in intense states of psychic disintegration prompted by severe mental illness or catastrophic events, which lead to intense feelings of emptiness and dread; or, an isolation from others, both internal and/or external. Loneliness can, also, be experienced as a loss; in grief or mourning—loneliness in the presence of others. The nature of loneliness can be understood by dimensions of duration (e.g., temporary or chronic) or by dimensions of disposition (situational or developmental). The dimensions of disposition offer a simple way to differentiate the painful affect of loneliness.

The first group, situational factors, can often lend to a sense of loneliness. For example, loneliness may be determined on a cultural level by those who experience the hatred of the dominant group. Living under the oppression of any form of government (e.g., fascism, despotism, dictatorship, or autocracy) especially if the individual is not in synch with the prevailing ideology, leaves that person at risk to live their life in fear and isolation; who would not have otherwise. In the same way, being the subject of racism, ethnic, gender or religious hatred leaves the individual profoundly alienated in his/her own community. Likewise, loneliness can be elicited from a brief but painful moment of isolation/loss. This can come about when one is leaving home, family and friends. Loneliness can be a prevailing affect as one enters and invests in a new life but has not yet developed the necessary substantial relationships needed to avert loneliness. Loneliness can occur with serious illness or ageing, especially if the illness leads to a loss of function. This leaves a longing for who one used to be. Loneliness can have an even more profound effect when the loss occurs from death, or even when it occurs in life, when the object of the loss is someone loved. Many of the authors in this volume express a similar notion that loneliness is the bedrock of becoming human, to understand loneliness is to understand the core of the individual. Winnicott (1969) tried to get at something similar by identifying the birth of the subjective as necessitating destruction of the mother, who manages to survive the attack. This repeated action transforms the subjective object into the subject and the object.

What determines the depth and duration of the agonizing emotional response has to do with the second group of experiences. These consist of life's developmental events (e.g., trauma, neglect) that have interfered with an individual's ability to fully develop a sustaining inner life. This often begins at a very young age (Winnicott 1958, 1969; Stierlin 1965–1966; Sullivan 1953). Many believe that it is this inner life that acts as an antidote to periods of isolation or aloneness. This group would include: Fairbairn 1963; Anna Freud,

1958; Fromm Reichmann, 1959; Jacobson, 1954, 1961; Klein, 1963; Mahler, Pine, Bergman, & Pine 1975; Stern,1985; Stierlin, 1965–1966; Winnicott, 1958; to name just a very few. It is in this group that we find Sartre's definition so apt. He proposed that loneliness was an essential feature of the human condition that arose from the conflict between the need to create meaning in life and the awareness of isolation or nothingness in the universe. So often this is defined by the nature of one's inner life. Sartre's contribution succeeds Rilke (1943) who also suggests that loneliness is an inevitable part of life, but understands its condition as made profoundly painful when the person sets one's will against it.

When we think of loneliness as temporary or chronic conditions we see yet another dimension of this affect. Chronic loneliness has been linked to genetic, physical (e.g., cancer, stroke, high blood pressure and cardiovascular disease) and psychological (e.g., depression and schizoid pathology, impaired cognition and personal determination, sleep disturbance, suicide, alcoholism and substance abuse) difficulties. As we can see from the variety of manifestations, loneliness is often a complex phenomenom in both its aetiology and presentation, which always presents uniquely to the individual.

These factors of loneliness help to define this painful affect as typically a destructive state. We can, however, also differentiate it further from other states of aloneness, e.g., such as solitude, that do not carry the painful anguish as part of its character and often serve constructive aims.

It is an interesting side bar that searching the Psychoanalytic Electronic Publisher's (PEP) database for titles concerning loneliness identified about 37 articles. Another search for "loneliness" as a key word or phrase in articles led to the identification of 4,125 citations. This may reflect what other authors have noted: that there are few publications that are dedicated to studying loneliness but it remains a powerful descriptor in our literature.

The aims of this book are to explore this vast domain of loneliness from a broad psychoanalytic perspective. The authors have put together 18 chapters that address, in four sections: loneliness creativity and the artist, the clinical dimensions of loneliness, loneliness in psychoanalytic training, loneliness in life events. Each section is preceded by an introduction and series of questions for each of the chapters. The final section is followed by a conclusion.

The book begins as four authors explore the topics of loneliness and creativity in the artist. This section opens with Lois Oppenheim's chapter, "A voice comes to one in the dark. Imagine.": Samuel Beckett's Search for Company. In this chapter, Oppenheim shows how a person can long for, while simultaneously be unable to tolerate, being with another person. She uses the work of Beckett to distinguish between loneliness and solitude and uses a part of his life story to reveal why loneliness, solitude, and isolation so dominate his work.

Chapter Two explores the Artists' Solitude and the creative process. In this chapter, Danielle Knafo, examines aspects of solitude in relation to creativity and personal transformation. She argues that solitude and relatedness are layered and interactive states and act as a core feature of the human condition. Knafo explores the uniqueness of women's solitude and relational needs that the art object serves for their creators. She closes the chapter with a consideration of the heroics of creative solitude.

Arlene Kramer Richards, in Chapter Three, turns to the question: What makes a woman? She employs the film "The Skin I Live in" as her vehicle for exploring this bedrock question. Key moments in the film occupy our thoughts as she reveals why, for Almodovar, loneliness and social isolation take the dominant role in the formation of becoming a woman, and becoming human.

In Chapter Four, "Forms and Transformations of Loneliness," Jeffrey Stern takes us back to the cinema to review *Hugo,* the story of a young boy and old filmmaker who save one another from the despair of their individual loneliness. Here clock and puppet repair are the metaphors for reparation. Stern expands this theme to the loneliness of monsters, represented in: The Phantom of the Opera, The Elephant Man, the fairy tale Hans the Hedgehog and in Shakespeare's The Taming of the Shrew. He concludes the paper with a brief consideration of Wim Wender's film "Wings of Desire".

Section II encompasses five chapters dedicated to working with loneliness in the clinical situation. The authors, in this section, address through case illustration the psychological and social dimensions of loneliness; treatment of loneliness in heterosexual men, the multiple expressions of loneliness, the intricate nature of loneliness and witnessing as the essential component of treatment. Beginning in Chapter Five "Shades of Loneliness: Psychological and Social Perspectives" Lucille Spira discusses the cases of Ms. A. and Ms. Y. to illustrate how biological, psychological and social events, past and present can contribute to a state of loneliness. Through examining the multiple components of loneliness Spira makes the case we will be better equipped to understand, constructively intervene and help these patients to overcome these painful states of experience. Going through each of these variables carefully Spira, also, shows how the social and psychological factors often intertwine and contribute to the persistent nature of loneliness.

"The Treatment of Lonely Heterosexual Men" is discussed by Jerome S. Blackman in Chapter Six. Blackman describes loneliness, as a multi-faceted problem, and in three cases of men (Anthony, Tom & Hank), he shows how pathological loneliness was accompanied by a sense of "giving up". Their divergent personality development was multiply determined and emphasized loss, neglect, and lack of (or symbiotic) attachment during early childhood and/or adolescence. Blackman explores the pathology and treatment of these three different men. He examines how their shared difficulties of empathy and trust interfered in their relations with women and was due to a loneliness, which could be determined as normal, as a defensive reaction to trauma, or as due to severe problems in object relations. In the treatment, he emphasizes the need for differential use of supportive, relational, and interpretive intervention strategies. Blackman posited the use of "object clarification" in cases of lonely heterosexual men, which involves: clarifying compromise formations that center on giving up, accumulate knowledge about the involved woman, and explain where possible potential reasons for the woman's reactions. Blackman discusses several other technical interventions and provides an elucidation of: unconscious defense, inhibition, and conflict; education regarding object relatedness and intergender relations in general and related to past life experiences with women.

In, "Exploring the Emergent Experience of Loneliness in Two Men During Their Psychoanalytic Journey," Chapter Seven, Anita Weinreb Katz demonstrates the nature and existence of loneliness. She sees loneliness as a universal condition that varies based on the awareness of it, the capacity to bear it, and the intensity of the experience itself. Relying on Ogden (1989), Winnicott (1965) and others she notes that loneliness is a developmental achievement requiring that one gain the capacity to be aware that s/he is attached to another, as well as an awareness that s/he may also be separate from the other. This separateness can fall between joyful to tormenting. To illustrate her point, she presents two cases: Bryan and Dan. These men share symptoms of protectively retreating into fantasy (sexual and aggressive) when their longing for an ideal object is thwarted (Richards and Spira, 2003). Both men carried intensely ambivalent feelings towards their fathers and traumatic early object ties to their mothers. Both develop phobic reactions to intimacy experiencing it as fear of the loss of breath and/or death. Though these symptoms were congruent the two men were distinctly different in presentation and disposition. For Katz the problem isn't in talking about loneliness the problem is in becoming aware of it. It is a phenomena rarely introduced by the patient but when proposed it is frequently recognized.

In Chapter Eight, Arthur Lynch takes the reader through the treatment of a young man whose complicated development was reflected in a series of character defenses that protected him from a subjective sense of his many losses. In this case, traditional analytic technique is used to identify the unconscious conflict and the multiple character defense structures used in a myriad of pathological compromise formations aimed at protecting the analysand from further pain. In this case loneliness acts as both a dreaded pain to be avoided and as a defensive constellation against an underlying state of depression.

Closing Section II is Jenny Kahn Kaufmann and Peter Kaufmann's chapter on "Witnessing: Its Essentialness in Psychoanalytic Treatment". The witnessing concept has been recognized for its important role in psychoanalytic treatment, which has proved especially useful in the work with individuals who have suffered severe trauma. The Kaufmanns review this concept and consider alternate practices of psychodynamic therapies often used with this population, with detrimental effects. They illustrate their ideas in the case of Lenore. In this treatment process, the use of witnessing and interpretation have helped her to face, feel, and integrate her painful formative experiences increasing her sense of self and availability to others.

Section III is dedicated to investigating the nature of loneliness/solitude endemic to the Psychoanalytic Training Process. This section consists of chapters by a candidate in training and three senior analysts who focus on the learning process in training. This includes the loneliness/solitude: of the candidates, with specific attention to the process of identification; from the chair of the supervising or consultant analyst/therapist; of the training analyst; and, in Institute life.

Jamieson Webster's "The Loneliness of the Candidate: Solitude and Solicited Identifications" opens the section with a chapter that looks at an elaboration of her personal passage as a candidate in psychoanalytic training, entwined with the story of another young analysand Rosine Lefort. Lefort who when beginning to treat psychotic children in a foundling hospital during her training analysis, felt she needed to leave her analysis for a period of time and work in almost complete solitude. These two stories emerge with theoretical considerations of Lacan and Klein shedding light on the question of loneliness and the experience of training to be a psychoanalyst.

Chapter Eleven introduces "Loneliness and Solitude in the Psychoanalytic Training Process—from the Chair of the Supervising Analyst." In this chapter Douglas H. Ingram looks at loneliness from the vantage point of the supervising analyst or consulting therapist; a term he uses to broaden the role to any supervising therapist. Ingram begins by providing a context for loneliness. Next he offers a case that demonstrates how waiting for a needed object/other provides a psychic substitution for the missing object/other and hence converts a lesser suffering for the greater anguish of loneliness. Ingram distinguishes and explores the therapist's solitude and loneliness from the patient and the therapist's solitude and loneliness with the patient.

Eric Mendelsohn, in Chapter Twelve, examines "The Loneliness of the Training Analyst." Mendelsohn focuses on the role and participation of the training analyst in the clinical setting and within the interpersonal world of the analytic institute. He understands loneliness as: a state of estrangement from self potentiated by an array of interpersonal circumstances. He then highlights the conditions that promote loneliness as a psychic state experienced by training analysts, and describes the clinical challenges and opportunities for clinical engagement.

The section concludes with Chapter Thirteen, "There Is No Place Like Home." This chapter takes its title from the Wizard of Oz as Dorothy expresses her wish to return home. This is a wish that Seiden (2012) believes is universal and more central to human motivation than all the other drive derivatives. Sandra Buechler borrowing from this allegory notes that the lonely analyst yearns for home. This home can be an internal refuge populated with relatively benevolent and caring supervisory images and other objects. This "internal chorus," she notes, can modify our more painful and alienating clinical experiences. Along with an example of an internalized supervisory object, this chapter suggests ways that institutes can become more welcoming homes for their candidates and graduates.

Section IV describes loneliness as it courses through certain life circumstances: the life cycle, widowhood, and life in the armed services. Chapter Fourteen investigates "Loneliness and the Life Cycle." Brent Willock examines the importance of loneliness with biopsychosocial factors that course through Erikson's life cycle. This work is expanded to include the two primary configurations of personality and psychopathology in relation to this life cycle. Willock argues that loneliness and longing, and their opposite state, are crucial emotional/relational constellations that are found in each phase of the life cycle and central to the overall constellation of the individual.

In Chapter Fifteen, Alma Halbert Bond captures "Marilyn Monroe, the Loneliest Person on Earth." Born to a woman suffering from schizophrenia and a father she never got to meet Marilyn Monroe was handed over to foster care at the tender age of 12 days old. This impossible beginning led to a life time of loneliness and ended in the tragic way that it seemed destined to. Alma Halbert Bond takes us through a glimpse of this life and shows how life's turns provided an extreme anguish in the midst of glitter and fame.

Patsy Turrini turns our attention in Chapter Sixteen to widowhood in "The Death of the Loved Spouse, the Inner World of Grief: A Psychoanalytic Developmental Perspective." Starting with Freud, Turrini reviews several psychoanalytic theorists' perspective on loss and mourning and concludes that painful normal mourning, as well as states of "separation anxiety" in adulthood can be partly understood in light of early painful losses and the emergence of the self. But the conviction of personal existence, of a self, is often connected to the availability of the external object (loved one) and the death of the loved spouse can cause a 'loss of one's sense of being.' Loneliness permeates a myriad of tortured biological developmental prewired experiences. Turrini expands our understanding of the inner world of grief and its composition of loneliness.

This section concludes with a rare view into the world of a soldier. Amit Goldenberg and Nathan Szajnberg, present "A Soldier's Loneliness" in Chapter Seventeen. Here they explore how a soldier can experience loneliness, solitude and aloneness when they are surrounded by their buddies and faced with enemies. The story of three soldiers from an elite combat unit is presented. From their experiences we learn about the continuum of loneliness, how one's pre-soldier inner life effects these critical moments reflecting ambivalence even with one's firearm, which as a rule must always be with the soldier. Listen to the soldiers themselves in this chapter and see how Goldenberg and Szajnberg organize these stories.

This volume concludes with an integrative summary and wrap up by Richard Gottlieb.

References

Fairbairn, W.R.D., (1963). An object relations theory of the personality. In: *From Instinct to Self: The Selected Papers of W.R.D. Fairbairn. Vol. I. Clinical and Theoretical Papers,* eds. E. Fairbairn Birtle & E.D. Scharff. Northvale, NJ: Jason Aronson, 1994, pp. 155–156.

Freud, A. (1958). Adolescence. *Psychoanalytic Study of the Child* 13:255–278.

Fromm-Reichmann, F. (1959). Loneliness. *Psychiatry* 22:1–15.

Jacobson, E. (1961). Adolescent moods and the remodeling of psychic structures in adolescence. *Psychoanalytic Study of the Child* 16:164–183.

Klein, M. (1963). On the sense of Loneliness. In: *Envy and Gratitude and Other Works 1946 – 1963,* New York: The Free Press, pp. 300–312.

Mahler, M.S, Pine, F and Bergman, A. (1975). *The Psychological Birth of the Human Infant: Symbiosis and Individuation.* New York: W.W. Norton.

Rilke, RM. (1934). *Letters to a Young Poet.* New York: W.W. Norton.

Seiden, H.M. (2012). On the Longing for Home. In: *Loneliness and Longing: Conscious and Unconscious Aspects,* ed. B. Willock, L.C. Bohm, & R.C. Curtis. London: Routledge.

Stern, D.N. (1985). *The Interpersonal World of the Infant: A view from psychoanalysis and developmental psychology.* New York: W.W. Norton.

Stierlin, H. (1965–1966). The Dialectic of Related Loneliness. *Psychoanalytic Review* 52D:26–40.

Sullivan, H.S. (1953). *The Interpersonal Theory of Psychiatry,* ed. H.S. Perry & M.L. Gawel. New York: W.W. Norton.

Winnicott, D.W. (1958). The Capacity to be Alone. *International Journal of Psycho-Analysis* 39:416–420.

———— (1969). The Use of the Object. *International Journal of Psycho-Analysis* 50:711–716.

Section I—Loneliness, Creativity and the Artists

Encounters with Loneliness: Only the Lonely begins in Section I with four outstanding chapters on loneliness, creativity and the artist. In Chapter One, "A Voice Comes to One in the Dark," Samuel Beckett's *Search for Company,* Lois Oppenheim carefully crafts an essay on loneliness in the work of Samuel Beckett. She traces Beckett's profound lifetime shyness, and the conflicts between his longing for—and his intolerance of—the company of others. She shows how deeply these psychic conflicts inform his work.

When asked to pose a question central to this chapter, Oppenheim offered us:

> How might the aesthetic rendering of solitude, as intolerance of intimacy, have served Beckett himself?

For our purposes, we might generalize this question to the clinical realm: How does solitude (i.e., intolerance of intimacy) enhance our patients' creative solutions in living?

In Chapter Two, Danielle Knafo presents the "Artists' Solitude and the Creative Process." In this probing chapter, she addresses the nature of solitude: what is the artist doing alone; women, solitude, and creativity; concluding with the heroics of creative solitude. Knafo poses the questions:

> What is the relationship between solitude and relatedness?
> How is solitude important to creativity?
> What is unique about female solitude?

To these we would add that she also asks:

> Is psychic pain inhibiting or adaptive to creative productivity? and,
> What facilitates a move towards creative productivity?
> Is it a relationship, an insight, or even success in the production itself?

In this chapter, Knafo demonstrates just how intricate the relationship is between solitude and the creative process.

In Chapter Three, Arlene K. Richards reviews the film *The Skin I Live In.* This insightfully provocative chapter begins with the question "What makes a woman?" Using Almodovar's film Richards opens up the question of female sexuality and the dilemmas of female development. She answers the basic question by shifting the bedrock from Freud's findings to that of loneliness and social isolation. She follows the film step by step showing how the skin is the filter of the physical and the ego is the filer filter of the psychological, allowing the emergence of the feminine image of one's self. This certainly makes us re-ask the questions:

> What is gender made of in its various biological, psychological and socio/cultural demarcations?

1

> Is loneliness the basis for one's understanding of the self (as man or woman)?
> Is loneliness an essential lens that some must pass through to become part of the person's sense of being?

Richards concludes with the idea that longing for whom one used to be may be more fundamental than longing for the other.
We may extend this to ask:

> Does loss of the other always diminish or create a sense of loss in one's self?
> Can insight bring that which is alienated back to self?

In Chapter Four, Jeffrey Stern presents "Forms and Transformations of Loneliness." Using loneliness as his motif, Stern explores the vast domain of loneliness in puppets and puppeteers; in a case: "Rose"; in the loneliness of Hugo, monsters, angels; and in Shakespeare's work and life. Reviewing this realm Stern sets up loneliness as a set of alternatives, both a cause (e.g., creativity, heroism, new relationships) and an effect that incites the damaged (monsters) to seek love and re-entry into humanity. Stern concludes that when early trauma overwhelms the developing mind, loneliness takes on a chronic state as illustrated by Rose and the "angels." When we read this fascinating account we wonder:

> Is there an antidote for loneliness?
> Is hope or love enough?

Chapter 1
"A voice comes to one in the dark. Imagine.":
Samuel Beckett's search for company
Lois Oppenheim, Ph.D.

Abstract:

It is the purpose of this paper to illustrate how one may simultaneously long for and be unable to tolerate being in the company of the Other. Taking the writing of Samuel Beckett, particularly his short novel entitled *Company*, as an example, the distinction between solitude and loneliness is articulated and this writer's preoccupation with isolation discussed. While avoiding the potential pitfall of speculation that is the risk of psychobiography, a significant feature of Beckett's life story is considered with a view to understanding the meaning of loneliness in Beckett's work. Key moments in Beckett's texts where the preoccupation is most explicitly rendered are noted in the effort to uncover why loneliness, solitude, and isolation so dominate his work and how an aesthetic rendering of them was psychodynamically of service to the author.

It has often been said that Samuel Beckett's images so shape his theater that they are more memorable, in a sense, than his words. As we fast-forward through much of his career in the theater, we mentally envision, for instance, the bowler-hat clad companions, Vladimir and Estragon, who, in *Waiting for Godot* (1953), occupy for the duration of the play a single non-descript space as they wait. *Endgame* (1957), much preferred by the playwright, offers the visually powerful tableau of the blind protagonist situated center stage in an armchair and the metaphorically powerful image of his parents confined to ashbins. In *Krapp's Last Tape* (1958), there is the enduring image of the lone character reviewing his life as registered on tapes containing his own earlier recordings. *Happy Days* (1961) reveals Winnie buried in a mound of earth. The characters in *Play* (1963), also morbidly confined, though this time to funerary urns, are unforgettable for that image which remains with the spectator long after the theater has been vacated. In *Ohio Impromptu* (1982), Speaker and Listener, seated at a table for the duration of the play, constitute yet another visually compelling composition. It is a single individual that is striking in his fragmentation into multiple selves in *What Where* (1983) and with *Quad* (1984) we have a haunting choreography, unaccompanied by any verbal communication at all, only hooded shapes pacing their prescribed routes as they assiduously circumvent the center. Interestingly, all the images from Beckett's work that remain steadfastly embedded in the mind's eye reveal a common thread of isolation and solitude, a feature so pronounced it disrupts the narrative dimension and liberates the figural element to render the image iconic (see Deleuze, pp. 5–6).

The tramps of *Godot* continually reunite but, once reunited, habitually return (despite their attempts at meaningful communication) to a solitary state as

5

they resume the wait. *Endgame*'s ashbin inhabitants are not only restricted in their movement but in their relational intimacy, a point made visually as well as verbally by the ashbins themselves: They are arranged so as to be touching while they keep the parents, one per bin, apart. "Krapp has nothing to talk to but his dying self," Beckett wrote in a letter to his director, "and nothing to talk to him but his dead one" (qtd. in Harmon, p. 59). Winnie's compulsive talking to her husband, who remains out of view throughout most of the play, elicits scarcely more than an occasional grunt from Willie. The characters in *Play* never so much as acknowledge each other as they alternate speaking in response to a spotlight shined on each of them individually. As one critic writing about *Quad* has noted, "the centre that the hooded wanderers have so fearfully to avoid is obviously the point at which real communication, a real 'encounter,' would be potentially possible but inevitably proves—by the very nature of existence itself—impossible" (Esslin, pp. 66–7).

Beckett's novels reveal the same preoccupation. Indeed, *Company* (1980), a short novel that is among the most celebrated of the author's late works and perhaps his most personal text, is a poignant if explicit expression of the very state of being that is solitude. "A voice comes to one in the dark. Imagine. To one on his back in the dark," the novel begins (1992, p.5). "The voice alone is company but not enough" (p. 7), we read, and thus additional ways, ways beyond the hallucinated voice, are sought to counter the isolation put in high relief in all Beckett's writing. Fantasies and also memories—the calling forth of images of others from the past—bring company, but, again, not enough, for memories, like the fables recounted by those who populate Beckett's texts, like the voices and visions as well, are but imaginings, and the "craving for company revives" (p. 45).

Yet imagining—whether storytelling or remembering—is precisely how Beckett's characters play with closeness, for it is an effective means of having it while also holding it at bay. However much it may be longed for, company is consistently too much to bear: "To be company," the author tells us, one "must display a certain mental activity. But it need not be of a high order. Indeed it might be argued the lower the better. Up to a point. The lower the order of mental activity the better the company. Up to a point" (p. 9). Up to the point where the dullest presence is company, but not too much. Remembering, when the company it evokes is too much to tolerate, is then put to rest. The description of photographs that appear in the mind of the speaker in the late play *A Piece of Monologue* serves to make the point:

> There was father. That grey void. There mother. That other.
> There together. Smiling. Wedding day. There all three.
> That grey blot. There alone. He alone. So on. Not now.
> Forgotten. (Beckett, 1984, p. 266)

With the obliteration of the image of the other is obliterated the memory of the deep loneliness felt even in the presence of the other. Loneliness yields to solitude, in other words, to the extent that togetherness signifies in the Beckettian cosmos unfulfilled longing and gratification not to be had.

Like so many of the author's early and mid-career works, *Company* is about the creating of voices devised expressly to diminish loneliness. This is not to say that the text is *about* the loneliness of a protagonist. Rather, it is a projection of the subjective experience of isolation, a phenomenology of the solitude that is sought to reduce loneliness, *the imagination's emptying solitude of its affective meaning by giving it form.* The questions for the reader or viewer of Beckett's work then become: From where does the author's preoccupation arise? Does his aesthetic, the shaping of solitude both in the theater and on the printed page, merely reflect the solitude endemic to the artistic endeavor, the solitude that is the *sine qua non* of making art, or something more? Is the making of art focused on extreme loneliness—and the imagination's continual striving to be rid of it—merely auto-reflective in the way modern art (early or late, neo or post) tends to be, or is it somehow therapeutic as well?

A firm believer that understanding art in terms of the artist's life is often highly reductive of the artwork, I also believe art to be fundamentally autobiographical not, as James Anderson has said, "in a trivial external way, not as a recitation of events and behaviors," but rather, as Anderson has written of fiction, "in the much deeper sense that it is a playing with, a musing on, an expression of what matters most to the individual." Over and above events drawn from the life of the artist, it is in the expression, implicit or explicit, of "struggles going on in [his or her] inner world" that the autobiographical element resides. "Writers try to come to grips with, to reconcile, and to find solutions to that which lacerates their souls," Anderson rightly observes (pp. 134, 135, & 136). Incidents from life may well appear in the work to enhance that effort, but they serve as support for the deeper telling the reconciliation entails and are not to be mistaken for it. Thus I would argue that there is a way in which artists *use* their art to ends that, in themselves, can be considered psycho-dynamically.

I have written elsewhere, for example, of the enhancement of agency the making of art affords the visual or literary artist (Oppenheim, 2012). In Beckett, the situation is more dire, with the vicissitudes of selfhood constantly at play: Indeed, writing served Beckett not only by enhancing his sense of agency, but also by concretizing his very sense of self. Beckett wrote himself into existence, in a sense, through the continual undoing of narrative constructs, and it is in this context that I would situate the isolation his persistent "fabling" brings to the fore (see Abbott, 1996). For the solitude that renders his story-telling a search for company implicates the self as other—which is to say, *the self as company*—so as then to internalize it as his own. In this perspective, the solitude that is endemic to Beckett's writing is not only a burden, the point of departure for the misery and longing that are the lot of the lonely, but liberation from the void of an absent self. In this perspective, solitude (isolation) and loneliness are seen not as one and the same; the former is a welcome reprieve, the latter merely more pain. To make the point, I will note in what follows an aspect of Beckett's biography that aids in our understanding of where for this writer solitude and loneliness part ways. I will point, in other words, to a significant feature of his life story played out in his work for the express purpose not of reducing his art to his life experience, but of exploring what was personally achieved for the author by his aesthetic rendering of solitude as both loneliness and relief from loneliness as well.

It is well known that Samuel Beckett was overly modest and pathologically shy. To meet with those he didn't know well, he needed to prepare by having a drink; he long had no telephone; and although he socialized (not infrequently with the art historian and son-in-law of Matisse, Georges Duthuit, and several of their mutual artist friends, and often engaged in late night/early morning drinking excursions with Giacometti as well), he had from childhood on a very great need to be alone. He regularly withdrew to his two-room home in the country, some 30 miles outside Paris, where he spent long periods in isolation and silence. "I seem to recuperate something in the silence and solitude," he wrote Tom MacGreevy, the Director of the National Gallery of Ireland and Beckett's closest friend (qtd. in Knowlson, p. 353). He was horrified to be awarded the Nobel Prize in 1969 (his wife's exclamation upon hearing the news—"Quelle catastrophe!"—was expressive of Beckett's own sentiments) and he sent his French publisher to Stockholm to accept the award on his behalf. Beckett suffered paralytic attacks of anxiety and depression and somatized his psychic conflicts readily. But it was the profound shyness notable throughout his life and how this timidity played out in his work—as both a longing for and intolerance of company—that interests me here.

As a child, Beckett loathed going to parties and would hide in his room to avoid having to go to them. In his teens, he was what his biographer James Knowlson calls "retiring," and in his early adulthood, though he could be drawn from his "cocoon of shyness and silence" by MacGreevy, his introversion and need for solitude were crippling. At the same time, however, Beckett loved to talk about music and painting and he did so making friends with those who shared his passions (Knowlson, pp. 40, 63, 98, 88, 183, 218). Indeed, though he intensely wanted to be alone and cherished his solitude, he was also fundamentally sociable, and it is this simultaneous pull toward isolation and sociability, the deep-seated need both to be alone and to be in the company of others, which fascinates in his work.

One form taken by this bifurcated need is the speaker's splitting of him or herself so as to protect the self in isolation while also providing company. Often, the speaking subject in Beckett's work is unable even to refer to him or herself in the first person. In *Company*, we read, "He speaks of himself as of

8

another," which is repeatedly replicated by the speaking of himself speaking of himself as of another. An extraordinary play from 1972, in which we see only Mouth, as she is called, recounting the tale of her own birth, is entitled, tellingly, *Not I*. Recurring throughout the fast-paced monologue is the frantic cry: " . . . what? . . who? no! . . she!" Beckett's remarkable penultimate work, entitled *Stirrings Still* (1988) begins: "One night as he sat at his table head on hands he saw himself rise and go." And in the remarkable play *Rockaby* (1981), we witness a woman seated in a rocking chair who speaks of the long- ing "for another," "another like herself," "another creature like herself," but the voice is on a recording. Her own voice is listened to by the woman as though it were, in fact, that of another and the taped monologue is interrupted only on four occasions by the woman uttering, not on tape, a monosyllabic plea for "more."

Thematically, the fragmenting of self characteristic of Beckett's work may serve a distinctly dissociative function, as in *Not I* where the inability to assume the first person pronoun (and even Mouth's logorrhea itself) appears as a defense against the shame of sexual longing. Though there are references to a rape, and the multi-leveled pain and suffering its memory causes, there are also intimations of intense desire, intimations as well of Oedipal wishes, and the denial of self is clearly meant to protect against them. Thus the disem- bodied mouth may be said to visually reference the vagina as the locus of the fulfillment of desire. At the same time, however, it references the orifice through which the self is brought into being: The pronominal insistence on the third as opposed to the first person—". . . what? . . who? no! . . she!"—is not only a protective negation of self, but the creation of the self as other for the purpose of reintegration. With the renunciation of 'I' comes 'she' and therein resides the irony: Fabling negates the self and creates in its stead the voice of the other; yet it simultaneously serves the isolated self as company, company that is as much completion of the self as it is the non-self of otherness.

Continually throughout his work, then, Beckett addresses the need to es- cape the loneliness of self for the company of the other and a concurrent need to free the self from the other as other, to take on the other as a part of the self. In *Rockaby*, as in *Krapp's Last Tape*, the woman seeks her self through the image created by her voice on the recording. In his celebrated trilogy of the 1950s, *Molloy*, *Malone Dies*, and *The Unnamable*, it is a quest for the other in its most primitive relation to the self that provides the narrative thread. *End- game*, the play of his that Beckett claimed to "dislike least," further exempli- fies (as does the better-known *Waiting for Godot*) not only mutual depend- ence, but coupling as the very completion of the self by the other. Reminiscent of Leo Stone's description of the "state of 'intimate separation'" that charac- terizes psychoanalysis, coupling in Beckett, very much like the analytic situa- tion, is what Stone called a "deprivation in intimacy" (qtd. in Malcolm, p. 44). Analysis does, in fact, constitute the central metaphor of *Company*, the voice

9

coming to one on his back being that of the interpreting analyst or even that of the analysand whose freely associating mind works both to repress and to recall at once: "Memories are killing," Beckett had already written in an earlier work. "So you must not think of certain things, of those that are dear to you, or rather you must think of them, for if you don't there is the danger of finding them, in your mind, little by little" (1967, p. 9).

As if to illustrate the danger of remembering in the service of seeking company (i.e., closeness), Beckett frequently recalls scenes from his own childhood modifying them from one text to another. Consider the narrator in *Company* who tells of emerging as a small boy late one afternoon from a store. Holding his mother by the hand, "looking up at the blue sky and then at [his] mother's face," he asks if the sky "is not in reality much more distant than it appears." For some reason the child is unable to fathom, the question angered his mother exceedingly: "[S]he shook off your little hand and made you a cutting retort you have never forgotten," Beckett wrote (p. 8). Almost three decades earlier, in his novel *Malone Dies*, Beckett had already written this:

> One day we were walking along the road, up a hill of extraor-
> dinary steepness, near home I imagine, my memory
> is full of steep hills, I get them confused. I said, The sky is
> further away than you think is it not, mama? It was without
> malice, I was simply thinking of all the leagues that separated
> me from it. She replied, to me her son, It is precisely as far
> away as it appears to be. She was right. But at the time I was
> aghast. (1959, p. 261)

And in the short prose text *The End*, here again we find the same, if slightly altered and somewhat more brutal, scene:

> Now I was making my way though the garden. There was that
> strange light which follows a day of persistent rain, when the
> sun comes out and the sky clears too late to be of any use.
> The earth makes a sound as of sighs and the last drops fall
> from the emptied cloudless sky. A small boy, stretching out
> his hands and looking up at the blue sky, asked his mother
> how such a thing was possible. Fuck off, she said. (p. 50)

Here the memory of closeness is more than one in need of company (imagined or real) can bear. The reminder of deep disappointment is a reminder that, at least at times, it is better to remain alone. Solitude parts ways with loneliness, then, in offering, as an existential and thereby affectless state, aloneness as a respite from pain.

10

We know that Beckett had a complex and, at times, turbulent relationship with his mother. May Beckett was of uncertain temper and suffered from powerful changes in mood and both separation from and closeness to her posed a threat for Beckett throughout his life. Did Beckett seek in his work a means of assimilating deprivation? Of resolving ambivalence? Of expiating the guilt aggressive feelings toward his mother may have provoked? These are questions that can only be answered speculatively. What I *would* venture, however, is this: It has been noted that "children who experience . . . massive early disappointments with their mothers . . . often develop a fantasy of a union with an idealized primary object—with the 'Good Object'—which they use to combat the traumatic deidealization." Yet "the prospect of merger with the primary object" may also be terrifying, "for the dedifferentiation it would entail would mean the destruction" of autonomy and individuality. "This fear of re-engulfment by the object" is repeatedly seen in Beckett's texts where "fusion" rather than "union" is the kind of love repeatedly sought by his characters and thus the need for separation a persistent threat (Whitebook, n.p.). In Beckett's early prose work *First Love*, the narrator goes so far as to change the name of his love object to maintain the much-needed distance. Ultimately, he leaves this woman once she has borne his child choosing once more solitude, aloneness, rather than risk the dissolution of self the oneness with her, as exemplified by their having made a child, implies.

So constant and so desperate is the anxiety of dissolution underlying the leitmotif of solitude in all his texts that the gratification Beckett obtained in writing might be qualified less as deriving from the need for object reparation than the projection of fear onto the outside world. In projecting his own fear of disintegration onto the characters he creates, it would appear that Beckett was able to situate the sense of impending debilitation and loss outside him, thereby potentially gaining some mastery of it. In light of this we can understand why, over and above his aesthetic intentions, Beckett once said, "I wanted to rupture the lines of communication to state the space that intervenes between the artists and the world of objects" (qtd. in Cremin, pp. 85–86). We can understand why Gilles Deleuze and Felix Guattari wrote of Beckett's work as exemplifying not only "schizoid sequences," but "schizophrenic disjunction" (see Abbott, p. 24).

Clearly, Beckett knew some form of that intervening space. The late Martin Esslin, long-time head of drama at BBC Radio, told of recounting to Beckett that a BBC producer on medical leave had suffered an apparently instantaneous decline in mental health. One moment this man was cashing a check in the bank and the next moment he found himself in the corner crying. Sometime later, this individual described what had happened in terms of a feeling that the world had simply disappeared and that he was completely detached from reality. "He had even written a little pamphlet about this when he got cured . . . ." Esslin told Beckett. Captivated, Beckett had responded, "This

11

is fascinating. Can you give me the title of this pamphlet? This is exactly what I was about" (qtd. in Knowlson, p. 535).

No doubt the author was referring to that most painful moment of his life in the early 1930s when walking down the street, he felt that he literally "couldn't go on moving. So I went into the nearest pub," he later said, "and got a drink just to stay still" (qtd. in Knowlson, p. 167). Severely depressed, anxiety-ridden, and in mourning for his recently deceased father, Beckett increasingly suffered physical symptoms, most of which were anxiety provoked and all of which were exceedingly anxiety producing. At the suggestion of a friend, he set off for treatment in London (psychiatry was not practiced in Dublin and psychoanalysis had few, if any, adherents) where he underwent a three-times-a-week therapy with Wilfred Bion, a treatment that would last just short of two years (though, interestingly, Beckett subsequently remembered it as lasting only six months). Beckett's correspondence reveals that, in the initial session with Bion, he spoke of "a bursting, apparently arrhythmic heart, night sweats, shudders, panic, breathlessness, and, when his condition was at its most severe, total paralysis," (qtd. in Knowlson, p. 169), a traumatizing state that I have elsewhere explored in relation to the stasis emblematic of his work, the "I can't go on. I'll go on" motif long explicated by the catch-all of mid-20th century Parisian existentialism (see Oppenheim, 2008).

How much the work with Bion helped him cannot be determined for little is known of the treatment and Bion had had only had two years of training when Beckett came to the Tavistock Clinic in 1934. ("I don't think I did him much good," Bion said, "but I probably didn't do him much harm either" [Francesca Bion, personal communication].) What *can* be said, however, is that Beckett repeatedly paid homage to psychodynamic therapy in his work: A semblance of free association is everywhere in his narrative and theatrical monologues; his logorrheic narrations are replete with resistance, with recurring symptoms, and with compliance as they recall the therapeutic alliance of the patient who speaks and is sometimes silent and the analyst who is silent and sometimes speaks (cf. Anzieu, 1983, p. 81).

What can also be said is that writing itself was, at the very least, stabilizing for Beckett. It allowed him to explore the boundaries of selfhood and better integrate psychic and somatic function. It regulated in some measure his depressive affect and the very articulation of words was calming: As long as there was language, as long as there was a voice to go on saying, there was company. As long as there was a reader of that voice, there was company. Whether the narrator is company for the reader or the reader company for the narrator is of no bearing (see Brater, 1983). The point is, rather, that the difficulties posed by self and other were given expression and that that expression provided a way for Beckett to articulate what he knew before he knew he knew it; namely, that solitude is distinct from loneliness and, at times, preferable to it; though there is a moment when the one morphs into the other.

Writing afforded Beckett a means of externalizing his simultaneous long-ing for and fear of the other and allowed him to play with the dichotomy, much as one plays with intimacy and separation in the analytic setting. "Little by little," we read in *Company*, "the craving for company revives. [. . .] The need to hear that voice again" (p. 45). And so he wrote. The "fabling" of *Company* and Beckett's work more generally is composed of autobiographical reminiscences, and in so being it is a re-gathering, for company, of those who had been company in actuality. But memories are always fictive, informed as they are by wish, cognition, and affect. Thus, however autobiographical the tale, what Beckett wrote was fiction, fiction in which a voice creates fiction to satisfy the non-fictive—indeed, all too real—need of the other, even when fear predominates. Only in this sense does the psycho-biographical element of the work have meaning. "The fable of one with you in the dark," Beckett wrote in *Company*, "The fable of one fabling with you in the dark." That, however, is but the penultimate close of the novel. The real end is this: "And how better in the end labour lost and silence. And you as you always were. Alone." (pp. 51-2). In a word, then, company for Beckett was better than loneliness. But soli-tude was better still.

References

Abbott, H. P. (1996). *Beckett Writing Beckett*. Ithaca: Cornell University Press.

Anderson, J. W. (2001). Is Fiction Autobiographical? In *Clio's Psyche* (Dec.).

Anzieu, D. (1983). Un soi disjoint, une voix liante: l'écriture narrative de Samuel Beckett. In *Nouvelle Revue de Psychanalyse* 28: 71–85.

Beckett, S. (1959). *Malone Dies*. In *Samuel Beckett: Three Novels. Molloy Malone Dies, The Unnamable*. New York: Grove Press.

Beckett, S. (1967a). "The End." In *Stories and Texts for Nothing*. New York: Grove Press Weidenfeld.

Beckett, S. (1967b). "The Expelled." In *Stories and Texts for Nothing*. New York: Grove Weidenfeld.

Beckett, S. (1984). A Piece of Monologue. In *The Collected Shorter Plays of Samuel Beckett*. New York: Grove Press.

Beckett, S. (1992). *Company*. In *Nohow On*. London: Calder Publications.

Brater, E. (1983). The 'Company' Beckett Keeps: The Shape of Memory and One Fablist's Decay of Lying. In *Samuel Beckett: Humanistic Perspectives*. Ed. Morris Beja, S.E. Gontarksi, and Pierre Astier. Columbus: Ohio State University Press, pp. 157–71.

Cremin, A. (1985) Friend Game. In *ARTnews*, 84:82–89.

Deleuze. G. (2003). *Francis Bacon: The Logic of Sensation*, transl. Daniel W. Smith. Minneapolis: University of Minnesota Press.

Esslin, M. (1992). Patterns of Rejection: Sex and Love in Beckett's Universe. In Linda Ben-Zvi, ed. *Women in Beckett: Performance and Critical Perspectives*. Urbana and Chicago: University of Illinois Press.

Harmon, M. ed. (1998). *No Author Better Served: The Correspondence of Samuel Beckett and Alan Schneider*. Cambridge: Harvard UP.

Knowlson, J. (1999). *Damned to Fame*. New York: Simon & Schuster.

Malcolm, J. (1981). *The Impossible Profession*. New York: Alfred A. Knopf.

Oppenheim, L. (2012). *Imagination from Fantasy to Delusion*. London and New York: Routledge.

Oppenheim, L. (2008). Life as Trauma; Art as Mastery: Samuel Beckett and the Urgency of Writing. In *Contemporary Psychoanalysis*, 44: 419–442.

Whitebook, J. Sigmund Freud: "A Philosophical Physician." Paper presented at the Association for Psychoanalytic Medicine, Columbia University Center for Psychoanalytic Training and Research, Feb. 2, 2010.

Chapter 2
Artists' Solitude and the Creative Process
Danielle Knafo

Abstract:

This chapter examines aspects of solitude in relation to creativity and personal transformation, especially as it pertains to artists and their objects. It argues that solitude is a core feature of the human condition and that it is inseparable from relatedness. Both solitude and relationship are layered and dynamically interactive states. The chapter also considers the relational needs that art objects serve for their creators and specifically addresses the uniqueness of women's creative solitude.

> *Ideas are like goddesses who appear*
> *only to the solitary mortal.*
> —Marcel Proust

> *I am a writer who came from a sheltered life*
> *A sheltered life can be a daring life as well. For all serious*
> *daring starts from within.*
> —Eudora Welty

The Diving Bell and the Butterfly (1997), a heroic and poignant memoir by French *Elle* magazine journalist, Jean-Dominique Bauby, describes his cataclysmic life after suffering a massive stroke that left him with a rare and horrific condition called Locked-In Syndrome. Bauby remained conscious yet unable to speak or move, except for one eye lid which he used to communicate. One would be hard pressed to find a more enforced solitary condition than this—a completely functional and active mind incarcerated in an immobile and nearly useless body. Understandably, Bauby felt intensely suicidal until he discovered the two gifts his stroke had not eradicated—memory and imagination. Little by little—one eye blink at a time, translated by Claude Mendibil into one letter at a time—Bauby wrote his memoir, *Le scaphandre et le papillon.* Even in such an extreme state of solitude, Bauby opted to make his world communicable. The diving bell refers to his deadened body sunk in the gloomy depths of immobility, while the butterfly is a metaphor for the flight of his imagination, delicate and ephemeral, rising above the dross of his despair.

Artistic creation, in essence, is a solitary vocation, usually not forced upon one as in the case of Bauby, but chosen and even cultivated. In his *Letters to a Young Poet* (1934), Rilke advised Franz Kapus to foster solitude first and foremost: "What is necessary, after all, is only this: solitude, vast inner solitude."

17

Indeed, the artist eschews social intercourse in order to engage the world anew through acts of imagination. Of course this is not only true of the artist, but of anyone engaged in an intricate creative undertaking. Scientists, scholars, and all manner of thinkers and planners may retreat from others to bring their ideas and creations into being. However, it is especially true of the serious artist who may spend the greater majority of his or her adult life in the solitary pursuit of creation. Perhaps only the lone mystic spends more time alone than does the dedicated artist.

Expressionist painter Agnes Martin (2005) said, "I paint with my back to the world." Françoise Gilot (2001), painter and one-time wife of Pablo Picasso, replied to her students who asked her how one knows if he or she is an original artist, "I can tell you that it's very simple. How many hours can you remain alone during a day, a week, a month, a year, a lifetime? If you can remain alone almost all of the time you can be a painter (p. 164)."

Nearly anyone who consciously retreats from the many to commune with the one, whether that one is oneself, nature, art, or even mystical possibilities, is practicing a disengagement that can have many benefits. In this chapter I examine some of the creative and transformative aspects of solitude, especially as it pertains to artists and their objects, while showing how both solitude and relationship are interrelated and layered states that exist in dynamic interaction.

The Nature of Solitude

I use the word solitude in the popular sense: that of physical and psychological withdrawal from others, a condition of being alone with oneself, either by choice or by dint of undesired circumstance. Naturally this begs further clarification. Firstly, let us note that radical or primary solitude, that is being alone in one's experience, is the ground state of human existence. Whether alone or with another, each human being maintains an existential aloneness throughout the course of life. Winnicott (1988) claimed that prior to the development of the "capacity to be alone" we exist in "a primary state of being," a "pre-primitive stage of development" that predates relationship (p. 133). Bollas (1989), too, states that "shadowing all object-relating is a fundamental and primary aloneness which is inevitable and unmovable. And this aloneness is the background of our being; solitude is the container of the self." (p. 20). Eigen (2009) calls this "boundless aloneness brought to us, in part, by who we are, an inherent ingredient of our basic nature." (p. 14). I cannot feel your toothache. You cannot taste my orange. I cannot live your life and you cannot die my death. You cannot love my love and I cannot hate your hate. You can never fully know what it is to be me, nor I to be you. At best, we can develop empathy for one another and know what it is *like* to be the other.

18

At the heart of human experience, solitude is the burden of that indescribable and impenetrable aloneness that drives us to reach our arms out from the solipsistic cage of our subjectivity and connect with others, whether through art or love or rage or the necessary goals of community. This movement itself is already an act of creativity, for each individual must find a way to deal with his or her own solitude. Therefore, creativity, too, is not an option; *it is a necessary condition of being radically alone*, in need of contact and encounter to realize and grow oneself.

Upon this radical foundation of human existence, two basic derivatives of solitude are found: enforced solitude and voluntary solitude. The former is a form of incarceration, either imposed by others or, even, by oneself, while the latter is the freely chosen retreat for the purpose of some project, artistic or otherwise. Both kinds may be productive and creative, though the latter is certainly the happier preference or alternative. Yet many prisoners, whether incarcerated by the state or by the self, have enjoyed creative production: Cervantes's *Don Quixote*, Malory's *La Morte d'Arthur*, Wilde's *De Profundis*, Genet's *Our Lady of the Flowers*, among others, were all penned in prison. Self-enforced solitude—as, say, in the case of a person who withdraws from others after suffering some personal loss——tends to be defensive, and yet it can also become highly creative. But voluntary solitude— as, say, in the case of an author who withdraws to write a novel—can also become defensive. (e.g., The writer produces a novel filled with rage against women after being rebuffed by one). Enforced solitude can become a blessing. Voluntary solitude can become a curse. And one form may evolve into the other.

Of course there is always a danger of solitude becoming degenerative and destructive, as when the artist or (hero) becomes malignantly blocked and remains unable to produce. Kurt Gödel, one of the greatest mathematicians of the twentieth century, literally starved to death in the last years of his life, overwhelmed by paranoid terror (Dawson, 1997). But relationships can also become degenerative and destructive.

What distinguishes artists from non-artists is their particular personal, historical and psychological response to experience. Artists are so affected by experience that they actually seek solitude to create something that stands apart from experience while conversing with it, revealing its myriad profiles and the possibilities embedded in its reality. The personal reasons artists create may be linked with awe, pain, loss, trauma or even some idiosyncratic aspect of character. Nevertheless the end effect is the same; they withdraw from the general course of life, returning to aloneness in order to create a product that speaks to others about existence in some new way. Small wonder solitude is a site of terror and delight, of harrowing self-diminishment and ecstatic self-expansion where human creation takes place, sometimes at the highest levels.

19

What is the Artist Doing Alone?

Few psychoanalytic writers have addressed the question of solitude. In particular, the abundant attention recently directed toward relational and attachment needs has eclipsed the need for and benefit of aloneness. Of course, Winnicott (1958/1968) is an exception, and his groundbreaking paper on "the capacity to be alone" stands nearly alone in its argument that solitude can be regarded as a developmental milestone that is "nearly synonymous with emotional maturity" (p. 31). Winnicott's understanding of this capacity, however, assumes that safe and secure mothering establishes the ability for the child to feel comfortable being alone. For Winnicott, being alone paradoxically implies that someone else—a good and reliable object—has been introjected and is therefore present. A graphic artist alluded to this state when she exclaimed, "Ah, the sweetness of walking into my silent studio space after being with people. It smells of me and my work. I almost call out, 'I'm home Mom!'" On a similar note, Modell (1993) claims that the muse, an internally constructed, mainly female and maternal presence, exemplifies the artist's continued connection to the mother despite apparent solitude.

Winnicott's assumption that only one who has had "good enough mothering" can attain such a capacity for aloneness is illuminating, yet I question its generalizability or universality, because it is known that many highly creative artists have experienced poor parenting and/or early trauma and loss (Eisenstadt, et al., 1989). The artist quoted above grew up in a home with an absent mother and a bipolar father. Keen on this aspect of solitude, Michael Balint (1968) wrote about the space of creation as one in which there is "no external object present, no object relationship and no transference." Although I disagree with this statement, in ways I will make clear shortly, Balint deserves credit for bringing attention to artists' creative regression from "harsh and frustrating" object relationships in order to "create something better, kinder, more understandable, beautiful, and above all, more consistent and more harmonious than the real objects proved to be (p. 68)." Along this line, Storr (1988) argues that artists' primary source of self-esteem and personal fulfillment often derive from their artistic output rather than from their interpersonal relationships. Likewise, artists often regard their own maturation in terms of the development of their art rather than according to changes in their relational world. Thus, self-understanding and self-regulation often take place in the privacy of the creative space. One poet recounted that when he was a young child, his mother kept him locked in a room for days at a time. "I had nowhere to go but inside," he said. It was during that time he developed a complex, imaginative world. Although he was "incarcerated for the crime of being a small boy," he cultivated a fertile, dynamic inner life that he later accessed for his writing. This is an example of how forced solitude can also lead to generativity.

So far we have two seminal ideas about solitude and creativity. For Winnicott solitude is an ability gained from being in the presence of a positive, nurturing mother, what Bowlby (1969) would call a secure attachment. For Balint solitude is a space of safety, predictability, and creativity to which one runs away from a frustrating or abusive environment. I would argue that both of these views are correct, and to them I add a third. Sometimes artists seek solitude to engage the bad object of their childhoods—Fairbairn's (1943/1952) unpredictable yet exciting objects—with whom they have unfinished business. Thus, there is a continued wrestling with one's objects even in the state of solitude, a need to seek resolution with the object world through the product of creativity. Austrian Expressionist artist, Egon Schiele, harbored enormous resentment toward his mother for neglecting him as a child. As an adult, he repeatedly killed her in a series of *Dead Mother* portraits (See Figure 1). Serving a dual purpose, these portraits expressed

Figure 1. Egon Schiele, *Dead Mother* (*Tote Mutter I*) (1910). Oil on wood, 32 x 25.7 cm. Museum Leopold, Vienna. Erich Lessing/Art Resource, NY.

his anger toward his mother, by killing her, as well as the inner deadness he experienced from her. Interestingly, most of these portraits include a baby—himself—inside the womb in an ultimate state of fusion (Knafo, 1993). During the time he created these eerie and compelling works, he lived alone and eschewed contact with others, except to spend time at his friend Dr. Graff's gynecological clinic sketching mothers and babies, both alive and dead. Later self-portraits would depict him as a lone monk, hermit and saint.

21

Figure 2. Frida Kahlo, *The Two Fridas* (1939). Oil on canvas (5' 8 ½ x 8 ½ in). Museo Nacional de Arte Moderno, Instituto National de Bellas Artes, Mexico City, D.F., Mexico. Photo Credit: Schalkwijk/Art Resource, NY. © 2008 Banco de México Diego Rivera and Frida Kahlo Trust. Av. Cinco de Mayo No. 2, Col. Centro Del. Cuauhtémoc 06059, México, D.F.

Many artists identify with their original objects in the creative process and thus embody maternal generativity, which obviously links to Winnicott's theory of the capacity to be alone (Knafo, 2002). For example, following a terrible accident at age 18, Mexican artist Frida Kahlo was forced to spend much time alone, in hospitals, in bed, away from friends and family. She offered self-portraits to her friends so they would not forget her. She also painted their portraits and surrounded herself with them to keep them with her (Herrera, 1983). In her largest painting, *Las Dos Fridas* (1939), two Fridas seated on a bench hold hands and face the viewer before a dark sky filled with ominous storm clouds (See Figure 2). One Frida has a broken heart and the other a heart that is whole. One Frida clasps a pair of surgical pincers in her hand to keep the other alive. Dispassionate and impersonal facial expressions produce an emotional remove from the poignant, emotional, near-death scene she is depicting. The artist informs us in this painting about the way she survived:

she kept herself together by appropriating the maternal function with which to nurture herself and by representing the ensuing self-containment of her world.

The work of art can additionally incorporate containing properties (Bion, 1959). The poet mentioned earlier, who was repeatedly locked in a room by his mother, clearly had a childhood filled with enforced isolation, trauma and abuse. He responded to my suggestion that he try to write about his mother by instantly writing a poem filled with profound longing, rage and despair, evident from the few lines quoted below:

> Then came the door, the door that would not
> open even when I had to piss, Mom, how could
> you, and the keyhole clogged with toilet paper
> so I could not see and the sheet stuffed beneath the
> door so I could not hear, while the man with the
> hatchet face became my next father as he hammered
> you into the mattress all summer and the heat baked me
> into a cinder. . . . Even when I got out
> I didn't. The room locked itself inside me and inside it
> I still am, still enclosed now as an old man . . . All the
> rooms I lived in after that, Mom, they were lifeboats,
> intensive care units, barrels thrashing over the falls . . .

After he wrote the poem, he rekindled what had been a very strained relationship with his mother. The poem, rooted in her solitary confinement of him, now contained all the toxicity of their connection, transforming the trauma into images and connections he created and controlled, thus allowing him to develop a more benign relationship with her in reality. He told me, "As a kid I was terrified of being alone. She'd leave to go to the store and I thought she'd never come back. She'd sleep and I was afraid she'd die. I hated my room. I hated being locked in. I hated being alone. Now I embrace my aloneness. It renews me. From it I draw out from myself that which is both beautiful and ugly. It is my aloneness in which I fully experience the terror of being a man with the wonder of being a man. If I couldn't be alone and create, I'd find it very hard to live."

Some artworks possess self-object properties (Kohut, 1971), and function in mirroring or idealizing capacities. American assemblage artist, Joseph Cornell, was a well-known recluse who worked in his basement from dusk to dawn creating his exquisite art boxes. He made boxes for women he admired from afar, like Lauren Bacall, Lois Smith, and many ballerinas. He was extremely shy and didn't have the nerve to approach these women, so he sent his boxes in his stead. The boxes he created clearly functioned for him as self-objects, both representing the women he longed for and interacting with them in ways he could not (Salomon, 1997).

In sum, whereas they are usually alone, artists are constantly talking to and creating for others, including, of course, a reader, a viewer, an audience. In the act of creating, art and audience are already presupposed; that is to say that just as one hears one's own thoughts, one experiences one's own production. In the moment of artistic creation, the artist becomes the first witness, the original audience of one. Indeed, the enjoyment of that very production and the belief that it is "good" provides the impetus to communicate it to others. The audience in effect is born from oneself and one's internal objects. One writer described the interaction and overlap of solitude and relationality that takes place in creativity thus:

> I am never alone (or lonely) when I write. When the going is good and the writing is white-hot, I am surrounded by my characters. They're huddled over my shoulders and around me, talking to me. That's one of the reasons I like to be alone: so I can hear them.

The poet who was locked in a room explained it thus:

> Paradoxically, my inner life demands both the presence and the absence of others. Without them my experience is barren and stark. I need them to live, to love, and to feel. But I also need to retreat from them as well, to turn away and turn inward so that I may understand what I did and what happened to me when I was with them. They necessarily return me to myself and my solitude necessarily returns me to them. *I need to be with them and to not be with them, knowing that I am still alone when I am with them and still with them when I am alone.*

Because solitude is connected with isolation, loneliness, abandonment and death, most people, including artists, fear entering solitary spaces or confronting difficult truths and affects. Yet they do so because they hope that the risks will pay off. One poet described the fear that accompanies her transition into solitude: "Going into solitude can be like snorkeling, which I always begin by reminding myself that I must now switch from nose breathing to mouth breathing and that this will not make me drown. There is a moment of hesitation and discomfort, almost fear, as I make the change, before I can descend into the joy of being alone underwater with the magical contents to be found there."

Being "underwater" means being immersed in another world, leaving behind a familiar one; it also implies the risk of drowning. Adam Phillips (1993) claims that "the risk of establishing one's solitude is the risk of one's potential freedom (p. 39)," and we know that freedom is something most people escape from (Fromm, 1941) but which many artists seek. Indeed, in order to gain access to such freedom, artists rarely create in the presence of others. Franz Kafka's fiancée once asked him if she could sit with him while he wrote, to which he replied,

> Listen, in that case I could not write at all. For writing means revealing oneself to excess; the utmost of self-revelation and surrender, in which a human being, when involved with others, would feel he was losing himself, and from which, therefore, he will always shrink as long as he is in his right mind . . . That is why one can never be alone enough when one writes, why even night is not night enough (Kafka, 1973, pp. 155–56).

Artists require privacy to regress in order to create. They must plumb their own depths. One cannot engage in a relationship with another when engaging in an intense relationship with the creative daemon, a relationship that demands everything and often risks everything.

The interplay of aloneness and relatedness brings to mind Ogden's (1994) conceptualization of a "third analytic space," created from projections and identifications of both the analyst and the analysand. He refers to the co-creation of an intersubjective space that transcends each individual and even the analytic pair. This third space, like Winnicott's potential space, is the space of creativity, the space where we discover and experience something new, where we transcend our own limits and knowledge. At the very least a third space can be constructed through the relationship with an assumed presence as an embodied act of imagination. The other is imagined as already being in a relationship with the artist. From the interplay between the mind and the figure of fantasy emerge new thoughts and feelings, ideas and images, situations and fabrications. In the movie *Cast Away*, Chuck Noland, played by Tom Hanks, imaginatively transforms a soccer ball smeared with his bloody handprint into "Wilson," a friend whose presence comforts him and even saves him from utter madness in his enforced solitude. So real is this relationship, and the space for dialogue that it creates, that Chuck nearly drowns trying to "save" Wilson when he comes loose from the raft and falls into the sea.

In his book, *The Invention of Solitude* (1982), Paul Auster beautifully portrays the intersubjective interaction taking place in the third space that exists between writer and reader:

> Every book is an image of solitude, the outcome of a great deal of time spent alone in a room. Literature is at once the product of an author's solitude and a means by which a reader reaches through his own and the author's solitude. In

25

> reading, an isolated individual becomes absorbed in something beyond his own preoccupations and communes with another mind. . . . It is possible to be alone and not alone at the same time. Reading literature creates a kind of companionship that preserves the solitariness of reading and writing (p. 136).

Auster and the other artists I have mentioned demonstrate that creative solitude is not necessarily an escape from the world but, rather, a different kind of participation in it.

Women, Solitude, and Creativity

Solitude for women is different than it is for men. Evolution and biology have shaped culture to place the female primarily in the caretaking role, and she is expected to be the more social, communicative, and nurturing gender. Even feminist psychologist Carol Gilligan (1982) writes about the female's self-definition in terms of her relationships, as opposed to the male's who finds his in terms of independence and achievement. French feminist psychoanalyst Luce Irigaray (1985) has gone so far as to locate woman's relationality in her labial anatomy—lips speaking to one another!

It is true that solitude cannot be isolated from gendered, cultural, and historico-political contexts (Miller, 1992/93). Its luxury has traditionally been linked to the wealthy and the upper classes whose resources of money and time lent access to books, education, and other forms of self-engagement. Solitude is also usually associated with men because of the independence and self-reliance implied by it—the privilege of the male, a rite of passage, a search for adventure and knowledge. The monastic tradition of leading a contemplative life while withdrawing from the mundane world has historically also been primarily a male prerogative.

Women in retreat, on the other hand, have been regarded with suspicion, perceived as dangerous or evil, a menace to society (recall the witch hunts), selfish, indulgent, irresponsible, neglectful of their duties as nurturers and caretakers, even miserable and pathetic (think of spinsters and old maids). Additionally, solitary women have been considered insane. Mr. Rochester's mad bride from *Jane Eyre*—hidden and locked in an attic—though nameless, has come to stand for the countless solitary women deemed mad by those around them (Gilbert & Gubar, 1979). Finally, the lone woman in old age is often presented as an ugly hag, horrifying and predatory. Emily Dickinson, who was a notorious recluse, is at times remembered more as an abandoned woman and invalid of love than the great poet she was.

Are these dominant cultural images of female solitude reflective of a more profound problem in women? Anthony Storr's popular book on *Solitude*

(1988) never once mentions gender differences, and nearly all of his examples are taken from the lives of men. Philip Koch, author of *Solitude: A Philosophical Encounter* (1994), devotes a chapter to women and solitude and concludes that two major obstacles block the path to female retreat: social norms and violence against lone women. Nancy Burke (1997) examines the psychological dimension of female solitude by applying the feminist psychoanalytic theories of Nancy Chodorow and Jessica Benjamin to explain why women may have greater difficulty developing the capacity to be alone. Burke argues that the mother's differential treatment of her daughters and sons results in greater difficulties for girls in the negotiation of separation and individuation. Accordingly, the bond between mother and daughter inhibits the development of strong self-other boundaries in the daughters, which makes it more uncomfortable for them to be alone. This discomfort is reinforced by cultural expectations that women be more social than men. Burke mentions borderline personality disorders and eating disorders as primarily female maladies and ties them to the difficulty women have in being alone.

Yet women can break free of the group and find themselves by themselves. When they do, they subvert social stereotypes and cultural expectations and challenge the idea of women as chiefly familial and relational beings. Women artists have even invented new words to describe female solitude, a state that involves nurturing of the self and of one's creativity. Alice Koller, author of *The Stations of Solitude,* isolated herself in Nantucket for three months and created the words "loning," "singling," and "instasis" for "standing inside oneself, in full and rapturous control begotten in doing one's work" (1990, p. 56).

Tillie Olsen wrote in her book *Silences* (1965) that most women writers have been unmarried and childless. Although this situation has changed since Olsen wrote her book, many women artists who are married with children, like author Ruth Setton, still have to steal moments from a hectic life to write, always in anticipation of interruptions, because "in a minute the door will burst open and a voice will cry, 'Mom, I'm home!' And I will wrench myself from [the writing world] while I return to the other world—the family world—where I am Mom and I have children and they need to eat and we're out of milk and I have to do laundry." Unsurprisingly, Setton adds, "Solitude is an aphrodisiac to someone who is rarely alone (personal communication, March 18, 2009)."

Women artists are solitary in another sense, too, because they lack lineage, a tradition of well-known and well-respected women artists who have made their mark in the art world (Miller, 1993/94). Significantly, women artists have had to fight for the space and time in which to create, for education and recognition. In her famous article, "Why Have There Been No Great Women Artists," art historian Linda Nochlin (1971/1988) answers her own question by explaining that for centuries women were denied access to art education. When they were finally admitted to select institutions, women were forbidden to attend anatomy classes. When I interviewed feminist perform-ance artist, Carolee Schneemann, she told me about the isolation she felt upon encountering the exclusion of women artists in her art history studies:

> In my college years I was outraged by the linguistic mascu-linization of all texts: "Man and His Images," "The Artist and His Materials," "Every student will remove *his* car from in front of the art building." I was automatically a girl gen-der criminal, because I didn't think that "He must empty his locker" really meant me. At the same time my creative es-sence was also denied its erotic core: there was no female genital sexuality . . . women's explicit sexuality belonged ei-ther to medical issues or to pornography. My lived experi-ence was taboo, occluded. (Knafo, 2009, p. 90).

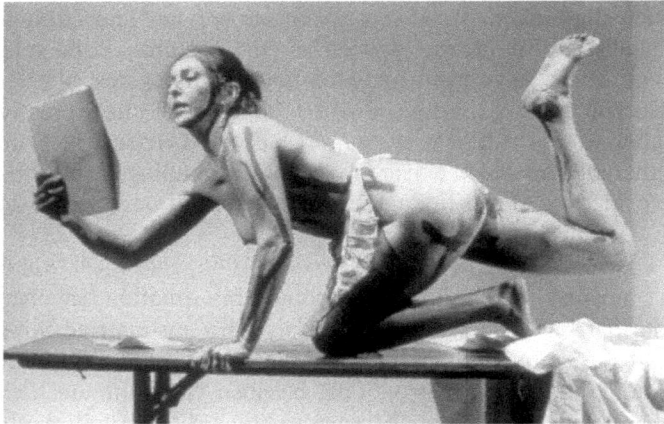

Figure 3. Carolee Schneemann, *Interior Scroll*, 1975. Photo collage with text: beet juice, urine and coffee photographie print; 72w x 48h inches. Photo: Anthony McCall. Courtesy of the artist.

Schneemann is best known for the instrumental role she played in launching nude female performance art in the 1960s and for advocating the validity of female sensual pleasure. She led the way for generations of women to literally put their bodies in their work (See Figure 3 above).

Recent progress notwithstanding, women artists continue to struggle to be taken as seriously as male artists and to have their works exhibited in major museums and galleries. Many women seeking creative lives, like Virginia

Woolf, feel the need to open a literal or metaphorical "room of one's own," a place of refuge and renewal, a crucible of interiority for delight, surprise, and transformation. Yet such a space, when not chosen freely, can be a prison, as in the case of French novelist, Colette, who was locked in a room by her husband and only allowed out when she had written the required number of pages. Her *Claudine* series, written under these conditions, was highly popular, but the author's name was her elderly husband's (Willy), not her own. Colette's case is another example of involuntary yet generative solitude.

Whether a room of one's own becomes a prison or a sanctuary naturally depends upon the circumstances, and we have seen that both have the potential to be generative. Virginia Woolf's "room" connotes a "stage for a single actor; a house of soliloquy; a studio of rich, internal echoes; a closet of expression; a safe cell for the incubation of ideas" (Malin & Boynton, 2003, p. 144). Author May Sarton wrote in her *Journal of a Solitude* (1973): "I am here alone for the first time in weeks, to take up my 'real' life again at last. That is what is strange—That friends, even passionate love, are not my real life unless there is time alone to explore and to discover what is happening or has happened. Without the interruptions, nourishing and maddening, this life would become arid. Yet I taste it fully only when I am alone here and 'the house and I resume old conversation'"(p.11). Sarton's house is her significant other, whom she names "Nelson," and refers to it as her bridegroom and host. Indeed, sometimes a woman's "love affair" with her home provides an alternative to a real person. Carolyn Heilbrun, famed author of the Amanda Cross mystery series, wrote in *The Last Gift of Time* (1997), "Solitude late in life, is the temptation of the happily paired; to be alone if one has not been doomed to aloneness is a temptation so beguiling that it carries with it the guilt of adultery, and the promise of consummation" (p.11).

Heilbrun's observation points to changes that take place with age in a woman's relationship to her solitude. Artist Erika Harrasch confessed that after her brother died when she was ten, she instantly became an only child and despised being alone. Many years later, when she became an artist, she began to enjoy her solitude. Harrasch calls her painting practice a "Labrynthic Solipsism," a space that is alternately "peaceful, meditative, exciting, and energetic" (personal communication, December18, 2009).

Figure 4. Käthe Kollwitz, *Self-Portrait*, lithograph, 1934. © 2009 Artists Rights Society (ARS), New York/VG Bild-Kunst, Bonn. Photo Credit: Art Resource, NY.

Storr (1988) writes of the increasing solitude that takes place in the "third period" of life and claims that as one ages, emotional dependency declines and one becomes preoccupied with internal concerns. The self-portraits of German artist Käthe Kollwitz represent a major psychological and formalistic shift as she grows old (See Figure 4). In her own words, she went from being a "revolutionary to being an evolutionary" (Knafo, 2009, p. 33). Whereas early self-depictions are of an ideological fighter, albeit one who is often forced to surrender to powerful external forces, later works focus on acceptance rooted in inner strength and faith. Storr explains the transformation that takes place with aging in terms of the individual entering a phase that allows the freedom to break free from attachments in preparation for loss and death. It is no surprise that as Winnicott (1988) aged, his attention to solitude increased and that the final essays of both Frieda Fromm-Reichmann (1959) and Melanie Klein (1963; 1975) were on the subject of loneliness.

Koch (1994) claims that women's art possesses unique qualities because women require different strategies of disengagement than men. Indeed, there is a gendered connotation to spaces, a spatial particularity to women's imagination. Erikson (1965) observed that the play of girls, unlike that of boys, is concerned with the creation of inner spaces, an interior well of resonance and being. Thus, women are not really strangers to solitude, for their bodies come with an inner space—the womb—the biological foundation for creation. The womb has its correlate in female experience as having space within for birth, both literal and figurative, a kinesthetic connection with a pulsing interiority rich with creative possibility.

Some thinkers remark on the highly personal quality in women's art, especially obvious in self-representational art (Knafo, 2009) and journal writing, a common form of female literary art (Buchholz, 1997). Between the covers of a journal is a set amount of pages, blank leafs that one fills with meaning, a textual offspring enclosed in white space. Anaïs Nin, famous for her journals, wrote: "Playing so many roles, dutiful daughter, devoted sister, mistress, protector, my father's newfound illusion, Henry's [Miller] needed, all-purpose friend, I had to find one place of truth, one dialogue without falsity. This is the role of the diary" (Moffat & Paynter, 1974, p. 14).

Writing in a diary represents permission for solitude and allows a private work for a private voice. Journal writing not only results in generative solitude; it also conveys the aesthetic aspects of women's daily lives. I would like to mention only a few of the better known works belonging to this genre. Most popular is May Sarton's *Journal of a Solitude* (1973), which offers an account of a feminist, lesbian, single child, writer, and poet. Sarton writes: "The fact that a middle -aged, single woman, without any vestige of family left, lives in this house in a silent village and is responsible only to her own soul means something." (p. 40) Annie Dillard's *Pilgrim at Tinker Creek* (1974), brings us to the Blue Ridge Mountains of Virginia; Doris Grumbach's *Fifty Days of Solitude* (1995) takes us to Maine; and Sister Karen Karper's *Where God Begins to Be: A Woman's Journey into Solitude* (1994), describes six years in the West Virginia backwoods. (Karper and her husband later founded a newsletter for hermits called *Raven's Bread*.) Stephanie Mills' *Epicurean Simplicity* (2002) reflects upon a life of solitude and simplicity and Jane Dobisz's *The Wisdom of Solitude* (2004) describes her 100-day experiment of solitude as enlightenment. All of these women, and many others whom I cannot name here, offer the kind of attention to detail and introspection specific to a female sensibility conversant with solitude. "By making my focus smaller and smaller," writes Dobisz, "everything is getting bigger and bigger (p.120)."

The Heroics of Creative Solitude

In sum, I wish to emphasize that solitude and encounter are in constant dialogue with one another. Specifically, the artist's solitude usually encompasses object relations in the creative process. But these relationships are not usually with the person present. It is important to recognize the different ways people choose to live their lives and to appreciate the constructive and productive aspects that solitary activities bring.

What most artists have in common is that they are in passionate pursuit of some private project. For many of them the most significant relationship, the very *causa sui* of their lives, is *the project*. Devoted wholeheartedly to their activity, they derive a primary sense of meaning and self-worth from their heroic endeavor, the creation of art. Even when such a person has a significant relationship of the romantic kind, it is often required that the partner fully accept the solitary pursuit, have one of their own, or support that of their partner. We must keep in mind, however, that the need for self-creation, self-expression, self-expansion and self-transcendence is being expressed. As Ernest Becker (1973) so astutely pointed out, all heroic quests, however conventional or unique, whether involving others directly or requiring long periods of aloneness, function radically as immortality formulas. Self-expression and the flight from death are inseparable—two halves of the same existential coin. Therefore, creation is *both* self-expression *and* flight from annihilation.

In the beginning of this chapter, I mentioned Jean Dominique Bauby's use of the diving bell because I believe it is an extreme metaphor for an essential aspect of the human condition. Indeed, we all have a diving bell locked within us, a state of dreaded isolation that exists just beneath the surface of our consciousness. It is what Bollas (1989) would call the "unthought known." This terror-filled emptiness quickly makes itself known, however, when one encounters the loss of a significant other or when one is faced with a terminal illness. It can be met when one is struggling unsuccessfully with a relationship or a job. It can peep out whenever one confronts one's own limitations, be they intellectual, physical, or creative. It becomes known the closer we find ourselves to death. The diving bell is always a human possibility and it underlies all human dread.

Bauby's brilliant and courageous response to his situation informs us about the desperation inherent in the human condition as well as the ways we attempt to transcend that desperation. The diving bell transports its passenger alone beneath the vast ocean, into an endless realm—not unlike the unconscious mind—of murky darkness, mystery, and the unknown. Plunged to the depths of a lonely solitude, Bauby nevertheless found beauty and great comfort in his memory and his imagination. He was trapped, "locked-in," yet he took flight, like a butterfly, into the realms of splendor. In my belief, though aging, loss, illness and death are our human inevitabilities, creativity allows us to fashion wings upon which we aspire toward immortality.

References

Auster, P. (1982). *The Invention of Solitude*. New York: Penguin Books.

Balint, M. (1968). *The Basic Fault*. NY: Brunner Mazel, 1979.

Bauby, J-D. (1997). *The Diving Bell and the Butterfly: A Memoir of Life in Death*, transl. Jeremy Leggart. New York: Vintage Books.

Becker, E. (1973). *The Denial of Death*. New York: Free Press.

Bion, W.R. (1959). Attacks on Linking. In *Second Thoughts: Selected Papers on Psycho-Analysis*. New York: Aronson, pp 93-109, 1967.

Bollas, C. (1989). *Forces of Destiny: Psychoanalysis and the Human Idiom*. London: Free Association.

Bowlby, J. (1969). *Attachment*. New York: Basic Books.

Buchholz, E.S. (1997). *The Call of Solitude: Aloneness in a World of Attachment*. New York: Simon and Schuster.

Burke, N. (1997). InVisible Worlds: On Women and Solitude. *Gender and Psychoanalysis*, 2:327–341.

Dawson, J. (1997). *Logical dilemmas: The Life and Work of Kurt Gödel*. Wellesley, MA: AK Peters.

Dillard, A. (1974). *Pilgrim at Tinker Creek*. New York: Harper Collins.

Dobisz, J. (2004). *The Wisdom of Solitude: A Zen Retreat in the Woods*. New York: HarperCollins.

Eigen, M. (2009). *Flames from the Unconscious: Trauma, Madness, and Faith*. London: Karnac Books.

Eisenstadt, M., Haynal, A., Rentchnick, P, De Senarclens, P. (1989). *Parental Loss and Achievement*. Madison, CT: International Universities Press.

Erikson, E. (1965). Inner and Outer Space: Reflections on Womanhood. In: *The Women in America*, ed. Robert Jay Lifton. Boston: Houghton.

Fairbairn, R. (1943). The Repression and the Return of the Bad Objects (with Special Reference to War Neurosis). In *Psychoanalytic Studies of Personality*. London: Routledge & Kegan Paul, p. 59-81.

Fromm, E. (1941). *Escape from Freedom*. New York: Holt, Rineheart & Winston.

Fromm-Reichmann, F. (1959). Loneliness. *Psychiatry* 22 1–15.

Gilbert, S. & Gubar, S. (1979). *The Madwoman in the Attic: The Woman Writer and the Nineteenth-Century Literary Imagination*. New Haven: Yale University Press.

Gilligan, C. (1982). *In a Different Voice: Psychological Theory and Women's Development*. Cambridge: Harvard University Press.

Gilot, F. (2001). A Painter's Perspective. In *The Origins of Creativity*. ed. Karl H. Pfenninger & Valerie Shubik. New York: Oxford University Press.

Grumbach, D. (1995). *Fifty Days of Solitude*. Boston: Beacon Press.

Herrera, H. (1983). *Frida: A Biography of Frida Kahlo*. New York: Harper Colophon Books.

Heilbrun, C. (1997). *The Last Gift of Time: Life Beyond Sixty*. New York: Ballantine.

Irigaray, L. (1977). *This Sex Which Is Not One*, transl. Catherine Porter. Ithaca: Cornell University Press.

Kafka, F. (1973). *Letters to Felice*. ed. Eric Heller & Hurgen Born, transls. James Stern & Elizabeth Duckworth. New York: Shocken Bookes, pp. 155-156.

Karper, K. (1994). *Where God Begins to Be: A Woman's Journey into Solitude*. Grand Rapids, MI: Eerdmans.

Klein, M. (1963). On the Sense of Loneliness. In *Envy and Gratitude & Other Works 1946-1963*. New York: Delta, 1975.

Knafo, D. (1993). *Egon Schiele: A Self in Creation: A Psychoanalytic Study of the Artist's Self-Portraits*. Cranbury, NJ: Associated Universities Press.

——— (2002). Revisiting Ernst Kris' Concept of Regression in the Service of the Ego in Aart. *Psychoanalytic Psychology* 19:24–49.

——— (2009). *In her Own Image: Women's Self-Representation in Twentieth-Century Art*. Cranbury, NJ: Associated Universities Press.

Koch, P. (1994). *Solitude: A Philosophical Encounter*. Chicago, IL: Open Court.

Kohut, H. (1971). *The Analysis of the Self*. New York: International Universities Press.

Koller, A. (1990). *The Stations of Solitude*. New York: William Morrow & Co.

Malin, J. & Boynton, V. (2003). *Herspace: Women, Writing, and Solitude*. New York: The Haworth Press.

Martin, A. (2005). *Agnes Martin Writings*, ed. Dieter Schwarz. Berlin: Hatje Cantz

Miller, L. (1992-1993). Alone in the Temple: A Personal Essay on Solitude and the Woman Poet. *Kansas Quarterly*, vol. 24/25, issue 4/1:200–214.

Mills, S. (2002). *Epicurean Simplicity*. Washington, DC: Island Press.

Modell, A. (1993). *The Private Self*. Cambridge: Harvard University Press.

Moffat, M. J. & Paynter, C. (1974). *Revelations: Diaries of Women*. New York: Random House.

Nochlin, L. (1971). Why Have There Been no Great Women Artists? In: *Women, Art, and Power and Other Essays*. New York: Harper and Row, 1988, pp 145–78.

Ogden, T. (1994). Projective Identification and the Subjugating Third. In: *Subjects of Analysis*. Northvale, NJ: Aronson, pp. 97–106.

Olsen, T. (1965). *Silences*. New York: Delacorte Press.

Phillips, A. (1993). On Risk and Solitude. In *On Kissing, Tickling and Being Bored: Psychoanalytic Essays on the Unexamined Life*. Cambridge: Harvard University Press.

Rilke, R. M. 1934. *Letters to a Young Poet*. Trans. M.D. Herter Norton. New York: Norton.

Salomon, D. (1997). *Utopia Parkway: The Life and Work of Joseph Cornell*. New York: Farrar, Straus & Giroux.

Sarton, M. (1973). *Journal of a Solitude*. New York: Norton.

Storr, A. (1988). *Solitude: A Return to the Self*. New York: Ballantine.

Winnicott, D.W. (1958). The Capacity to be Alone. In: *The Maturational Processes and the Facilitating Environment*. New York: International Universities Press, 1968.

———— (1988). *Human Nature*. London: Free Association Books.

Chapter 3
The Skin I Live In
Arlene Kramer Richards

Abstract:

This horror film by Almodovar shows us the making of a woman. It uses loneliness and social isolation as metaphor and as bedrock for the process of becoming a person. Where Freud posited penis envy as the bedrock of femininity, Almodovar posits a very different beginning and a very different process for the formation of a woman and by extension for the formation of a human being.

What makes a woman? The Hebrew bible tells of the creation of woman: Eve is created because Adam is lonely. She is made for his companionship, to accompany him and give him pleasure. This idea has persisted in Western civilization as the foundational myth of femininity. Female sexuality is made for man's pleasure. Their roles are not equal; their purposes are different. Modern women have been insisting that our sexuality and our own selves are just as important as those of men. But it is an uphill battle. I will discuss a movie that opened up for me the question of female sexuality once again and that seems to me to illustrate the dilemma of female development in a new social context.

The horror film *The Skin I Live In* by Almodovar shows us the making of a woman. It uses loneliness and social isolation as metaphor and as bedrock for the process of becoming a person. Almodovar calls her "Vera"; Vera means truth. Where Freud posited penis envy as the bedrock of femininity, Almodovar posits a different beginning but a very familiar process for the formation of a woman and, by extension, for the formation of a human being. Both Freud and Almodovar posit the woman as having been a castrated boy. Where Freud went for the internal and the "dark continent," Almodovar goes for the external as window into the soul. The story he presents is one of sorrow and mourning. A scientist loses his beloved wife in a car accident that burns her skin off. He develops artificial skin that would have saved her if he had it to use while she was dying. The skin is flawless and impervious: It will not burn. It does not feel.

How does he use this wonderful invention? We see him drive his expensive car to his palatial house. In it he has a lab where he performs surgery, and a rehabilitation clinic where a beautiful and mysterious patient lives. Her skin is flawless and is kept perfect by her second skin: a flesh- colored leotard. But she lives in near total isolation. She has contact only with a motherly woman who feeds her via dumbwaiter and provides her with books to read, also delivered by dumbwaiter. She exercises and she reads, but she does not get out of her room.

As the film unfolds we learn that she is actually a person who was once a man but has had a sex change. Yet she is not a usual trans-sexual. This change was not done in the usual trans-sexual way, with hormone treatments and gradual reversible steps leading up to the permanent change of surgery. Instead, the young man had penile ablation and an artificially created vagina first. In this, Almodovar is mimicking the creation of a woman rather than a trans-sexual. The woman is created on the basis of a female genital, not by changing the secondary sexual characteristics that would present her to the outside world as a woman. She starts out as a genital female, then gets the smooth hairless face, soft skin, breasts, hips and female suppleness that actual women develop at puberty.

But how is she to become a psychological woman, how can the feminine image become her way of seeing herself? The book we first see her reading is written by Alice Munro, a Canadian feminist author. She lives with art made by Louise Bourgeois, a French feminist sculptor. She is taught by women artists what it means to be a woman. She is isolated from actual women except by the intercom connection to the woman who feeds her from a distance and supplies her with art materials from a distance. Her social isolation is carefully dosed with female ideas. This is the adult equivalent of giving little girls baby dolls to play with so as to prepare them to think about themselves as nurturers and caretakers, and giving them fashion dolls so that they can think of themselves as becoming ladies of fashion. Her skin is the interface between self and environment, protecting her self against the impingements of the outside world and at the same time keeping her self together, protecting her self from leaking into the outside world. In developing this impervious skin, she is confined to a solitary room. The price of protection is high: her skin isolates her from the world.

We find out that when the surgeon's wife recovered from her terrible burn, she saw a reflection of herself with horribly scarred skin, jumped out a window and killed herself. We now know both how and why the impervious skin was so important to the surgeon who invented it. But the story is even more complex. The isolated woman is in solitary confinement. She lives in a prison, in the most punitive of all prison situations. She is all alone, almost all the time. Who can she identify with? Who is the witness to her life? Only the surgeon sees her. Only the surgeon has the power to keep her in her prison or release her from it. Only the surgeon represents the outside world to her. His will determines her fate. His choice of how she is to live determines her only possibilities. Isolated and alone, she can only long for his visits. She lives an exaggerated version of the life of 1950's housewives described by Betty Freidan (1963) ; alone in a beautiful suburban house with nothing to do all day long but take care of her body and wait for her lord and master to come home. He puts her in a situation which maximizes her loneliness and minimizes her possibilities, yet it is also a situation that seems luxurious and is similar to what upper- middle class housewives choose for themselves in the twenty-first century. She has the smooth skin that so many women achieve through injections of poison and through plastic surgery. Her yoga practice is her only consolation. She believes the televised yoga teacher who promises that it will give her a way to reach her inner core. Yoga gives her some semblance of choice. She can do it without having it imposed by the surgeon. What she does not have is another person who wants to know what she feels or wants to listen to her thoughts. This makes her lonely and also makes her a non-person.

Psychologically, the skin is the border of the self. It is the first boundary. Being stroked, held, caressed, slapped, cut, burned, beaten is experienced through the skin. It is the organ of feeling. It is the edge of me/-not- me and is implicated in perversions as pleasure inches over into pain and pain becomes pleasurable. When the surgeon gives his patient impermeable skin, he is depriving her of both her vulnerability and her capacity to blemish her humanity.

The surgeon has been coaxing her to use dilators to enlarge her vagina so that she will be capable of sexual intercourse without pain. The movie shows the surgeon's brother as his cruder alter ego. The brother rapes her, hurting her but shocking her into life. She complains. The surgeon promises her pleasurable intercourse. But this is not to be. She has feelings. She is shown brutally raped, then tenderly cared for and consoled. She shows herself frightened and weakened by the pain of first intercourse experienced as rape. She has taken on what the environment showed her as her place.

Yet, in the end, the surgeon is not successful. Vera is physically a woman, but psychologically still a man. In the end she will go back to her mother's second-hand ladies clothing shop and reveal herself as the mutilated version of his moher's son. Psychologically this person is still a man. The irony of her situation is underscored by her mother's occupation. She runs a store in which she sells women's second-hand clothes. She is her mother's second-hand woman.

Almodovar tells a modern version of the Tiresias myth. Tiresias lived as a man, was punished by the goddess Hera by being turned into a woman for seven years, and rewarded for a good deed by being returned to his life as a man. Asked about the sexual pleasure he experienced as a man as compared to that of a woman, Tiresias replied that a woman has ten times as much pleasure as a man. The hero- victim of Almodovar's story had no such satisfaction in being a woman. For her, it is pain and ultimate calamity. At the end she has returned to being a man just as Tiresias did.

The loneliness of living in an artificial skin is unbearable. Anzieu (1989) proposes a parallel between the psychological function of the mental image of the skin and the physical function of the bodily skin: the psychological skin ego skin serves to keep in everything needed for mental health and functioning, while at the same time keeping out everything that could harm the self, just as the bodily skin keeps in the other body organs and keeps out what could harm them. This implies that the skin ego is necessary for sexual function. It seems to me that the act of sexual intercourse becomes frightening when it is seen as intrusion on the body in the same way that psychological intimacy threatens to intrude on the self. To ward off this danger one needs to keep away from others who might intrude. Self- imposed social isolation that leads to unbearable loneliness protects both against being intruded upon and intruding on others. The theme of intrusion is taken up by Lemma (2010) in her study of body modification. She describes several cases in which people sought plastic surgery even though the their surgeons thought that the their body parts would not be substantially improved by the procedures. The patients insisted that the changes they wanted made were important to them because they chose them. The body they were rejecting was that provided by the mother who was experienced as either too intrusive or too neglectful, or as alternating between these two noxious extremes. The modifications of the body were felt to be assertions of a separate self that had nothing to do with the mother and therefore would free the patients from the anxiety of intrusion as well as the depressive affect associated with abandonment.

Among the artists who modify their bodies as a form of art Lemma cites Orlan, a woman who has had multiple plastic surgeries recorded on video and broadcast to show the extreme procedures which induce horror and revulsion in the viewers; and a man named Stelarc, whose art consists of mutilating his body by adding extra functional parts like a third arm. Orlan's form of change is a change in being, and Stelarc's is a change in function. Orlan's is passive in that she provides the face and the image of the face, while the surgeon and the viewer provide the action. For Stelarc, the body is modified to produce new action on his part. Stelarc himself, as quoted by Lemma, says:

> I've moved beyond the skin as a barrier . . . Skin no longer
> signifies closure. . . The hollow body becomes a host. . . . It
> is time to recolonize the body. (p.127)

Lemma sees this as a fantasy of using the body as a womb, thus undoing the experience of having been enclosed in the mother's womb so that the artist can undo the loss of the mother by becoming a mother. In all, Lemma sees bodily mutilation as a way to either: deny separation, attempt separation, cover shame, defend against fear of fragmentation, or to retaliate against the parent. She thus offers many avenues to explore with patients who mutilate themselves or who, like the surgeon in the movie The Skin I Live In, are motivated to mutilate others.

In the movie, the surgeon lost his wife some years earlier when her skin was burned beyond repair in an automobile crash. He very recently lost his daughter to a rape-murder. Having lost his entire family, he lives alone. He is doubly castrated in having lost both of the women he loved, his wife and his

42

daughter. He is utterly lonely. By first castrating and then isolating the young man who raped and killed his daughter, he is leaving the person who isolated him as helpless and alone as he has become. The story equates castration and social isolation with femininity. The young man becomes a woman by being rendered helpless and alone. After completing the transformation from male to female, the surgeon tries to teach the young woman he has created how to become a sexually functioning woman. His attempt fails because the young woman longs for her mother, longs to return to her life as her mother's son. Yet his mother's work as the purveyor of second-hand womanhood seems to have doomed him from the start to his fate of becoming a second-hand woman.

The theme of the second-hand woman appears in Gilbert's (Sander 2010) version of the myth of Pygmalion and Galatea. In the original myth, Pygmalion is a sculptor who falls in love with a statue he makes of a woman and his love causes her the statue to come to life. In Gilbert's version, he makes the statue using his own wife as the model; and he falls in love with the statue only after he experiences loneliness and longing when his wife leaves him for a day with the promise that his sculpture of her will keep him company as he waits for her to come back. Unfortunately, the newly alive statue falls in love with him and he, in response, falls in love with her as well. Only when she is frozen back into marble will he achieve peace. The surgeon in The Skin I live In has also created a woman to substitute for the wife who left him. But his creation does not fall in love with him. He must suffer his loneliness without a substitute.

Another variation on the theme of creating a woman to love is shown in Shaw's *Pygmalion,* and again in Lerner and Loewe's *My Fair Lady* (both the stage and movie versions), a musical based on Shaw's play. In all of these, the creator of the woman, like the surgeon in *The Skin I Live In,* ends up alone and lonely as does the surgeon in *The Skin I Live In.* The creator is the father who must see his daughter go off with another man to a life of her own with a love of her own choosing. But the surgeon's creation, the woman he has made for himself, goes off leaving both the surgeon and himself devastated. In the end, he experiences the ultimate loneliness: he longs for himself as a man. By longing for his former self s/he experiences what is impossible to fulfill, he must be lonely for the rest of his life. In this movie, Almodovar has shown us a form of loneliness that no one has ever seen before. To the ideas of longing for a specific object (Brenner, 1959), longing for an empathic object (Kohut, 1977), longing for acceptance in an elite group (Proust, 1997), and longing for a national or racial group's acceptance, Almodovar has added longing for oneself. This idea is implicit in Freud's assertion that narcissistic love can be longing for one's former self, longing for one's ideal self, or longing for one's mirror image. But Almodovar gives us a picture of someone longing for his former sexual and gender identity in a way that was not possible in Freud's time; because the possibility of sex reassignment surgery was not available. The closest thing to it that could be achieved was adopting the gender role of the opposite sex in life and the sexual role of the opposite sex in love making. So a psychological change was possible. Castration was possible, but trans-sexuality like that of Tiresias only became possible with modern surgery.

What has all of this to do with clinical practice? When a Chinese person gets a divorce, he or she may say: "I have lost my skin." When he or she is disillusioned or disappointed, he or she may say something similar. Skin has the meaning of a layer of protection from the world. The skin provided by a spouse is a reassurance that one is a wife and therefore a female or that one is a husband and therefore a male. Our sexual roles reinforce our gender identity. And our gender identity reinforces our sense of self. To have a gender is be a person. If a man speaks as a husband, it reinforces his sense of self; if a woman speaks as a wife, that reinforces her sense of self. To lose that status is to lose a part of oneself.

When angry at another person one says in English that the other person is "getting under my skin." The expression conveys the feeling of being intruded upon that causes psychic pain to the person who has been aroused to anger. The other person who has "gotten under" her skin is an alien presence that does not fit with the image of herself that she values and wants to protect. And nothing is as important to protect as one's sexuality. But, by contrast, a popular song of the last century by Cole Porter called "I've Got You Under My Skin" describes being in love as having the other person inside oneself but again against his own will and better judgment.

Concealing sexuality and concealing one's sexual organs are part of most societies. In both China and the west, modesty is based on covering the sexual organs. That part of the skin that covers the sexual organs is both the most delicate, the most abundantly supplied with nerve endings, and most to be protected from intrusion. In this sense sexuality is the basis and foundation of the innermost self. And the skin is the organ of touch, and touch is the sensation of sexual arousal. The senses of smell, sight and hearing are involved in the earlier stages of sexual arousal, but the skin on skin contact of sexuality is the essential part of both arousal and fulfillment. So the skin stimulates, and the nerves it shields and stimulates are the road in to sexual experience and to the sense of oneself as a sexual being.

The sense of being a sexual person is crucial to adulthood for most people. Whether one sees oneself as heterosexual male, homosexual male, heterosexual female or homosexual female, having a firm sense of being one of these helps makes most people feel grounded in their own bodies. Some people believe that they are free to choose and to change their sexual choices as they meet new possible lovers. They still feel themselves to be male and potent with male partners, for example, even though they also have female partners. Blechner (2009) argues for the consideration of any sexual desires as non-pathological as long as they give pleasure to the persons who practice them. He thinks that psychoanalysts harm their patients when they categorize any forms of sexuality as abnormal.

But this attitude, while sounding modern and cool to New York City therapists, limits psychoanalysis to a way of thinking that fits a particular society at a particular time. What about sex with children? With patients? With students? All of these can cause harm. One way of dealing with this problem is by limiting what we consider normal to what happens between two consenting adults. But this standard does not fit into everyone's way of defining limits, and it is not recognized by societies with different moral standards. Psychoanalysis faces a crisis whenever we try to fit our concepts to a new social reality. Blechner (2009), among others (e.g., Dimen, 2005), is trying to widen our horizons to accommodate a widening social acceptance in the United States of the rights of homosexual people. Marriage between two men or two women is already socially acceptable and legal in several states in the United States including New York and Massachusetts, where many analysts practice. The shame that used to attach to homosexuality is gone. The blame for feelings of sexual desire has stopped. Men and women are publishing their same-sex marriages in *The New York Times,* our most prestigious newspaper.

At the same time, young people who are starting their adult sexual lives worry about their sexual orientation. They tease homosexuals and even push some of them to suicide (Parker, 2012). Young people are anxious about their new sexuality. Are they going to be good lovers? Will someone want them? Will they be attracted to the right sort of person? Will the right sort of person be attracted to them? Are their bodies disgusting? Do they smell bad? Are they too hairy? Not hairy enough? Are they too fat? Too skinny? Too short? Too tall? Is their nose too big? Too small? Are their eyes the right shape? Do they look too pimply? Will they do well in the preliminaries? Will they be too fast? Or too slow? Will they be able to sustain sexual contact long enough? These worries, and many others, make them vulnerable to disappointment in their own sexuality.

When people feel vulnerable in these ways, one way to protect themselves is to find others who are less attractive or less popular, or who have sexual preferences that are different from those of most people. If most people are heterosexual, then homosexuals make good targets for teasing and put downs. People who do not fit the model of sexual attractiveness of their society may also easily become targets.

If "blonds have more fun," then darker hair or darker skin makes a good target. The idea that different is worse makes the alienation of the other, especially the other of a different skin color, a permissible target of for rejection, ridicule and persecution. People who do not fit the model of sexual attractiveness for their society may also easily become targets. Adolescent sexuality pushes young people into cruelty because they project their uncertainty and anxiety about their own attractiveness onto anyone with less socially valued attributes and features.

The social value of sexual attractiveness is a combination of innate and socially differentiated elements. For example, all known social groups value symmetrical features, almost all value the look of health. These traits seem to belong to an innate system of values. By contrast, only very special circumstances make obesity or extreme thinness sexually attractive; although there are some social groups in which obesity in women is seen as a sign of fertility and therefore of sexual attractiveness, and there are groups in the western world that value the extreme skinniness of fashion models. Young people are extremely sensitive to these values and go to extreme lengths to alter their bodies and their faces to achieve what they see as the ideal of sexual attractiveness in their society. And many older people are willing to go to great expense and take great risks in order to try to look young and sexually attractive (Sinkman, 2012). Like the surgeon's wife, they are disgusted and repelled by the signs that age and experience have left on their skins. Like her they would rather die than look scarred. They prefer to risk their lives and tolerate pain and discomfort rather than risk the social isolation and loneliness that they see as inevitable concomitants of wrinkled skin, droopy muscles and white hair. They are willing to risk looking ridiculous, in clothing worn by much younger people, shoes that torture older feet, hairstyles that require hours at the colorist and more at the stylist's. They work at looking younger as if their very lives depended on it.

Ironically, Eco (2011) shows that ugliness in women is represented in art as old age masquerading as beauty by hiding behind cosmetics, seductive clothing or seductive poses. This idea has particular relevance to our current aging society. More and more, women past menopause are unwilling to see themselves as ugly. Yet it is not age, but the attempt to imitate youth that is seen as ugly. But Eco reminds the reader that what is beautiful in art may not be the same as what is beautiful in life. A beautiful woman may be painted by Picasso with green cheeks or a single eye, yet a woman in life who had such features would be ugly. So we cannot take what is represented in art as a depiction of what would be beautiful in life. The girl who starves herself to look like a model in a fashion magazine does not get elected homecoming queen. The old woman who uses cosmetic surgery and/or chemical cosmetics may or may not look beautiful to her aging husband or her children or her grandchildren. They may want her to look the age that fits the role she plays in their lives. Yet to her friends and even to her age mates she may look wonderful when she looks young enough to make them feel young also. The role of cosmetics and plastic surgery may be to enhance a woman's attractiveness or these may make her look fake and even frightening.

Often, by rejecting one's body and face as they have been, one manages to alienate the body from the self, leaving a person lonely in the most radical way imaginable, lonely for oneself. Aging forces this alienation on the person, especially in adolescence when the secondary sexual characteristics change one's body and face, and again in the process of aging when menopause or male climacteric change the body and face. Longing for who one used to be is a kind of loneliness that is even more radical than longing for another person. Plastic surgery offers the possibility of rejecting the newly acquired changes but at the cost of still further alienation from the self, and still further loneliness and longing for the self she once had, but can never really recover. Almodovar has shown us in this film a wonderful instance of the complexity of changing one's body and the loneliness for the former self that transcends the social aspects of this exquisitely painful feeling.

References

Anzieu, D. (1989). *The Skin Ego.* New Haven: Yale University Press.

Blechner, M. (2009). *Sex Changes.* New York: Routledge.

Brenner, C. (1974). On the Nature and Development of Affects: A Unified Theory. *Psychoanalytic Quarterly* 43:532–556.

Dimen, M. (2005) Sexuality and suffering or the Eew! factor. *Studies in Gender and Sexuality* 6:1–8.

Eco, U. ed., (2010). *On Beauty.* New York: Rizzoli.

——— (2011). *On Ugliness.* New York: Rizzoli.

Friedan, B. (1963). *The Feminine Mystique.* New York: Norton.

Kohut, H. (1959). Introspection, Empathy, and Psychoanalysis—An Examination of the Relationship Between Mode of Observation and Theory. *Journal of the American Psychoanalytic Association* 7:459–483.

Kohut, H. (1977) *The Restoration of the Self.* New York: International Universities Press.

101Lemma, A. (2010). *Under the Skin.* London: Routledge.

Parker, I. (2012) The story of a suicide. *The New Yorker*, Feb 6, 2012.

Proust, Marcel. (1896–1919). A race accursed. In: *On Art and Literature,* transl. Sylvia Townsend Warner, introduction Terence Kilmartin. New York: Carroll & Graf Publishers, Inc. pp.210-229, 1997.

——— (1913–1927). In *Search of Lost Time.* (6 volumes), transl. C.K. Scott Moncrieff & T. Kilmartin, rev. D.J. Enright, introduction Richard Howard. New York: Modern Library Edition, 2003.

——— (1956). *Letters to His Mother,* transl. & ed G.D. Painter with an essay by Pamela Hansford Johnson. New York: The Citadel Press.

Richards, A. K. & Spira, L (2003). On being lonely: Fear of one's own aggression as an impediment to intimacy. *Psychoanalytic Quarterly* 72:357–375.

Spira, L. & Richards, A.K. (2003). The "Sweet and Sour" of being lonely and alone. *Psychoanalytic Study of the Child* 58:214–227.

Sander, F. (2010). *Created in Our Own Images.* New York: IPBooks.

Sinkman, E. (2012). *The Psychology of Beauty.* New York: Rowan, Littlefield.

Chapter 4
Forms and Transformations of Loneliness
Jeffrey Stern

Abstract:

This paper will explore several sorts of loneliness and responses to loneliness that are taken up in works of film and literature. Martin Scorsese's film *Hugo* which is about the loneliness of a bereaved little boy and an old film maker who save one another from despair is taken up in some detail, and via an automaton the old filmmaker has built and the boy endeavors to restore, leads into thoughts about puppets as a hedge against loneliness and perhaps something about the loneliness of puppets themselves. The discussion of Hugo also opens into a consideration of the loneliness of monsters represented in such works as The Phantom of the Opera and The Elephant Man and the fairy tale Hans the Hedgehog and in Shakespeare's The Taming of the Shrew. The paper concludes with a brief consideration of what might be called the loneliness of angels figured in Wim Wenders's *Wings of Desire*.

In *Beyond the Pleasure* principle Freud famously describes how his eighteen-month-old grandson Ernest threw a wooden bobbin up from the floor onto his cot and sadly uttered the word "fort!" (gone!) (Freud 1920: pp. 14–15) when it disappeared from view. And then he reeled it back, excitedly exclaiming "da!" (there!) when it reappeared. This is perhaps the first discussion of loneliness in our literature, as well as the first magic trick ("now you see it, now you don't!"); and the first use of a puppet, insofar as the piece of wood represents a person, his mother, which he controls with an attached string. In this paper I want to talk about loneliness, magic, and puppets—specifically, magic and puppets as responses to loneliness; or, more broadly, art as a response to loneliness and loss, and the loneliness of puppets themselves. I will try to suggest that transitional object play enabled by 'good enough' internal objects (or, if you prefer, self-structure) offers a bulwark against unendurable loneliness, and the hope of union or reunion with the longed for other. As loneliness, magic, puppets, and art are at the heart of Martin Scorsese's recent film *Hugo*, we will consider this movie in some detail; the paper will also touch on the loneliness of monsters, angels and Shakespeare.

I.   Loneliness and Puppets

In Walt Disney's lovely 1940 film *Pinocchio*, the old woodcarver Gepetto creates a marionette out of his longing for a son. For a little while he is completely happy dancing the little puppet around the room. But a transitional

51

object is an imperfect cure for loneliness, because it is completely under the self's omnipotent control—which is to say that we can only *pretend* that it is loving us back. If we desire the nurture of its actual love, we have to set it free. But once it's free, it's free to leave us. And this, of course, is exactly Gepetto's fate. He wishes on a star that Pinocchio might be transformed into a real boy, and the Blue Fairy grants his wish. But after Pinocchio is freed from his strings, he runs away from home. But Pinocchio misses his father and longs to be reunited with him. And the story has a happy ending because Gepetto is able to endure the disappointment—Winnicott would say the destruction (Winnicott 1971; pp. 88-89).– that loving a real boy requires.

But can puppets themselves be lonely? Puppets, it might be said, are only not lonely when they are completed by the hands of the puppeteer. Dolls and teddy bears are perfectly happy to sit on shelves or pillows all day, waiting for their children to come home, but puppets and marionettes only come into being when connected with their humans. There is no word like puppeteer for dolls and teddy bears because dolls and teddy bears exist independently. Puppets need us entirely. We merge with them and they with us. The moment we put them down, they lose their shape, their integrity—they fall out of being. But I think for a puppet to be truly lonely rather than, say, in a state of patient or impatient waiting, it would have to sense that its child had a broken imagination, that its child was too lonely or heartbroken to play. This I think is why the automaton in *Hugo* seems sad.

Genesis offers a story like that of *Pinocchio*. God creates Adam and Eve to relieve his loneliness but sees that their connection to him can have no meaning unless they have free will. And, of course, because they do, they sin and he banishes them from the garden, which leaves them pining for reunion with him. Because he is able—perhaps just barely—to withstand their transgression without destroying them, mankind endures.

Much of what we are about as parents has to do with reenactments of these stories of children wishing to cut apron strings and proclaim their independence, and our struggles to survive and contain their ambivalent emotions and our own depression, rage and loneliness.

The Case of Rose

Rose was a woman unable to survive such destruction. Her parents were alcoholics who either ignored or clung to her. She needed them to pay attention and respond to her on her terms, but everything they did they seemed to do for their own purposes. Their idea of closeness was to drag her to social events that had no meaning for her, and to leave her to her own devices once they arrived. Sometimes they forgot about her when it was time to go home because they were too drunk to remember they'd brought her. At other times they would leave her for months at a time in the care of a governess she had probably just met while they traveled. To soothe and enliven herself she spent much of her time imagining herself in a fairytale world where she was loved by handsome princes and watched over by fairy godmothers. As an adult, she longed for love but felt afraid of every man she met. Her yearning to be taken care of was so intense that she imagined herself becoming any man's puppet on a string. Like a child unable to avail itself of a transitional object because lacking the *secure enough* attachment to lose itself in play, she couldn't open herself to the dangers of any relationship she couldn't control. In her effort to be the one pulling the strings, she created a world in which all of her significant others were in her employ and governed by strict rules of professional conduct. She had therapists, accountants, lawyers, bankers, stockbrokers, pilates instructors, hair stylists, and a personal assistant, in addition to the people who worked in the small insurance agency she owned. Her days were given over to appointments with people who could be relied upon to treat her as she demanded because if they didn't, they would be replaced—at least in theory. In fact, she found it almost impossible to replace any of them, and frequently felt that she was the puppet on a string rather than the other way round. Not surprisingly, Rose was chronically lonely, although she was able to keep her loneliness split off much of the time because she was always seeing people.

In the film *A.I.*, Steven Spielberg appears to transform the theme of puppets as responses to loneliness into a meditation on the loneliness of puppets, but the film is really about the loneliness of an abandoned little boy. David is an advanced robot developed by a future society as a "replacement child" (Anisfeld & Richards, 2000) for bereaved parents. The family that acquires him has a child with an incurable disease. This child is preserved in suspended animation while a cure is sought. David is different from other such machines because he has the capacity to love if his mother, Monica, programs him to do so by speaking certain words to him. When a cure is found for her "real" son, Monica's husband insists that David be taken back to the robotics company for destruction. Because the heartbreak of losing his family exceeds the emotional intensity level that his psyche has been designed to tolerate, Monica can't bear to go through with the plan and so instead abandons David in the woods. He believes that she has done so because he is not a "real" boy and dreams of asking the Blue Fairy—Monica has read him the Pinocchio story—to make him into one. The irony of course is that despite being made of plastic and wires, he is more human than his human brother because he is driven entirely by longing and love. The programming Monica performs is, of course, entirely metaphorical: every child is programmed to love by the special words it hears from its mother. Despite the fact that fate takes David away from Monica and thousands of years go by, he never stops missing her and dreaming of the day that they will be reunited—which finally and briefly happens. He is supremely capable of surviving destruction, the (object) constancy of his devotion unwavering. Spielberg seems to be saying that our loneliness—

defined as our ability to love in the face of loss, privation and impossibility—is what makes us human. Even when—as in the case of David or E.T.—we aren't.

Homer suggests something similar in *The Odyssey,* where Odysseus's longing for his wife, son and kingdom drives him to overcome unimaginable obstacles to his returning home. His is a very different sort of loneliness from that of Rose, because, like David's in *A.I.*, it is based on powerfully good internal objects. Odysseus holds the memory of Penelope and his kingdom and child within him from the moment he leaves Ithaca. Loneliness for him is not a reason to avoid life and its dangers; it functions like a radio signal that guides him home. Even when he is offered love and immortality by the nymph Calypso, he pines for his aging Penelope and Telemachus. One wonders if his men—all of whom perish during the ten-year voyage—do so because they lack the sort of inner bonds Odysseus has to those they leave behind.

II.   The Loneliness of *HUGO*

Hugo is all about the loneliness and grief of Hugo, a small boy, and Melies, an old filmmaker (played brilliantly by Ben Kingsley). They are fellow travelers, or, perhaps more accurately, nontravelers—because anchored in depression—who live (Hugo) and work (Melies) in the great Paris railway station Gare Montparnasse. It is also about a puppet without strings, an automaton. Hugo isn't lonely because he lacks 'good enough' internal objects, or the capacity for object constancy, he is lonely because he is friendless and an orphan. When we first see him he is looking at the world through the number four of the huge station clock within which he sits. Kohut (1971, pp. 136, 158) would say that the lonely child merges through his eyes with the denizens of the railway world below, and critics have likened him to the frail asthmatic child Scorsese was himself, a child who watched the children he couldn't play with framed by his bedroom windows and later watched his actors framed by the lens of his camera.

We learn that Hugo's father, Monsieur Cabret, was a clockmaker, and that Hugo adored him, but that he died tragically in a fire at the museum where he sometimes worked. Cabret's drunken brother Claude takes Hugo to the railway station where he lives in an apartment within the walls and teaches Hugo to wind and repair the station's great clocks. But Claude soon disappears—we learn that he has drowned in the Seine—leaving Hugo entirely alone. He lives by his wits stealing food from the station's concession, terrified that he will be tracked down by the Station Inspector's frightening Doberman, Maximillian, arrested and sent like a criminal to the orphanage where all of the homeless children caught at the station end up.

Hugo has one possession that he cares about and that ties him to his father, the beautiful and sad looking automaton that his father found abandoned in the attic of the museum and with Hugo's help was working to restore when he died. The automaton holds a pen, suggesting that its purpose is to write, and Hugo believes that if he can get it to work, it will produce a message from his father. It is thus a sort of double transitional object: something that Hugo hopes will help him to feel less lonely and a go-between linking himself and his father. The only place Hugo knows where he might find parts for the automaton's broken clockwork is the toy booth at the station. Since he has no money he steals them as the forbidding old proprietor—Georges Melies—is aware. Melies pretends to doze to lure Hugo to his counter, and when the boy reaches for a windup mouse, he grabs him and demands that he open his pockets. One contains stolen wheels, springs and gears, as Melies knew it would, the other a notebook of drawings Hugo's father made of the automaton. The notebook is not something Melies expects, and it clearly upsets him.

Melies demands to know who made the drawings, but Hugo refuses to tell him, whereupon Melies insists that he has stolen it and announces his intention to burn it. Desperate to save the one thing he possesses in his father's hand, Hugo follows Melies home where he meets Isabelle, the old man's goddaughter. She promises Hugo that she'll make sure the notebook is safe, but the following day Melies hands Hugo a handkerchief full of ashes. When Isabelle sees Hugo weeping, she assures him that it's only a trick: the notebook is safe. Why the old toy seller should wish to play so cruel a trick on a small boy is a mystery.

Hugo refuses to leave the toy booth without his notebook, so Melies orders him to fix the broken windup mouse. When Hugo easily does so Melies tells him that he will allow Hugo to work off what he has stolen and possibly to earn back the notebook. As soon as Hugo takes up a broom, however, Melies begins practicing card tricks, which of course draws Hugo to him like a moth to a flame. And then, suddenly, Melies is teaching him his magic. What is going on?

We will learn that Melies had been a young man like Hugo, one who loved fixing mechanical things which had led to a career in magic with its array of "fort-da"—"now-you-see-it-now-you-don't"—illusions. But although happily married Melies had no children, no son, the reason perhaps that he built the automaton, which like Gepetto's Pinocchio he tenderly loved. With the invention of film Melies realized that he could create far greater magic on screen than he could on the stage. Indeed, he felt that he could transform his dreams into the dreams of his audience. "If you ever wonder where your dreams are made," he tells the young Rene Tabard who visits his crystal studio and will one day write a book about his work, "they are made here."

Melies explains that his wife, Jeanne, was his star, muse, and amanuensis and that they were completely happy translating the luminous world of his imagination into film with their crew of actors, artists, and technicians. These served in effect as transformations of the automaton performing Melies'

55

commands to the letter and connecting him to the audiences that flocked to see the 500 films he made. The world was Melies' oyster until the First World War ended everything by shattering the psyches of his audience. They had seen too much reality to take pleasure any longer in his whimsical dream works, and so they stopped coming to his movies. The loss of his mirroring audience is devastating for Melies. As a filmmaker their approval is essential to his sense of self, tantamount in effect to what Kohut calls "the gleam in the mother's eye." (Kohut 1971, p. 116). With them he is everything, without, more than lonely, he begins to doubt his very existence. "What am I?" he asks his wife, "Nothing but a penniless merchant! A broken windup toy!" Recall King Lear ignored in his daughter Goneril's household: "Does anyone here know me?" (1.4.223) he asks. "Who is it that can tell me who I am?" The Fool answers, "Lear's shadow" (1.4.227-8). Without his audience to complete him, Melies loses what Hugo calls his purpose. His business collapses and to pay bills he has to fire his actors, close his studio and sell his films to be melted into chemicals for the manufacture of women's shoes. Ashamed at his helplessness and the indifference of his public, Melies becomes narcissistically enraged with himself. He burns his sets, props and costumes and abandons his crystal filmmaking palace. In his despair he donates his automaton to the museum.

This is why he is so heartless and mean to Hugo: he can't bear to be reminded of what he has lost, so when Hugo appears with sketches of his beloved automaton, he freaks out. And yet he doesn't burn the notebook, as he had burned all of his filmmaking equipment, he only pretends to, and he allows Hugo to enter his life. Evidently a split-off part of himself remains intact—and recognizes a chance to be brought back into being by the boy who reminds him of the boy he had once been himself.

It might appear that loneliness is not the issue for Melies but depression. He is not physically alone of course living as he does with a loving wife and goddaughter. But he is lonely for his lost life as an artist with its vitalizing connections to his actors and filmmakers and audience and the feeling that his life's work has meaning. At some level he realizes that he needs Hugo to put him in touch with his forgotten power to create, enchant and connect with others through the medium of his art.

Hugo completes repairs on the automaton's clockwork but can't wind the mechanism without a missing heart-shaped key. The missing heart key makes the automaton a sort of Tinman and suggests that what it needs to function is love. Hugo discovers that Isabelle wears the key around her neck—(it's her godmother's charm)—and the key indeed brings the automaton to life. But the real key is Isabelle's loving friendship. Hugo is too lonely and sad to lose himself in imaginative play. So the automaton appears to be lonely too, sitting inert and downcast, like a toy an unhappy child can't make use of as a transitional object until Isabelle comes into Hugo's life.

The automaton, as it turns out is itself the key to the identity of Melies, because with its pen and inkwell it draws an advertisement from one of his greatest films: *A Trip to the Moon*. This isn't of course a message Hugo's father wrote to him, but it is a message Hugo recognizes, because his father had seen this film and had told him about it. The drawing thus leads the children to discover who Melies was. And Hugo believes that by showing Melies *A Trip to the Moon* he will be able therapist-like to shock him out of his melancholy.

The night before he is to do so, however, Hugo has two nightmares. In the first he sees the heart-shaped key to the automaton on the train tracks and jumps down to retrieve it: the words "Cabret et Fil Horlogers" are written on it. When he looks up a train is bearing down on him. It jumps the station rails to avoid hitting him and barrels through the station until it smashes through the wall and the engine crashes to the street below. (This, incidentally, is Scorseses's recreation of a famous actual early train accident.) In the second dream Hugo opens his eyes upon awakening from the train nightmare and discovers himself morphing into the automaton.

The dreams seem to be about Hugo's anxiety over his wish to become like a son or grandson the next day to the Melies Isabelle calls "Papa Georges". The automaton has revealed itself to be a literal transitional object linking Hugo's father, who watched *A Trip to the Moon* and Melies, who made it. The connection is further inscribed in the automaton that Melies invented and Hugo's father worked to repair. In the first dream Hugo sees the key he had found around Isabelle's neck on the tracks with the words "Cabret et Fil Horlogers" written on it, suggesting that Melies is the key to the recovery of his relation to his father. This thought is evidently overstimulating to Hugo, because immediately upon finding the key the train leaps the rails and runs unstoppably and uncontrollably through the station, a perfect metaphor for the failure of Hugo's psyche to contain his excitement and anxiety.

In the second dream Hugo sees himself morphing into the automaton, the object then of Melies, who designed it. Hugo dreams of this reversal of the Pinocchio metamorphosis from marionette into real boy, because if it were to occur he would never again be lonely. At the same time his wish to morph into the automaton terrifies him because it would mean entirely losing his sense of agency and indeed his very humanness. He would be a machine entirely in the control of Melies. This in effect restages Rose's stark construction of the relationship dilemma: to be free but lonely, or attached but a thing.

The final element of Melies psychological cure is his reconnection to the film audience that he has been so desperately lonely for and which completes the circuit of his reconnection to his lost artistic self. The film professor Rene Tabard stages a retrospective of his work at the film academy after recovering more than 80 of his films. When Melies is introduced to the audience they stand and applaud, and he addresses them in what he says is their essential being as wizards, mermaids, travelers, adventurers, magicians—in effect twins of his own grandiose self. "Come," he says to them, "and dream with me."

Like so many therapists the lonely and broken-hearted Hugo in repairing the lonely and broken-hearted Melies repairs himself. At the end of the film Melies tells the Station Inspector who has finally caught up with Hugo and is about to send him to the orphanage that the boy belongs to him.

III. The Loneliness of Monsters

Having said all of this, there is more to say about *Hugo*. Let us consider the Station Inspector, Gustav (wonderfully played by Sacha Baron Cohen) whose cruelty to Hugo and the lost boys and girls of the station recalls Melies' initial cruelty toward Hugo but goes quite beyond it. With his war ravaged leg supported by a creaking brace that he needs to oil with an oilcan reminiscent of the Tinman's in Oz, he is initially another kind of heartless automaton. Nonetheless his shyness and stilted awkwardness, especially in the presence of the flower girl, Lisette, makes us wonder if we haven't misjudged him, as does the suspicion that his fearsome Doberman, Maximillian, may actually be sweet-natured.

It appears that Gustav's social like his physical clumsiness, is an effect of the war, but we discover that it is really due to the fact that he has had no parents and was brought up in the very orphanage that he sends the station's homeless children to. "You don't need a family!" he screams at Hugo. Like Melies, it appears that he is unable to empathize with the children because doing so would force him to remember the loneliness he would like to forget. Despite what he says, having had no mother has left him as inwardly damaged as having been shot has damaged him outwardly. He never learned to smile and has no idea what to say to the flower girl Lisette for whom he pines. He asks her if her flowers are "smelly" because he doesn't know to say "fragrant", and he speaks absurdly of the perfectly formed udders of the cows in Bordeaux when she tells him it is her home, because he doesn't know how to tell her that he thinks she has a beautiful figure.

While he talks to her, the brace on his leg seizes up, leaving him mortified with shame, and he tells her that he had been wounded in the war and that the wound will never heal. What he means is that he will be forever too damaged to appeal to her as a suitor. She then tells him of a wound she has that will also never heal: her brother was killed at Verdun. And she gives him a flower. Thrilled that she accepts him—because unlike Gustav himself Lisette is capable of empathy—he begins to heal.

We will see that both Gustav's loneliness and its transformation follow the pattern of what we might call the loneliness of monsters—such beings as the phantom of the opera, the elephant man, beauty's Beast, Hans the hedgehog of Grimm's fairytale and the recent French novel and film to name but a few. In these works the protagonist hides from a world that considers him monstrous due to his physical and or psychological deformities. The phantom of the opera is a brilliant "angel of music" who conceals himself because half of his face is hideous. The hidden half face is doubtless meant to symbolize the intolerable feelings of hatred, rage, envy and depression that shame him. The kiss of his beloved Christine transforms his hatred and self-loathing into self-sacrificing kindness. John Merrick, the "elephant man," too is saved from unbearable loneliness by the actress Mrs. Kendall, who allows him to see her naked body. Her willingness to offer her most intimate self to his adoring gaze seems to undo the effects of his years of forced and humiliating exposure in the freak show to the stares of the leering patrons.

The fairytale hero *Hans the Hedgehog* is born with quills because he recognizes from the first that his father doesn't love or want him. The quills protect his sensitive skin from the pain of this knowledge. He becomes a lonely and solitary musician like the phantom of the opera as well as a warrior and herdsman. But his coat of quills falls away when he finds a woman who agrees to marry him despite his appearance, because he has saved her father's life. The novel and film that transform this tale tell the story of a lonely and dowdy middle aged French woman who works as a concierge in an apartment building and begins to come emotionally alive in response to the warmth and respect she experiences from a new male tenant who appreciates and shares her interest in literature and from a suicidal girl who discovers in her a tender soulmate and defender. *Beauty and the Bea*st is another such tale in which a hero's ugliness is a sign that he has been scarred by rejection, ill-treatment, or loss. His isolation represents his attempt to protect himself from the re-traumatization that he expects to suffer should he attempt to re-enter the world. The cost of safety, however, is nearly unendurable loneliness. Only the love of a woman able to see the wounded human soul languishing within the beast's exterior can transform the creature into the "prince" he was destined to be.

The Taming of the Shrew is Shakespeare's version of this motif. Kate exists in a state of perpetual rage because she has no mother and her father makes no secret of his preference for her accommodating younger sister Bianca. Indeed as Kate may at some level conceive it, Bianca has not only stolen her father's love, she has in being born deprived her of her mother. (I am imagining that Kate's mother dies in childbirth or soon after because there is no mention of her in the play.) So she is full of black emotions that drive everyone away from her until Petruchio shows up to court her. Unlike everyone else she has ever encountered he is undaunted by her rage. Indeed, he is like Kohut's model oedipal father (Kohut, 1977, p. 230) in that he takes pride—even delight—in her angry assertiveness even as he sets about to limit and control it, or Winnicott's "good enough" (Winnicott 1973, pp. 17, 44) mother in that he is able cheerfully to survive her destructiveness. Kate finds that

Petruchio not only doesn't fear her strength, he seems turned on by it and takes pleasure in striving to match it. When she sees that he intends to play with her until she stops fighting, and—perhaps more importantly—that he has no intention of abandoning her, she begins to fall in love with him, her shrewishness and loneliness falling away like the hedgehog's coat of quills.

Kafka's *The Metamorphosis* offers an opposing example, one in which a man is transformed by loneliness and the absence of love into a monster. Gregor Samsa devotes his life to the support of his family by working as a salesman for a soulless company. The dehumanizing treatment he endures transforms him literally into an insect, and when his family ceases to recognize him as the son and brother that his exterior conceals, he dies of despair.

IV. The Loneliness of Angels

Wim Wenders's beautiful 1987 film *Wings of Desire* is about the loneliness of angels. These angels move usually without wings through the black and white streets, circuses and libraries of Berlin. They ride trains, sit in cars, and watch the city atop tall buildings. They hear what people are thinking and reach out to touch them when they are in pain, but they can't actually make contact. And sometimes their efforts to console fail altogether as in the moment when a man the angel, Cassiel, tries to save from despair with his tender empathic presence jumps unheeding to his death. The angels know one another, but they seem to take no emotional sustenance from each other, and it gradually dawns on us that they are lonely.

Wenders's angels have always reminded me of the opaque and formal psychoanalysts I was trained by, who sat unseen and largely unknown behind their couches saying almost nothing. Like Damiel and Cassiel, they heard the most intimate and secret thoughts of their patients and suffered with them empathically, although their patients—like the humans the angels try to lift with their empathy—often never realized it. These analysts barred themselves from the sort of ordinary human contact that the angel Damiel comes to long for. Many of course still do. We probably tend not to think of psychoanalysts as lonely, but perhaps we are. Perhaps the reason we spend our working lives alone with lonely people who seek desperately to connect with us speaks as much to our loneliness as to theirs.

Fascination with a beautiful circus acrobat leads Damiel to realize how lonely he is and eventually to decide to become a mortal: he wants to feel what humans feel when they taste food, or drink coffee, or bleed or smoke, or rub their hands together for warmth, or when they see colors, or above all when they take one another in their arms. So he gives up his immortality and his wings and falls into the world, a person. Peter Falk, playing himself, greets him warmly telling Damiel that he too was an angel before becoming a man, an actor, a father, a husband, an artist, rumply Columbo. I cannot help but wonder if at least something of today's increasingly relational psychoanalytic technique didn't—at least to some extent—grow out of the desire some of us felt to break through the conventions of our classical training—conventions that required us to be blank screens to our patients and denied us the sight of their faces and them the sight of ours, conventions that in a word compelled us to be too much like Wenders's angels and too little like ourselves.

V. Loneliness in Shakespeare

As a magician, a dreamer and a dreammaker, Georges Melies provides a ready link to Prospero ("We are such stuff/As dreams are made on" [4.1.156-157]), Shakespeare's magical creative artist of *The Tempest*. But before we think of Prospero and loneliness, we should first think about *King Lear*, because Shakespeare in *The Tempest* seems to be trying to solve the problems of loss and loneliness that make *King Lear* a tragedy. At the start of the play, Lear needs to marry off his daughter, Cordelia, to a continental prince (evidently the Duke of Burgundy) because she has come of age. He has already given away his two older daughters in marriage, and Cordelia is his last and best, his joy. He doesn't want to do it. Losing Cordelia for him will mean losing everything that has made his life worth living. In an effort to undo the marriage that it is his duty to bring about, he devises a stratagem—the love-trial—whose purpose, as I read the play, is to force her to stay with him in Britain (Stern 1990). And this as we know reaps the whirlwind. Lear's actions are often seen by psychoanalysts in terms of occulted incest wishes, but it seems to me that what is at the heart of his tragedy isn't his unconscious wish for sex, but his very conscious terror of loneliness. "I loved her most," he says bitterly, "and thought to set my rest/On her kind nursery" (1.1.123-124).

What then of *The Tempest*? Prospero, banished from his dukedom in Milan, becomes like Melies a great magician and maker of illusions on his island in the New World. His actors are spirits, who, automaton-like, serve to body forth his illusions with absolute obedience to the omnipotent gestures of his will. But he seems not to need them very much until his daughter, Miranda, like Cordelia comes of age and needs to be married. Unlike Lear Prospero realizes that there is no way to avoid this necessity, despite the fact that he too sees only loneliness and sorrow in its wake. He thus makes peace with his enemies and gives her to Ferdinand even though he imagines his "every third thought" in the aftermath "will be [his] grave" (5.1.315), and he sees that he will die alone. How is he able to do this? Kohut might see him as one who has been able to transform his narcissism into wisdom (clearly something Lear couldn't do: the Fool tells him: "Thou should'st not have been old till thou had'st been wise"[1.5.43-44]) meaning one who has been able to accept the inevitability of death and to identify with the greater cycles of time and generation. I think, however, that he is able to bid Miranda farewell because he believes that despite the distance between them, their internal bond will remain unbroken. Lear imagines no such thing. He is convinced that if Cordelia sails away, his internal attachment to her will disintegrate. Prospero nonetheless imagines that loneliness will overwhelm him if he fails to reconnect with the world that exiled him. In the Epilogue he asks the audience to release him from the isolation of his "bare island" (Epilogue. 8)—his "I-land"—"with the help of [their] good hands" (Epilogue.10)—with their applause. Like Melies he needs to feel appreciated and affirmed by those he sought to please "or else" (Epilogue. 12) as he says, "my ending is despair" (Epilogue.15).

VI. Shakespeare's Loneliness

Hamlet was written in 1601, the year Shakespeare's father died. The play is about a prince who bears virtually the same name as Shakespeare's son, Hamnet, who died in 1596. Other plays feature boys who die or exist in the realm of spirit: Puck in *A Midsummer Night's Dream* is of course a fairy and so not of our world. This play may or may not have been written after Hamnet's death, but it was certainly written long after Shakespeare had left him in Stratford to pursue his life in the London theater. Mamillius in *The Winter's Tale* is his father's favorite but dies when this father, Leontes, becomes psychotic. And there is the witty son of Macduff and Lady Macduff in *Macbeth*. Hamnet was a twin, the brother of Judith, which brings to mind Viola's (apparently) dead twin brother Sebastian in *Twelfth Night*. Perhaps Shakespeare saw his lost son's face in Judith's face. Perhaps the wish to see a boy in a lovely girl has to do with the fact that Viola, Rosalind (*As You Like It*), and Imogen (*Cymbeline*), all disguise themselves as boys, and are thus in effect their own twins. Some of Shakespeare's most beautiful poetry is written over the bodies of dead boys—like these lines spoken over the body of Fidele in *Cymbeline*:

> Fear no more the heat o' the sun,
>   Nor the furious winter's rages;
> Thou thy worldly task hast done,
>   Home art gone, and ta'en thy wages:
> Golden lads and girls all must,
> As chimney-sweepers, come to dust. (4.2.261–166)

Or the lines a bereaved mother speaks in *King John*, probably written just after the death of Hamnet in 1596:

> Grief fills the room up of my absent child,
> Lies in his bed, walks up and down with me,
> Puts on his pretty looks, repeats his words,

Remembers me of all his gracious parts,
Stuffs out his vacant garments with his form . . . (3.4.93–97)

Prospero says he uses his art to open graves. And it is in *The Tempest* that the most arresting spirit boy—Ariel—appears. Hamnet dies in his twelfth year. Ariel spends twelve years with Prospero and then must, according to their contract, be set free. When Ariel leaves him, Prospero renounces his art altogether. *The Tempest* is by tradition Shakespeare's last play, his farewell to the theater. What this might suggest is that Shakespeare's writing for the theater, the writing that allowed him to dwell in a world of magical and transitional play, may have functioned—in part at least—to protect him from the unendurable loneliness that followed the death of his only son. Perhaps it allowed him in fantasy to deny that death, that "Gone!" and keep Hamnet "There!" even as Ernest Freud did his mother with his "Fort-Da!" puppet play. This is to imagine that for Shakespeare the theater itself may have become a "Fort-Da!" game—one that became painfully addictive ("release me from my bands" [*The Tempest,* 5.Epilogue.5]) and that he can only stop playing when he writes *The Tempest*, because writing *The Tempest* enacts his decision to undo his denial of Hamnet's death and let his spirit go. Shakespeare hints that his refusal to do so has been a kind of sin for which writing *The Tempest* represents a kind of penance—sufficient he hopes to win him forgiveness. Thus with his final words Prospero appeals to the audience: "As you from crimes would pardoned be/Let your indulgence set me free" (5.Epilogue.20).

Conclusion:

In this brief survey I have looked at several of the faces of loneliness. These break down into a set of alternatives with loneliness as a cause or loneliness as an effect. When the self is reasonably cohesive, that is to say, when internal object relations are strong enough, loneliness is a cause of creativity (Ernest Freud, Gepetto, Melies, and Shakespeare); heroism (Odysseus, and David in A.I.); and new relationships (Hugo and Melies). When the self is damaged by rejection, cruelty, and shame loneliness is an effect. Yet it still impels the "monsters" of this discussion—the elephant man, the phantom of the opera, Hans the hedgehog, and Kate the shrew—to seek the love of an essential mirroring other who will allow them to become strong enough emotionally to rejoin the circle of humanity from which they have fled or been exiled. Finally, when early developmental trauma to the self reaches a threshold that leaves it in danger of fragmentation and thus unendurable levels of anxiety and depression, loneliness is an effect that seems endless. People like Rose are certain that they will be unable to survive the destruction of relationships that exist outside the realm of their omnipotent control and thus sadly, avoid them. Wim Wenders's angels appear to epitomize this type, and yet they suggest that there may be hope even for these loneliest of the lonely, because they—(some of them, at least)—find themselves unable to resist falling in love with people they can see and hear but never touch and only rarely influence. Their empathic connection with these souls makes them human, and so they crash into Berlin, utterly vulnerable, yet certain they will survive.

References

Anisfeld, L. & Richards, A. (2000). The Replacement Child: Variations on a Theme In History and Psychoanalysis. *Psychoanalytic Study of the Child*, 41:299–308.

Bevington, D., ed. (1992). *The Complete Works of Shakespeare*. New York. Harper.

Freud, S. (1920). Beyond the Pleasure Principle. *Standard Edition* 18.

Kohut, H. (1971). *The Analysis of the Self*. New York. International Universities Press.

———— (1977). *The Restoration of the Self*. Madison: International Universities Press.

Stern, J. (1990). King Lear: The Transference of the Kingdom. *Shakespeare Quarterly* 41: 299-308.

Winnicott, D.W. (1971). *Playing and Reality*. London: Tavistock Publications.

———— (1973). *The Child, the Family, and the Outside World*. Middlesex, Da Capo.

Section II - The Clinical Dimensions of Loneliness

This section contains five chapters dedicated to working with loneliness in the clinical situation. In this section, the authors address through case illustration the psychological and social dimensions of loneliness; the treatment of loneliness in heterosexual men; the multiple expressions of loneliness; the intricate nature of loneliness; and witnessing as the essential component of treatment in cases where loneliness is a predominant characteristic.

Section II opens with Lucille Spira's "Shades of Loneliness: Psychological and Social Perspectives." In this chapter, she identifies specific conditions that create risk for states of loneliness. She begins with a discussion of the pain of loneliness and then moves into a review of loneliness from a bio-psycho-social point of view. Completing this overview, she turns to the psychoanalytic perspectives and surveys: being alone; overvaluation of the past; other longings; inner states of aloneness; aggression, fragmentation and loneliness; contributions from Melanie Klein, and effects in later life. Spira presents two cases (Ms. A.& Ms.Y.) to illustrate her points and places special emphasis on the power to assuage loneliness, and the sense of self and its loss in loneliness. Because of the broad spectrum loneliness entails, Spira ends by highlighting the multi-determined nature of loneliness and advocates for a clinical understanding and intervention-strategy that is based on this complex nature. For Spira the question isn't what causes loneliness, rather she asks what wishes are unsatisfied and what fears are expressed; how does the emotional state of loneliness reflect an adaptive possibility by finding solutions to enjoy when alone; what are the moral components and self-punitive trends of one's loneliness; and how does one defend or avoid knowing their loneliness?

All these and more go into the complex of bio/psycho/social factors that make up this uniquely painful state.

In Chapter Six Jerome S. Blackman discusses the "Treatment of Three Lonely Heterosexual Men." Blackman examines how these men have difficulties with empathy and trust in relations with women. In the treatment he emphasized the need for differential use of supportive, relational, and interpretive intervention strategies. Blackman brings us to several important questions:

> How does one intervene in a case where loneliness is the predominant conscious problem?
> Are the forms of intervention based on differences in pathology or on the level of severity?

Blackman applies supportive, relational and interpretive intervention strategies and applies them differently depending on his assessment of the patient's needs.

> Are these classes of interventions all necessary in cases of loneliness?

67

Is there a greater clinical need for "object clarification" in cases of loneliness than in other types of symptom presentation?

In Chapter Seven, "Exploring the Emergent Experience of Loneliness in Two Men During Their Psychoanalytic Journey" Anita Weinreb Katz posits that the intrapsychic state of loneliness is related to developmental challenges and failures, which vary based on the awareness of loneliness, the capacity to bear it, and the intensity of the experience itself. Two cases (Bryan & Dan) of middle-aged, single men are discussed. Katz illustrates how early trauma and intense affect states present in these two men, focusing on their inner state of emotional isolation, paranoia, addiction to fantasy, and guardedness.

This paper raises the question: Is loneliness an essential aspect of human growth? Or is loneliness always the derailment of development representing trauma and ongoing conflict?

"The Complex Nature of Loneliness" is explored by Arthur Lynch in Chapter Eight. He examines the case of James, a 30-year-old living an isolated but somewhat productive life. James reveals in his inner life a series of compromise formations that lend themselves to containing his sense of self as he struggles with a harsh and at times unforgiving environment. It was the unfolding of these compromise formations in his regression in treatment that led to an understanding of his unconscious fantasy, an amalgam of his wishes and fears. This understanding was the basis for insight that began an integrative readaptation to his world, as he attempted new ways of living and participating. Initially, he uses the transference as both a "selfobject" function and a testing site to explore possibilities. As the material progressed, the transference became more a site for infusion of unconscious conflict.

Here Lynch is asking: Can cases of loneliness be understood as derived from conflict and can conflict theory paradigms adequately address these problems?
What is bedrock in cases where loneliness prevails?

In Chapter Nine, Jenny Kahn Kaufmann and Peter Kaufmann explore "Witnessing: Its Essentialness in Psychoanalytic Treatment." Witnessing has been recognized for its important role in psychoanalytic treatment, especially in severe trauma cases. The Kaufmanns review this concept and consider alternate practices of psychodynamic therapies that are often used with this population with detrimental effects. They illustrate their ideas in the case of Lenore. This superb case illustrates how the use of witnessing[2] and interpretation

---

[2] Poland (2000) notes that witnessing "reflects the patient's advancing self-other differentiation, both a growing self-definition and an increasing regard for otherness,

helped Lenore confront, experience, and integrate her painful formative experiences, increasing her sense of self and availability to others.

This case raises some interesting clinical questions. Lenore was prematurely forced into an early self-individuation process through the trauma of parental loss by death and emotional desertion. Her sense of self is well-defined but fragile or brittle in nature and requires the attentive holding environment that the analyst so carefully negotiates. As Lenore descends into her unformulated angst, the strain of the heartbreaking losses yield a longing and loneliness accompanied by frustration, disappointment and rage at the way things turned out. The analyst uses holding and witnessing to contain both the anxiety and rage, helping Lenore to hear the voice of her own heartache. She is unable to bear, at this point, the persistent destabilization from persistent interpretation that is used with more integrated patients (Arlow & Brenner, 1990))[3] with similar pathological compromise formations. Likewise, she is unlikely to benefit from the intense transference-focused interpretations, which often highlight aggression, with more fragmented patients (Kernberg et al., 2008). [4] Clinically one wonders:

Can witnessing be used as effectively in these different kinds of cases? How does the analyst using witnessing address the threatening aggressive drive derivatives when frustration stimulates them or when they dominate the affective field?

The Kaufmanns' paper suggests witnessing has a bigger technical role than has previously been explored.

---

seemingly separate processes that are intrinsically unitary. Thus, analytic witnessing . . . brings into the open the connection between *self*-definition and the fabric of human *inter*connection" (p.18).

[3] Arlow, J., & Brenner, C. (1990). The Psychoanalytic Process. *Psychoanalytic Quarterly* 59:678–692.

[4] Kernberg, O.F., Yeomans, F.E., Clarkin, J.F., & Levy, K.N. (2008). Transference Focused Psychotherapy: Overview and Update. *International Journal of Psychoanalysis* 89:601–620.

Chapter 5
Shades of Loneliness: Psychological
and Social Perspectives
Lucille Spira

Abstract:

This paper is an overview of particular variables that contribute to a person being alone, lonely and socially isolated. Clinical vignettes are used to highlight the multiple elements that might contribute to a patient's loneliness such as developmental history, a person's overall psychic structure including the state of the self and intervening social factors. Hopefully by examining different components of loneliness we might better help our patients to understand and to overcome their struggles with this potentially very painful affect. One main idea is that the psychological and the social intertwine in contributing to persistent painful loneliness. (I include material from published papers that I co-wrote with Dr. Arlene Kramer Richards.)

"The port from which I come is the port of my loneliness."
Henry James (Quoted by Stanley Kunitz: *The: New York Times*, 6/10/02)

The Pain of Loneliness

Why is it so difficult for some people to make friends and find the connections that they say they want? Without structure and an obvious script, there are many lonely people who cannot engage comfortably with others. This was true for Ms. A, a lonely and socially isolated, obese woman. Despite progress gained over the years in other areas of her life, and very unhappy in her solitude, she continued to avoid almost all social contacts. At some point in her mid-40's, she recounted the following:

The two young women across the hall asked me to join them for coffee. I was really surprised that they asked me; they're young and pretty. I almost told them no, but I accepted. I suppose I was flattered. We decided to have coffee at the Starbucks on the other side of the park. As we walked into the park and came to a bench one of the girls suddenly jumped over it. The other girl quickly did the same. It looked like the most natural thing to do. Before I knew it, I jumped too and landed full force on my arm and injured my elbow, it really hurt; that's why the cast. After I fell, we had to go to the hospital emergency room. I don't know what I was thinking when I jumped over that bench. I wasn't thinking. I was feeling lighter--happy--being with them, until this: she points to her cast. I think that now they think that I'm a pain, a bit crazy.

Despite Henry James' conviction about the source of his loneliness, loneliness or the pain of social relationships is not so easily understood. Are they lonely because they long for someone? Or are they lonely because they cannot imagine loving someone or having someone love them? Do they believe that they will always suffer unrequited love? Or even do they believe, like Ms. A, that being with others is unsafe (Spira and Richards, 2003)?

Psychoanalytic theory suggests that emotional growth takes place in the context of a relationship. When a patient's social isolation and loneliness persists, it alarms the therapist. When the patient longs for a family, our rescue fantasies are mobilized. Often, we are anxious that time will pass these people by. Over the years, at our APsaA Discussion group-- "Towards an Understanding of Loneliness and Aloneness"-- it has become clear how challenging it is to help patients to overcome persistent painful loneliness and social isolation.

My patient, Ms. A, believed that relationships were too risky and that no one she would want would want her. She saw herself as damaged because of a chronic illness and as unlovable because her mother had told her so. Of course, unconscious factors played a role in her loneliness and social isolation (Spira and Richards, 2003a.)

When Ms. A told me about the incident in the park, she was telling me that she was not ready to allow herself new attachments lest she get hurt. Most importantly, I could see how when she is with others, it is she who hurts herself. She finds it is safer to long for companionship than to seek out friends or romantic attachments.

For some people, of whom Ms. A is one, being with others stirs intolerable and/or forbidden feelings such as envy, shame and guilt. Even more worrisome, for her, trusting another person can put you at risk; she became seriously ill following her first romantic encounter many years ago. Where boundaries are not firm, a person can lose her sense of self when under the thrall of the other. Where one is starved for contact, as they begin a new relationship, they easily are over-stimulated. Phillips (2001) pointed out how gay male teens might become overwhelmed when exposed to the male nudity that typically occurs in the everyday life of the male adolescent. Although Ms. A is not gay, I thought that she was over-stimulated by these young women. They did not ask Ms. A out again; nor, did she approach them. Their disengaging from her did not make her unhappy.

Loneliness: Points of View

Cacioppo and Patrick (2008) suggest that a person's genetic endowment is a powerful determinant in whether or not they become lonely or socially isolated. This biological approach to understanding loneliness posits that we are born with more or less tolerance for being alone. Then loneliness--longing for object connection--results when a person's need for attachment is out of sync with his/her actual or perceived social opportunities.

A psychoanalytic view of loneliness might consider character type, developmental history, self-relations, internal and external object relations, the power of the drives, and capacity to regulate affects--an ego function--as all playing a role. Dr. Dan Buie, in his 2012 Plenary Address at the APsaA Meeting, delineated the core issues of those with a personality disorder. His conceptualization precisely captures the emotional state and self-experience of many of the profoundly lonely patients whom we see in psychoanalytic treatment. He said about personality-disordered patients,

"To a significant extent: They are lost in terms of knowing who they are. They feel a dark aloneness. They feel a grim sense of worthlessness. They feel no warmth for themselves. They do not feel like a whole person with a genuine place with other people" (p. 1).

Whether or not we think of our patients as personality disordered, when one suffers with the cluster of variables pinpointed by Buie (2012)--in short, a predominance of a bleak self experience and a sense of alienation--that person is at risk for profound loneliness.

The social science literature suggests that almost anyone can become lonely, but old age, femaleness and, particular life events, like becoming a widow or widower, can increase the likelihood of loneliness (Weiss, 1973.) Olds and Schwartz (2009) show how economic factors might put a person at risk for social isolation; i.e., the rich suburbanite, without connections to community, who lives in a large home spread over many acres, in his self-imposed isolation can fall prey to loneliness.

The single over 35 educated female, who wants a male partner, frequently finds it difficult to meet a suitable one (Lieberman, 1991). Men in their age category often choose younger women. Being a large young woman, in this thin-obsessed culture, makes finding a male lover more challenging (Hirschmann and Munter, 1988.) Some eating problems in adolescent girls derive from an unconscious need to be large to remove themselves from the risks that they associate with sex and intimacy (Bruch, 1958); this defense can contribute to a person being lonely.

Those who are part of a disparaged minority group are also at risk for loneliness. Lesbians and gay people, for example, can experience loneliness when the environment promotes a "don't ask don't tell policy" (Goldstein and Horowitz, 2003). Having been excluded from a social group based on social demographics and/or body type, when we recall the pain associated with that memory, we may project or displace that experience into new situations. Thus early negative experiences of being socially excluded set the stage for our later avoiding situations associated with past exclusions. This increases the chances of a person becoming lonely. Cacioppo and Patrick (2008) suggest that such avoidant behavior is related to a person's cognitive style. A psychoanalytic view might consider that our cognitive style is influenced by our psychology as well as our interpersonal and broader social experience.

Almost all of us have significant experiences of being excluded in our families. As children, we are left out of the parental bed and the intimate relations of the married couple. When a child becomes an oedipal victor, or, has the illusion of being one, later, as an adult, that early victory impairs his chances for mature love relations (Lasky, R., (1987); Gil, H. (1984); Halberstadt-Freud H., 1991.) The psychological, biological and the social intertwine in determining a person's loneliness.

Psychoanalytic Theory and Loneliness

Loneliness may be widespread but, until *Loneliness and Longing* edited by Willock et al. (2012), contemporary psychoanalytic contributions that illuminate the dimensions of loneliness have been relatively few. As part of his work on affects, Brenner (1974) understands loneliness as an affect reflecting longing for the return of a specific person. Brenner's idea of loneliness shows how it differs from depression; in his view loneliness implies the hope of return, while depression results from loss of hope. H. Kaplan (1987) builds on Brenner and others whose work suggests that loneliness is a longing for the past. He labels clinging to the past as "pathological nostalgia", and believes that it is often accompanied by elation. A person who cannot mourn losses or acknowledge that time has passed, misses opportunities for present day intimate relationships. The ego growth and self-esteem gained through new identifications, and new social interactions, is compromised.

Being Alone

While for many people being alone provides an opportunity to commune with the self, pursue hobbies or produce artistic works (Buchholz, 1997), for others being alone is a way to avoid any pain associated with inner conflict. Alone, a person may believe that they can avoid the fear of being swallowed up or being a greedy swallower. Aggressive and sadistic behaviors that otherwise might be directed toward others can be attenuated. The person who cannot satisfactorily resolve the conflicts connected to particular developmental phases might use avoidance to defend against overwhelming anxiety. But defensively avoiding relationships also can result in loneliness, depression and loss of self-esteem.

Overvaluation of the Past and Loneliness

Ms. A, referred to above, typically dressed in a much younger and messy style. She spoke in a little girl shaky voice that seemed at odds with her large size. In the vignette I discussed, her confusion about whether she is a woman or a girl can be inferred from the way that she refers to her new companions, first, as young women, and later, as girls. Together we considered that being selected by these idealized "girls" caused her to regress and impaired her judgment. Suddenly, she was sporty, agile, light and maybe younger. Did she see herself as more powerful with these possible new self-objects and not the helpless and sickly person that she typically imagined herself to be?

Other Longings

Are chronically lonely and isolated persons who believe that they want a partner only longing for lost or past objects? Zilboorg (1938) believed that some lonely people long for someone to mirror them. Here, unlike for Brenner (1974), the longing is more for a particular function rather than for a specific person. Zilboorg characterized these people as narcissists and believed that their aggression pushed others away.

Inner Loneliness or Aloneness

Fromm Reichmann (1959) focused on the seriously lonely patient--the person who suffers from a sense of inner aloneness or emptiness; the experience of feeling without inner objects. To her, inner loneliness is rooted in failures on the part of the mother in her relationship with her infant. Though attachment theorists might focus on the adaptive aspects of loneliness, patients lonely in the way described by Fromm Reichmann, mentally flee by becoming depressed and even psychotic. Here, the psychotic state is the seriously lonely person's attempt to people his/her inner world, a way of counteracting the perceived barren internal landscape. She gives an example of a patient who experiences herself as encased in a block of ice with no way to break out or to see or to connect with an other. The analyst's or therapist's overarching interpretation is to communicate her presence to signal that the patient is not alone with her sense of alienation or isolation.

It is the eccentric thinking of the psychotic person that Lotterman (2011) believes causes psychotic people to be isolated from interpersonal relationships. He found that helping a patient give meaning and voice to his hallucinations or delusions connects the person with an empathic other. That understanding might allow the person to break out of his isolation.

Aggression, Fragmentation and Loneliness

A person's internal world, with its good and bad objects, impacts the degree to which that person suffers painful loneliness (Adler and Buie, 1979). And, how a person perceives others also depends upon the integration of his inner objects. As one formerly very lonely and seriously depressed patient put it: "My interest in my genealogy comes from my wish to feel connected, not just floating or suspended in space. I'm less lonely when I see myself as part of a long line of others, even if some of those others are no longer around." For some time, this person's intimate connection was with dead people, not with others who are alive. The patient's living relatives, significantly more financially successful than the patient, aroused shame and envy, and were defensively avoided. Feeling less than the other family members was a lifelong preoccupation for this person. My patient was barely aware of any aggressive feelings toward them as such feelings were directed inward. Later, this patient's knowledge of the family genealogy helped the patient to connect with family; now, my patient, in some small measure, had something special to interest the family. Here, shame, envy, low self-esteem and a harsh superego contributed to the depression and loneliness. The societal and perceived familial value on material possessions reinforced this person's low self-esteem.

Klein's Contribution

In Klein's (1963) formulation the baby's aggressive instincts cause the baby to see the mother as bad or frustrating and pull away from her. To her the longing of the lonely is for the perfect internal state; an understanding without words characteristic of the idealized relationship with the mother. Cohen (1982) builds on Klein and describes loneliness as a painful fragmentation that can occur even when one is loved. It arises from the fantasy of losing parts of the self, as may occur in psychosis and with some elderly people.

Loneliness in Later Years

Ms. Y, a single woman, then age 65, came to treatment because she was feeling anxious about her future. She had recently retired from a career in design. Ms. Y, born and reared in Canada, lived most of her adult life in NYC. She had no relatives. When I met with her, she did not have a real social network. The typical social outlets, easily available, she saw as not good enough. Being a "top" girl and being among "top" girls was important to Ms. Y; it was what her mother had wanted for her. Her looks, and perhaps her wit and intelligence, had made that possible. Ms. Y, for years, was in conflict about whose ideals and wishes she should pursue—her goals, or those of her mother. Throughout her childhood she submitted to her mother's demands. She told about how she suffered through endless sessions of painful hair-straightening as her mother thought she looked best with straight hair rather than her own natural curly style. Beginning at a very young age, she suffered as a soloist at music events to please her mother. This relationship paradigm that she had

78

with her mother continued with her lovers; her intimate relationships typically were not collaborative ones; submission and rebellion was a theme.

I believe that the theme of dominance and submission came into her treatment at the outset. About an hour before her first session Ms. Y called to tell me that she felt a cold was coming on. She asked me if I still wanted her to come in to her scheduled session. I told her that I wanted her to do what she felt was best for her as I could not tell how soon she needed to get started, nor how badly she felt,—only she could know that. She chose to postpone our first meeting until the following week. Ms. Y told me that she was glad that I was flexible about the appointment; I had taken her needs into consideration. This led us to a discussion about her past experiences with others and whether or not she believed that they could recognize and accept her separateness and individuality. We considered: Whose voice counted and why? Although the goals her mother set for her caused her intense anxiety, for years she passively mirrored her mother's interests and ambitions. As she described her relationship with her mother—first conforming then uncomfortably rebellious--we could see how it impacted her present day life and loneliness. What she experienced as her mother's value of perfection was internalized. The high standards she set worked for her in her career but her too high expectations in her personal life were hurtful.

Ms. Y: The Power to Assuage Loneliness

My patient wanted to figure out what might be possible for her in a relationship; she knew that in relationships she could not easily compromise. In a relationship, she could be nurturing but also provocative. I learned that over the last few years, her two close friends, both older than my patient, died. She anticipated difficulty in making new friends and finding an intimate companion. Loss of friends is typical for the older adult as is the reality that it might be hard to make new friends. This belief can spark a crisis in those who are without family supports and/or, like Ms. Y who suffer from poorly resolved self and object relations.

The Sense of Self and Loneliness

In one session, Ms. Y brought in a photograph of herself from when she was about 30 years old. She was vague about why she'd brought the photograph. As I looked at the photograph, of a young beautiful woman, I saw only a faint resemblance to my patient. I knew from prior discussions that she was in pain about how she had aged. She told me that she could barely connect herself with the woman in the photograph. I thought that she wanted me to admire her image there so that she could reconnect affectively with the self that she felt that she had lost. It was this longed for lost self that she believed had empowered her. Then, when love soured with one companion she could easily find another.

We discussed her life during the time of the photograph how in what ways now she was different and how also, she might be the same. It was important to help Ms. Y mourn, not only for her lost friends, but also those aspects of her self that she believed lost. Mourning is more tolerable when you are not alone with painful feelings and when you believe that you can replace some of the loss with new experiences and people. Fleshing out one's memories and putting words to the feelings connected to those memories reassures us that residues from our past are within us; we are not devoid of either objects or self experience (Richards and Spira, 2012). Hopefully, mourning in the context of a therapy relationship can help the mourner to feel less alone. A person can be helped to find new ways to feel empowered.

Ms. Y eventually developed a nurturing and platonic friendship with a much younger "top" girl that was a source of pleasure. In that new relationship, my patient enjoyed being valued by a woman whom she also valued. My idea is that as she helped her new and younger friend to develop her artistic voice, she experienced herself more positively. Our sessions were filled with Ms. Y discussing artistic works. She could see that I valued her opinions and knowledge; assets that she had a tendency to easily dismiss.

Hopefully, her therapy had lessened the harshness of her superego as it also provided mirroring for her unique attributes, ones she had, in some degree, overlooked or devalued. As she both valued herself more and also became better able to accept her own "imperfection," she became more comfortable with others. Ms. Y's increased tolerance made her fellow volunteers at a local food coop more acceptable and allowed her to be more comfortable in that group.

Defenses and Loneliness

Although he did not put forth a theory of loneliness, Freud (1916/1917) discussed the fear of being alone in his chapter on "Anxiety." He illustrates with a charming anecdote about a child who fears the dark except when his aunt speaks to him. The child says: "If someone speaks, it gets lighter" (p.407).

What happens when our patients do not believe, or do not want to believe, that they have an "aunt" or an inner voice to comfort them in their moments of anxious loneliness? How do they defend themselves? Jarvis (1965) observed how children, when they see their mother's as disengaged, turn to compulsive behaviors. It may be that the unproductive compulsive behaviors reported by our patients, partly, are attempts to ward off restless loneliness.

I return to Ms. A. who used compulsive eating to disengage when she experienced too much pain and when she felt helpless--a feeling that made her angry. In her words, she "stews." It was difficult for her to put words to her aggressive feelings and to elaborate aggressive wishes. Over years, Ms. A acted as if she were the alone and neglected child of her early childhood when no one responded to her voice; her mother had left the household when the patient was about two and returned a year later. Her parents divorced when she was a teen and her father became less available. She longed for him and for his approval. She blamed herself because she did not get it.

My point here about Ms. A, and some others, is that the sense of being alone—a mental state--can be about the current situation, a reemergence of real past experiences, or fantasies of past experiences. Being without others, though sometimes a defense, can stir feelings as well. Anger and hurt that often accompany the feeling of being alone, lonely, abandoned or unwanted can be about the present. Such feelings simultaneously can be connected to suppressed or repressed feelings from the past. Ms. A constantly has to work to maintain a view of herself as "good enough." Now, though Ms. A has made several solid friends with whom she can share feelings, ideas and activities, she doubts a man would ever be interested in her as an intimate partner. She says that she is sad about that but not enough to try to find out the veracity of her belief. When she feels alone she is better able to reach out or to rely on her inner voice, though she finds this an ongoing challenge.

Conclusion

The port from which the lonely come is only part of the story. The other part is the intermediate ports on their voyage to the first therapeutic encounter. There are many variables that might contribute to a person's being lonely, alone or suffering from inner aloneness. Nurture, nature and social factors likely contribute to intense and persistent loneliness. The longing of the lonely can include a yearning for a mature intimate connection, a social group, or for an idealized or real object from the past, or, even, for aspects of the self. Others may long for mirroring. Different factors in one person might drive their longings and overall emotional state. Loneliness transcends diagnostic categories. Interpretations and interventions that recognize the contribution of a person's overall psychic structure, including the state of the self and situational factors, might all be useful. As much as a person says that he wants a relationship, being intimate with another person may provoke more anxiety or pain than being alone. For long periods of time, the therapist may be the only intimate connection that some seriously lonely people can allow, until they are able to make the changes that might help them to be less lonely, less isolated and/or without the sense of internal objects. As an interim compromise formation some people may be helped to feel pleasure in their solitude.

References

Adler, G. & Buie, D.H. (1979). Aloneness and borderline psychopathology: The possible relevance of child development issues. *International Journal of Psycho-Analysis* 60:83–96.

Brenner, C. (1974). On the nature and development of affects: A unified theory. *Psychoanalytic Quarterly* 43:635–654.

Bruch, H. (1958). Developmental obesity and schizophrenia. *Psychiatry* 21:65–70.

Buchholz, E. (1997). *The Call of Solitude: Alonetime in a World of Attachment.* New York: Simon & Schuster.

Buie, D. (2012). *Core Issues in the Treatment of Personality Disordered Patients.* American Psychoanalytic Association Plenary Address.

Cacioppo, John T. & Patrick, W. (2008). *Loneliness: Human Nature and the Need for Social Connection.* New York: W.W. Norton & Company.

Cohen, N.A. (1982). On loneliness and the ageing process. *International Journal of Psychoanalysis* 63:149–155.

Freud, S. (1916–1917). Introductory Lectures on Psycho-Analysis. *Standard Edition* 16:392–411.

Halberstadt-Freud, H.C. (1991). *Freud, Proust, Perversion and Love.* Berwyn, PA: Swets & Zeitlinger.

Gil, H. 1987. Effects of Oedipal triumph caused by collapse or death of the parent. *International Journal of Psychoanalysis.* 68:251–260.

Goldstein, E.G. and Horowitz, L. (2003). *Contemporary Psychotherapy and Lesbian Identity.* Hillsdale, NJ: Analytic Press.

Hirschmann, J.R. & Munter, C. H. (1988). *Overcoming Overeating.* New York: Addison-Wesley.

Jarvis, V. (1965). *Loneliness and compulsion. Journal of the American Pschoanalytic Association* 13:122–58.

Kaplan, H.A. (1987). The psychopathology of nostalgia. *Psychoanalytic Review* 74:465–486.

Klein, M. (1963). On the sense of loneliness. In: *Writings of Melanie Klein 1946–1963.* New York: New Library of Psychoanalysis, 1984, pp. 300–13.

Lasky, R. 1984. Dynamics and problems in the treatment of the Oedipal winner. *Psychoanalytic Review* 71:351–374.

Lieberman, J.S. (1991). Issues in the psychoanalytic treatment of single females over thirty. *Psychoanalytic Review* 78:176–198.

Lotterman, A. (2011). Psychotherapy can benefit schizophrenic patients. *The American Psychoanalyst* Vol. 45, No. 4. Fall/Winter. pp. 12 –16.

Olds, J. and R.S. Schwartz (2009). *The Lonely American: Drifting Apart in the Twenty-First Century.* Boston: Beacon Press.

Phillips, S. (2001). The overstimulation of everyday life: New Aspects of male homosexuality. *Journal of the American Psychoanalytic Association* 49:1235–267.

Richards, A.K. & Spira, L. (2012). Proust and the lonely pleasure of longing. In: Loneliness and Longing: Conscious and Unconscious Aspects, ed. Willock, B., Bohm, L.C., & Curtis, R.C. London & New York: Routledge.

Spira, L. & Richards, A.K. (2003a.), The "sweet and sour" of being lonely and alone. *The Psychoanalytic Study of the Child* 58:214–227.

——— ——— . (2003b). On Being Lonely, Socially isolated and Single: Multiple Perspectives. *Psychoanalysis and Psychotherapy.* Vol. 20:3–21.

Weiss, R.S. (1973). *Loneliness: The Experience of Social and Emotional Isolation.* Cambridge, MA: MIT Press.

Willock. B. et al. (2012). *Loneliness and Longing: Conscious and Unconscious Aspects.* London & New York: Routledge Press.

Zilboorg, G. (1938), Loneliness. *Atlantic Monthly* 161:45–54.

Chapter 6
"Object Clarification" in the Treatment
of Lonely Heterosexual Men
Jerome S. Blackman

Abstract:

Although common American ideals of masculinity include some use of pseudoindependence and isolation of affect, emotionally healthy heterosexual men are able to effect satisfying, close relationships with other men and with the opposite sex. Loneliness accompanied by a sense of "giving up" characterizes a type of psychopathology.

Loneliness in the three men I describe below seemed to have several roots. Loss, neglect, and lack of (or symbiotic) attachment during childhood and/or adolescence had caused divergent personality development. Defenses managing multiple traumas during development sometimes played a role. They had all also experienced interference in the development of close relationship(s) with women as adults.

Their inner conflicts were aggravated by a history of actual disappointments, and resulted in a variety of maladaptive defensive operations: withdrawal from objects; grandiose or autistic solutions; avoidance of social activities (although all three had sublimated interests); generalization about standard rejections and disappointments; rationalization and projective blaming regarding "real" personality features in the women they had known; inappropriate timing of expressions in the social arena (Case 1); inappropriate quietness (Case 2); and inappropriate wishing and hoping (Bacharach 1953, Akhtar 1996) (Case 3)[1]. All three showed a startling lack of social knowledge and skill. All three sought sexual pleasure that did not run the risks of frustration or disappointment in whole-object ties.

With these cases as examples, I hope to demonstrate several techniques I used to help them overcome their problems. Besides explaining their unconscious defenses, inhibitions, and conflicts, I added explanations about object relatedness, intergender relations in general, and the reactions of the particular women they had encountered. This latter (supportive) technique, which I call "object clarification," addressed their impairments in reality testing in relation to women. Some "relational" (Renik 1999; Mitchell, 2000) technique also seemed necessary for them to stabilize and

---

[1] All the cases described are amalgams of several people, and identifying information is highly disguised.

87

develop trust in me. The results of treatment varied from poor (Case 1), to fair (Case 2), to good (Case 3).

When Anthony, in his first session, asked me to "teach [him] how to live without a woman" (*see below*), I had one of my first clinical experiences with a lonely man who had given up on finding a mate. Since then, I have evaluated and attempted to treat a number of men in this category.

As single men mature toward a stage where they desire mutual empathy and emotional commitment with one woman, they frequently experience frustration with women they date[2]; the frustrations may be due to differences in ideals, poor "fit" of their personalities, faulty timing in their respective development, poor social skill in their early interactions with any woman, discovery of serious mental disturbance in the women, and sometimes just bad luck in who they meet.

Men often experience reality frustrations and inner conflicts about women with whom they have contact. But how they resolve those conflicts and re-adapt to the realities of a new relationship varies. This chapter addresses the phenomenon of men who have "adapted to" their frustrations and conflicts via painful loneliness, and how I endeavored to help them. The results were variable.

After each case I describe below, I give a brief discussion of my formulations about their pathology and of my technique. In the Summary at the end of the chapter, I address a bit more about theory and technique regarding loneliness in heterosexual men.

Case 1: Anthony

Anthony, 37 and never married, began his evaluation by saying, "I want you to teach me how to live without a woman."

I told him I had never heard that request before, and asked him how he had come to the conclusion that he should live without a woman. He complained that women rejected him, usually after one or two dates, and he was tired of getting hurt. He had had one girlfriend during his twenties. They dated, off and on, for less than a year. They had sexual intercourse a few times. She then decided she didn't want to do that, but never would explain her decision. He had not had sexual relations since.

Since she dumped him, he sometimes had dates when one of his male friends fixed him up. He had also asked out some women who dealt with his family's business, for which he had worked since graduating from high school. After two or three dates, the women he dated found excuses and would not go out with him again. His reality testing was good enough that he knew

---

[2] Similar to the frustrations of women who have reached this stage

88

ation" in the Treatment of Lonely Heterosexual Men—Jerome S. Blackman

they were making excuses and rebuffing him, but he couldn't figure out what had gone wrong.

After explaining this much, Anthony again asked me to teach him to be happy living alone—he detested being lonely. At this point, I decided to test his treatability: I told him I could not fulfill his wish because I did not know how to do it. I offered to help him think about his dating failures, if he would like, to see if I could help him understand them—maybe then he could find someone he liked. He tentatively agreed.

During the next several weeks, Anthony described himself to me much in the same manner as he had with the women he had dated. In fact, after he told me about himself, he explained that this was the same way he had approached women. He listed his strong points:

- "I'm tall [about 6']
- I'm clean [clean shaven with short hair]
- I'm fit [he worked out three times a week and played golf, alone or with his friend, Ryan, once a week]
- I have an expensive, cool car [a new BMW sportscar]
- I own a beautiful house on the lake [with no mortgage] and a nice boat
- I have a good job [middle management in his family's business]
- I have a lot of money
- I'm gentle
- I'm not a pervert
- I like to talk
- I want a family and children."

"What else would any woman want?" His rhetorical question was infused with bitterness. Since nobody seemed to want all that, he felt he might as well give up and learn to live alone.

As Anthony told me all this, I noticed no loose associations, no bizarre thinking, and no paranoia, although his concreteness about "what women want" was obvious. He was dressed casually but neatly: his short-sleeved shirt was pressed; his khaki pants had a crease; his shoes were polished.

His parents were shy people; he had dinner with them on Sundays after church. He had never had much to do with his brother, 10 years his junior, who also worked for the family business.

To "reconstruct the present," (Kanzer, 1953) I expressed confusion (Blackman 2003, 2012) about the course of Anthony's interactions with women. He then gave me an example. A month previously, Ryan gave him Tina's phone number; Anthony called and invited Tina to dinner at a *very* expensive restaurant, a fact he mentioned to Tina as they walked in. At dinner, in response to Tina's questions about him, he ran through the list above. He then

89

told Tina he would like to show her his house after dinner, take her for a ride in his boat, and maybe take a swim in the lake. She politely demurred and instead told him she had an early morning and needed to go straight home; maybe some other time . . . . Again, he understood she was rejecting him, hid his pain and confusion, and drove her home. He had no idea why she didn't like him.

Through the way Anthony expressed himself, I could see the enormous gap in his social awareness. I wondered if he might be schizophrenic in spite of his organized thinking and relatively good abstraction ability in other areas. I decided "his relationship to reality" with women was somehow lacking, so I decided to use Frosch's (1988) technique—to "reality test" for him and see what happened. I told him, "I now see what happened." Anthony looked incredulous. I continued: "By inappropriately mentioning the priciness of the restaurant and telling her about your wealth, you made Tina feel like you were trying to buy her; then, when you asked her to see your house and take a boat ride, that made her suspicious. When you mentioned swimming, which would involve taking off her clothes (even if you picked up a swimsuit from her place), she had to suspect you were crassly inviting her to have sexual activity—which, from the way you approached her, she thought you wanted to buy." I tried to convey, as directly and dramatically as possible, that most women would not want to feel that they had to have sex with a man just because he had money.

In spite of what I thought was direct, Anthony first responded, "I thought that's what women wanted! I've read a lot about this. Are you sure?" I admitted I of course could not be 100% sure. However, I thought Anthony did not understand what I had said. Since I thought his problem here was concreteness, I explained that, the way he described their interaction, he had either caused Tina to think he was a sex maniac—which frightened her, or that he saw he saw her as a whore (for sale), which insulted her. Anthony paused, and then said, "You're a genius!" I responded that what I had told him was not a deep secret, but he again countered that he had read many books about dating; most suggested that women wanted the 11 qualities he told them about, and supposedly were impressed with a man being "confident." He had tried all those approaches, and they didn't work.

In following sessions, I learned that Anthony's parents had harbored rather simplistic notions of dating. They had been introduced to each other by their parents at church, and had never dated anyone else. Anthony was the kid who sat in the back of the class in high school and never spoke to anyone except Ryan. Nobody made fun of him; nobody noticed him.

Because of the apparent deficit in his social skill development, I also answered other questions for him. I advised him: to ask women more about themselves; when joking, not to joke *about* the woman; to limit his descriptions of himself (avoid bragging); and not to ask them to his house until he knew them for a while. I also suggested he not pick a very expensive restaurant to start, (to allow the woman to feel freer), and that he not talk about money very much.

Anthony decided he would stop telling women about himself so much, and would ask them more questions. After about 6 sessions, he said he had learned enough, and wanted to practice for a while without my help. Two years later, he came back for one session. He was depressed and back to square one. He had "tried" for two years and failed. Although women would see him for more dates—now up to four or five, they still all rejected him. He had given up. If I could not tell him how to live alone, he would just try it, himself. I expressed understanding of his pain, and offered to help by understanding his failures. He did not want this, left, and did not come back.

Discussion of Anthony's Case

Anthony was, as Koontz (2003-2010) might say, "odd." I could not find any overt psychotic functioning, and was never certain of his capacities for closeness and trust (object relations features). His relationship to the reality of dating was clearly damaged, although briefly responsive to my attempts to help him with his reality testing—object clarification—and to teach him some social skills.

Raised in a home with parents who were relatively simplistic and concrete about relationships, Anthony, himself, mirrored that attitude. It was not clear how much of his concreteness was caused by identifications with his parents. His hermit-like withdrawal in high school seemed to have been caused by anxieties about closeness. His persistent social awkwardness, besides a failure to learn the usual social skills, seemed to reflect delay in his development of empathy, trust, and mutual closeness with other human beings.

Technically, I felt the disturbance in his ego functioning (i.e., his limits in relationship to reality, judgment, anticipation, and executive functioning) needed attention. He did respond to my initial clarifications of disturbed perceptions, but not with enhanced introspection (mentalization) or new material. Rather, he "learned" from me. Unfortunately, his limitations in object relatedness persisted in causing him to be rejected.

He eventually resolved his conflicts and relieved his pain by consciously deciding to forego finding a mate.

Case 2: Tom

Tom was 55 when he came to see me, and moderately depressed. He was boyish looking, slender, fit, clean-shaven, and impeccably dressed in a suit and tie. He had just sold his appliance business to a national chain for over $5 million (this had been reported in the local newspaper), but he was unhappy (though not suicidal). He had never been married, and had not had a relationship with a woman since he was 30. He had "given up" on that. Women were too much trouble, and "most of them are crazy and just think about themselves." He also thought all women were socialistic or, at best, Democrats, and therefore unable to understand his values as a self-made man—a capitalist. At this point, he didn't want therapy; he just wanted to know if I had some ideas about how he could feel better.

I decided to answer his question (Blackman 2012) : I told him my initial impression was that his business sounded like it had been an important part of him[3] for over two decades. He confirmed this and added, "It was me; it was like my family; it was everything." That's why he regretted selling it. I pointed out that he must still be grieving—the loss would make him feel down for a while. He was surprised you could grieve over something like a business, but quickly saw that since the business had meant so much to him, it was logical that he would be mourning over it, in spite of his delight in making so much money. I also suggested that perhaps he needed a new project, and he agreed. He had some ideas.

I did not hear from him for over two years. When I saw him again, he reported that he had become involved in a charitable organization, and was busy. Tom had made many male friends over the years. They all stayed in touch with him; he frequently traveled to see them. He had dinner two to three times a week with different groups of male friends, most of them married to "left-wingers" who disliked discussing international events (and might say, condescendingly, "Why don't you men just put away your guns!") and otherwise nagged their husbands. These observations fueled his anxiety about dating women and led him to prefer isolation and loneliness. Tom played golf well and jogged 3-5 miles every morning. He enjoyed and cared about his male friends. Men liked him and would give him the shirt off their backs; he'd do the same for them.

But: He had just had an interview with a local newspaper, during which he had mentioned something negative about the government's slowness in implementing certain elements of the program he was now involved with. He was now afraid someone in the government would read this and that he'd be sued for defamation. After hearing more details, I was able to ascertain that Tom had not mentioned anyone's name. I "tested reality" for him, explaining what I thought he already knew: that in the United States, you can criticize the government with impunity. I did not think he was in any danger. I further opined that he somehow felt guilty about how angry he was feeling toward

---

[3] I.e., part of his self-image. According to Kohut (1971), when there is a rupture of the self-image (like when the business, which had been part of him, was lost), there can be a breakthrough of "aggressive breakdown products," which can then be projected or turned on the self, causing depression (Blackman, 2010).

some specific people (in the government), and that he was then imagining he would be punished with a lawsuit. He was relieved, and said he'd like to see me for another session.

When I saw him a few days later, he told me he had been thinking about his guilt. He now confessed that he felt guilty about calling phone numbers where young women were paid to talk about sex. He had made these calls periodically because he was lonely. This had not worked well, however, because the woman he talked to would typically make salacious remarks; he would then ask the woman just to talk with him about herself. The woman would then explain that she was not supposed to have personal discussions with people who called, and he would hang up in frustration. He was now afraid one of the companies might blackmail him by calling him back and threatening to expose him. I again explained that I thought his fear was caused primarily by him feeling he needed to be punished[4], and I was doubtful that a sex-line-girl would call him back, at all. Again he felt relieved, and we set up a regular treatment schedule.

Over the next few months, he revealed he had used prostitutes since his girlfriend, Sarah, had broken up with him when he was 30. He never touched the prostitutes. He would have the prostitute disrobe; he then just conversed with her "nicely." He would pay her, have her dress and leave, and then masturbate while recalling their discussion.

Tom and I discussed his problems in therapy over the next 11 years. In a nutshell, here's what I learned and how I tried to help him.

Sarah was the only woman he had ever loved. She had worked for the same company at which he worked at the time. After they dated for two years, she, without discussion, avoided him. Months later, she sent him an invitation to her marriage to a different man. When he received the invitation, Tom banged his head on the wall and considered suicide, but toughened himself, instead.

Some months before Tom returned to see me (27 years after they had parted), Sarah had started emailing Tom. He showed me the emails, which appeared friendly, newsy, and slightly suggestive. He had responded blandly. Tom theorized that Sarah was unhappy with her husband, and might be reconnecting with Tom because she was thinking of leaving the husband. Tom turned out to be right: she did leave her husband about 3 years later and obliquely invited Tom to visit her. He briefly considered this, but could not bring himself to see her after the horrible pain he had felt at her hands when he was 30. She stopped emailing. When I clarified that Tom seemed to secretly derive pleasure in having disappointed her, he said it was no secret to him. He knew he enjoyed rejecting her; but he also couldn't imagine putting himself in a situation, again, where she could break his heart.

---

[4] Externalization of the superego (Blackman, 2003).

Tom's loss of Sarah at age 30 seemed to have been an organizing trauma—his reactions to it consolidated resolutions to earlier and later conflicts, as well. The earlier problems surrounded his mother. She had been alcoholic since he was a small child. His father, a corporate executive, traveled frequently, and was almost never home. Tom lettered in football, basketball, and baseball in high school, and played freshman baseball in college. His father never saw him. Tom's tendency toward extreme independence was partly a reaction to his aloof, drunken mother, and partly a defense against his feelings of loss and anger toward his father. His teammates became like brothers, and he maintained 50-year-long relationships with many of them.

His mother's drunkenness was so severe that Tom could not bring high school friends home. His mother was "disgusting:" she rarely got dressed; she hung around the house in her nightgown, and when drunk, she would fall down, and sometimes reveal parts of her body. He felt severe disgust and embarrassment as he remembered these incidents—which he reported only after we had looked at his resistances to discussing his mother.

Some years after Sarah disappointed him, Tom became more successful financially. Once he started his own company, things took off. He then dated several women, and a few times, had sexual intercourse. However, he reacted with 'disgust' to seeing those women lying naked on the bed after sex. At one point, he moved his company from Boston to Phoenix. One woman he had briefly dated in Boston wanted to accompany him. When he demurred, she, unbeknownst to him, moved to Phoenix. After an unpleasant phone call with him, she killed herself with an overdose, leaving a suicide note referencing his rejection. He was briefly interviewed by the police. He then was more terrified of any woman: he added "crazy" to "disgusting." He went back to calling sex lines, and sometimes got women to talk to him about other things aside from sex. He had given up on the idea of any committed relationship with a woman, though he still masturbated with thoughts of a woman talking nicely to him.

Repeatedly, I discussed with him how he sexualized his wish to talk to a woman; when he got prostitutes to talk to him, he would then reject them and avoid his disgust and fears of being ignored or rejected. He deftly avoided humiliation, rejection and guilt at the same time he found gratification of his desire for emotional closeness with a woman—while convincing himself it was "just" a sexual game. We discussed how his feelings of disgust and criticism toward his mother were transferred onto other women in various situations.

After several years of treatment, Tom began dating again. First, a 57-year-old woman, whose husband was dying from cancer, invited him to dinners and parties. But she showed overt interest, in front of her sick husband, in starting something with him before her husband died. He was disgusted by her humiliation of her husband and her obesity, and avoided her.

Next, a friend's wife fixed him up with a divorced friend. This "tubby" woman, reportedly, spent most of their time at dinner talking about her grown children and grandchildren. He could not relate. He listened for a couple of hours, patiently, then drove her home.

I thought I noticed a pattern. I decided to explain this pattern to Tom in terms of his behavior and what I thought the woman's reactions were to it ("object clarification"). I pointed out that Tom was quiet on these dates, which I suspected caused the women to regress and become too aggressive or chatty (to handle his withdrawnness). Tom acknowledged that my observation was accurate. He confirmed this character trait, again, after a pleasurable first meeting with a different woman, 50 years old and divorced, at a friend's house. Tom took her to dinner. He was excited because she had in common with him a love of sports (!). At dinner, however, she revealed all her family soap opera and her financial straits, and asked nothing about Tom. After Tom dropped her off, he was afraid she would call him. Again, he was right: she called him twice before his polite excuses enabled her to recognize his rejection. Again, a woman had regressed in the face of his quietness[5].

The fourth date, a few months later, was with another middle-aged woman. She got drunk during dinner. Of course, Tom got disgusted (reality and transference from his mother). When she wanted him to take her to a local bar to drink more, he dropped her at home instead.

Finally, on a trip to see his accountant in Phoenix, he met a "beautiful" woman, probably in her late 30's. They had a lively discussion. She was the first woman he had mentioned who expressed interest in him, and now Tom was more open. They had better give and take, and he thought she got to know him. He was pleased that she left him her phone number in Phoenix and he gave her contact information in Virginia Beach. A few months later, she "surprised" him by showing up at his house without having called first. In tow were her husband (he didn't recall noticing her wearing a wedding ring on the plane) and her obese, overtly sexually suggestive mother. The mother, who

---

[5] Jeb, A different man, age 60, once consulted me because of confusion. He had learned to be "a good listener" to women he dated (who were between about 45 and 60). Often, after two or three dates, these women invited him into their bedroom. He had sex with them, but felt guilty because he could see that their warm feelings for him were based on his sham of pretending to be interested in their "prattling on." He felt guilty about seducing them this way, and sometimes would get caught in a relationship he didn't want, to relieve his guilt. On the other hand, he enjoyed his conquests and the sexual activity. In both Jeb's and Tom's cases, their "listening" seemed to produce both transferences (that the man was like a loving father/mother) and projections (the man fit their wishes) in the women. Jeb was conscious of this effect, whereas before therapy, Tom had not been aware of what was causing the discrepancy between his polite withdrawal and the woman's fervor.

Tom thought was a bit inebriated, after a few minutes of chatting, invited Tom to return to Phoenix to stay at her home. Tom correctly assessed her as having interest in him, but was disgusted at her approach, and angry at the daughter, who did not seem to have realized he had been stimulated by and interested in her, not her mother. Again, Tom wanted to give up. I took the opportunity to mention to Tom that he seemed to have neglected to ask the daughter if she were married during his first discussion with her. To be sure, she had not mentioned it, whatever that meant (I agreed it was a bit odd); nevertheless, he could have saved himself some heartache had he asked—he had made a social faux pas.

Over the next several years, Tom became friendlier with me. His interest in several of my community activities and my simple responses to his interest seemed to foster a better mood in him, and seemed to be transferred into his relationships with new women he met. He gradually gave up some of his pessimism, but still never wanted to get married. Toward the end of his therapy, he was dating occasionally and had stopped his phone calls to sex lines. He had desisted from calling prostitutes. The periodic contact with women as dates seemed sufficient. Interestingly, a few who were interested in his life, his feelings, his career, etc., were married to his friends. Some women in their 20's invited him to lunch; but they mistakenly saw him as a father figure (while he secretly was pining for them to love him). Tom correctly assessed the younger women's misperceptions, but did not dispel these women of them because he didn't like being lonely.

Discussion of Tom's Case

Tom suffered a number of depressing traumas. These included his mother's alcoholism and her overstimulation of him during his childhood and adolescence. Though he loved sports and excelled at almost all he tried, his father was never there and did not seem interested. Tom's surprise rejection by his first serious girlfriend was complicated by guilt related to another woman (whom he knew later), who committed suicide after he broke up with her. He adapted defensively to his pain and guilt by avoiding women, working hard, staying friends with men, and relieving his sexual urges by masturbating after talking to call-girls.

Analysis of the conflicts that had led to the maladaptive solutions seemed necessary but not sufficient. Due to his character trait of interested/polite listening when interacting with women, some women seemed to attribute affectionate feelings to him when he, in reality, was bored with them. I felt that he needed help in understanding a variety of women's responses to his polite quietness; I engaged in "object clarification" to help him get a better perspective on these interactions. Sadly, after he began to correct this character pathology, he had a frustrating, highly annoying, and somewhat humiliating interaction with a woman who had seemed to be interested in him.

Tom did not achieve an optimum resolution of his conflicts. Part of reason for this was that he was well into his 50's when he began treatment (Freud, 1905); and although that was not the biggest of his problems, it should not be overlooked. Many of the women he dated had been homemakers, involved with children and later grandchildren. He had not had those experiences, so it was difficult, though theoretically not impossible (Buie, 1981), for him to relate to those women. Also, many of the older women he met were overweight and unathletic—which was not compatible with his interests in fitness and athleticism. Although many senior citizens are quite capable of forming new relationships, and can be treated with analytic techniques (Settlage, 1996), the social situation Tom faced was no doubt actuarially more difficult than if he had been 30.

His situation was made trying and painful by his long history of neglect and trauma in regard to women. He had resolved his father hunger (Herzog ,1981, 2001) through displacements onto male friends and later onto me. It is true that, during treatment, there was a change in his compromise formations (Brenner, 1975, 2006): he no longer used the phone sex-lines and prostitutes. His new compromise formations included periodic contact with women who were interested in him—but nothing intimate and ongoing.

Case 3: Hank

Hank was lonely. A lean, good-looking 26-year-old man, he had a good job as a third-year associate at a moderate-sized law firm. He worked hard and was popular with the partners. He had had a serious girlfriend in high school, but that broke up when she cheated on him sexually. He had dated in college and law school, and had sexual intercourse a few times. Hank had lived in his fraternity house in college, so he had not been lonely. In law school, he shared an apartment with three other men. They had their problems, but there was usually somebody around to "shoot the shit."

He liked the law firm; and he liked the idea of living almost 1,000 miles away from his parents. He at first liked the idea of living alone in an apartment, where supposedly lots of "upscale singles" lived. But gradually he realized that the "hype" about the place was just that: the apartment complex contained families, elderly, and a few young adults who were living together. He was lonely.

After a year of drowning his loneliness in working 80 to 90 hours a week, he met Priscilla. She had finished a year of law school and had been hired by his firm as a "summer associate"—to work at the firm for two 4-week blocks. The first Saturday of the summer, the firm had a cocktail party to welcome the summer associates, and he and Priscilla hit it off. They talked for a couple of hours, and he felt he had found his soul mate. She was pretty, funny, and liked him. They shared tastes in music, laughed about the "sport" of curling, and flirted with each other. Hank started seeing her almost every night for dinner, often spending the evening after that walking along the boardwalk at the beach. After a week, they had a rip-roaring good time in bed, and that continued, almost nightly.

At the end of the eight weeks, Priscilla moved back to Williamsburg (William and Mary Law School), about an hour away. For a while, Hank drove to stay with her on weekends or she drove to see him. Sometimes, they saw each other during the week, but otherwise, they enjoyed talking on video-conferencing almost every night. Hank was excited, and reported he had once mentioned marriage and having children with her some day; Priscilla had been surprisingly reserved in her response, but Hank chalked that up to nerves.

Just before Thanksgiving, Priscilla dropped a bomb on Hank: she wanted to "take a break" from their relationship. She said she needed space. When Hank pressed her, she admitted she had been seeing Bob, an old boyfriend from her first year of law school, and felt she "owed him a chance." Hank's response of "Bullshit!" was not persuasive. She insisted he was "not fair," and blamed him for being "immature" because he couldn't wait for her to make a decision. Hank consulted his friend, Jeff, who advised Hank to "play it cool." Jeff theorized that Hank had been "coming on too strong" to Priscilla, apparently based on a book called *The Game* (Strauss, 2005). Briefly, Hank tried to believe this.

Since then, Priscilla had called Hank a few times, as Jeff had predicted. She wanted to talk, and joked about sexual things as well. It was in the middle of this turmoil that Hank came to see me. He could not disentangle his "love" for Priscilla although she was "driving [him] crazy." We embarked on once-a-week therapy that lasted about a year, to try to figure this out.

I began by looking at the various factors in Hank that were causing him trouble. He, himself, wondered if he had turned Priscilla off somehow. It seemed to me that he was trying to figure this out without having any data from Priscilla, an observation I shared with him. He confirmed he had felt a bit shy about "pinning her down." This turned out to be partly an inhibition he felt because he did not want to lose her. We connected this fear of loss to a fantasy of punishment he had felt, for years, over being nosy. He had avoided asking his mother or any girl too much about themselves because of his own adolescent sensitivity to being invaded (he projected his own sensitivity onto the girl and then treated her "nicely"). I also pointed out to him that he might be afraid to hear the reality of Priscilla's opinions about him—they might not be complimentary.

Following these sessions, Hank called Priscilla to ask her what he might have done that had led her back to her old boyfriend. Priscilla was adamant that he had done nothing that she disliked—she loved him, but she also felt her old boyfriend needed "another chance." It was not clear to me whether Priscilla repeated this as a polite rejection of Hank.

After a couple of weeks of not hearing from her, Hank called Priscilla. She was again standoffish. However, she continued texting him funny, sexy comments, and he responded. Following on those exchanges, he called and asked if she had had enough space. She said she still wasn't sure, and asked him to be "patient." At this point, he expressed anger, called her a "controlling bitch," said he never wanted to talk to her again, and hung up on her. He was depressed, but felt it was over.

Hank was grieving the next time I saw him. I agreed with him that although it was difficult to tell if Priscilla's reasoning indicated true confusion, severe self-centeredness, or a more serious mental illness, it looked more adaptive to me that he had recognized that her approach was eating him alive and that he had taken steps to stop the pain. He now confirmed that he had been avoiding loneliness by holding on to her—although he insisted her sense of humor was "awesome."

The following Saturday night, after working until 9 pm, he stopped for a burger, and was walking into his apartment around 10 when he received a text from Priscilla. She was in his parking lot and wanted to talk. Reluctantly, he agreed. When he saw her, he was no longer angry; she looked "hot." One beer later, they were in bed. After a pleasurable round of sex, they were lying next to each other, when Hank said he was glad she was done with Bob. This set off a firestorm in Priscilla, who now accused Hank of being presumptuous and self-absorbed. Hank attempted to argue with her, to no avail. She finally dressed, and around 4 am, stormed out of his apartment.

When I saw Hank for his next appointment, he was shaken. He and Priscilla had not spoken after that Saturday. He asked me what was wrong with her. They had such a great time, they loved being together, but she wouldn't give Bob up. I now decided some "object clarification" was both possible and necessary. I explained to Hank that there are certain kinds of people who cannot sustain close relationships. They can get into one, and be a lot of fun (including sex), but the emotional closeness makes them nervous. They then do something to create distance (like going back to Bob). But after a while, they don't like the closeness with the new person, and want to get away. They may call the first lover back, so that when they get "space" from the second lover, they are not alone.[6] I explained that such people are like

---

[6] I.e., they avoid selfobject fusion anxiety with one object by leaving; but they also avoid separation-depressive affect by having a new object to hold onto, at least for a while.

comets, swinging in close, then swinging out into orbit for some period of time.[7]

Hank's reaction to this was, "That fits! Oh my God! She's a wacko!" I explained that she didn't seem entirely a wacko. She obviously had a lot to recommend her, which was attractive to Hank. And he didn't want to be lonely. I further opined that his wishes to marry her and have children with her, which he mused about at some point, may have aggravated her anxiety about closeness with him—sort of the opposite of what you would predict in a normal woman who was wrapped up in a torrid sexual affair with a man whose personality she enjoyed. If there had been one thing that may have provoked more distancing from her, it was likely his stated interest in settling down and starting a family.

Hank, in later sessions, said he had not previously understood so clearly the type of woman he was looking for. He had been lonely. Priscilla had seemed to be a balm for that, and a lot of fun. He now could see that he was not interested in a woman who did not want marriage and children. He needed to be more selective, no matter how lonely he was.

Priscilla called him one more time. She was now apologetic about having hurt his feelings. He told her that he was actually looking for someone who was ready to settle down. Priscilla claimed she would "one day," and then, on the phone, virulently attacked Hank for not being "patient" while she pursued her affair with Bob. Hank told me, "I could see in that five minutes the same pattern that had gone on for almost a year!" He told her not to call him again.

Hank now connected with some male friends from law school, and they decided to have rotating parties at each of their apartments every few weeks. Through these parties, he met several young women. At the time he stopped treatment, he did not feel lonely. He had dated several women briefly, and was sorting out how he felt about each. He had not found his soul-mate yet, but seemed to be well on the way. At that point, by mutual agreement, we stopped his treatment. He sent me an email about a year later, saying he continued to be successful in his firm, was continuing to date, and was feeling optimistic about his future.

Discussion of Hank's Case

Hank had not clarified his ego ideal—that he actually was ready to settle down with the right woman and start a family. He suffered the "normal" loneliness that single people generally experience once they are out of school and working. He had initially used some obsessional defenses (workaholism) to relieve his painful loneliness, and as is often the case, these defensive opera-

---

[7] More about comets (based on some ideas of Vamik Volkan's) in Blackman (2010)

100

tions, in conjunction with his training and intellect, served him well in adapting to his work situation in the law firm.

Priscilla had, at first, seemed like a dream come true. It seemed to me that neither she nor Hank had been particularly clear about plans to marry or have children. In addition, Hank had been too passive as a left-over adolescent defense regarding invasion and "TMI" (too much information). He therefore fell in love with Priscilla before he really knew much about her character functioning and her life goals. What appeared to be, at best, her pathological ambivalence about a committed relationship (if Hank were to take her at her word) only became clear during the quite painful, sadomasochistic interactions into which she had embroiled Hank. It took some time before this pattern became evident. When I thought we had spent enough time on Hank's defenses and inner conflicts, it seemed to me that "object clarification" (as I describe in the Abstract [above] and in the Summary [below]) could be of use to him. In fact, that clarification led the way toward his recognition (consciously) of his own ego-ideal (about marriage and children) and aided him in dating. He then stemmed his loneliness with male friends who were in the same position that he was. Together, they came up with a plan to search "for the perfect woman." (Volkan, 2009)

Summary

We owe a debt of gratitude to Frieda Fromm-Reichmann (1959) (Mendelson 1990) for drawing our attention to the serious problem of loneliness in psychotic and near-psychotic people. Others have widened our understanding of the problems in older adults and in homosexual men (Cohen 1982). Arlene Kramer Richards and Lucille Spira (2003a &b) have furthered our understandings, not only in their articles, but in the long-running discussion group they have chaired on loneliness at the meetings of the American Psychoanalytic Association.

In this chapter, I have first tried to illustrate some differing etiologies of loneliness in single, heterosexual men. Loneliness can be normative, as when men are just out of school and working. Another possibility is defensive reactions to multiple emotional traumata. Finally, serious object relations problems may be at the root of men's difficulties in establishing an empathic, trusting, emotionally close relationship with a woman.

Through the examination of elements of the pathology and treatment of three very different men who were all lonely, I have also attempted to demonstrate the use of supportive, relational, and interpretive techniques in respect to different etiologies of their loneliness.

Finally, I have shared a technical suggestion: that in cases of lonely heterosexual men, whether they have severe, moderate, or mild social difficulties, some amount of "object clarification" may be necessary by the therapist. This technique involves: (1) clarifying the compromise formations (involving defenses and wishes) operative in the man that cause him to give up; (2) accumulating knowledge about the woman with whom the man is involved; and (3) explaining to the man, as best as possible, the reactions in the woman which he does not understand—either based on his behavior with her or on her own psychopathology, if applicable.

One cannot speak of this technique without cautioning the therapist about concordant and complementary identifications in the therapist (Racker, 1953): unconsciously picking up the attitudes of the person you are treating, or siding with objects in that person's life as they are represented in the mind of that person. Other distortions by the person you are treating must also be considered (Blackman, 2012).

Keeping those *caveats* in mind, the therapist may want to use object clarification when there is some disturbance in a person's relationship to reality (Frosch, 1988). In the case of more severely damaged men, clarifying the effects of their behavior on women may be taken as a correction of their reality testing. In men with personality disorders, clarification of women's reactions may aid in highlighting those men's maladaptive character features—of which they previously had been unaware. Finally, in normal-neurotic men, object clarification can become involved with their insight into their compromise formations, and help them clarify their ego-ideals in regard to relationships at different stages of their lives.

References

Akhtar, S. (1996). "Someday . . " and "If only . . " fantasies: pathological optimism and ordinate nostalgia as related forms of idealization. *Journal of the American Psychoanalytic Association* 44:723–53.

Bacharach, B. (1953). "Wishin' and Hopin'"
http://www.onlinesheetmusic.com/wishin-and-hopin-p120860.aspx

Blackman, J. (2003). *101 Defenses: How the Mind Shields Itself.* New York: Routledge.

———— (2010). *Get the Diagnosis Right: Assessment and Treatment Selection for Mental Disorders.* New York: Routledge.

———— (2012). *The Therapist's Answer Book. Solutions to 101 Tricky Problems in Psychotherapy.* New York: Routledge.

Brenner, C. (1975). Alterations in Defenses during Psychoanalysis. *The Kris Study Group of the New York Psychoanalytic Institute,* Monograph VI, ed. B. Fine & H. Waldhorn. New York: International Universities Press.

———— (2006). *Psychoanalysis: Or Mind and Meaning.* New York: Psychoanalytic Quarterly Press.

Buie, D. (1981). Empathy: Its nature and limitations. *Journal of the American Psychoanalytic Association* 29:281–307.

Cohen, N. (1982). On loneliness and the ageing process. *International Journal of Psycho-Analy*sis 63:149–155.

Freud, S. (1905). On Psychotherapy. *Standard Edition* 7: 255–268.

Frosch, J. (1988). Psychotic character versus borderline. *International Journal of Psychoanalysis* 69:347-357.

Herzog, J. (1980). Sleep disturbance and father hunger in 18- to 28-month old boys—the Erlkönig syndrome. *Psychoanalytic Study of the Child* 35:219–233.

———— (2001). *Father Hunger: Explorations with Adults and Children.* New York: Routledge.

Kanzer, M. (1953). Past and present in the transference. *Journal of the American Psychoanalytic Association* 1:144–154.

Kohut, H. (1971). *The Analysis of the Self: A Systematic Approach to the Psychoanalytic Treatment of Narcissistic Personality Disorders.* New York: International Universities Press.

Koontz, D. (2003–2012). *Odd Thomas* series (novels). New York: Bantam Books.

Mendelson, M. (1990). Reflections on loneliness. *Contemporary Psychoanaly*sis 26:330–355.

Mitchell, S. (2000). You've got to suffer if you want to sing the blues. *Psychoanalytic Dialogues* 10:713–733.

Racker, H. (1953). A contribution to the problem of countertransference. *International Journal of Psycho-Analysis* 34:313–324.

Renik, O. (1999). Playing one's cards face up in analysis: an approach to the problem of self-disclosure. *Psychoanalytic Quarterly* 68:521–539.

Richards, A.K. & Spira, L. (2003). On being lonely: fear of one's own aggression as an impediment to intimacy. *Psychoanalytic Quarterly* 72:357–374

Settlage, C. (1996). Transcending old age: Creativity, development and psychoanalysis in the life of a centenarian. *International Journal of Psycho-Analysis* 77:549–564,

Spira, L. & Richards, A.K. (2003). The "sweet and sour" of being lonely and alone. *Psychoanalytic Study of the Child* 58:214–227

Strauss, N. (2005). *The Game: Penetrating the Secret Society of Pickup Artists*. New York: It Books. http://www.stylelife.com/.

Volkan, V. (2009). *Searching for the Perfect Woman: The Story of a Complete Psychoanalysis*. Northvale, NJ: Aronson.

Chapter 7
Exploring the Emergent Experience of Loneliness
in Two Men During Their Psychoanalytic Journey
Anita Weinreb Katz

Abstract:

I hope to demonstrate the nature and existence of the lonely
position. It is an intrapsychic state, and is not defined by external behavior. It is a position that is related to developmental challenges and failures, (Klein, 1963); specifically the
lack of empathic holding by the caregivers (Winnicott,
1965). I will discuss two middle aged single men who are
very different on the surface, but both represent the lonely
position. My aim is to demonstrate how the lonely position
manifests itself in these two men—focusing on their inner
states of emotional isolation (as contrasted with physical isolation), as well as paranoia, addiction to fantasy, and guardedness. During the course of analysis both of these men developed the strength to tolerate their inchoate feelings of
loneliness, which had been split off, repressed, and defended
against.

Loneliness is a universal condition, although the awareness of it, the capacity to bear it, and the intensity of the experience varies greatly among people. It is a developmental achievement because it is an awareness that there is
another (at first the mother) to whom one is attached, but can also be apart
from. Being apart can be a sad or angry experience, or a pleasing and enjoyable one. Like all other emotions, loneliness may be defensively repressed or
split off and never mentalized—that is, not known or felt at all. Winnicott
(1965) and Lacan (1949) write about the stage of development—when the
baby realizes he is separate and no longer a part of the mother—an extremely
traumatic and sad moment for the child.

Ogden (1989) explains awareness of loneliness as a developmental
achievement. A distinctly new form of anxiety is generated: the anxiety in part
is due to believing that one's anger has driven away or harmed the person one
loves.

In this paper I will draw on Ogden's understanding of the developmental
achievement of experiencing the loneliness of missing a significant other. I
will discuss two men, Bryan and Dan, who both came to me in their forties
and were stuck developmentally, unable to mourn the losses and injuries they
each experienced in their childhoods.

Richards and Spira (2003) discuss the frustrated "longing for an ideal object with whom one would never have to feel aggression and from whom no
aggressive actions would have to be tolerated" as a source of loneliness. Both
Bryan and Dan retreat into fantasy—including intense aggressive fantasy—
when their longings for an ideal object are thwarted. They feel very guilty

about these fantasies, but these fantasies protect them from painful longings and feelings of loneliness.

Although Bryan and Dan were strikingly different in demeanor and initial presentation, in the course of the psychoanalytic process their underlying deep loneliness emerged. Dan was overtly bitter (but portrayed a dark sense of humor that mercifully broke the heaviness of our sessions). He led a constricted life, alone much of the time except for work, playing golf and frequent calls and visits to his mother. His work life was a struggle, riddled with disappointment and failure. Bryan was an outgoing man with an extended social life and a successful but unfulfilling career. Yet romantic and intimate fulfillment eluded both of them. Neither man ever experienced a secure and empathic link with his mother, despite having a strong attachment to and idealization of her. Both men harbored intense disappointment and anger at their fathers– along with love. Both eventually developed phobias related to intimacy, love and sexual relationships. Both men spent a great deal of time in extended fantasies. Both men had fears and symptoms involving breathing, and were fearful of losing not only their breath but life itself.

Neither man spoke of loneliness as a reason for seeking help from me.

These men sought help for different reasons and related to me differently. For the first few years of analysis, Bryan was charming, seductive, and entertaining, and Dan was angry, sarcastic, bitter, critical and cynical. I will explore the analytic journey of these two men, and hope to shed some light on their underlying loneliness, its etiology, clinical manifestations and the analytic work that enabled their underlying loneliness to emerge and be experienced.

Bryan

Bryan was overtaken by an incapacitating depression—so disabling that he could not work. His visits to the psychiatrist for medication left him unsatisfied, and he told me in his first session that he wanted someone to talk to, not just prescribe pills.

Initially Bryan was unable to travel alone to his sessions, and was always accompanied. After a few months he recovered from his acute depression and inability to travel alone, and resumed his work as an executive in a prestigious firm.

For the first couple of years of therapy, he was engaging, seductive, funny, and charming. I later learned that this was a persona he had developed in his early twenties. It enabled him to be socially successful, and funny. But this was not satisfactory for him because he knew that the popular man was not the authentic Bryan. He was hiding his darker, angrier self from others

Well into our third year of analysis, he acknowledged that his behavior with me was a performance —a persona. I had been taken in and charmed by his persona. I now understand that this persona was connected to his deep feelings of loneliness —loneliness because he did not feel that his authentic self was acceptable; who he was needed to remain hidden. He gradually began to exhibit and explore another part of himself —the tortured obsessive-compulsive, angry and withholding self. He resisted my invitation to lie on the couch. We sat facing each other, but he would hardly ever look at me, explaining that was the same as lying on the couch. During this phase of the analysis I felt bored and shut out. His need to control was so great that he wrote notes in preparation for what he would say in each session. When I suggested trying to come without a prior agenda, he insisted his notes were helpful to making the best use of our sessions, and he continued this practice for several years. Underlying this practice, as I learned later on, was an intense fear of making a mistake and being severely punished.

A turning point in our work together occurred when he shared some of his intrusive thoughts—"Dirty Spic" referring to the Puerto Rican doorman with whom he enjoyed chatting,—and "Rich Jewish Bitch" referring to me. Instead of feeling insulted, I felt he was developing trust in me and in my willingness to accept and not judge or punish him for exposing his hateful and shame-riddled self. I acknowledged with compassion his hatred of paying me, and his distrust of me.

Bryan had many friends and frequent social interactions both at work and in his leisure time. He hosted regular poker games, got together with guys to watch sports, and after breaking up with his girlfriend he started dating other women. Although enjoying sex with these women as well as incorporating them into his sexual fantasies, ultimately he rejected the women who desired a committed love relationship with him. He pined for the tantalizing, unavailable women (Fairbairn, 1954)

He had frequent visits from friends who often stayed in his apartment. He was and continues to be connected to his widowed mother and favorite brother by weekly phone and Skype conversations. While being very social and seemingly comfortable with people, he was easily hurt and angered.

His eight year relationship with Erin (with whom he had lived) was stormy. His controlling behavior and her desperate desire for autonomy, led to her closing up both emotionally and physically. In their apartment, he had a separate bookcase, which was designated as off limits to her. Although she accepted his limits and prohibitions, she unconsciously established limits for him with her body. Her vagina was so tight that penetrative sex became excruciatingly painful and impossible. When he broke up with her, he gave her the down-payment for a coop, since he had an excellent position and prided himself on his generosity. They are still very close friends but, not surprisingly, fight a great deal, each often feeling misunderstood by the other.

Bryan used to tell me that when he was a child, he and his mother were best friends, played, laughed and had fun. It took many years of our work together for him to even entertain the idea that she was not able to mother him in an empathic, comforting way. Also, he repeatedly rejected my attempts to gently suggest that she was the first love of his life—both seductive and rejecting. He gradually has been able to share stories with me of her insensitive, even sometimes cruel treatment of him. He is still a very faithful, loyal son and has empathy for her, realizing how cruel and rigid her own mother was; however, he is now able to access his anger and disappointment in her as well.

A memory with his mother has become poignantly significant for him; it became a metaphor for her lack of attunement to him. When he was a young adolescent after being rejected by a girl he liked, he went to his mother to complain about his nose. Instead of recognizing his anxieties about being unattractive to girls, she made a joke of it, saying. "Okay, lets go to the doctor and see if he thinks there is something wrong with your nose." She and the doctor laughed in his presence about his "nose problem." He was mortified. In a much later session, he and I replayed this scene, with my playing the role of the empathic mother, reassuring her crestfallen son that he is an attractive young man, and that he *will* find a girl who would be happy to be his girlfriend. He smiled and seemed grateful.

His father, though very successful and well respected in the community, was a very strict, rigid man. Bryan felt that his father preferred his older brother. When his brother did something wrong, Bryan was inevitably blamed for it.

When Bryan was about twelve he found a dog he loved and took care of for three months. One day, his father said he must get rid of the dog. Begging and sobbing to no avail, Bryan's father and mother in the front seat of the car, and Bryan and his beloved dog in the back seat were driven twenty miles from their home. Neither tears nor pleading could stop his father from dragging the dog out of Bryan's arms and abandoning him in a field. Bryan cried, watching his dog get smaller and smaller as the car pulled away.

One night, when Bryan was a young boy, the whole family stayed up late to watch the Olympics. After everyone was in bed, Bryan became very frightened and knocked on his parents' bedroom door, crying and pleading for comfort. They said "You will have to take care of it yourself." His attempts to awaken his brother failed, and he was left all alone with his terrors. Freud writes that for children the first phobias are transformed into fear of the dark. "... if someone speaks it gets lighter" (Freud, 1919). To this I add, if someone speaks with compassion, it gets safer.

From adolescence on, Bryan handled hurts, failures, emotional insults, sexual and romantic longings, and feelings of abandonment or rejection by retreating into fantasy. In these fantasies there would be long stories about being successful and powerful in work and love, romantic fantasies, or voyeuristic fantasies of seduction scenes between Erin and either a man or a woman or sometimes a triangle. Fantasies of getting respect and/or berating people whom he felt "threw him under the bus" would sometimes go on for as long as 4 hours at a time. We named these extended fantasy sessions "fantasy marathons."

Analytic Treatment

Early in our work together, Bryan told me: "I am *buried deep down in a haystack and nobody knows I am there—nobody finds me.*" He did not know if this really happened, or was a dream or fantasy. It became a significant metaphor. I understood that the haystack is a safe place where he is protected and nobody can hurt him, but it is also an extremely lonely place, where he is lost forever. Although he rarely returned to this image in our therapy, it stayed with me as a metaphor for both the safety of being hidden, and the terrifying loneliness he lives with. The image of the haystack relates to

Klein's (1963) understanding that the state of internal loneliness "is the result of a ubiquitous yearning for an unattainable perfect internal state" (pp. 300-313).

Bryan had many dreams of violently expressed rage against his brother. These dreams frightened him. Along with Richards and Spira (2003), I believe that Bryan needed to have space and freedom to feel angry at me and not abandoned or punished. Richards and Spira (2003) suggest that the interpretation of the patient's fear of his acting out his aggression, and the experience of contained aggression in the analytic relationship are reparative and generative. While Bryan at times feels understood by me, he also gets angry with me and pushes me away. Gratitude is expressed, but then negated. He told me "I feel like you don't give me credit for the hard work I'm doing, just like my mother, you don't have empathy for my struggle, you look for the solution." I said, "So you feel I dropped you." And he said, "I'm telling you how much my heart was aching, you did not acknowledge how painful it was, like my mother." I said with humility, "I know, I'm not perfect, perhaps you feel that is not a good thing". He said, "It brings to my mind my repeating myself. It is hard for me to believe that I am being heard." And I said, "That is connected with loneliness, not feeling heard or being held. A very lonely position." He said, "Yes as a child I know that loneliness was an enormous issue, nowadays it is much less so." It was less so because these feelings had been cut off.

Bryan had been unable to cry for at least twenty-five years—since his early teens. It was after five years into our work together that he cried for the first time. He experienced this as a powerful achievement. After this, he had more access to crying as well as to his feelings of sadness. The first time that Bryan experienced feeling lonely was six years into his analysis when his brother said goodbye after a visit. Bryan felt as though he had crossed into some new important place in his capacity for feeling. He felt very good about this. The power of feeling lonely for Bryan meant that he was a connected person, capable of loving and missing a loved one.

For Bryan there is some confusion between fantasy and reality—he believes that the fantasy can lead to something that will happen in reality. He feels that fantasies about married women can lead to cheating and he therefore feels guilty about these fantasies. Rather than feeling informed by the fantasies of his unfulfilled longings, they become dangerous predictors of the future. When I distinguished between fantasy and reality, he objected, saying these fantasies were sometimes precursors of sexual acting out. I believe that this is an example of his magical thinking about the power of his fantasies.

Recently Bryan proudly told me that he now has three plants on his window sill. He is enjoying taking care of them and seeing them grow. He is trying to let himself experience things such as enjoying his plants. I wonder with him if this is I wonder with him if this is a way for him to connect with a more nurturing father, whom he had previously described as crudely forcing him to work in the garden. He then recalled a memory he often talks about. When he was a teenager, he called his father, asking him to open up the clubhouse for him and friends; his father refused. He was in a rage. Immediately, the power and admiration he had hoped to get, turned into humiliation and castration. When I interpreted the good nurturing father he responded with rage, remembering the stern, rigid, depriving father.

Eventually in our analytic sessions, Bryan developed a more nuanced understanding of his father's refusal to open the clubhouse for his friends. That is, his father would have liked to help him out, but his internal rigidity stopped him from bending the rules. I was impressed with his newfound compassion for his father's internal conflict and the pain he imagined his father felt when he disappointed his son. For the first time Bryan expressed a feeling that his father loved him. I was very moved by Bryan's new understanding, and told him: "Good work Bryan about your new understanding of your father as a separate person with his own conflicts and rigidity." Bryan answered: "I learned by talking about it to you. Before, I was figuring things out as I go along (i.e. by himself). It's interesting how talking about something to you brings new understanding." Bryan can now leave room for two people, for me and him, and for his father and himself—and feel less lonely. He is becoming less trapped in his own psyche (Bach, 1985). He is beginning to look at me a lot more. He is now more connected to me, and both of us are not so lonely. He is able to trust me more and tell me details of his life.

Bryan recently told me, "I used to be furious at Dylan (his popular older brother), because he did not help me be more successful with girls. He was not the mentor I wanted. When I cried because I couldn't get positive attention from girls, he said "If this is what drinking does to you, you should stop drinking." Now I am more understanding about him. Dylan was very uncomfortable with my crying." Recently, Bryan expressed empathy and understanding of Dylan's own anxieties. I said, "That is quite a change in your perspective about Dylan." At the end of this session he commented about how this was a great session and that he learned two things, being aware of loneliness and learning he can cope with people as they are and not have so many rules and scenarios in his head for how things should be.

Bryan is struggling with the dangers of getting what he wants, a connection to somebody, and a desire for separateness—can you have both? In a recent session, he told me of the exchange between Erin and himself in the kind of detail that was new—an indication of greater openness and trust in me. Erin and he were having dinner at an outside café and there was a lot of street noise. He couldn't hear her and he kept saying, "What, what? She got annoyed with him and criticized him for "not listening." He said, "I can't hear, it's too noisy." It escalated into the two of them feeling unheard, disrespected and uncared for. He walked away furious, and he was going to send her an email saying that he wasn't going to talk to her for a month. I said, "So, both of you had feelings of not being heard, and listened to." I wondered what would have happened if he could have stepped back from revisiting his own trauma and understand that she was revisiting her trauma of feeling abandoned. I suggested that he say to her, 'Erin, I want to listen to you. I know that you are feeling very upset because you feel I don't want to, but I do want to be here for you.' It was at first hard for him to hear that. And I said, "That is why both of you are such lonely people because you feel that nobody wants to listen to you or understand you." He said, with compassion, "She had a more traumatic childhood than I did. This is a new way to think about and to process things. Thank you." And I said, "You know something feels very different, and this isn't the first time, but it has been gradually feeling this way. You look at me much more, you are much more open to being connected and present with me," and he said, looking at me with warmth, "Thank you very much."

Dan

Dan was 46 years old when he began his analysis. In the first phase he was angry, depressed, bitter and sarcastic with me. He was overweight and had bad posture. He seemed uncomfortable and resentful. The one redeeming trait was his sense of humor which helped me and other people to stay open and connected to him. Dan lives alone and leads a relatively isolated life. Besides his colleagues at work, and his golf buddies, the only other person he is in touch with on a regular basis is his mother.

His first job was in the financial industry, making cold calls with the hope of realizing his dream of making big money quickly. This was a dream he shared with his father--a dream that never materialized for either of them. He then decided to get a masters degree to equip him for a new more stable profession, and it was in the fifth year of this career that he sought psychotherapy with me. Unfortunately we did not have enough time or connection to work on and understand his self-defeating patterns, including his rage at any criticism from his supervisor and his resistance to the supervision offered to him on the job. He was given an unsatisfactory evaluation, and was terminated from this position. He felt that this was unfair and paid a lawyer several thousand dollars to unsuccessfully fight this. His present job is low paying, dangerous and boring. Although he has the skills to branch out on his own to earn more money, until very recently he has resisted pursuing this route.

His parents married when they were both teenagers, and had a stormy relationship—divorcing for the first time when Dan was about 3 years old, and then remarrying and divorcing again in his early teens. His mother rejected his father's attempts to marry her a third time.

Dan remembers when, as a young boy, age 11, his father woke him up at 4 AM to help him set up and sell at the flea market. For the first year or two, Dan loved this special place and time with his father, but then he began to resent it bitterly. My hunch is that the time spent at the flea market became more about him taking care of or admiring his father, than his father parenting, guiding, supporting, and mentoring him.

His mother is "the love of his life"—he carries a photo of her in his wallet—a beautiful woman. He showed me her picture. Early in our work together he told me that he could not forgive her for having sex with men—except perhaps allowing that if she hadn't had sex with his father, he would not exist. For the first two years of psychoanalysis, she was the only one he called on the telephone—sometimes several times a day. During this time he also had hardly any early memories of his mother. Much of his past was a blank—and even if accessible to him, was not shared with me.

While growing up, his mother always worked, and from the age of five he was left in the home of a woman who cared for him but also scared him with some of her strange beliefs.

In his early forties, he dated a woman for six months, his only sexual relationship (he had premature ejaculations). Right after his mother and grandmother told him to marry her, he broke up with her.

Analytic Work

Although his attitude in sessions was angry, sarcastic and sneering towards me, he consistently came to sessions on time and paid on time as well. He often responded to questions with a grimace as if I was touching a wound that hurt too much. I realized how fragile and vulnerable he was and that his excess weight was a kind of armor to protect him. His attitude even towards people who were outwardly friendly was suspicious and guarded. In every session, even now, he brings a drink. He has to feed himself, not trusting that he could get a good feed from me.

It was at least a year and a half into our work together that I sensed there was value for him in coming to see me. He showed his appreciation for one of my interpretations in the second year of our work together (mimicking a member of the mafia, in "Analyze This") by pointing his finger at me, "You, you are good!" I laughed with relief and joy and he said, "You didn't see that movie?" This became a way for him to show some gratitude.

After a year of therapy he became interested in cooking and loved to share his recipes with me and what he would eat that day. Perhaps this was a way for him to symbolically feed me and not be alone while he was eating. I expressed interest in his recipes. It was cooking and golf that enlivened him and I appreciated this. Dan complained about not being able to lose weight and I recommended a nutritionist. He took my suggestion and gave up sugar completely. He lost forty-five pounds within a year. His waist size went down from 46 to 34. Still, there was always tea or coffee without sugar in his hand. He described to me everything he eats in a day. I believe this was one of the first ways for him to be intimate with me. The lonely child feels heard and cared for by the analyst mother. I think the work I did with him in the beginning was a lot of listening and showing appreciation for his accomplishments and for the hard work he was doing.

Since Dan was so isolated from women I recommended that he take dancing lessons as a way to be gently connected to women. And he started Argentine tango classes. But even after nine months of lessons, he was still having trouble learning. . I suggested that he take a few private lessons, but he never did. Perhaps private lessons felt scary because of the intimacy. I asked him if he usually had trouble learning new things and he said yes. I said to him that his guard was so strong in order to protect him, that it's hard for him to let anything new in.

Another indication of this was his fear of asking his mother for details when she confessed to him that she owed him a huge apology for the way she treated him when he was a young child. When I asked him, "Do you know what she meant?" he grimaced and only at my urging did he ask her for details of the mistreatment. In the following session he told me that she said "When I was very little, three or four, she was in bed during the day and couldn't go to work—she was very depressed. She was in her bedroom behind closed doors. I stood at her bedroom door and I screamed, 'I hate you!' She came out of the bedroom, crying hysterically, and then went into the bathroom and locked herself in. And I cried". So I said, "You felt so guilty for expressing your feelings for feeling abandoned, for feeling alone. Of course you hated her. And then adding insult to injury she became hysterical and then locked herself in the bathroom so she was even more inaccessible to you. How scary that must have been for you, and how guilty you must have felt. So you had a normal response of expressing hatred towards your mother because she was not available to you. But by expressing your feelings she became even less available." I empathized with his fears, his loneliness and hatred. He was an abandoned child—who felt both rejected by and destructive of the one he needed the most. I told him "We need to know more about this—more about your childhood and maybe your mother has more to share with you that would be helpful".

In the recent yearly reunion with his four high school friends, he felt excluded when two or three people were talking. Uncharacteristically, he inserted himself and said, "what are you talking about?" He wanted to know and I was surprised that he could be that assertive. He then could feel less lonely when his friends included him. He hates being left out. And I think that connects with his mother's depression. As he spoke about asserting himself with his friends he came alive in a way that was new for him.

In another session he told me a story about going into a store to get a bagel. He said that when he sees someone going into the bagel store before him, he does not go in because he is afraid the person before him is going to take so much time. He goes into a long monologue about the person in front of him taking too long. He gives up what he wants because somebody else is going to take too long. He has very low frustration tolerance. I told him that it was very hard for him to wait and to not get what he wants immediately because that made him feel unnoticed and uncared for. I suggested that this might be connected to his mother being unavailable when he was a little boy.

In psychoanalysis, I am a self object (Kohut, 1971; Bach 1985) supporting his growth, development and expansiveness. I also use words that loosen him up, although they also scare him. When I first asked him, "Do you masturbate when you have fantasies?" He painfully grimaced, saying, "I hate saying that word —masturbate!"

Since I know that he is musical and plays the drums, I asked him if he had fantasies about the drums. He said that he had fantasies about being a rock star. When I asked him if he has ever played with a group he became annoyed with me. I interpreted this as me bringing him out of his fantasy to talk about reality. The fantasies are so much more exciting than the reality.

In a recent session after I whimsically decided to put a one inch purple streak in my hair, Dan reacted with horror and terror to this change. The reaction was so extreme I was shocked. I asked him, "What's going on?" "That's weird," he spewed!—I believe this stirred up deep feelings of abandonment and confusion. The therapist he was used to and the therapist that he trusted did not have a purple streak. The change was traumatic for him, and he felt alone and unbearably lonely. This underlined for me how terrified he was of not holding on to the continuity of the maternal object in reality or in transference. After a week passed, I checked to see whether or not he was still thrown by my purple streak. He was more comfortable and he seems to be aware that I am still the same person. His reaction to the purple streak was related to his fear of my abandoning him, which is very familiar to him because this is what he experienced with his mother when she was psychotically depressed. He then proudly told me that he doesn't call his mother every day like he used to.

I shared with him my belief that this had been his way of reassuring himself that she was not dead and abandoning him.

One of the men that he golfs with invited him to go to Costco to buy almonds (after Dan told him almonds are his standby when he's hungry—non fattening snack.) Dan said he couldn't go, and then the man said he would buy him some when he goes, and Dan refused this offer. When I asked him why, he said, "If I accept, then he will expect that I do something for him." He explained that accepting the offer makes him feel trapped into having to give back. I reflected upon his distrust of any offer of friendship. His underlying wish is to be unconditionally cared for, including by me.

In the next session, we talked about his conflicts in love and work in relation to his lonely but addictive attachment to his mother, and his lonely, submissive attachment and identification to his father. He remembered that when he was alone with his mother, and she was shut off in her bedroom, he threw toys over the eighth floor balcony of their apartment. The police came up, and reported this to his mother. This was both a very angry gesture, but also a cry for help and attention. He said remembering these things boggles his mind. He is amazed that he didn't turn out as a severe anti-social, aggressive and violent kid. I said, "I guess that wasn't all there was—you must have also gotten some good stuff along the way."

It is clear that Dan is becoming stronger—more able to remember and feel the painful trauma of his early childhood. I asked how come you waited so long to seek therapy. He replied, "I guess I had to hit rock bottom."

He looks good—he has better posture, and is less angry with me. I told him I had been thinking about him for a long time over the weekend, and realized that he was so in love with his mother because she was elusive due to her serious depressions when he was a toddler and preschool child—so he carries her picture in his wallet.

And his career problems, I realized, are related both to identifying with his father—a compulsive gambler who never made it in the work world—and to his fear of surpassing him and being a success—an oedipal victory that feels murderous.

When I told him I had been thinking about him over the weekend—wondering whether his relationships to his father and mother—internal now—were related to both failures in love and in career, he said "That's bullshit." I was hurt—or was it totally discouraged, hoping that this could become some kind of breakthrough. He is very sensitive to my reactions, and so explained, that the insights regarding his father and mother/ career and love were "priceless," but it was bullshit that I spent time over the weekend thinking about him. We spent the whole session on this—his distrust of me—his still longing for the loving, empathic mother he never had and his conviction that I too easily forget him.

His expectations of being hurt and rejected are so deeply rooted and intense, that to overcome his fears—which he is working on and gradually doing—is a very hard struggle. I feel close to him at this moment, and in spite of how difficult it is for him, he is sticking it out in therapy and working hard.

Recently, Dan has trusted me enough to share explicit details of his fantasies.

He is a rock star, playing the guitar. The lead singer is a woman. The song is about love and a swindler. He is attracting two young women in the audience—they are both former colleagues of his. In the fantasy they are swooning over him. Then he is playing the drums. Swindler reminds him of his father. As a teenager he felt swindled by his father—not genuinely cared for—either seen or mentored by him. This fantasy about being a rock star is returned to over and over again.

In one remarkable session, he criticized me for being impatient while he wrote his check in the waiting room. Rather than feeling welcomed by me—he felt criticized.

The session turned out to be an extremely moving one. I asked him if he felt lonely (I felt very lonely—misunderstood and accused by him) He said, casually "No".

He said Matthew loves to tell bathroom and sexual jokes, and did so at a recent dinner with three other couples present. Dan was embarrassed by this but said nothing.

When he was 19 or 20, he used to go to bars with Matthew who inevitably picked up a woman and bragged the next day that he got layed. After learning that Dan did not get layed, Matthew told him: "You couldn't get layed if you were in a whore house with a $100 bill sticking out of your mouth." Matthew knew that Dan was a virgin. I said "That's very cruel." I asked Dan how that felt, and he said—"The hardest words for me to say are 'That hurts me.'"

I gradually processed his unexpressed—and not really experienced terrible hurt and shame about not being able to stand up for himself, and his despair that there will ever be anyone else who will stand up for him. I became sad and tearful. I said—I'm feeling the sadness you are unable to let yourself feel." He looked uncomfortable—reflected this, and I said—"it's ok—I'm feeling what's hard for you to feel with me." As Bollas says, "if our own sense of identity is certain, then its loss within the clinical space is essential to the patient's discovery of himself" (Bollas, 1983). I told him that I now know why he never calls Matthew. "He has been so cruel to you—he obviously is very competitive and insecure—but he has behaved terribly with you, and you were unable to defend yourself and tell him off."

At the end of the session I asked him how he felt. He said "good." I experienced this as an acknowledgment that we had connected and that he felt understood by me.

118

In the next session, the following day—Dan wanted to get back to what happened the day before—very unusual for him. He was very moved by the session, and I was happy to hear this rather than his past response of warding me off with sarcastic comments or humor. He spoke of a movie with Robert Redford that he has watched many times, and it always makes him cry. I asked him what the movie was about. He then told me the story of a famous baseball player (Redford), who got shot and became a player on the second string. Fifteen years forward, he once again rose to the top, and during a base-ball game [at this point it was difficult for Dan to talk—his voice cracking up, and he wanted to stop, but I encouraged him to continue] he received a note from a woman in the bleachers. She wrote that he had a son who was now about 15 years old. In the last scene, Redford, the woman and their son were together in the middle of the field. Dan cried for the first time in my presence (four years into our work). At first I thought tears represented his longing for a wife and son—but later realized that the threesome represented his enduring longings for his mother, father and himself to be united. He confirmed that the latter is what he longs for.

It is probably also significant that the wounded father reminds him of his damaged father, and the reunion—the dream of the intact family—keeps him stuck, unwilling to accept his loss, mourn the heartbreak of the broken family, and give up his mother as the one and only love of his life.

Hopefully, his attachment and growing trust and intimacy with me will give him a chance to endure his grief and mourn his painful childhood, and open up to the uncertainties and dangers of a present intimate connection.

This feels like a new chapter in our work together—deepening of trust in me allows him to remember and talk about his past experiences. With this emerging trust in me, he told me that he dated a girl when he was 19 years old. They went on a couple of dates—hey even kissed, and Dan enjoyed it. But he was so uncomfortable and anxiety ridden that he broke off the relationship. At this point, he seems to be more in touch with his loneliness, and wants me to understand and help him with the barriers and terrors that keep him alone and lonely. I believe that our future work will include his becoming aware of his deep longings for the early cuddly mothering because this was something his "dead mother" could not provide (Green 2001).

In his present job, Dan is getting positive feedback. This is new. Dan re-cently spoke more reflectively than usual: "On the one hand I feel like I'm just nothing, I'm inferior, I hate everybody, but there is the other side to me, I feel they are all a piece of shit, and I'm better than everybody." I've talked to him about how he comes into sessions and how he greets me. I said to him, "Is it so hard to smile?" And he's been working on it. "Recently instead of just star-ing down at people, I've decided to smile." So he is less guarded and gradu-ally risking being open and welcoming to people. He has been smiling and people smile back. (This brings to mind Izard's theory [Shrlich1973], that at

119

first the mother's smile is imitated by the baby and then the baby experiences pleasure.)

Conclusion

As I started to think about this conclusion, I found myself feeling lonely—connected, perhaps, to my own existential loneliness. It is lonely to think alone, and write alone, to wonder if I will find any listeners who care about what I say here, and who will engage with me in agreement or disagreement, in teaching or learning, to ultimately have an experience of mutuality that will enrich us both. Significantly, with both Bryan and Dan my loneliness was exacerbated by their distancing themselves from their own feelings of loneliness and rejecting my attempts to understand and empathize. And they felt dropped and alone when my attempts at understanding them did not exactly mirror their feelings.

The last subphase of separation individuation is termed *on the way to* (from about 24 to about 36 months) an associated self. This subphase is characterized by the emergence of a more realistic and less shifting view of the self. It is also characterized by the consolidation of a deeper, somewhat ambivalent, but more sustained internalized maternal representation, the libidinal attachment to which is not seriously compromised by temporary frustrations.(Mahler, et al., 2000, Akhtar, 1999). Neither Bryan nor Dan had a secure attachment to their mothers, so they could not bear the fluctuations of connectedness and separateness. They had different ways of submerging their feeling of loneliness. For Dan, it was telephoning his mother several times a day; for Bryan it was joining alternative religious groups and doing a lot of volunteer work. Both of them were very distrustful of those who were kind to them or interested in them, and tended to desire women who were unavailable and romantically rejecting (Fairbairn, 1954).

Both Bryan and Dan are struggling with traumatic early object ties to mother, especially—and to some extent also to father. They both feared, both within and outside of the analytic relationship, that an intimate attachment to a love object would open up their vulnerability and repeat the pain of earlier experience of abandonment, failures in empathy and harsh criticism.

Ehrlich (1998) states that comfortable intimate relationships involve a balance of "being" and "doing". He defines "being" as a state of merger of self and other—an experience of feeling one with the other (p. 144); and "doing" is a state in which self and other are distinct and separate entities (p. 143). My inference is that when there is a rupture in both these modalities, starting with infancy—both with maternal preoccupation with the baby (Winnicott, 1965); and with maternal facilitating the baby's separate powers—the problem of pathological loneliness is generated. I believe this to be the case with both Bryan and Dan.

To soothe themselves, they entered into an alternate self-constructed world of fantasy, fulfillment, power and security. Along with other feelings associated with a healthy maternal and paternal attachment, feelings of loneliness were unmetabolized,—and instead they resorted to escape into fulfilling fantasies. The ability to both empathize with and separate from their parents was a developmental achievement in our work Their strengthened sense of self and self worth enabled them to endure missing the loved one and experience feelings of loneliness and paradoxically to feel less depressed and less dependent upon fantasy.

The analytic work involved both transference connections and the real relationship. Satran (1961) states that the real relationship between patient and analyst has been ignored for many years. Stone (1961) underscores the legitimate gratifications a patient is entitled to in analysis and how certain stilted maneuvers may impede rather than enhance the crystallization of transference" (p296).

Satran's (1961) statement that "a lonely child would have a tendency towards social isolation" applies to Dan, but not to Bryan.

Fromm-Reichmann (1990) emphasizes that most people have difficulty talking about their loneliness. I would like to emphasize that many people are not even aware of their loneliness. For Bryan and Dan, achieving the capacity to feel loneliness felt wonderful. They each felt more connected in a genuine, deeply emotional way—perhaps they felt more human.

In my experience, loneliness is rarely introduced by the analysand. I have found that when I introduce the patient's loneliness in the context of the content of a session, the door is opened, and then they are able to speak and eventually experience their lonely feelings. Paradoxically, this is experienced as a welcome achievement.

References

Akhtar, S. (1999). *Inner Torment, Living Between Conflict and Fragmentation.* New York: Jason Aronson.

Bach, S. (1985) *Narcissistic States and the Therapeutic Process.* New York and London: Jason Aronson.

Bollas, C. (1983) The Expressive Uses of the Counter-Transference—Notes to the Patient from Oneself. *Contemporary Psychoanalysis* 19:1–33.

Ehrlich, S. (1998) . On Loneliness, Narcissism and Intimacy. *American Journal of Psychoanalysis* 58:35–162.

Fairbairn, W.R.D. (1954) An Object-Relations Theory of Personality. New York: Basic Books.

Fromm-Reichmann, F. (1990). Loneliness. *Contemporary Psychoanalysis* 26:305–329.

Freud, S. (1919). The Uncanny. *Standard Edition* 17: 219–256.

Green, A. (2001). The dead mother. In: *Life Narcissism, Death Narcissism,* transl, A. Weller. London and New York: Free Associations Books.

Izard, C.E., (1971). *The Face of Emotion.* New York: Appleton-Century-Crofts.

Klein, M. (1963). On the sense of loneliness. In: *Writings of Melanie Klein 1946-1963.* New York: New Library of Psychoanalysis, 1984, pp.300–313.

Kohut, H. (1971) *The Analysis of the Self.* New York International Universities Press

Lacan, J. (1949). 'Le Stade du miroir comme formateur de la fonction de Je, telle qu'elle nous est revelee dans l'expérience psychanalytique', Revue français de psychanalyse 1949:13:4.

Mahler, M, Pine, F and Bergman, A (2000) *The Psychological Birth of the Human Infant: Symbiosis and Individuation.* New York: Basic Books.

Ogden, T.H. (1992). *The Primitive Edge of Experience.* Northvale, NJ: Jason Aronson.

Richards, A.K. & Spira, L. (2003). On Being Lonely: Fear of One's Own Aggression as an impediment to intimacy. *Psychoanalytic Quarterly* 72:357–374.

Satran, G. (1978). Notes on loneliness. *Journal of the American Academy Psychoanalysis* 6:281–300.

Stone, L.(1954). The Widening Scope of Indications for Psychoanalysis. *Journal of the American Psychoanalytic Association* 2:567–594.

Sullivan, H.S. (1953). *The Interpersonal Theory of Psychiatry.* New York: W.W. Norton.

Winnicott, D.W. (1965). *The Maturational Processes and the Facilitating Environment.* New York: International Universities Press.

Chapter 8
The Complex Nature of Loneliness
Arthur A. Lynch

Abstract:

This chapter follows up on the theme from the introduction to the book—Loneliness is a universal emotion that is both intricate and unique. Loneliness is an emotion that probably lies within a spectrum from solitude through intolerable and desperate isolation. It is an emotion that reacts to loss in the manner of anguish and that continues in the longing for the lost other through self-reflection. "I am without the other and it is intolerable to me." It is this reflection that organizes the individual's attention that s/he is alone and unable to fill the void with those around him/her. Loneliness may or may not be part of the mourning process as the concerns vacillate between the anguish of the impact on the self of being without the other and the intolerable state of living in a world without them.

This chapter addresses the question of whether loneliness, an experience known to most people, can be addressed as a single phenomena or whether it is a complex affect state. This exploration will occur by reviewing the progress of the case of James as he struggles in treatment with the uncertainties he seeks help for, and the torment that underlies his life. The presentation of the case will be followed by a brief discussion on some concepts relating to the analytic process.

The Case of James

James is a 30 year-old, single man. He entered analysis with concerns about his sexuality after his pregnant psychotherapist interrupted her practice to give birth and become a mother. It was at her urging that James sought analysis at this time.

James is a research scientist and currently a principal investigator in a laboratory that has several junior fellows and staff under his management. I have been working with James for over two and a half years on a three times a week basis. James lies on the couch and associates freely. His case is packed with details, most of which cannot be included. Instead, James' treatment will be condensed into a story-line that attempts to capture the relevance of the case to loneliness as a complex affect.

When James began treatment, his complaints included: a confusion of sexual orientation, the belief that he was in some way female, childhood intestinal illnesses that required ongoing medical attention, concern about the size, structure and function of his penis, and intense anxiety about being assaulted and about being alone. His constant worry about these symptoms and their relationship to one another led him to an understanding that he was a homosexual man and that because of his cultural, religious and familial beliefs he was destined to be alone in this life. James recognized the irrationality in his thinking and continued functioning in his daily life with extraordinary competence in several areas.

The onset of the symptoms occurred, James recalled, when he was in college and he fell in love with his roommate, George. It was in this relationship that the symptoms gradually unfolded. The first episode occurred with a crisis, when in an inebriated state James confessed his love and desire for George. George, in turn, flatly rejected him, leaving James disgusted with himself and desperate to have George's friendship back.

This event precipitated intense separation and castration anxiety as James sought frantically to correct his misstep. The two men found a way to reconcile after this incident without ever speaking about it, but the relationship had changed and would never be the same. James continued his deep passion in private, longing for George's love but fearing further rejection. After graduation both men went on to graduate school in different parts of the country but they remained in touch. In his early reports on this relationship, it was clear that James felt he needed to make the major effort if the relationship was to survive. After graduate school, James sought weekly treatment from Francine, a psychology lecturer he met while in graduate school. She was a little older than he was, and had begun psychoanalytic training. When she became pregnant and needed to interrupt her practice, she suggested to James that he enter analysis.

His analysis began with the emerging narrative of a tormented childhood. James reported life with a very disturbed mother and a remote father, both of whom managed to communicate, albeit indirectly, their love and admiration for him; which, as one might suspect, was conditional and demanding. His mother was infused with fears about all the people in her life. Among other things, she worried persistently about her husband's fidelity, her daughter's sexuality and her son's masculinity. Her father, James' maternal grandfather, had lost his own mother at a very early age (around 2) and was described by James as an alcoholic, a violent bully and a pervert. James had been taken care of primarily by his maternal great aunt, who he loved quite deeply and who lived near the family, from his birth until the age of four. During this time he would see his parents in the evenings. Both parents worked long days and, often, weekends. He recalled frequent fighting at home often involving his grandfather, who also lived near the family.

Typically, his grandfather would get drunk and start fights with the other family members. James remembers his maternal grandmother as "nice enough" but uncaring and disinterested in him. At the age of four, his mother's sister moved into his family's home and remained there for the next

126

seven years. It was during this period, when James was six and a half, that his father left the home. His business had collapsed into bankruptcy and he left the home seeking employment in nearby cities to pay off his debt and provide some financial means for the family. During this period James lived on and off at home with his mother, sister and aunt; as well as, at the home of his great aunt. These chaotic living arrangements were necessitated by his mother's absence due to repeated hospitalizations for psychotic decompensation. His aunt proved an unreliable caretaker during these years for both him and his sister, often becoming violent and beating them. She moved out of the home to marry when James was 11 years old. Initially, James was welcomed to visit at his aunt's home and was treated well by his new uncle; but this too transformed when his aunt gave birth to her first son. At this point, James reports, everything changed. His aunt and uncle no longer had any real interest in him and he was perceived as a burden to their family.

These were confusing and shameful times for James. He was deeply embarrassed and angered by his father's business failings. Members of the extended family did not help financially, nor talk about his situation. In fact, his father was never mentioned during family gatherings. James' life descended into extreme poverty during this time and he recalled sleeping on a roll-up mat on his great aunt's dining room floor. James' "sister"—his cousin from the family of his mother's older brother—arrived when he was five. She is formally his cousin from the family of his mother's older brother. She came to live with James and his family when his maternal uncle's family fell apart and he was unable to provide care for his daughter. Distraught, he planned to place her in foster care; but it was at James' mother's insistence that she came to live with their family. This stands out as an important memory of pride that James held for his mother's strength and conviction. He remembers, however, being distressed over his "sister's" arrival, and he began to develop a fantasy that his parents wanted a daughter rather than a son. This distress later manifested itself in two ways. First, James developed a childhood intestinal illness that required frequent trips to the hospital for injections. As he was a young child his father had taken over the care of these illnesses. James remembers his father's loving, attentive care. He would take James to the hospital and hold and comfort him through the injections. Secondly, James developed a view of himself (a self-construct) as intellectually superior to his family. This idea was born out of his need to compensate for his perceived loss. It gave him a better understanding of his feelings of alienation and protected him from his loneliness by providing a sense of safety from his belief that he, as a male, was unwanted.

These fluctuating living arrangements continued through his latency and adolescent years. James lived between homes until his last year of high school when he moved in permanently with his great aunt. High school for James was particularly painful, with a mixture of shame, guilt and alienation. This was underscored by his family's extreme poverty. In the years prior to his father's bankruptcy, the family had been financially secure and had, at times, thrived. After the collapse, James remembers not knowing where his clothes came from, and he was frequently embarrassed because they were often ill-fitting and never in fashion with his peers. James remained quite isolated socially, unable to develop a deeper social engagement with his peers; but he nonetheless excelled academically and demonstrated a proclivity for math and the sciences. This fueled his "gifted identity." During this time he was able to manage his feelings of alienation by immersing himself in the problems of the family. This helped to contain his feelings of loneliness, and it wasn't until he left home for college that this containment ruptured.

It was during his college years that his symptoms began to emerge, but they were somewhat attenuated by his relationship with George. It was only after their graduation, however, that his symptoms took on their full force. James came to treatment with the deep conviction that he was a gay man who was unable to ever have a meaningful relationship. The initial phase of treatment was characterized by the setting of the frame, scheduling, fees and an appreciation for the early themes of James' deep devotion to both Francine and George.

These attachments presented both in the service of self-soothing and resistance, which was manifested in multiple relationships in James' life, including the emerging transference with the analyst. In the opening phase of treatment, the transference question was: Was I a suitable replacement for Francine, and secretly in the shadows, maybe even for George; or would I be the failed and broken parents? The answer to the question flowed back and forth between his fear of me and the formation of a trusting relationship. George and Francine had provided him with the acceptance and affirmation he needed to feel better. They were able to enter into a "selfobject relationship."[8] I treated his feelings owards George and Francine respectfully but also curiously. In doing so, I always took the time to recognize and highlight their adaptive importance before further exploring their conflicted nature. George, and Francine, differently, let James view himself as "good enough." With them, he felt like a young man of value and promise. But they both also represented a conditional

---

[8]Here the use of selfobject falls within the definition provided by Skelton, R. (Ed.), (2006) in The Edinburgh International Encyclopaedia of Psychoanalysis. Selfobject, "denotes a sense of oneself in relation to the other that is needed for the sustenance, vitalisation, or enhancement of the self. A selfobject is neither self nor object, but the subjective aspect of a self-sustaining function performed by a relationship of self to objects who by their presence or activity evoke and maintain the experience of selfhood. The selfobject experience, the selfobject transference, as well as the selfobject relationship, are variously co-created by patient and analyst." For original definition see Kohut & Wolf, 1978, p. 414.

and limited form of love that, when made apparent, would torment James with deep suspicion and self-hatred. After several months of exploring the loss of Francine, James stated: "I spoke with Francine last night. I had to tell her that I was angry with her. This was very difficult. It was very difficult and I was afraid but I said: "'I am angry that you cannot be there for me, too. I am afraid my telling you this will hurt you and your baby, but I am angry.'"

James was surprised at her response. Francine was initially silent, but after some time apologized in a sincere and meaningful way. James understood her to mean that she was sorry he felt this way, sorry for anything she did to make him feel badly, sorry for all the bad things that had ever happened to him. She was, in a way, saying: 'You can be angry at me. It's all right. I understand and I can take it.'

I believe his understanding of her intention was an idealized wish for her statement of "Sorry" to mean this much. This may well have been his way of relinquishing his wishes and needs for her, and beginning to make room for our relationship. After telling me this, he cried for a long time and realized that he really had no choice in the matter, just like as he really had no choice growing up. He said: *"I had to take care of either my mother or myself. I was way too small to take care of myself. So I had to take care of her."* This became a theme in our work for several months, when James announced that he had phoned his mother and told her: *"Mother, you have to start taking care of yourself better. I can't be there for you any more. I am a grown-up man now and I have to take care of myself."*

It would take another six months before he could begin to let go of his devotion to Francine, as she regularly visited us in the turmoil of our sessions, and James would remind me how she might do the work differently and subtly better. Concerning his devotion to George and his mother, we had just scratched the surface.

In this period of the early work, I wondered with James if he felt alone in these struggles, to which he replied: "No, because now I have you." When I asked how that made him feel, he replied: "This makes me feel much better. I can now say goodbye to Francine. We will still be friends but in a different way." This seemed to be both a wish and fear, reflecting a part-object usage in the transference as James had not yet found a way to really trust me. For James, I was still more of a fantasy object, used mostly to defend against a deeper anguish, sense of alienation and loneliness. In this process, it felt like he was scrambling to let go of Francine before he was abandoned, and was establishing an idealized transference to compensate for the absence of trust in our relationship; all designed to guard his inner sense of well- being (i.e., homeostasis). Adaptively, this acting out offered two important advances: (1). It invited, more fully, the transference into the treatment; (2). In being infused with an idealized transference, I was also provided with the potential to help create a space where we could meet.

As one might suspect, this dynamic in the relationship was compounded by the emergence of a competing and compellingly apprehensive and mistrustful transference configuration. James, at this point, viewed me as strong and potentially harmful, and himself as weak, fragile and dependent.

This can be seen in a dream James reported: "A middle- aged man is yelling at someone: 'Why do you say unpleasant things about me to others!' He then throws something in his hand and it hits with the sound of metal." It was the ring of his alarm bell that woke him up. When I asked James what his thoughts were about the dream he stated that he recognized the man in the dream as a teacher he had had. This man's name began with the letter "A." He said: "I remember your name contains an A, no it has two A's. "Is he you? Mostly, I have felt comfortable with you. Your temperament is like my father's, but your age is like my Grandfather. I've told you he is a pervert and very paranoid. That sounds more like the man in the dream. I suddenly feel very uncomfortable telling you all of this." There is much more to this dream, but in the end I noted it seemed important that in the dream the image of the man throwing a metal object was like his grandfather and that I seemed to be about his age and that telling me this made him uncomfortable for some reason. I told him that this all seemed important to me.

As we explored these struggles, he gained insight into an unconscious childhood image of his grandfather, aunt, and mother as anxious and dangerous people. Their demands, with the clear directive that he must be compliant, resulted in the loss of any expression of his autonomy. He is still in the process of becoming aware that he fears that successful independent action will lead to an intolerable increase in suffering and eventually the loss, primarily of his mother. This was further complicated by his identification with his submissive father. The delicate transferential balance that he and I had to navigate in the treatment, in all its ramifications, falls between his ambitions and his sense of illness, his success and self-esteem recovery, and his death and defeat.

Success was as alarming in sexual activity, as it was with work. Our exploration in the early phase of treatment was to look at his sexual anxieties as a means of avoiding all contact and social participation. He was afraid of being involved. The treatment issues around his sexuality were, and remain, intense. This work was ushered in when James recalled a visit he had made to see George. He returned from this visit angry and disappointed. After their initial meeting, George did not return his calls. He thought: "Maybe I should say goodbye to my hopes of ever having George as a boyfriend." This powerful fantasy of "waiting faithfully" for George served many purposes, including barring him from pursuing others out of fears of infidelity. At one point in this period he said: "I see myself as less important than he or even others are. I take what I can get. Straight men do not think like gay men. They can't understand. Do you understand me?" Now I thought that was an interesting question: Here James is approaching a possible erotic transference with all its excitement and fear, but is only aware of the wish for affirmation. These forms of parallel communications were frequent during this period and I usually explored them further. "Yes, this is the question you have been asking. What do you think?" was my response.

James had another and different thought. "I read on the internet about a gay psychoanalyst named Sullivan. Did you know him?" I interpreted this as a defensive move away from the initial question, and said: "He was a very interesting analyst who we can talk about, but, before we do that, you had asked me if I understood you.

"Yes, you're right," James responded, "I believe you understand me but I am looking for something. I looked for it in my relationship with George. When we were sitting around his apartment I looked at his new iPhone. He had an iBook on what dreams mean. I asked him about this and he said he wants to be able to read people's minds. He thinks this will help him in his business. In the past, I would have told him it was a great idea; but this time I told him I thought it was stupid!" James is beginning to cast out the magical world that he hoped would save him. He went on: "We started to talk seriously and I told him why I fell in love with him. I said: "'my mother was like yours, George. She did not treat my father very well. She was afraid that all men would be violent, like her father. She could not deal with me as a little boy, so she made me her little girl. She needed me to be a son but not a boy. She needed me to be a son who was a daughter.'"

He went on to tell George: "I was also a daughter/little girl to my father, who needed the affections of a woman in his life, and I took care of him the way a little girl would. When I met you I realized that, like me, you needed a mother and so I became a mother for you. I didn't know I would fall in love with you." Our time was coming to an end and I asked James: "How long have you known this?" He responded: "I think it is something I have always known but it never came out like this before, not even with Francine." As the session ended, I did not want James to leave feeling too vulnerable with this topic. I told him: "How you feel about this is very important, but we have to stop for today. Let's see if we can get back to it on Friday."

As the weeks went on, we further explored this dimension. James became aware that his sexuality was always discouraged by his mother, and he believed that the reason for this was because his interest in another woman would inevitably lead him to leave her. He reported that his mother would not allow him to urinate standing up, and always told him to sit. Even as an adolescent she would yell: "Are you sitting down?" Again, these same feminine identifications have protected him from the dangers of a sexual relationship with a frightening woman, as he entertained fantasies of being a submissive lover to a male.

131

In a later part of the treatment, as James began developing a greater sense of separation from his mother, he integrated this aspect of identification into a larger picture. In his own reconstruction, he notes: "It reminds me of my mother. She told me girls want to destroy your future. I lived in her shadow for many years. She believed that all women are seductive and destructive. This comes from her father's desire. He was out of control sexually and she may have been his desire, and she repelled it by seeing women as seductive and bad because that is what she felt from his desire. Then she left him and brought these fears first to my father and then to me, feeling it was wrong to feel desire for or be with women. She was obsessed with my father's fidelity and I don't think he ever did anything wrong. As a teenager she would take me out at night and search for my father, who had long since moved out, to see if he was with other women."

This explanation evolved into a much more complex fantasy containing both positive and negative oedipal determinants, and in the context of his case I understood James' desire to renounce any sexuality as the defensive aspect of an unconscious fantasy that helped him avoid any movement toward autonomy and an active personal involvement. As we addressed this question of avoidance, James began flirting with both men and women. Then he became infatuated with a female colleague. Finally, towards the end of our second year, James came back from a conference where he met Mia. She was a graduate student, finishing her degree in a health related field, and who had attended his presentation. She was gushing with praise for his work, and soon enough the two began dating. Although there remain many questions about his sexual identity, he made clear progress on the question of his involvement.

Discussion

What I am addressing in this treatment is how conflicts stemming from the unpleasure of James' experiences have influenced his unconscious mental organization. Only by understanding the structure of his defenses against this unpleasure could the nature of James' symptoms, transference, and relationships with others be understood in an insightful manner.

There were, at least, six decisive childhood experiences that have emerged in the course of treatment: (1) the multiple and at times chaotic caretaking until he was four years old, and the need to adapt to a violent unpredictable environment; (2) the move to bring his aunt's into his mother's home, and the confusing parental lines that moved back and forth between the mother and the aunt until age 11; (3) His mother's caring but volatile nature and the departure of his father from the home; (4) the parents' extreme admiration for his intellectual achievements and his intellectual triumph in school; (5) the disapproval, by both parents, of his masculine activity, and his mother's fear of women; (6) the arrival of his "sister," accompanied by the traumatic loss of his special position with his parents. These experiences led to a symptom formation that created the illusion of a special ongoing but separate relationship with his mother and his father. To have his needs actually met, however, he had to meet their needs first, i.e., to take care of them. Within these more complex needs were the simultaneous fears and defenses (i.e., against these fears of their loss, the loss of their love, becoming a woman and penile damage, and self-loathing). Here the childhood illness accomplished this compromised state with his father, who cared for him while sick. He returned to being sick whenever threatened by perceived threats. Another dominant threat, the fear of castration, was managed in three ways: (1) with regard to his desire to be like his mother, there was a complex unconscious fantasy where he identified with her by refuting his masculinity; (2) oedipal wishes were also opposed by the belief that he was too "weak, ill, impotent or female"; (3) by identifying as the beloved daughter to his father. Each of these solutions contained aspects of depressive affect[9] that helped explain his overall emotional state, loneliness, but left him free from recognizing the true state of loss. These complex compromise formations were barely adequate solutions to the myriad of fears that tormented James growing up, but they became woefully inadequate when he left home.

All of this emerged in the treatment in a fragmented and chaotic way. Often these factors would arise in relation to one another as James struggled to understand and avoid the pains these feelings brought about. While at home as a child, the emergence of the grandiose self-construct was a pathological compromise formation that maintained both adaptive (i.e., feeling special) and defensive functions. Within this narcissistic symptom the defenses of grandiosity; idealization, splitting, projection and devaluation all took their place within this narcissistic symptom. What became clear over time was that this grandiose self-construct was not the primary source of pathogenesis, but a solution designed by James with the arrival of his "sister" to protect himself from a sense of further loss. In the initial phase of treatment, the reflections of this grandiose self were the most prominent in the expression of both defense and transference. As such, it was the feature that drew most of our early attention. My initial stance to these narcissistic engagements was empathic, and I soon learned that there was more substance and stability to James' inner life than these symptoms suggested. Initially he saw me with great skepticism.

---

[9] Brenner's (1982) most succinct statement on this can be found in his chapter on affects in *The Mind in Conflict.* He states: Psychic conflict ensues whenever gratification of a drive derivative is associated with an unpleasurable affect that is sufficiently intense. The affect may be of two kinds, either anxiety or depressive affect. Anxiety is unpleasure plus ideas of danger, i.e., ideas of impending calamity. Depressive affect is unpleasure plus ideas of a calamity that has already occurred, a calamity that is a fact of life." (page 70).

How could I possibly be a replacement for Francine or George? They had been "good enough" to meet his early maternal longings and were now enshrined in his mind as the necessary standard for future relationships. As we reviewed my shortcomings regularly, we began to see both our participations in the experience. Repeatedly wondering with James how it was to work with such an analyst helped to destabilize the equilibrium of the narcissistic character defense structure. This gave way to the emergence of other transference patterns and facilitated the broadening of his previously restricted organizing function. James was now able to engage me in a fuller object state with the reduced need to take flight in criticisms or aggrandizements. Slowly these transference patterns transformed into a new, differentiated transference, which Kernberg (1970, 1974) has found as counter-indicative to core narcissistic character pathology. This was not a steady progressive path, but one that was frequented by regressive swings when James was disappointed in the therapeutic hour (e.g., any lateness or misattunements), disappointed with his significant others in the outside world, fearful of uncertain material arising in the hour (e.g., becoming aware of tender feelings for people he felt he only previously hated). During these times James would present a brief divergence from the work, or express hopelessly his deep disappointments. I found it best to follow him during these times until he indicated he could hear the purpose of this digression.

By analyzing the narcissistic character defense we were able to make room for a more painful affect of loneliness that lay at its base. This defense structure allowed James to feel special; but more importantly it allowed him to avoid feeling lonely, uncared for, unwanted. If left unanalyzed, it is highly likely that this defense structure would keep him frozen in this state of feeling fraudulent. Now, however, he was beginning to see that he had real value based on real talent.

The newly found aspect of his life, his loneliness, was not, however, the core pathogenic factor either. It too, took on the complex nature of the other solutions, which in this case allowed James to simultaneously feel what he didn't want to know. What emerged more clearly was an unconscious fantasy of the "poor lonely boy."[10] Exploring the varied themes of this fantasy led to many painful states, all signifying loss. This was the fundamental loss in his

---

[10] Interestingly enough, what also transformed here was a movement in the analyst's intervention from working with the manifestations of the conflict (defense and transference interpretations) as it appeared in consciousness (Gray, 1973, 1996; Pray, 1996) to understanding the derivatives of unconscious aspects of compromise formations as manifest in unconscious fantasy (Arlow, 1979; Arlow & Brenner, 1990). This shift was not a conscious one but followed the presentation of the clinical data. See Paniagua (2011) for an interesting discussion of the blended techniques.

life: the loss of those he loved, the loss of a life he believed was fuller and kinder when he was a child and his family was doing well and caring for one another, the loss of the family home and place in the community. Recognizing this loss meant working through how he lost these attachments; how the collapse of his father's business and his mother's mental illness made them unavailable; and more painfully, recognizing how his parents' personal traumas led to their wishes/desires impinging upon him, for their fulfillment, and how that alienated them further and left him further from his own center of being. The loneliness was a form of knowing what he couldn't allow himself to know. So, as the bard says: "What you don't know you can feel somehow" (Bono and U2—It's a beautiful day).

The treatment process has also led to some affective transformations. Solitude has replaced the subjective loneliness in some of the analytic hours. Quinodoz (1996) elaborates on the role that "taming the sense of solitude" plays in psychic integration during treatment. He writes: "The capacity to transform the anxious sense of solitude into one that replenishes the wellspring of the subject's being and benefits relations with others can be acquired during the course of the psychoanalytic process, in particular by working through the separation and loss-of-object anxieties that punctuate the analyst—analysand relationship" (1996, p. 482). Recognizing and mourning these losses, and the depressive affect associated with them, is the work of the end of the middle phase of treatment. These unmourned losses lay at the base of James' struggle. Mourning will bring resolution, if not forgiveness, and recognition of the delays created in his life. As these emerge, it is likely, he will continue to be challenged by castration and separation anxieties, as well as abandonment, depression and the haunting fears of being left. This work has as its aim to enhance integration and the acquisition of "buoyancy" (Quinodoz, 1993, 1996) or " a sense of ego integration that corresponds to the internalization of a well developed capacity to be alone" (1996, p. 492), with each participant able to enjoy the other.

To conclude, the features of James' psychopathology revealed, at times, to fall between a moderate and severe range. James suffered from complex narcissistic conflicts that were deeply rooted in his fear of being alone and the anguish he felt from loneliness. These were compounded by an intense state of depression with masochistic features. Yet, throughout his psychological struggles James maintained an ability to function on a very high level of competence in several areas of his life. He also had the capacity for meaningful object relations, which eventually led him into several strong professional relationships and, more importantly, a love relationship.

What appeared at first impression to be an individual struggling with severe narcissistic pathology changed over time. This initial state gave way to a deeper recognition of his profound sense of loss, compensatory attachment to a brutal irrational composite other, with a consequential baseline affect of in-

135

tolerable depression and personal isolation (experienced as alienation). This reflects the unevenness in mental functioning that Richards (1981) has discussed in some detail. In the treatment situation, this defensive constellation acted more as a petrified state and was found less frequently as the focus of treatment transitioned toward the underlying depressive affect; while erupting, as abrupt grandiose expressions, during times of significant disappointment. This recalls Fenichel's conceptualization of defense as: "The forces which at one time opposed each other are now wasted in the useless and hardened defensive attitudes of his ego; the conflict has become latent" (1940, page 190).

References

Arlow, J.A. & Brenner, C. (1990). The Psychoanalytic Process. *Psychoanalytic Quarterly* 59:678–692.

Arlow. J.A. (1969). Unconscious Fantasy and Disturbances of conscious Experience. *Psychoanalytic Quarterly* 38:1–27.

Brenner, C. (1974). On the Nature and Development of Affects: A Unified Theory. *Psychoanalytic Quarterly* 43:532–556

————(1979). Depressive Affect, Anxiety, and Psychic Conflict in the Phallic-Oedipal Phase. *Psychoanalytic Quarterly* 48:177 –197.

————. (1982). The Mind in Conflict. Madison, CT: International Universities Press.

Fenichel, O. (1940). The study of defense mechanisms and its importance for psychoanalytic technique. In *The Collected Papers of Otto Fenichel.* Second series, pp. 183–197. New York: W.W. Norton.

Gray, P. (1973). Psychoanalytic Technique and the Ego's Capacity for Viewing. Intrapsychic Activity. *Journal of the American Psychoanalytic Association* 21:474–494.

.————(1996). Undoing the Lag in the Technique of Conflict and Defense Analysis. *Psychoanalytic Study of the Child* 51:087–101.

Kernberg, O.F. (1970). Factors in the Psychoanalytic Treatment of Narcissistic Personalities. *Journal of the American Psychoanalytic Association* 18:51–85.

.————(1974). Further Contributions to the Treatment of Narcissistic Personalities. *International Journal of Psycho-Analysis* 55: 215–240.

Kohut, H & Wolf, E.S. (1978). The Disorders of the Self and their Treatment: An Outline. *International Journal of Psycho-Analysis* 59:413–425.

Paniagua, C. (2011). Psychotherapy and Close-Process Technique. *International Journal of Psychoanalysis* 92:43–56.

Pray, M. (1996). Two Different Methods of Analyzing Defense. In *Danger and Defense: the Technique of Close Process Attention,* ed. M. Goldberger. Northvale, NJ: Jason Aronson.

Richards, A.D. (1981). Self Theory, Conflict Theory, and the Problem of Hypochondriasis. *Psychoanalytic Study of the Child* 36:319–33.

Chapter 9
Witnessing: Its Essentialness in Psychoanalytic Treatment
Jenny Kahn Kaufmann and Peter Kaufmann

Abstract:

The witnessing concept has come into prominence in terms of helping people who have suffered through major histori-cal-social trauma (such as the Holocaust) in their recovery process. But, as several recent psychoanalytic writers have recognized (Poland, 2000; Orange, 2010), witnessing plays an important role in the psychoanalytic treatment process, especially for individuals who have experienced formative trauma in their own private lives. In this paper, we are going to review definitions of witnessing and generalize about the crucial functions and benefits that it provides in treatment. Witnessing involves the recognition of what the patient has done and experienced from the analyst's position as an ac-knowledging but separate other that enables the patient to ac-cept and integrate their history. Then we are going to con-sider the alternate practices that sometimes occur in psycho-analytic therapies and their detrimental effects. Sometimes, analysts minimize the patient's actual experience and stress explanatory formulations and/ or compensatory behavior that are designed to fix the patient and place him or her on a more adaptive path. As well intentioned as these strategies may be, they frequently lead the patient to dissociate crucial aspects of their experience and to compromise their resulting sense of self. To illustrate our ideas we will review the case of Lenore in which she had not been witnessed in several earlier treatments, but finally benefited from the facilitation and witnessing in her current therapy. As a result of her earlier "fix- it" treatments, Lenore had become more dissociated from her traumatic past and from related aspects of herself. She felt disconnected from her more vulnerable sides, and thus couldn't fully enjoy her current life or resonate with the vulnerability of others, including her children and close inti-mates. Her "fix-it" treatments unwittingly repeated the inhu-man treatment she had experienced as a child. In her current treatment, the process of witnessing as well as interpretation gradually enabled her to face and fully feel her painful for-mative experiences and gradually integrate a more "whole" sense of self. In Winnicott's terms, she went through a re-experiencing of the breakdown that she had suffered before but which had never been recognized (Winnicott, 1974). De-riving this sense of self corresponded to and came from her ability to build a more complex, "accurate" narrative of her life (Schafer, 1983; Stern, 1985).

Introduction:

Fundamentally, this is a paper about extremee, practically unbearable aloneness. It is about the aloneness that comes from early object loss, secondary abandonment from the surviving parent and, especially, the feeling of loneliness, alienation and despair that comes from failed analytic treatment(s). When I first met Lenore, she had already undergone two analytic treatments, first as a child and then as a young adult. Neither analyst had been able to witness her experience; consequently Lenore had practically given up on ever being seen or getting better.

Definition of Witnessing:

We begin our discussion with a review of the concept of witnessing as put forth by Warren Poland (2000). Poland begins by positing, "It takes two to witness the unconscious" (p. 17). He goes on to clarify his position that the analyst must be a separate person, with his/her own separate center of subjectivity, a person who is present in the room with the analysand as an observing, interested, empathic, *comprehending* person, but a person who is an "other" just the same. The point is that the analyst is not over-identified with the patient, or confused in any way about where he/she ends and the patient begins. The analyst is not tangled up or merged with their patient. At times the analyst may perform holding functions; at other times, the analyst may perform interpretative functions, but there is something essential about his/her otherness that allows the analysand to be seen in his/her entirety.

Poland writes, "My intent now is to focus on the analyst's participation in observing that evolving testimony, and specifically on that part of the analyst's function that strengthens the patient by recognizing the patient's mastery of solo flights, as it were." We believe this is a very important point, as it underscores the analysand's need to feel like they are the pilots in control of their own life. Perhaps the case could be made that when the patient isn't witnessed, and when other, "extra-analytic" techniques are used, the patient will not be sufficiently strengthened by their analysis, and consequently, will not feel as though they are in the driver's seat. They may feel helped in some ways, yet be unseen in other ways, particularly in ways that have to do with a true witnessing of their unconscious life.

Poland underscores the point that being witnessed is more than being comforted by being affirmed. It may be useful to be affirmed, but in the end, it is true recognition that is comforting. Ultimately, the patient will feel better because they are known, both in the mind of the analyst and in the patient's

142

own mind. Poland writes, "We strive in our work to analyze, not anesthetize, pain."

We believe that when extra-analytic techniques are used, and patients are not witnessed in their analytic treatment, this can lead the patient to despair. Furthermore, we believe that patients who are not witnessed in their treatments may feel even more despairing than they did before embarking on analysis. Examples of alternate detrimental practices that sometimes occur in psychoanalytic therapies include times when analysts minimize the patient's actual experience and stress explanatory formulations and/or compensatory behaviors that are designed to fix the patient and place him/her on a more adaptive path. At times, this has been described as a corrective emotional experience. Comments such as, "that was then; this is now" set the person up to minimize the significance of the past, and to believe that the past can simply be overcome. We believe that William Faulkner got it right when he wrote, "The past is never dead. It's not even past." At best, the trouble with corrective approaches that minimize the patient's actual experience is that the past never gets integrated. At worst, the patient can feel profoundly depressed about not having been seen, and can become even more hidden and dissociated. Even worse, when the patient has been encouraged to "find a new start," they may feel painfully disconnected from the self that they were, the self they knew themselves to be. Perhaps even more than the painful, terrifying experiences that led these patients to seek out psychoanalysis, the experience of not being witnessed—and here we really mean the experience of *being not witnessed*—can lead patients to feel even more lonely, isolated and alone than they were. We might even say that the experience of not being witnessed by a separate other can lead the person to an experience of practically unbearable aloneness.

Perhaps patients who have experienced formative trauma in their own lives—especially only children who have experienced very early parental loss in the first few years of life—are especially susceptible to the experience of not being seen or witnessed. There are multiple reasons why this would be the case. One reason is that these individuals are frequently so alone in the world that their experience is unthinkable, unimaginable—perhaps even incomprehensible. A young child without a parent is so alone and so defenseless that comprehending just what they have been through can be disorganizing for the psychoanalyst. Another reason why these patients may be hard to reach is because that they frequently suffer from secondary abandonment by their surviving parent. There are many reasons for this—reasons we can speculate about but that are beyond the scope of this paper. In any event, these patients are used to being on their own, and are particularly adept at hiding their more authentic self. In Winnicott's terms, these patients may adopt an accommodative, "false self" organization that exists for the purpose of hiding and protecting the individual's "true self." These patients are in hiding, and unless the analyst knows the territory, these patients may be hard to find. The patient, of course, is ambivalent about being found. On the one hand, the patient longs to be found; on the other hand, the patient is terrified of coming out of hiding. But we believe that patients who sign on for psychoanalytic treatment—with all the demands that psychoanalytic treatment places on individual resources—*DO* want to be found. It is of course not unusual for treatments to become stuck. But when this happens, it is imperative that the patient /analyst-dyad devote themselves to the task of understanding the impasse so that treatment can go forward. We believe that when treatments become ineluctably stuck, the patient can become filled with despair.

To illustrate our ideas we will review the case of Lenore, a patient who had not been witnessed in several earlier treatments, but who finally benefitted from the facilitation and witnessing in her current therapy with Jenny. As a result of her earlier "fix-it" treatments, Lenore felt more lonely and alone, despite the advantages of her current life. She felt disconnected from her more vulnerable sides, and thus couldn't fully enjoy her current life or resonate with the vulnerability of others, including her children and close intimates. Her "fix-it" treatments unwittingly repeated the inhuman treatment she had experienced as a child. Part of the inhuman treatment that she experienced as a child can be traced to her experience of being in child therapy from the ages of 9 to 16. Furthermore, the impact of that treatment, and the way it set her up on a lifelong missive to perfect herself, and a mistaken belief that the purpose of psychoanalytic treatment was to perfect herself, was never understood and was inadvertently repeated in her psychoanalytic treatment. In her current treatment, the process of witnessing, along with interpretation, gradually enabled her to face and fully feel her painful formative experiences and to gradually integrate a more "whole" sense of self. In Winnicott's terms, she went through a re-experiencing of the breakdown that she had suffered before but which had never been recognized (Winnicott, 1974). We will turn now to the case of Lenore in order to illustrate these ideas.

The Case of Lenore

When Lenore came to see me she was in her mid-40's, in a long-standing marriage, with two teen-age children. She complained that her life did not feel like her own, and she felt more confused and unhappy as her children were growing up. She'd had a lot of treatment but was still very unhappy. She wasn't sure treatment would work for her. Her father had died when she was three years old. She'd been very close to him and really missed him after he died. Her mother had remarried and Lenore and her mother had moved to another city. Lenore had a problematic relationship with her stepfather, and never felt like she was part of the new family her mother had created. It had been very important to her to form a family of her own, and she'd had children when she was relatively young. She was having a hard time as her kids were growing up and struggling to separate. Lenore wondered if her problem was that she'd never worked through the death of her father. It felt like a fact to her that she knew about, but somehow the reality of the loss had never come to life. Lenore let me know she had doubts about whether she could benefit from psychoanalytic therapy.

"I find it hard to be with another person, and to be honest about what is going on with me. Sometimes I get so over-stimulated sitting in a room with another person that I can't think straight. I get overwhelmed, and start thinking I love them, and want to merge and be held by them. I'm sensitive to other people's needs, and I always end up taking care of them. It's hard for me to get seen, or get my needs met. I think I was seen—at least in some ways—when I was in child treatment. Maybe I was seen too much in some ways, and not enough in other ways—like close-up, but out of context. But when I was in analysis in my 20's, I would leave sessions and realize that I never got to the really hard stuff, the stuff that had been on my mind before I got to the session. On the one hand I was upset about it, but I was also relieved. I was scared to bring in the difficult material. Sometimes I couldn't even remember what we talked about."

I wondered what conditions would help Lenore to be in treatment, and asked her what she thought? "I need you to be very still and quiet. I might need to write down what's been going on with me and read it to you. That way I can be sure I won't forget the most important stuff. Would that be okay?"

I reassured Lenore that that would be okay, and I would do my best to give her the space she needed. I realized that to not impinge on her I would need to be very quiet. I tried to stay very still and keep my movements to a minimum. Lenore came to sessions prepared, always bringing a lot of material with her. I didn't have a problem with the material, or with her reading it to me, but I had the feeling that she was presenting a picture of herself that she thought I wanted to hear. I told her I had the impression she was presenting herself to me. Lenore started to cry, and I asked her about it.

"I think you're onto something. I feel like I've been presenting myself my whole life."

"That's interesting. Can you say more?"

"Mom was always introducing me, presenting me to other people. She was so concerned with how I looked and what I wore. I knew I had to make a good impression, no matter what was going on with me."

"So you learned to present yourself, starting from an early age?"

"Yeah, whatever was going on with me, I couldn't let my mother know. I learned to hide my thoughts and feelings. I think I'd just cut off from them when I was around her. I only felt like myself when I was alone. It's very hard for me to feel like myself with another person in the room."

I let Lenore know that I understood she needed to present herself to her mother and that this was upsetting. But I still wondered what was upsetting her now.

"I think I'm crying because you really do want to see me, and I feel like myself when I'm with you. I've been hiding my whole life. I wonder if I feel with you the way I did with my dad. . . ?"

"It's almost as if you can't remember him *per se*, but you remember how it *felt* to be with him."

"Exactly. I was so young when he died—I can barely remember what he looked like. But I've seen pictures of him. Mom told me that dad and I listened to music together, and that was important to him because he was a cellist. I'm not sure how, but somehow I know he really loved me, and he wanted me to feel comfortable being myself. It's funny that I have that dad feeling when I'm with you. You're a woman and I'd think that being with you would feel more like being with my mom, but somehow you remind me of my dad."

Lenore worked well in treatment for several months. We had a short break when I went to a professional conference, and where I got a phone call from Lenore. She had woken up in a panic, having had a nightmare. In her dream, Lenore was sitting in a small room with a man who was a musician. The man had been a friend of her father's and the two of them were in a small space listening to the Philharmonic Orchestra together. Lenore was watching all of the different musicians in the box—there were musicians playing cellos, violins, flutes, and violas—even a woman playing the harp! In the front there was a man who appeared to be the conductor. He was waving his baton in every direction, somehow keeping track of the entire orchestra. The scene shifted. Suddenly there was a giant tsunami and the music was gone. Everything was gone, and in its place was chaos and debris: trees, houses, bodies and body parts everywhere. The orchestra had been wiped out and the man who had been sitting next to her was gone. Lenore was jolted from a deep sleep with her heart pounding. It was the middle of the night, and she was terrified. She was frozen in fear, and could barely move. By a sheer force of will, she got out of bed, wrote down her dream and called me. We talked on the phone.

Lenore could barely get the words out. "This was a terrifying dream. I'm so scared. Having you be away is so disruptive. It feels as if my entire life can come to an end."

We processed this dream for months. This was how Lenore felt after her father had a massive heart attack and died when she was three years old. The man who sat next to her and kept her feeling safe was gone. Also gone was the father who could help orchestrate her life, keeping track of the totality of her. Without her father, and without me in the transference, Lenore was left with a terrible feeling of absence, terror and nothingness. But after processing the dream, Lenore started to feel better in a deeper way.

146

"I really am starting to feel better. At least now I know what happened to me. When my father died, it felt as though there'd been a tsunami. My dad's death was a cataclysmic event. It changed my life forever."

Lenore realized that she didn't register the full impact of her father's death all at once. For a while, she lived with her grandparents, and that still felt like a safe place to be.

"I loved being with my grandparents, and I knew they loved me. Their house was aesthetically pleasing. I loved the sights, sounds and smells of their home. I particularly loved the smell of furniture polish. My grandparents had a cook, and she made pot roasts and soups and homemade pies. The house was so pleasing. There were large French windows, and they let in streams of light."

For weeks, Lenore remembered the feel of being with her grandparents after her father died.

"My father was gone but at least I had my grandparents. My grandfather was a judge in the local courthouse. I loved to take walks with him, and listen to him talk. He knew many poems by heart, and he loved to recite them to me. He also quoted from Shakespeare, and told me how our legal system was structured. He wanted me to understand how the world worked, and he cared about my character. He wanted me to develop patience, resilience and humility."

Lenore remembered this time period happily. It was a good time in her life. But as she got older, she remembered trying to talk to her grandparents about her father and his sudden death. She could talk to her grandparents about almost anything, but that subject was off limits.

"My grandmother said, 'You're too young to be thinking about death.' I know grandma meant well. She really believed she was doing the right thing, protecting me from feeling upset and sad. But her mum approach didn't help me feel better. I may have been too young to know about death, but I was *living* with it, and I could have used some company. I think it was my grandmother who couldn't talk about my father's death, but she put her discomfort into me."

"You were alone with it and you had to hide your thoughts and feelings from everyone, even your grandparents. You had to protect them from your sadness and pain."

"I couldn't stop thinking about my father, and I couldn't find him anywhere. It would have helped if my mom had been a bit sensitive to my needs. If only I had a picture of him in my room, or even if I'd been left with his cello! But no—all traces of my dad were wiped out. I was supposed to move on, but I couldn't. After my mother remarried, and she and I moved to Toledo, I hardly saw my grandparents anymore either. They came to visit once a year, and I went to visit them in the summers, but there was a big hole where they'd been. My mother expected me to simply adjust to this new life, with a new father and then a sister and brother! It was way too much for me. It was over-whelming—just too fucking much.

"Too fucking much of everything; not enough of anything."

"Exactly. And I didn't feel like I belonged. It's as if everybody else was part of a cozy, happy family and I was on the outside, looking in. When I asked my mom questions about my father she became irritated with me. She didn't want to talk about him. I think she wanted to forget he ever existed. I was a bother to my mother. She wanted me to snap out of it, but I couldn't. I clung to fantasies about being with my father."

As Lenore got in touch with memories of how miserable she'd been in Toledo, and how much she'd been in a state of longing—she remembered how much time she had spent in therapy as a child.

"I don't get it. I spent so much time in therapy, and it should have helped me get better. I should be over my father already. How could I have spent so much time in therapy, and still not have mourned?"

"Did you talk about your father when you were in therapy with Dr. W? What do you remember about that treatment?"

"There were parts of it I liked. I had the feeling that Dr. W was really thinking about who I was and what was going on inside of me. She was a psy-chologist. I drew pictures about what was going on at home, and even pictures about my father, and my fantasies about how he had died. I remember I was worried about where he was, physically. I knew his body was buried in a cemetery, and I wanted to make sure his body was safe. I was scared about animals eating his body, or his body getting attacked or corroded. Dr. W paid more attention to me than anybody else did. She really was interested in who I was, and I think she wanted to help me. I know I was really angry, and it felt safe to express my anger in therapy. She could see my anger, but she couldn't help me with the situation at home."

I asked Lenore to say more about that.

"Well I remember one time my parents came and we had a check-on-Lenore's-progress-in-therapy session. Dr. W was explaining to my parents how we were working on my ego strength. My mom got annoyed because she didn't understand what Dr. W was talking about. But rather than own that it was *her* confusion, or *her* issue, mom put me down. In this really dismissive, derisive way, she said to Dr. W, '*Lenore* doesn't know what that means.' And Dr. W explained what she meant. I felt betrayed. Dr. W played right into mom's hands. That's the sort of stuff mom did to me all the time. I understood exactly what we were doing in therapy, and I knew what Dr. W meant when she said we were working on my ego strength. It was mom who didn't get it. Maybe she was pissed off that nobody was working on *her* ego strength. She put her venom into me. And Dr. W just went along with mom. She didn't stand up to her. It's like nobody could see it, or stand up to mom."

"I can see why you felt let down by Dr. W. She could see you in therapy, but she couldn't stand up to mom. She couldn't help to change what was going on in the family."

"I know she helped me a lot. She definitely did help to strengthen my ego. But my ego sort of existed on its own, like a free-floating ego, outside the family context. That doesn't make sense. I had a strong sense of self, but my sense of self didn't exist in a context. I knew when I was angry, and my anger propelled me. That's how I've been able to accomplish so much. I was always able to get a lot done, working off the anger fumes. But there's some way in which I didn't "work through" my father's death, and I never came to terms with the "new" family. Of course the new family was really a joke, a fantasy. In the end, that family didn't hold up any better than my first family, with me, and my father and mother. Let's not forget that my parents were separated before my dad died, or that mom left her second husband. And those kids are even more messed up than I am!"

"One thing always bothered me about my treatment with Dr. W. One day I was talking about my parent's wedding, when I was a flower girl. I said to Dr. W, 'When *we* got married.' Dr. W sort of seized on the phrase and kept talking about it. She was harping on the fact that it was *my mother* who got married (not me.) Maybe she thought I was confused, and didn't know the difference between my mother and me. Or maybe she had some theory that I was jealous and competitive with my mother, and I was fighting with her for my stepfather's attention. But this comment really irritated me, and I felt misunderstood. I feel like Dr. W was trying to fit my experience into some theory, some Freudian theory about Oedipal dynamics or something."

"She had a theory, but she didn't understand your experience."

"Right. When my mother got married I was 6 years old, and it had felt as if we were a unit. Mom was the only parent I had. But then it felt like she just dropped me. I'd been clinging to her for dear life—I had to because she was so unpredictable—and then when she married my stepfather I felt abandoned."

"I wonder why you were sent to therapy? Do you know?"

"I've often wondered about that. I should have been sent to therapy because my father had died, and I was heartbroken and devastated. I mean, what three-year-old can deal with the death of a parent?"

"Your dad meant everything to you. He was part of you."

Lenore began to sob. "It's true. He made me feel safe in the world."

"You needed him. After he was gone, you felt lost, and you clung to your mom."

"I did. But it wasn't the same. Mom never felt like my dad."

Lenore stayed with this material for many months. Her feelings were very raw, and she felt incredibly vulnerable during this period. It became clearer to her than ever before that her dad was her primary parent, and her mom was second best. Lenore never felt the same way with her mom as she did with her dad. She began to process more fully how self-involved her mom was, and the degree to which she felt dropped and alone when her mother remarried. Lenore also began to process how thrown away she felt when she was sent to therapy. This was confusing because she did benefit from being in therapy, even though she realized she was sent for the wrong reasons.

"Mom just wasn't that tuned into me. I should have been sent to therapy because I was devastated by daddy's death. But I don't think that's why I was sent to therapy. Mom felt like there was something wrong with me and she wanted me fixed. I was a bother. I was sullen and withdrawn, and I think my depression was getting in the way of this big happy family. Also, I wasn't doing well in school. I don't think mom really noticed or cared—it almost feels like she liked that I was having trouble because that way she got to feel superior to me. This is so sick." Lenore sobbed for the rest of the session.

We talked about Lenore's experience in child therapy for many months, and off and on for a long time. I let Lenore know that I thought she was probably right about her assessment of the treatment—that it did seem as if being sent to Dr. W wasn't really about helping her, but was another way of getting her out of the way.

"Yeah, mom sent me to Dr. W so I could get fixed and she could enjoy her marriage to my stepfather. It's not as if that marriage even worked out . . . But it was convenient for mom to blame me for their problems."

Then Lenore shifted, and began to talk about her experience in analysis when she was a young adult.

"When I was in treatment with Dr. S, in my 20's, I began to wonder why I had been sent to therapy in the first place. I thought it was because I was bad, and it may have started me on my lifelong tendency trying to be perfect. I guess there are a lot of reasons for that, but this was one part of it. Anyhow, I went to see Dr. W and asked her why I had been sent to therapy? It was interesting. It was good to see her, and she was curious to know what had happened to me, where I had gone to college, etc. Like, how did I turn out? I answered her questions but there was something weird going on. It goes back to when you said I was presenting myself to you. There was some way I was presenting myself to her when I went back to see her. Like I was presenting an image of the person I thought I should be, trying to impress her, trying to 'pass.' That may have even come out of the treatment with Dr. S. I'm not sure. I just know I didn't feel like myself, the way I do now, working with you. Anyhow, Dr. W told me I went to therapy because I was trying to break up my parent's marriage. That really shocked me. I was mad, but I couldn't put my finger on what I was feeling, or why I felt that way."

"I think you were mad because your mom told her you were interfering with the marriage, and she bought your mother's version of what was wrong. She didn't understand how much your mother was pinning the blame on you, and trying to get you out of the way."

"Yeah, you're right. W bought it, hook, line and sinker. Why couldn't she see how much I was struggling, not only because my dad was dead, but also because mom was out to lunch? It felt like mom just couldn't see me. Sometimes she could, but only when my father and siblings weren't around. If they were there, mom forgot I existed."

"Your mom forgot about you, and that was the piece Dr. W couldn't see."

"Yeah, its weird though, because there were ways that Dr. W did see and help me."

"I agree. She taught you to attend to what was going on in your own mind."

"I did, and I learned to pay attention to my dreams, too. But there's also a way I got too caught up in my unconscious process."

"Yes, sometimes you can get lost in yourself."

"It's true. I get lost in my own process, and I have trouble seeing the big picture. Sometimes I'm so in the trees that I can't see the forest. But I also feel like that's starting to change, working with you. "

"You feel seen."

"I don't understand why this didn't happen to me before. When I went to Dr. S, and he suggested that we start psychoanalysis, I felt so hopeful. I thought we'd get to the bottom of my problems and I'd really feel better. But that never happened."

"You felt better in some ways, but not in ways that freed you up."

"It's hard to know what happened. Of course there are ways in which he helped me a lot. I know that. I began to focus, and learned I was smart and could do well in school. I learned to stay with subjects, and understood how knowledge builds over time. I gained self-confidence. But I never got to the bottom of my anxiety. I felt better because Dr. S was always there (or he was there four days a week, when our appointment was scheduled) and it was the first time in my life I could count on somebody just being there. Because our appointments were scheduled at 5:30 PM, I began to get a sense of rhythm and continuity, and learned about the seasons of the year. It was the first time I realized that the days got longer in the summer and shorter in the winter. Unbelievable, but true. I thought maybe you got better in psychoanalysis just because somebody's there."

"Well it does help to have somebody there."

"Yeah. It helped that S was also encouraging, but just the mere fact of his presence helped me see myself. I also learned that I had a body. I started to run half marathons and became a pretty good swimmer."

"You learned there were all sorts of things you could do, and that helped you feel better about yourself."

"You know, I really liked going to therapy even though it disrupted whatever I was doing during the day. I was kind of used to having to stop whatever I was doing anyway, from mom. But there was something good about getting out of my house, and looking at things from a different perspective. Dr. S often had helpful suggestions and advice. But that's not psychoanalysis, right? You're supposed to get to the bottom of things."

"You needed to get clear about where you'd come from, who your parents were, how you'd come into the world."

"I never could figure out how psychoanalysis was supposed to work. Before we began, I thought we would talk about my father's death, but Dr. S gave me the impression that was off limits. He asked me about it in the beginning, but then he sort of dropped it."

"Once again, you were left holding all the feelings about your dad. You saw Dr. S four days a week, but you couldn't talk about the thing that was most on your mind. It was your grandparents all over again."

"I think the fact that I was in psychoanalysis AND we didn't talk about my father's death made me feel worse about myself. It was bad enough that I couldn't talk about it with anybody else in my life. But the fact that I couldn't talk about it in analysis made me feel awful. I think it may have even left me feeling worse about myself—maybe better in some ways, but worse in others. Oi!! What is wrong with this picture?"

"A lot is wrong. But I think the main thing is not being able to talk about your dad's death. You ended up feeling like you had such an awful secret, that nobody could hear it."

"Yeah, because it was something that couldn't be talked about, it left me feeling defective. It made me feel like I needed to hide the fact that I didn't have parents, and that it was a big joke that children are supposed to have parents. I know it's crazy, but I ended up feeling like there was something so wrong with me that I couldn't parent my own children."

"Your children needed you, and you needed your children."

"Yeah. I guess there's no crime in that. But in my experience, children just get dropped. That's what happened to me, and that's what I did to my children. It even got repeated with my therapists. You'd think I would have gone back to Dr. W rather than starting with someone new when I was in college. After all, I saw her till I was 16 years old. But once we ended I felt like it was over. Just gone. I knew I needed to be in treatment, but it never occurred to me to go back to her."

"Goodbyes have felt so unsettled and unsettling for you. Things end, but you're left feeling like, what happened? You've experienced separations without any sense of resolution. They've been very ragged and confusing for you."

"That's exactly right. I ended up feeling like attachment was bad, so I learned to just tune out the person. Move on and don't look back. I was just like my mother—oh, what a misery! But it's weird that Dr. S didn't ask more about my previous treatment. I'm not sure he realized I'd spent so many years with Dr. W. I definitely told him, but somehow, it didn't register. Even when I

152

was in treatment with him, and I went to ask Dr. W why I was sent to therapy, he wasn't that interested. He made some stupid comment about not believing in child analysis because the child is tied to their home environment. Like they're not when they're grown up? Anyway, who cares—I was in child therapy! And the thing is, I think that treatment with Dr. W affected my entire analysis with Dr. S."

"I'm sure you're right. You never got past the feeling that something was wrong with you."

"Right. So I used the treatment with Dr. S to try to perfect myself. I just kept driving myself harder and harder. When Dr. S wanted to know what I was going to do with my life, I felt like something was wrong with me because I didn't have any idea. He told me, 'From now on, everything you do counts. Everything you do is part of your permanent life resume.' I think he thought I was a spoiled rich kid. So I got my life resume in order. I thought, if I work hard enough, I can jump onto the life-wagon now. I worked really hard. I got a career and I started a family right away. But we never made sense of what had happened. Dr. S glossed over how abandoned and thrown away I'd been. So that became my dirty secret, and not being able to talk about it just left me in this awful place where I was doomed to repeat the past. In the beginning Dr. S asked me lots of questions about my history and early life, and those questions made me feel hopeful. But he didn't put the story together; he didn't connect the dots. He gave me advice and directives, and I did everything he told me to do. But it didn't make me feel more in charge of my life. In fact, it left me feeling more confused, and more pulled apart. I went further into myself."

"Yes you did. And at the same time, you felt like you had to be perfect in your job, and perfect as a mother. But you couldn't find your own center."

"Yes, I felt hollow. I'm starting to come back to life again. With you, I know I can say anything and you'll make some sense of it. I know I'm sitting with somebody who's working hard to create meaning. I never get the sense that you're trying to stay awake. I know you're thinking. I can *feel* you thinking! And suddenly I'm beginning to understand my own story. Lots of pieces of my life are falling into place, and I feel like I'm coming to life from the inside, not from the outside. Being able to talk about my father's death is important, but it's only one piece of the story. When you can't tell your story, you start to feel like you're not even human. No wonder I had so many dreams with reptiles in them. When you can't picture the two people who gave birth to you, you start to feel like you don't come from anywhere—like you're just not human. It's such a scary, lonely place to be. When you're that alone, it's downright terrifying. It's more than anybody should have to bear."

"You've had to deal with unbearable aloneness. When you went into treatment with Dr. S, you were desperate to be seen. You thought you were getting psychoanalysis, but you ended up with fix-it therapy. There were all these things you were supposed to do. Each time you did a new thing, you held out hope that this time you could live. But it never happened. Time after time, you felt disappointed, and when things didn't work out, you felt like you were crashing."

"Right. I was so hungry to feel better and make a life that I listened to everything Dr. S had to say. I was a good student, and my life did get better in real ways. But there were other ways I shut down. When I first started to see Dr. S, I used to come to sessions with a cup of coffee. Dr. S told me, 'a cup of coffee is like a tit'. So I felt ashamed—for bringing the coffee and for wanting a tit. The message was loud and clear—no mom or dad for me!"

"You had to be perfect baby."

"You mean perfectly self-sufficient. When I was with Dr. S, lying on the couch a million miles away from him, I felt as if I was in the room by myself. In some ways my life got better, but I also got disconnected from who I was. Thank you for never saying anything about my bringing coffee to sessions."

"I think Dr. S was uncomfortable with the coffee, but he didn't deal with his own discomfort. Instead, he shamed you."

"Thank you for saying that. The other thing I keep thinking about is how when I went into treatment with him I had elaborate dreams. I was tuned into my unconscious, and I knew how to remember my dreams. But Dr. S didn't want me to bring in something I'd prepared. You're supposed to be spontaneous and free associate in sessions. Those were the rules. So I stopped bringing in dreams altogether. I shut down. Therapy is supposed to make you feel more put together, but it left me feeling pulled apart and disconnected. I accommodated to Dr. S. It was another version of being with my mother. He had all of these ideas about what I should do. I did what he said, but I ended up feeling more disconnected from myself. I could never figure out what **I** wanted to do."

"Remember when I first came to see you and I dissociated so much, and I thought I'd never be able to tell you what was going on in my life? I was so worried you'd be critical of me."

"You felt so ashamed of yourself that you couldn't let yourself remember. You needed to be sure it would be safe in here."

"I have felt safe here, and seen, for the first time. Remember how I did nothing but cry for the first two years? I'd walk into your office door, and I'd start to cry. Wow! It's like I've been trying to get back to some core sense of self my whole fucking life, ever since my dad died. Thank you for not imposing your stuff on me."

"You've been imposed on way too much in your life."

"Dr. S kept telling me that he was a psychoanalyst, and he loved telling me the technical difference between being a psychiatrist and a psychoanalyst. Who cares whether he'd had four additional years of training? He'd had the training, but he wasn't a psychoanalyst. I'd tell him I couldn't sleep at night,

154

and he'd tell me I would be able to sleep if I just kept coming to analysis. But it never happened. I just stopped being able to sleep at all. Wow!"

"You've been imposed on so much. Dr. S meant well, but he ended up becoming yet another voice in your head."

"Right. I learned a lot from him, but he couldn't see me. Thank you for seeing me."

"I'm glad I could see you."

"It's so weird though. Because even though there are a million ways in which my life wasn't witnessed, I still feel a lot of good came from my analysis. Dr. S was a really a decent guy. I'm not sure I'd be alive today if it weren't for him. And I've been a decent mother to my kids in spite of myself. On the one hand I wasn't sure I was allowed to be a mother to my own kids, and on the other hand it's been hard to see them as being separate from me."

"You are starting to see them more clearly now."

"It's true. I feel seen by you, so now, for the first time, I can see my kids. It's as if we've all been rolled up in one big undifferentiated mass."

"The mass is starting to break apart."

"It's also good that I no longer feel the need to be perfect. Before, I was trying so hard to be perfect, and I was trying to get my kids to be perfect too. That caused everyone problems. It doesn't even feel good to be perfect!"

"You needed to be perfect because things were so messy and chaotic. You got rid of the mess, but you also lost some of the vitality."

"Yeah. Who cares if things are messy? It feels so much better to feel *alive*! It's also interesting to me that my husband and I have stopped fighting altogether. We used to bicker and get into a lot of fights because I was sure there was a right way to do things. Now I know there are lots of ways to do things, lots of ways to skin a cat. I think what's happened is that I've felt accepted by you, and my husband feels more accepted by me. So that helps too. We can really join forces as parents. Not in a dictatorial way—like it's our way because we're the parents, but I really feel like we're working together to figure out what's best for our kids. Not so easy—there are no right answers—but at least we're working together."

Conclusion

In reviewing the case of Lenore, we've presented how the process of witnessing evolved between Lenore and her therapist and how Lenore benefited from this process. It helped her to formulate and express what had happened in her life and to gradually build a narrative that enabled her to feel that she was not only real, but also worthwhile. This process also allowed her to overcome the profound sense of loneliness that had afflicted her since her father's traumatic death. From that time on, Lenore had struggled with painful experiences that could not be witnessed by others and thus could not be formulated and integrated into a meaningful perspective on her history. She thus felt cut off from significant aspects of herself in ways that affected her capabilities, her relationships and her overall sense of self. What may be most remarkable about Lenore's case is that she not only needed witnessing concerning the most painful aspects of her childhood history, but also witnessing regarding her previous therapy experiences, that had provided some gains, but had also reinforced the primary trauma. Unfortunately, it cannot be said enough how often childhood and adult treatment can inadvertently traumatize vulnerable patients who in turn are too ready to accommodate to therapists who are oriented towards pursuing preferred formulations or corrective agendas. In following their therapist's leads in order to maintain needed ties, these patients then become even more dissociated from vital aspects of their experience and come to feel even more lonely and alienated from others and even from the prospect that psychoanalytic therapy can help them in the fundamental way that they need. The importance of witnessing has been most emphasized in helping people to recover from social catastrophes such as the Holocaust or the effects of apartheid in South Africa. We want to stress that this process is also vital in helping patients in treatment to recover from their own more private catastrophes that can involve not only childhood trauma, but also their previous treatment experiences as well.

Having highlighted the vital role of witnessing, we also want to acknowledge that with patients like Lenore there are dangers of fostering and maintaining an idealization of the therapist of the sort that promotes devaluation of previous treatments and prevents the patient from fully individuating when they are ready. We believe that with Lenore the idealization of the therapist was an expectable result of the therapist's ability to be with Lenore in the process of formulating and presenting her painful past. This may also be true for other patients like her. We still trust, though, that Lenore will shift towards asserting herself more and that the quality of the transference will shift accordingly. Likewise, Lenore's awareness of what was lacking in the previous treatments reflects some aggressive devaluations intermixed with her more "objective assessment." But we see her striving for that assessment as being the predominant factor here, as indicated by the perspective she has already attained and in which she's able to balance her criticisms of each therapy with an appreciation of what each one offered her.

References

Gerson, S. (2009). When the Third is Dead: Memory, Mourning and Witnessing in the Aftermath of the Holocaust. *International Journal of Psychoanalysis* 90:1341–1357.

Orange, D.M. (2010). Recognition as: Intersubjective Vulnerability in the Psychoanalytic Dialogue. *International Journal of Psychoanalytic Self Psychology* 5(3):227–243.

Poland, W. (2000). The Analyst's Witnessing and Otherness. *Journal of the American Psychoanalytic Association* 48:17–34.

Schafer, R. (1983). *The Analytic Attitude*. London: Hogarth Books.

Spence, D.P. (1982). *Narrative Truth and Historical Truth: Meaning and Interpretation in Psychoanalysis*. London and New York: W.W. Norton.

Stern, D.N. (1985). *The Interpersonal World of the Infant: A View from Psychoanalysis and Developmental Psychology*. New York: Basic Books.

Winnicott, D.W. (1974). Fear of Breakdown. *International Review of Psycho-Analysis*. 1:103–107.

Section III—Loneliness/Solitude In the Psychoanalytic Training Process

Section III offers an extraordinary account of loneliness and solitude in the psychoanalytic training process. The idea for this topic, which was first introduced at the panel of the Symposium 2012, came from Dr. Richard Gottlieb who wondered how this important affect influenced psychoanalytic training. The authors of this section engage this question in four chapters, which cover the loneliness/solitude: of the candidate, with specific attention to the process of identification; from the chair of the supervising or consultant analyst/therapist; of the training analyst; and, in Institute life.

In Chapter Ten, Jamieson Webster grapples with "The Loneliness of the Candidate: Solitude and Solicited Identifications." In this chapter she addresses the central question: Does the encounter with the inevitable loneliness of being a psychoanalyst play a critical role in training and how can an institutional structure support or hinder the passage from candidate to psychoanalyst?

Webster talks about the inevitable sense of loneliness that occurs when working analytically and that must be transformed into a state of solitude as engagement occurs. Courage and fortitude are all one has when taking responsibility as a psychoanalyst. To illustrate this Webster uses the story of Rosine Lefort, an analysand of Lacan, which resonates with her own story. Here Webster captures the "fierce" connection between desire and the inevitable loss of the desired, which underscores our dependency on external reality. Clinically, Rosine is guided by the question, which we all must ask: What gives life to the subjective, (i.e., "the genesis of the subject") what marks separation? Webster takes this further. She views loneliness as desire's negative underside and wonders what sublimates loneliness into new creative possibilities. She relies on Lacan and Klein to answer these important questions.

In addition she addresses two other decisive questions: Can we encourage our trainees to explore their desire for psychoanalysis from the inception of training, and create an environment that allows this exploration without demands of compliance or indoctrination? Moreover, how do we as clinicians sustain a link to the field of psychoanalysis as a whole to contain and sustain our clinical work?

In Chapter Eleven "Loneliness and Solitude in the Psychoanalytic Training Process—from the Chair of the Supervising Analyst" Douglas H. Ingram asks:

> How does the analyst/therapist facilitate a needed object/other role as a psychic substitution for the missing object with the aim of creating a lesser suffering for the greater anguish of loneliness?
> Can this action take place in the transference?
> Can this be done in the patient's external environment?

159

Among other matters, Ingram considers the adaptive function of *waiting*. Might the anguish associated with waiting, he asks, serve as the lesser anguish when the horror of abandonment and ensuing loneliness is the alternative? Isn't it better to wait by the phone for an errant lover to call than to collapse into a dreaded loneliness?

Then, he wonders if there might be two very different kinds of loneliness that therapists experience: loneliness *from* the patient and loneliness *with* the patient. He asks,

> What might be the personality configuration of the therapist that would lead to a tendency to feel loneliness from certain patients? Is it possible for the therapist and patient to feel so bound that they become a duo so intimate and so merged that they become isolated from the ambient world? What can this lead to? How dire can this be? And finally, how can it be identified and encountered constructively?

In Chapter Twelve "The Loneliness of the Training Analyst," Eric Mendelsohn explores and enumerates the many potential and often unavoidable conflicts of interest between the analyst and analysand during training. He wonders:

> In what ways do the intrinsic role conflicts of the training analysis, along with the social organization of institutes, predispose the training analyst and the candidate/analysand toward loneliness (i.e., away from the necessary solitude Webster earlier suggested is an essential training transformation)?

The section comes to a close with Sandra Buechler's Chapter Thirteen entitled "There Is No Place Like Home." In this chapter, Buechler addresses the connection between a profound state of loneliness and an intense desire for a home. This often translates professionally into a yearning for an analytic home. She explores three important ideas related to this: "First, we all yearn for a (professional)[11] home, where we feel less lonely because we know we are fundamentally accepted and safe. Second, the next generations can do better to create a respectful community of analytic homes. Third, there is nothing that can substitute for such an environment. In other words, there is no place like home." In addressing these ideas, she generates a series of questions that are as important to our professional life as they are to our field.

> How does the internalization of our training enter into our practice?
> Who is actually in the consultation room with us?
> What are the conditions necessary to move loneliness to aloneness?
> How do these translate into the necessary elements for an open and welcoming atmosphere in our institutes?

---

[11] Parentheses added.

Chapter 10
The Loneliness of the Candidate: Solitude
and Solicited Identifications
Jamieson Webster

Abstract:

Is the experience of being a candidate in analytic training one of inevitable loneliness? Is the encounter with loneliness fundamental to the task of learning to work psychoanalytically? In what ways does loneliness pose problems with regard to shifting identifications with one's analyst, institution, or the field more broadly? How might the institution of psychoanalysis thwart an experience of loneliness and solitude crucial to the passage from candidate to psychoanalyst? These questions are wrestled with through an elaboration on my own experience as a candidate in psychoanalytic training, woven together with the story of a young analysand of Jacques Lacan's—Rosine Lefort—who, when beginning to treat psychotic children in a foundling hospital during her training analysis, felt she needed to leave her analysis for a period of time and work in almost complete solitude. These two stories, together with theoretical reflections on Jacques Lacan and Melanie Klein, hopefully shed light on the question of loneliness and the experience of training to be a psychoanalyst.

I don't think I've ever felt as lonely as I have felt in analytic training. But a characteristic of loneliness is its egocentric magnitude, accompanied by amnesia for any other time of having been lonely, as if loneliness lifts by virtue of repression only to descend again with implacable immediacy. Speaking about loneliness feels intensely labored, like slow pouring molasses in darkness. There is something unspeakable about it. I feel I have to be incredibly careful around this topic. If there is a singular quality to the loneliness of being a candidate in analytic training, something I'd like to try to say something about, it will be a difficult if not potentially contradictory enterprise. How can I speak for everyone, no less or even myself? Perhaps in allowing myself to take on this challenge, ripe with inevitable pathos, a claim might be heard about the difficulty of taking on the solitude of the psychoanalytic listener. Perhaps a movement, from loneliness to solitude, can be found, one critical to the act of learning to listen, learning to use one's unconscious life, to take bearing there. Perhaps even a question of how analytic training might support or hinder the transformation of loneliness could be wrestled with, tentatively, but not without great importance.

On first glance, the intensity of loneliness that I've experienced as a candidate seems ripe for an interpretation of repetition. How did you experience being in school? Disappointment more generally? What were your expectations? Where did those expectations come from? Were you a lonely child?

What did analytic training wake up in you from your past? Behind questions like these however—important though they may be for any individual to ponder—is a more structural question: What does it mean to be a candidate? What can we say about the experience of being a candidate, of being in the middle of that strange, difficult, and absolutely unique experience of taking up the position of the analyst for the first time? It is on this knife's edge between the personal history that one brings with them to psychoanalytic training and the history of psychoanalysis itself, its formation of a training system, and the very real task of becoming an analyst, that we must ask this question about loneliness.

I remember an email that went around my institute by a fellow candidate who spoke with eager enthusiasm about how proud she was to be part of this historic place and its many masterful clinicians, evoking a potent image of family and lineage. A lingering despair about training and institutes always hit hard at moments like this, along with a certain amount of guilty rage, self-accusation, and, that bugbear, intense loneliness. Why didn't I feel this way? Wouldn't everything be so much easier for me if I did? Why was I so lonely? Where was my gratitude? I felt left to imagine what it would be like to announce *my* membership, a membership I, for some reason, still didn't understand, let alone feel.

There is a lot we can say about one's personal myth—in the sense that Kris (1956) lent to the concept in the great paper of the same name—and how psychoanalytic training can feed them imaginary oxygen for an idealized fire. But we shouldn't be so quick. We don't want the institutes to burn down, she says with negation, at least not before we can ask a question about their role in the mitigation of the loneliness of training to be a psychoanalyst. Certainly, whether one feels palpably like an outsider, or one turns training into a family romance fantasy, both are undergirded by a powerful sense of loneliness. I have my own myths.

When I was first invited to speak about the loneliness of the candidate, my own mythic story kept surfacing in my mind, one that has acted like a life raft during taxing times throughout training. I return to it again and again. I realized, while reflecting upon it, that it was a story of the anti-candidate, a story of a non-training training, if only because there was really no where to train, no institute, and only the slightest idea of what psychoanalysis should make possible. In imagination, absent these structures, the desire for psychoanalysis seems to have had an inordinate amount of room to take shape. This is what gives it its mythic character: rising from the ashes, on the edge of the birth of something new.

The necessary courage and fortitude, in the face of the inevitable loneliness of working analytically for the first time, is an obvious source of transformation in this story. The story is about the utmost point of solitude present when taking on a case, taking responsibility as a psychoanalyst, which can be seen so clearly because there are almost no extant supports. We need extremes not to establish a middle road but to clarify what is universal. This is what I find so extraordinary about Freud's methodology, taking perversion and establishing the place of psychosexual development in all human beings, taking dreams and situating the unconscious, taking psychosis even and delineating the power of desire in both defense and cure. So while what I will come to say about my own myth will be laden with a certain amount of fantasy, my hope is that something more structural could be heard in doing a little work. Would working through be taking matters too far? You'll have to decide that for yourself.

For now, I'll take some time and tell you this story of mine. A woman named Rosine Lefort, thirty years old, begins her analysis with Jacques Lacan in Paris in the early 1950s. A year and a half later she begins work in the hospital *Fondation Parent de Rosan* under the direction of the pediatrician, and soon to be psychoanalyst, Jenny Aubry (mother of the great historian of French psychoanalysis and a psychoanalyst herself, Élizabeth Roudinesco). Rosine was to work with children between the ages of one and four who were either abandoned by their families or left for too long because of an illness in their only parent. The hospital did not understand the difference between physical and mental illness and these children were left in bed for most of the day. Rosine describes the children having to watch a nurse feed other children one by one, each knowing full well their place in this line. Crying, watching, waiting, three times a day this is how meals were taken.

Paris, as you may know, was a little behind the times with respect to psychoanalysis because of the Second World War and a general resistance to psychoanalysis that didn't exist as strongly in the Germanophone and Anglo-American worlds. In anticipation of the occupation, the psychoanalytic society of Paris was entirely dissolved. But, it must be said, even in its minimal existence before the war, it had very little impact on the hospital systems which were dominated by a long and very orthodox tradition of French psychiatry going back to Charcot and Janet, and including figures like de Clérambault and Henri Claude. The hospitals were seen as places for expanding the knowledge and research of French psychiatry and its classification systems more than treatment centers. Psychoanalysis was a huge source of contention in this regard.

Jenny Aubry was working with Francois Dolto, one of the first child psychoanalysts in France, who would come to be a very important public figure of the likes of Winnicott in England. Both Jenny Aubry and Dolto were consulting with Anna Freud, Melanie Klein, Donald Winnicott and the Tavistock more generally. They were interested in the work of Rène Spitz and John Bowlby, the latter directing an international study on hospitalized children that partially funded Aubry's work and which must have served in the financial support for Rosine's position at the hospital. They were also working with Jacques Lacan.

Jenny Aubry (later to include Rosine Lefort) was writing an important book titled *Enfance abandonée* looking at the exacerbation or creation of illness in these children by virtue of their prolonged "hospitalization." She was hoping, obviously, to change the way the mentally ill were treated in France. Rosine Lefort, beginning her work, takes four children into psychoanalysis who seem on the verge of psychosis. The work with her first two cases, the 13 month old Nadia in particular, is incredibly intense. Work with Nadia—which one can read about in the most extraordinary and unprecedented detail— seems to demand that Rosine use all of herself to help this child whose health was alarmingly in decline in the manner of a failure to thrive. Something in her eyes, the pleasure she takes in looking and playing at exchanging gazes, despite an almost total passivity, draws her to work with Nadia first. There was some contact that she still wanted to make; there were signs of life. Rosine takes her down to a playroom for sessions five times a week.

In the beginning months of treatment Rosine interprets that Nadia is attempting to extract an object from her body that she can tolerate as separate. If it is acknowledged as separate it could be a source of desire. For Rosine, this is an encounter with a point of loss that is nearly unbearable for her, this case giving us something of the fierce link between being able to desire and having to inevitably confront loss in doing so. We want what we do not have, desire shows us our dependency on outside forces.

Alone in our desires, we must reach outwards towards the world, a fact that Rosine sees as literally giving us an inside and outside, marking the difference, the crucial gap between the two. For her, desire gives birth to us as human beings, creatures formed in a knotting of drive, desire, and loss. Childhood psychosis, psychosis in general, refuses to allow this knot to form, taking instead the route of a kind of dispersal of these threads in drive diffusion, de-differentiation, and autistic-like encapsulation. Desire, as a subject-forming force, is foreclosed.

The scene that comes most readily to mind is when Nadia, finally building up the courage to have more contact with Rosine, seeks out her mouth, tracing it, and putting her fingers into it, and then touching her own. She bites off the corner of a cracker and then has Rosine do the same. Confronted with this minimal differentiation between her mouth and Rosine's—finding her own mouth by taking in the image of another's—she becomes incredibly violent, clawing and scratching at her neck; Rosine interprets this as both as a defense against having registered the place of her mouth (there is no hole in one's neck) and a primordial symbolization of what she just encountered.

It is important to see this act of symbolization even in negation and violent acting out. It was a decisive step in the treatment, a possibility opened up in the transference where objects could enter into an economy of exchange, as

166

Rosine sees it, in the form of oral, anal, and phallic signifiers. Nadia had to refuse, but in this first act of refusal she recognizes a gap between herself and what she wants. In this wanting, she begins to structure her self-image. The mouth was her first critical object, important since Nadia was barely eating, didn't use her mouth to suck, and seemed to take little to no oral pleasure, which was a situation so severe that her health was in rapid decline in the manner of a failure to thrive.

In sessions Nadia had pulled at Rosine's fingers, her teeth and skin, but the mouth increasingly became the center of her attention, proving to be hollow, a ready-made gap for an investigation of what cannot be filled. Having been filled passively by nurses for the majority of her life, treated as an inert body, one begins to see what is at stake. Rosine conjectures that in the pull towards psychosis, there is no mouth, no orifice that acts as a site of exchange. There is no hole in the body, which, taken in this psychotic totality acts like a smooth surface with nothing lacking. Psychosis is a denial of separation whose smooth surface anchors nothing, no self-image, no other.

Rosine has to work against this regressive pull, to open a space for desire and wish. But aggressivity immediately erupts in Nadia when desire is felt. Rosine writes of this experience:

> I was only too sensitive to the limits she imposed on me, having myself suffered from neurosis. It had been through my body that I had experienced this suffering intensely; a body, which, as always in such cases, I could only cope with by allowing it to become the object of care and attention. Nadia, for her part, only had her body insofar as it was the object of care and attention. The ambiguous solicitations of care givers, whether in the family or in an institution, can leave the subject in the totally derelict state of being physically manipulated in the real, without a single word to acknowledge her position as subject. As a result of this painful experience, I was reluctant to become a maternal figure for her, that is to say, to give additional care and attention and, inconsiderately, to bring into play the Real of bodies, of the child's and mine. . . In the analytic relationship that established itself, Nadia put me in a position where she showed me the Real character of my body, while at the same time forcing me to renounce it. It was in this position that I was to let her challenge me, to listen to what she had to say, to let her speak death in order to live. (Lefort, et al, p.7–8).

Rosine works for a little over a year trying to reverse the consequences of Nadia's illness, and we can see that in it she is already making reference to her own 'neurosis', to something she knows about how a body feels in neurotic suffering. Through this, she is able to recognize the first rumblings of desire—speak death!—in the unfolding of their relationship in the transference.

Nadia must emerge as a subject in her own right, but illness is such that despite the fact that this is exactly what she needs, it is exactly what she refuses. Rosine understood how this child neurotically solicited (already at the age of thirteen months!) exactly the care inapposite to what is required in this task of becoming a subject. Rosine could not confuse this register of acknowledgment with mothering this little girl, reducing listening to an exchange of caresses that would silence her. Doing so meant a certain kind of renunciation. These are renunciations we all have to learn to make when taking up the position of the analyst, but here, we see specifically how it takes place on the level of the body. Yes, this is a pre-verbal child, but Nadia, I think, shows us the original principle of abstinence, the necessity that a demand for bodily exchange be exchanged, at all costs, for words born of desire. It is only in them that we may hope to find ourselves. Nadia brings Rosine to this basic psychoanalytic truth.

One could imagine that *only* psychoanalysis—ensconced in the mythic proportions I have lent to it—could make this possible. Only psychoanalysis could bring a child back in this way, refusing to confuse care in the form of mental hygiene with what must more enduringly take place. And it is not simply 'better care' than that of the nurses. It is not the well-ordered ministrations of a doctor. Psychoanalysis cannot participate in this form of morality. The question of what gives birth to a subject, separate from a body, separate from simply biological life, is the guiding question for Rosine.

This is what is so astonishing in this work: as you read you read her traversing this edge between a care that makes passive and silences, and this other thing, X, called psychoanalysis. You watch Rosine invent psychoanalysis by figuring out how to differentiate the two. It isn't obvious, and what you also learn is that it wouldn't be so even for the 'fully' trained psychoanalyst, a reassuring fact for a candidate no doubt. That Rosine is able to do so is what saves Nadia. Inventing herself as a psychoanalyst becomes synonymous with this child's cure. Their fates are completely intertwined.

It is here, in this moment, that the stage is set for the mythic action in my story—a scene in a hospital between a first time analyst and young, very sick, little girl. This is the point where what Rosine is in the process of inventing will be shown to enter into her life more broadly. Forming herself as a psychoanalyst becomes an operating force whose lines read like the lines of fate. Isn't that always how a myth unfolds? An action is taken that will come to shape a life with the force of destiny, already foretold by an oracle of some kind like a message from Cassandra that no one can hear. Doesn't fate always unfold from a moment of critical choice, Rosine standing at the crossroads?

This choice point brings itself to bear on her very life: the intensity of Rosine's work with Nadia (and soon to include three others) is so great, calls on her to use her own experience of illness to such an extent, that she feels she cannot continue with her personal analysis at the same time. The choice feels like an either/or, either her analysis or theirs. The two cannot co-exist. Rosine decides she has to leave her analysis until she feels like she can handle both again. She chooses Nadia over herself and, perhaps, over Lacan. The hiatus lasts for13 months, the time that she is working in the hospital with these four children.

This is the moment I return to again and again in my imagination. I've thought about the choice she felt she had to make, the position she put her analyst in. Did Lacan interpret this decision as a defense, as a part of the transference neurosis? Did he make her feel that the antithetical choice was part of her illness or a counter-transference that must be analyzed? Did he support her desire to leave and its connection to what was so painful about keeping her self and these children in mind simultaneously? Was the work itself seen as a reasonable substitute for a period of time to establish her analytic identity? Did he affirm her position as psychoanalyst, where desire is precisely a force that calls on you to make a decision, one that hangs in the balance like life and death? What did Lacan do? While I have it all mapped out, just as I'm telling it to you now, the strange irony is that very little is actually written about this moment by Rosine Lefort herself.

Looking at her work I was surprised by how sparse the indication of this moment really is at the exact point at which she mentions it, compared not only to my imagination of it, but to what it is in distinction to the immense work on the cases themselves (Nadia's, over two hundred pages alone). Rosine writes,

> Nadia's treatment was the first chronologically. It will be shown how I started it. This treatment lasted approximately ten months, from October 1951 until July 1952. By October 1951 I had been in analysis for eighteen months. My analysis had been imposed by the need to overcome neurotic suffering and for that reason it was very difficult for me. It was difficult to the point that during Nadia's treatment I felt, over a period of several months, that it was impossible for me to attend the sessions of my own analysis regularly. The treatment of Nadia, and indeed of the other children which I commenced successively in the course of the following three months, in some way performed the function, therefore, of a substitute in my own analytic process, within which it came to be inscribed. (Ibid, p. xvii).

With that she ends her preface. I realized that it wasn't what she said about her analysis, or her own suffering *per se*, but what one reads *from* this, between the lines of the case, that finally gives you an indication of the profound passage she is making. She gives you the hint and you follow the scent in the unfolding story of her work with Nadia.

If one thinks of myths—and clearly I am working with their classical form—life-changing passages are traversed by virtue of forced solitude or exile, confronting the necessity of sacrifice, a dangerous odyssey, or simply the unknown. Oedipus, Orestes, Odysseus, Orpheus . . . I could go on. But this change of order always involves a radical separation from ancestors, family, and home. The passage indelibly inscribes something in its *passant*. My thoughts turn here because the final word that Rosine uses in her preface is "inscribed." Something needed to be inscribed—a word whose dual meaning is to carve, write, or mark, in an enduring way, and to name, dedicate or sign, coming from the Latin *inscribere*.

We know that Freud spoke of the unconscious as a kind of writing, as a magical writing tablet, whose traces form a matrix of wish and memory. But, these memory traces in the unconscious are also organized around traumatic moments, in particular, inevitable experiences of loss in the context of one's developing (sexual) self. Trauma, lest we forget, means wound, puncture, opening, and is tied to the body. We erase some of the original meaning of the unconscious as traumatic writing in a contemporary ideology that positions trauma as simply bad against those who are supposedly "not" traumatized. For Freud, sexuality is inevitably traumatic even in the very force that drive exerts upon mind. Wrestling with these forces can bring about something new in subjectivity.

Attempting to return to this original meaning, I would say that Rosine's act of leaving her analysis does just this. It punctuates or marks by creating a gap, and this gap provides as space, an opening, for her desire as a psychoanalyst. It was no doubt traumatic in the sense just described, something that was exerting force from the inside, and Rosine had to find whatever way possible to sustain this tension, to live through it. Her pioneering work with children, through this absence, is inscribed into her analysis, and her analysis, circumscribes this moment, absent though she was, when she takes up the position of the analyst.

The image is like that of a circle with a hole, a figure like that of the mouth, or any orifice whose rim-like structure psychoanalysis has shown as the erogenous sites of sexuality. The rim is a threshold between inside and outside. Allowing the drive to circumscribe this threshold, to symbolize and signify a point of interchange, the body becomes a written body, a body with a potential for language, creativity, sublimation. It is, as Rosine poetically puts it, the writing of a hole, like what it means to see with one's mouth, as Spitz characterized the baby once.

Try though we may, all erogenous zones starting with the mouth are hollows that ultimately cannot be filled. Trying—why call this desire anyway?—forms a subject with an inside and an outside. Lacan spoke of this formation once, as a glove turning inside out, a moebius strip's inside surface that traversed simultaneous to its outside edge. The most basic self-image is formed thus and it is a radical act of naming, of being called into being. Freud wrote that the ego is first and foremost a body ego, and Rosine means to find these earliest moments when the body first becomes a written body, binding drive in the nascent structure of the ego. Lacan, of course, elaborates these concepts theoretically in his paper on the mirror stage.

Rosine writes about a slip in her notes where she forgot to mention Nadia wanting her to help her look in the mirror before the end of the session,

> I can say that Nadia's treatment, in the full sense of the word, was a part of my own analysis, since it was with and through her that I was to come to grips with my own specular image, or rather with its relations with the Other. It was an exemplary illustration of, on the one hand, the place of the analyst as the one who is taught by the analysand; but much more than teaching, it was a question of the essential unconscious passage that this baby-analysand was to cause me to make. After treating Nadia, standing in front of a mirror was quite a different experience for me (Ibid, p. 110).

A dual inscription indeed! If the analysand is not the one to teach the analyst, then how can this dual inscription take place? This kind of unconscious writing—what she calls an unconscious passage—is how Rosine Lefort will come to define analytic work. The self-image of analyst and analysand are mutually altered.

Reading her text in this way, one can imagine her analysis as this very form of traumatic writing, an intense dialectical movement following the patterning of the drives: in her analysis, and in its absence, in work with Nadia, and back again in her analysis . . . impossible suffering, impossible conviction . . . Fort! Da! . . . here, gone . . . absence marked, presence regained . . . the traces are formed. Looking in the mirror will never be the same as it was.

Once you have the action that crystallizes a myth it is important to understand its aftermath, the trajectory of what it has set in motion through this inscription, like everything that follows in the wake of Antigone's decision to bury her brother, Polynices, in defiance of Creon's laws. Lacan encouraged Rosine to present some of her work four years later in his newly formed seminar that would serve as the foundation of the *École Freudienne de Paris*. These cases were seen as an important and inaugural application of French psychoanalytic ideas to work with severely ill children. Jenny Aubry, François

Dolto, and Rosine Lefort continued to expand child psychoanalysis in France in the 1960's and 1970's.

François Dolto spoke on the radio to parents, opened nurseries known as *Maisons Verte,* which now exist across Europe, wrote parenting handbooks and children's storybooks that dealt with difficult topics, created a method for intervening with pre and post partum parents, as well as, writing countless books and articles for clinicians working with children in the neurotic *and* psychotic spectrum. In a personal reminiscence, she recalls that Lacan used to say to her often, "you don't need to understand what I say because without theorizing about it you say the same thing" (Rudinesco, p. 241). Only one book, *The Case of Dominique,* is translated into English as of yet. Such, we might imagine, is the imaginary power of group dynamics.

Rosine joins another heroic figure in my mind, Maud Manoni, in her experiments with in-patient settings and the treatment of severe illness from pseudo-mental -retardation to schizophrenia and autism in an experimental center in Bonneuil. Manoni wrote extensively on working with families and within institutions, developing a place for psychoanalysts in the most divergent of settings, showing how psychoanalysis is uniquely situated for the most crucial interventions in these settings. Figures like Deleuze, Guattari, and others came to Bonneuil—which became legendary—to work and develop their ideas on psychoanalysis and its relation to a whole host of disciplines, including theatre, politics, art, and philosophy, creating a public intellectual space for the discussion of psychoanalysis.

Most importantly for our purposes, Rosine Lefort publishes these cases as a book with her husband, Robert Lefort, also a psychoanalyst, but only 30 years later. They traced her incredibly detailed notes step by step and added theoretical reflections on the clinical data, as well as addressing broader questions concerning "the genesis of the subject," what marks separation for a child, what can we learn about the functions and structure of the psyche from psychosis. The work is titled *Birth of the Other* or, *Naissance de l'Autre.*

Fascinated by the idea that she waited until theory caught up with what she had unwittingly found herself in the midst of, waited perhaps until another could support her in going back to a time that must have been harrowing, lonely, deeply ambiguous, and tied into her analysis in an important way, is certainly another part of what makes this story mythic. It takes her life and it gives it this kind of magical arc, starting with a moment that constitutes the birth of a psychoanalyst and suturing that moment to an end point where a lifetime of experience as an analyst, as well as an important partnership with a loved other, provides an avenue for further reflection and perspective. Seeing this arc, you know that she never could have calculated its endpoint, especially not at that critical moment when she abandoned her analysis and took on work with these children in almost absolute solitude.

I would reiterate that I do not and would not make a judgment on Rosine's analysis—she certainly doesn't—for this need to leave it. In fact, precisely the opposite, since what she uniquely transmits in this text is the powerful desire of a psychoanalyst that she alluded to having been born there. One could even say she demonstrates this as a desire that lasts a lifetime. Transmitting this desire through a written text is a difficult task and is, in my opinion, rarely communicated; this desire easily blotted out by one's theoretical allegiance, institutional commitments, or simply the heavy weight of fetishized knowledge. If you want to convey desire, there is very little room for the super-egoic whose shape shifting prose properties within a discipline should be carefully examined. Rosine, to my mind, manages, and I cannot but conclude that her personal analysis made this possible.

Something new must be created at all costs and the unconscious passage necessary for this creation is harrowing and often very, very lonely. The difficulty of sustaining the analytic position in the face of the youngest of patients in an extreme situation is what I find so path-breaking in her work. And this, in particular, by an analyst who could have no guarantee for her position, for her work, or even of her status, being without formal training, having abandoned her own analysis, shy of most conceptual developments in France with respect to theory and technique.

The pull of a pernicious rescue fantasy could only have been incredibly intense and yet, as she would have known, this would have been a total violation of the analytic frame. I can only imagine the pull between this fantasy and her identification with the principles of a psychoanalytic process, one that she had only begun to experience herself eighteen months previously. How did she do this? She develops a laser- like focus, finding any way to allow the objects—whether it is food or toys or parts of her own body—to take on a symbolic dimension in the transference. It is the most intimate and minute of confrontations with these objects treated only as signifiers in the transference that seemingly brings the child out of their impasse.

What this means is that these objects are not taken as objects to fill a lack, to stuff a body, but heard as signifiers that she marks not only through interpretation but by attention, for example, to her presence in distinction to that of the nurses on the ward. She creates the treatment and its frame. The frame isn't there already, as if by calling yourself an analyst it just exists, the magic power of a couch! The frame is something you create through listening as a psychoanalyst with only the conviction of what it must make possible.

Psychoanalysis is an act of creativity, one taken on in absolute solitude, and I think, or rather I know from experience, that it feels inordinately lonely, *especially* in the beginning. The easiest way to deal with this loneliness—the self-reliance and sense of one's own illness that is called on—is by thwarting the analytic process and replacing it with something that *feels* more substantial. A fantasy of rescue raises its head in the dark. . . . and the call to the child would be to speak to me, for me, not for his or her self.

It is this intensity that I think Rosine is referencing when she speaks of having to leave her analysis. The parallels that can be drawn between the work Rosine does with her patients and what I imagine took place in her analysis, using this skeleton that she offers to us, are fascinating. Both Rosine and her patients are finding a way to speak: the child literally, either coming out of mutism or finally advancing developmentally, and Rosine in relation to her interpretive voice as an analyst. So too her analysis was seemingly born by virtue of the creation of a gap, the same space that she introduces in her work with these children.

If Lacan supported this desire, then he must have allowed this act to signify what it would, even if only in its sheer form as marking an absence. Reading between the lines of Rosine Lefort's slight and modest remarks on her analysis and the detailed cure of a little girl that parallels the implications of what it means to be a psychoanalyst, we witness Lacan's support of her desire to be an analyst, *avant la lettre*. My reading is suggestive of a transformation of loneliness in Rosine Lefort that we can only infer—"my impossible neurotic suffering"—into the solitary struggles of the psychoanalyst.

If loneliness runs like a flat line, an insomniac night, all pervasive and unending, then there is something important here about what disrupts a state of things, what breaks into loneliness and transforms it, what makes loneliness a force of creativity. I would say it has something to do with desire's sublimation form. Desire's negative underside is loneliness. One is inevitably lonely in one's desire. To desire is to accept loneliness in the form of solitude, which finally gives birth to new possibilities.

The message in the end, as I see it, is threefold: Rosine uses her analysis, *even when leaving it*, in order to sustain her transferential work with these children. Doing so creates her as a psychoanalyst and creates a link to the field as a whole. This is how French psychoanalysis would eventually come to understand (years after the case of Nadia) what they call "the desire for psychoanalysis" that binds analysts in their impossible profession. Though we work in solitude, alone in our offices, maintaining this social link is important. But it is seen as nothing more than desire, founded on a profound confrontation with loss. What this means is that it cannot be something of the likes of a false object to fill a hole in the form of identifications with power, prestige, or even, family that are a denial of loss, loneliness, and the necessity of solitude.

Finally, if desire is transformed into a desire for psychoanalysis, then it is one that we have to let trainees invent for themselves. Becoming an analyst requires this kind of precarious invention, and if training lapses into indoctrination in any form, into a prescribed way of doing things, it thwarts this process: training would amount to a silencing of the candidate's desire. All institutional troubles follow from failing to make this differentiation. We should take our lesson from Rosine and her work with Nadia—this differentiation is no easy matter and it has resonance with the very task of psychoanalysis.

The symbolization in the transference of what is irrevocably lost, what we must accept separation from, is a dimension Rosine unfailingly tries to engender—this gap allowing these children to separate and come alive as subjects in their own right. The question "what does this Other want?" brings with it the important question, "what do I want?" But these questions can only be asked when the Other as analyst knows that they have nothing to give but the unique gift of psychoanalysis, the gift of listening to and for desire. Hence the title, *Birth of the Other.*

It is this unique gift that Rosine gives that could be held up as a mirror to the present state of our field. There is an odd, maybe even apt, metaphor in Rosine's work with Nadia concerning the question of the contemporary training of the psychoanalyst. It is a message for the Americans as much as the French, even French Lacanians (or especially for them), who have the same institutional troubles we do. This early moment that I am characterizing using Rosine's situation in France is true of psychoanalysis in its earliest periods in America, England, Germany, and Vienna. Something extraordinary takes place, is given birth to, in its most nascent moments—the Wednesday Psychological Society, Tavistock, the wild inventive splits in the American frame of psychoanalysis, Paris in the 60s.

So I would say that psychoanalysis seems to me to have a choice: either it can treat candidates as inert bodies to be filled—by knowledge, with solicited identifications, varieties of quasi-maternal attention, the supposedly rescuing structure of an authority—mistaking this kind of care for helping candidates find their way as analysts, or, it can work to create or open a space in which it hopes, but cannot know, that a desire for psychoanalysis will be born. It is a rigorous psychoanalytic principle. This desire is something we all know to be born from an experience of personal analysis, with working with one's own unconscious and "neurotic suffering," learning to listen there. When this is supported by one's personal analysis, in particular by it being precisely psychoanalysis and nothing else, the experience *will* transfer into a way of working with patients.

Have we lost our conviction in this particular fact? Do we pretend that it is anything else? 4–5 years of classes? A control experience with a patient who comes four times a week and lies down? Graduation? Successful integration into the analytic community? Simply the name, rightfully conferred, of psychoanalyst? Have we lost our ability to structure analytic training in accordance with what we know about the engendering of desire? When one cannot locate a space for desire in one's training, it is created through a massive split. The next generation finds a voice, but questions of an enduring transmission of psychoanalysis between generations are left in the wings, the field fragmenting, generation after generation. Are we caught in the infinite creation of psychoanalytic institutes? This begs the question of what Institutes understand about what it is they do, but I am certainly begging that we ask that question. It is important, as I hope I have shown, for the transformation of the loneliness of the candidate.

Lacan and Melanie Klein, despite wildly diverging clinical languages, are the two thinkers that I have found who speak about loneliness and seem to do so in connection with the very ethos of psychoanalysis itself. It is a great help to an analytic candidate to read work that connects what we are hearing to what we are doing in a way that positions us as subjects in the process of something inevitable; that what we are learning is not some application of a piece of knowledge to this or that patient, held by this or that analyst (something to fill a lack, I might say, in the model of care doled out in this foundling hospital in Paris), but a work that applies equally to patients, as to candidates, if not to the field as a whole. It is important to hear in our theory that our process is a process of mobilizing this thing we call psychoanalysis in a way that speaks more broadly to what it means to be a psychoanalyst. It helps bind the generations in a structure of inherited desire.

Loneliness, even exclusion, is fundamental to Klein and Lacan, and their way of conceiving subjectivity. This is, I suppose, closer to an existential condition than any psychopathology per se, or rather, psychopathology is closer to a refusal of these basic existential facts, their covering over. Loneliness, Klein says in her paper "On the Sense of Loneliness," comes from the impossibility of achieving any final integration, "a ubiquitous yearning for an unattainable perfect internal state" (Klein, p. 300). Not belonging has deeper meaning, for some parts of the self cannot be regained "contributing to the feeling that one is not in full possession of one's self, that one does not fully belong to oneself or, therefore, to anybody. That lost parts too, are felt to be lonely" (Klein, p. 301). Loneliness can be mitigated but not eliminated.

For Lacan, desire is essentially a lonely experience. It is always beckoning towards an object that is never its match, working with words that only ever half-articulate it. Desire, he says, is impossible, and the analyst's desire no less so, or, to flip this around, all the more so. In his characteristic negative pomp, Lacan writes,

> Whoever cannot carry his training analyses to this turning point—at which it is revealed, with trembling, that all the demands that have been articulated in the analysis (and more than any other the one that is at its core, the demand to become an analyst, which now comes to maturity) were merely transferences designed to keep in place a desire that was unstable or dubious in its problematic—such a person knows nothing of what must be obtained from the subject if he is to

be able to ensure the direction of an analysis, or merely offer
a well-advised interpretation in it (Lacan, p.531).

The analyst has to place himself beyond loneliness in a realm where solitude can take on the strength of a desire that is beyond fear and beyond pity.
Rosine Lefort could not have allowed herself to feel pity for these children she
was working with if she was to keep to the frame of what psychoanalysis was
to try and open. She had to rely on her desire.

Of course, for both of these thinkers, as well as for Rosine, as we have
seen, this work is tied to the act of symbolization. Symbolization is for them
no willy-nilly easy once-and-for-all matter. For Lacan the symbolization of
desire means you confront the most fundamental of losses, as well as, find the
courage to face the super-egoic social pressures that like to keep symbolization and pleasure in check. For Klein it means you are able to get one foot out
the door of unavoidable paranoid splitting while still facing the harangue of
depressive anxieties. A harsh super-ego will never forgive destructive impulses, and the harsher the super-ego the greater will be one's loneliness and
need for defence. This amounts, for Klein, to an imperative to find a way to
allow enjoyment to mitigate destructive impulses even when that is at the cost
of the hopelessness and disappointment of de-idealization.

Lacan and Klein have shown me what psychoanalysis is in a unique position to recognize, in particular what is crucial in the transformation of loneliness in the creation of the psychoanalytic listener. The kind of creativity and
capacity for pleasure that psychoanalysis must constantly reinvent in order to
move forward is an idea that I feel has supported me in the darkest moments
of training. It is why I've written or endeavored to speak on occasions like this
one, a task I differentiate from any of my identifications with institutional life,
my analysts and supervisors, and even with the wider community. This is one
reason the story of Rosine Lefort is so important for me.

Rosine's transference transfers to psychoanalysis itself, to its internal
principles in their most basic form—co-ordinates that could serve as the beginning of an entire life. It is for this reason that I imagine she can practice as
a psychoanalyst in the most divergent of settings, settings that compound the
loneliness of the psychoanalyst. She ends her case with Nadia in this fashion,

> On May 20th she gave me the most poetic image of herself:
> through the window, I saw her in the garden, playing with
> her shadow, clapping with joy at the way it changed shape.
> Death was there, although she did not know it; it was life she
> was applauding . . . This is the point Nadia had reached . . .
> the transference was not the enactment of the unconscious
> but the place where the unconscious could emerge, the place

177

> where Nadia as subject could emerge . . . Hence she was able to detach herself from me . . . At the time I said, 'we have nothing more to do together'. (Lefort, et al, *selected text from* p. 211–213).

Death could be contained in an image she allowed herself to animate, like Antigone animating her brother's still-living corpse with her desire. The work is a kind of shadow play. Only psychoanalysts know with profundity the applause into life that is the creation of a space where the unconscious can emerge. I hope we continue to find a way to give this gift for the sake of the next generation of analysts, for candidates. I hope our institutes, their training systems, form themselves accordingly, for the love of psychoanalysis. Love, Lacan said, is to give what one does not have to another who perhaps doesn't want it. Psychoanalysis is this impossible gift of love.

References

Klein, M. (1984). On the sense of loneliness. In: *Envy and Gratitude and Other Works, 1946–1963*. New York: Free Press

Kris, E. (1956). The personal myth—A problem in psychoanalytic. Technique. *Journal of the American Psychoanalytic Association* 4:653–681.

Lefort, R., (1994). *Birth of the Other,* transl. M. Du Ry, L. Watson, & L. Rodriguez. Chicago: University of Illinois Press.

Lacan, J. (2006). *Écrit,* transl. B. Fink. New York: W. W. Norton.

Roudinesco, E. (1997). *Jacques Lacan*, transl. B. Bray. New York: Columbia University Press.

Chapter 11
Loneliness and Solitude in the Psychoanalytic Training Process—
from the Chair of the Supervising Analyst
Douglas H. Ingram

Abstract:

The loneliness of the therapist in his or her work with patients is considered from the perspective of the consulting therapist or psychoanalytic institute supervising psychoanalyst. A case history demonstrates how waiting for a needed object provides a psychic substitution for the missing object and hence substitutes a lesser anguish for the greater anguish of loneliness. The therapist's loneliness from the patient and the therapist's loneliness with the patient are distinguished and explored. The therapist's experience of solitude is similarly considered.

In approaching a consideration of loneliness and solitude from the supervising analyst's perspective, I encountered one or two issues that I had not expected and that seemed surprising. Yet as I began to drill down on them, I came to an understanding that however odd these considerations seemed initially, I concluded that it might also prove fruitful to pursue them.

Still, since it is always best to start at the beginning, I want to consider first some points of terminology that will then be followed with a clinical case that reaches back to my own days as a candidate-in-training. The case addresses loneliness and the psychic function of waiting for something. Though had it not been for the consultant's straightforward advice, the opportunity for me, if not my for patient, to gain useful understanding would have been lost. This will then lead to a brief consideration of what the role of a consultant is. I will need to confide a dilemma that one may legitimately suppose casts doubt on my standing to say much of anything on this topic of loneliness. Then, I will take up the issues I described as odd and surprising: I will draw a distinction between *loneliness from the patient* and the oxymoronic *loneliness with the patient* and I will plunge into an account of each. Before summarizing and concluding, I will briefly consider solitude, which I admit seems to me much less engaging than loneliness, perhaps as Dante's Paradiso is much less engaging for most than his Inferno, and for the same reasons.

Terminological Considerations

By *loneliness*, I mean the feeling of being psychically distressed by a sense of aloneness either when one is isolated from others or in the presence of others. The term *alone* is neutral. The capacity to be alone entails ego-relatedness (Winnicott, 1958) and enables *solitude* with its creative tilt and quality the dimension of personal choice.

Also, by way of terminological clarification, I will refer to the supervising analyst as the "consultant," the candidate analyst as the "therapist," and the analysand as the "patient." My reason for these definitions is my wish to subtend an arc that extends our discussion beyond the formal training of the psychoanalytic institute.

Clinical Case Presentation

As mentioned, this clinical material dates to my own days as a candidate. The patient was a successful academic. I was the analyst-in-training, the therapist. By her ego strengths, wit, scholarship and fluency (these which I was impressed me—she was my first really smart control case) I was encouraged to suppose that she would be able to solve her problems if I mostly stayed out of the way, limiting myself to the rather conservative prescription of seeking out and solemnly interpreting transference resistances and displacements.

My patient was in love with a man who, after a brief affair, seemed to lose interest in her, though without altogether terminating their relationship. My patient would literally sit by the phone (we are in the 1970's). She'd wait for his call. My careful interpretations of this presumed transference displacement, that perhaps she was waiting for my call, for something from me, came to nothing. I felt increasingly distant from her, alone *from* her. Impatiently, I asked my supervising analyst, "Why doesn't she go out and do something else and just not wait for his call? Are there other dynamic processes I am overlooking?"

The supervisor, or consultant, considered my impatience with him, paralleling my impatience with my patient, which, in its turn, paralleled her impatience with her errant lover. The consultant recognized my patient's strengths and correctly assumed that allowing me to lapse into errors of psychodynamic ignorance and technical sloppiness would do no damage to her and might even prove instructive for me. Perhaps wisely, he said, "Why not ask her—but you might be surprised at her answer."

I did ask her, and even now in its recalling this I feel embarrassment at my clinical innocence. "So," I said in my next session with the patient, after arranging my face with appropriate gravity and compassion, "What is in it for you waiting for a phone call that hardly ever comes when you could be out doing other things and meeting other people?" I was startled by the tearful and angry answer, "Because, doctor," she erupted, leaping off the couch with a glare at me, "I would feel terribly lonely. As long as I am waiting for him to call, I don't have to feel that terrible loneliness. He is with me in my mind as long as I wait and I am not alone."

The point of instruction for me was that the distress of waiting defers or eclipses the far greater distress of abandonment and loneliness. Placed in a theoretical formulation, waiting enables the subjective self to imaginatively connect to the absent and needed object. The needed object may even be functioning as a certainty that dispels the apprehension of not knowing, even of not knowing if an outcome is good or bad. In waiting, there is the soothing belief that sooner or later relief will come. A good lesson. Now, decades old, my experience with that patient drew me into an understanding that compounded over the years and led me to give thought to how time figures psychically, how the psychology of duration inheres in our treatment sessions, how the time-keeping function of the therapist is to be appreciated, and that how we operationalize time-keeping deserves our thought. (Ingram, 1979).

Many of our patients are waiting for something—a person, a promotion, a school acceptance, a lottery ticket to come in, the other shoe to drop, Godot. Mostly, this presents little difficulty. But sometimes, the clinician is recruited or even conscripted into the agony of the patient's waiting, as I was with that professor. I could not wait with her. I could not stand it. I did not understand that waiting may be a constructive defense that wards off the pain of loss and intolerable loneliness. After her retort, I was silenced and mortified. We had briefly reversed roles and we were both the better for it, myself more than she.

There is more to the story. In my training analysis, and this should come as no surprise, I discovered my frustrated impatience was triggered by my own competitive jealousy. I was excluded. I wanted her to be preoccupied with her analysis, with me—not some other guy. I was frustrated and impatient. She was alone *with* the image of her lover, but alone *from* me.

The Role of the Consultant

The consultant or supervising analyst wishes to accomplish three things. The first function of the consultant or supervising analyst is to appreciate the extent to which the therapist or candidate-in-training is characterologically disposed to enter into dialogue with the patient or, on the other hand, is disposed toward a more traditional analytic posture. The more traditional analytic position may expose the therapist to a sense of loneliness, though the therapist is, at the same time, psychically protected from that loneliness by the injunction to avoid expressing countertransference reactions. Of course, the orientation of the training institute and training analyst bear on this question. The dialogic orientation, as I am using it here, does not mean more utterances by the analyst, but that those utterances not be seen as "interventions." If the consultant analyst can swing either way, all to the good. If, however, the match between the supervising analyst and the candidate is too strikingly at odds, the candidate deserves a supervisor more in keeping with his or her own characterologic orientation or preference.

Second, the consultant or supervising analyst wishes to establish a trusting dialogue with the therapist or candidate in order to impart insights of a psychodynamic nature and techniques useful to accomplish forward therapeutic motion—most commonly, what to say to the patient. Identifying circumscribed countertransference manifestations that impede analysis is often nec-

185

essary (Arlow, 1963). With experience, the interiorization—I prefer Bakhtin's usage (1984) —of the therapist's dialogue with the consultant establishes increasing confidence in the therapist's capacity to adequately encounter difficulties that patients may present in the future. The interiorization of that dialogue and its gradual and complete unselfconscious integration into the psychic repertoire of the therapist is the aim.

Third, the consultant wants to establish that beyond the current supervision itself, consultation about a patient is easy and useful. Many experienced therapists maintain an ongoing relationship with a consultant or participate in peer supervisory groups. In this, the experience of loneliness engendered by a patient may be the affective trigger for discussion. If the consultative sessions are scheduled weekly, no affective trigger may be needed. Accompanied by an ongoing psychodynamic consultancy, the loneliness that may arise for being alone from or with a patient is likely to be much less.

A Dilemma

Here, I think it is necessary for me to say something about myself. Fact is, I am not disposed to feel lonely from patients or the therapists whom I see in consultation. I may feel anxious, distressed, worried, loving, angry, frustrated, hateful, and the textured and shifting marbelized amalgams of these and other feelings. But loneliness is not among them. Nor have I found that those whom I supervise feel lonely in sessions with their patients. Distant, perhaps. Removed, possibly. But not so removed that the term lonely applies. I cannot recall a supervisee complaining about a feeling of loneliness engendered by a patient. At the same time, I acknowledge that perhaps those who consult me and that I, myself, may defend against loneliness or enact behaviors to ensure it does not reach awareness. Perhaps the clinical case I presented earlier is an example. Perhaps my impatience intercepted and masked feelings of loneliness with regard to her. Still, I must consider the empirical findings of my personal experience. I felt impatient, not lonely. If I am to find loneliness in my experience, I need to back into it, to infer a loneliness I did not feel.

So, I speak theoretically. I appreciate the dilemma, or more dramatically put, the arrogance of speaking about something that I have little immediate feel for. Yet I think that I can tentatively offer something useful despite my lack of immediate experience with loneliness in a clinical context. With this qualification, which I hope is not a fatal one, I will soldier on.

My early training was at the American Institute for Psychoanalysis, founded by Karen Horney. Horney had a definition of what she called basic anxiety, the "feeling of being isolated and helpless in a world conceived as potentially hostile" (Horney, 1950, p. 18). The three essential terms in that formula are *'isolated'*, *'helpless'*, and *'hostile'*.

186

By way of inference, we may find that anxiety can primarily organize subjectively as helplessness for some, as aloneness for others, and as hostility for still others. We want to acknowledge that mostly these may present in some combination, though often one or another—helplessness, aloneness, or aggression—will dominate. Also, we want to recognize the disruption in cognitive and affective competence and even perception that may accompany basic anxiety. That is, the therapist's distress may take different affective colorations, depending on the therapist's character organization, the patient, and the context. Some of us may experience difficulty with a patient by feeling helpless, others by feeling aggressive, and others by feeling lonely from or with the patient, often in some complex combination.

Loneliness From and Loneliness With

I want to draw a distinction that may have some value as we approach this topic. I wish to distinguish "loneliness *from* . . " and "loneliness *with* . . ." In speaking of the therapist's loneliness *from* the patient, I am referring to that distinctive experience that although the patient is present in the therapist's analyst's consulting room, the therapist feels alone—and not merely alone, but painfully alone. As I have said, this is outside of my personal experience. Thankfully, Sandra Buechler (1998) has amply explored this phenomenon and I will consider her contributions shortly. The therapist's experience of loneliness *with* the patient is strikingly different. Admittedly, that seems like an odd and paradoxical construction, feeling lonely *with* one's patient.

Yet this is an experience that clinicians do have. I have had it and therapists who have consulted me have had it. Here, theoretical formulation for me flows from experience far more directly. The therapist and patient are together with each other but, for reasons we will recognize shortly, are distressingly separated from their usual worlds. Therapist and patient are together, but adrift and at sea. In its most extreme form this state of loneliness finds the therapist *with* the patient insofar as the patient is a continuous psychic presence. It is in Fromm-Reichmann's (1990) consideration of loneliness that we find foundation to explore this extreme form of loneliness. For those of you who saw the movie, *Castaway,* we observe the splintering of cognition, of ego fragmentation as a result of the Tom Hanks' character's unfathomable loneliness. That is, mentation becomes monologic and speech consists of short disconnected phrases that suggest psychotic incoherence. In creating through dissociation a kind of fire god whom he can address, dialogue is restored and, with it, cognitive competency. The protagonist is dreadfully lonely, but he is lonely *with* a dissociated persona that enables effective dialogue and cognition (Ingram, 2001, from Cacioppo and Patrick 2008).

187

My patient of so many years ago that I described serves as another example of this kind of loneliness. Separated from the world, she was painfully alone with the imagined vision of her lover.

Regardless of how loneliness engenders a unique psychic terrain in the therapist, the therapist's feelings *from* or *with* a patient should be regarded as a trigger to seek consultation (Cacioppo and Patrick 2008).

The Therapist's Loneliness *From* the Patient

Buechler (1998) thoughtfully considers how we may feel lonely with different kinds of patients—or, as I am semantically reconstructing it—lonely *from* different kinds of patients.

—The narcissistic patient may be so taken up with him- or herself that the analyst may feel left out of the equation and, hence, lonely.

—The schizoid patient may be unavailable to anything we say or do, to seem so utterly indifferent that we may feel lonely.

—The borderline or psychotic patient may treat us as so differently from how we feel about ourselves that we may feel lonely.

The acknowledgement and exploration of these feelings in the consultative session can go far towards remediating this distress in the therapist and enable the therapy work to proceed. Buechler notes that the consultant needs to be aware of how loneliness in the therapist might manifest. For example, the narcissistic therapist may need more admiration and adoring engagement from a patient than the patient gives. Feeling lonely, though not quite in touch with the feeling, the narcissistic therapist behaves in a fashion that engenders much-needed admiration. The more obsessional therapist is likely to prefer patients who likewise rely on obsessional character defenses. The more affectively charged therapist, reciprocally, may feel more alone from the intellectualized patient and seek to assault intellectual defenses to keep loneliness from the patient at bay.

Hopefully, the therapist—each of us, really—is aware of the need for connection. Not to be aware of that need for connection can lead to defensive inattention to loneliness in our patients.

As I have said, loneliness *from* a patient is more likely to occur in those therapists who are prone to experience basic anxiety as mostly structured by a lonely feeling. If the therapist is not given to feeling lonely, characteriologically, distressing countertransference feelings may simply not show as loneliness. Some examples:

—One therapist-supervisee was startled when a narcissistic patient objected to the therapist's use of the term "we." The patient insisted there was only one person in the room, and that was he, himself, the patient. The therapist was not to be counted as a person. The therapist experienced not loneliness, but curiosity and even amusement.

—Another supervisee who was viewed as a monster by her patient, experienced hatred towards her patient, not loneliness.

—A therapist complained that a highly obsessional patient was boring her to death. Loneliness was not an issue.

Buechler anticipates these concerns and adds to them how the institutional or personal analytic theoretic stance may affect how our patients engender loneliness in the countertransference.

The Therapist's Loneliness *with* the Patient

This feeling, "lonely *with* another," occurs when the presence of the other as a presence or psychic presence creates a wedge between the therapy dyad and others outside the clinical engagement. This experience of loneliness is, in my experience, far more common. Somewhat arbitrarily, I will divide this group, "loneliness *with* the patient," into three. These are really points along a spectrum. The first is benign and limited to the work with the patient. The second is a meaningful and a legitimate preoccupation with the patient's clinical status, and is warranted. The third creates a loneliness that overflows the therapy and threatens to globally engulf the clinician.

First, an example in which loneliness with the therapist is limited and benign: Imagine you are working successfully with a patient. Initially, payment was assured by a family member, a parent or a spouse, but well into the therapy the payments become tardy and then seem to cease altogether. You explore the matter with the patient, but soon nothing that either the well-intended patient or you, yourself, can do will speed up or assure payment. You are alone with the patient. There are no good options. In your helplessness, you experience humiliation, anger, helplessness, and a cascade of associated fantasies. You are alone "with" your patient, not "from" him.

In the course of a training analysis—and this depends on the traditions of practice of each institute and of each training analyst—the therapist may explore with the training analyst the feelings and associations that contribute to the dilemma. The analyst does not offer ideas on how to proceed. It may be understood that giving ideas on how to proceed is not the training analyst's role. That is the job of the supervising analyst, i.e., the consultant. So, though the extent of the painful countertransference reaction is detoxified through one's own self-exploration, being "alone *with* the patient" continues. The therapist may still be unable to think the matter through clearly enough to devise a plan. Can the supervising or consulting analyst help? Of course.

The consultant may help in considering how the payer, the third party, wishes to exert control, or perhaps sabotage the therapy because the patient is derivatively regarded as an oedipal rival, or enviously wishes to join the therapy, or suffers from some global characterologic unreliability, and so forth. So, in exploring these and other possibilities with the therapist, who may in turn explore them with his or her patient, the consultant joins with the candidate who is now no longer "alone *with* the patient."

The countertransference experience of "loneliness *with* a patient" as described so far has loneliness as circumscribed. Consider, next, the second category of loneliness *with* a patient. Here, concern and worry about a patient fantasizing about suicide or about some other highly destructive behavior, or the patient who stokes powerful erotic feelings in the therapist, the loneliness the therapist may feel threatens to cause overwhelming difficulty for the candidate, or beyond candidacy, for the experienced psychodynamic therapist and analyst. Recall that patient of mine so many years ago who was preoccupied with the image of her uncaring lover, so much so that she was separated from the world. She was alone *with* him. So, too, that kind of loneliness can occur for the therapist highly preoccupied with the patient.

The third category concerns circumstances in which loneliness *with* a patient more powerfully drives a wedge between the therapeutic dyad and the circle of colleagues, friends and family, and the wider collective that further constitute one's world. This is palpably a different kind of matter.

When a patient is considering in a more immediate way suicide, murder, spousal abuse, pedophilic activity, sadistic behavior, or other substantially unlawful or unethical acts and includes the therapist in his or her thinking, the expression 'being alone with the patient' blazes with new meaning.

Here, the quality and intensity of loneliness induced by clinical circumstance is virtually unbounded. There is continuous limbic flooding within the therapist. Acknowledgement *to anyone* of the difficulty one has with a patient may seem unacceptable. This is especially likely if the supervision is within the framework of formal psychoanalytic training because it may carry immediate institutional censure. Strikingly unprofessional conduct with a patient is the usual matter—a therapist's sexual or other exploitation of the patient. Additionally, the therapist's fear of becoming the object of potentially criminal activity, violent or otherwise, can precipitate a sense of loneliness with the patient who is foregrounded in one's mind, deeply coloring all other thought and disturbing somatic functions such as sleep and appetite. Other causes of this kind of isolation include: the possibility of government sanction or investigation, the threat or involvement in a lawsuit, untoward high profile publicity, investigation by insurance fraud units, Medicare, hospitals or licensing agencies, ethics committees, and even (believe it or not) Homeland Security. Again, the loneliness is the separation from others, the isolation that accompanies fantasies of, or a real potential for, an ignominious exile from the professional, familial and social group.

From the point of view of the psychoanalytic training process, thankfully, patients who would create clinical circumstances of this description are unlikely to gain status as suitable control subjects for candidate training. But it can and does happen, and woe to the candidate and supervising and training analyst if it does. Indeed, the entire institute of training can be rocked by matters such as these. The loneliness engendered by what for most of us are highly exceptional clinical challenges can be overwhelming. The role of clinical consultant, or, here, the supervising analyst, is necessary to defang the fear, helplessness, shame, and loneliness of the clinician's psychic experience. It is in cases such as these that the consultant must also feel, himself or herself, alone with the therapist. That is, the consultant has also become a party to something egregious and must seek help. That help may include supervision or consultation from colleagues and, often enough, attorneys.

Solitude

Can it be that solitude, like loneliness, is something the therapist also has *from* or *with* the patient?

The dialogic orientation as I am applying it here is one in which solitude is determinedly regarded as *with* the patient. Perhaps this is another oxymoron, "shared solitude," but so be it. The analyst and patient share a solitude open to the universe of explicit memories, reports, associations and emotions of the patients and, while though they are generally unspoken, is necessarily open to the same from the therapist. The certainty of the duration of the therapy session, uninterrupted and unfailing, enables a creative and shared solitude in which the world, including time itself, falls away. The sessions transcend time, where the moment and eternity fold together, and where the sessions may merge seamlessly as though erasing the intervals between them.

Conclusion

In summation, I have sought to explore an approach to loneliness and solitude from the perspective of the consultant, or, in the context of the analytic institute, the supervising analyst. Early on, I presented a case in which waiting is illuminated as having a defensive function, that although distressing, may be far less distressing than the abandonment and loneliness that is a consequence of losing the psychic presence of the object. Borrowing from Horney's concept of basic anxiety, the therapist's anxiety in a difficult therapeutic encounter may be experienced or enacted as helplessness, aggression, or as a sense of being uncomfortably alone, as lonely in the analytic sessions. I described this as the therapist's being alone *from* the patient. I acknowledged my own inexperience with feeling alone from patients or its reported presence in supervisees.

In other difficult clinical circumstances, it is more helpful to regard the analyst as lonely *with* the patient. The patient is intimately bound with the therapist so strongly that the therapy dyad feels too isolated from others. This feeling of loneliness, which in most cases is limited and contained, is mitigated by the consultant who joins helpfully with the therapist in the offer of understanding and technical counsel. More troublesome and more likely to cause a sense of being alone with one's patient occurs when there is a clinical case of extreme urgency, say, the real possibility of suicide. In still more disturbing cases, as when the therapist is engaged or threatened to be engaged with unprofessional behavior such as patient abuse, the feeling of loneliness may be consuming and terrifying. Here, the therapist is tied to the patient such that the sense of loneliness with the patient has a malignant quality of separating therapist and patient from the community. Consultation is necessary to ward off therapeutic failure and irredeemable damage. Here, even the consultant may seek consultation.

Turning to solitude, I argued similarly but affirmed that solitude is an experience shared with the patient. The therapeutic space is isolated from the world and in its certainty and constancy transcends the quotidian and elevates therapist and patient with what we might call a shared psychic sanctity, enduring and reliable.

References

Arlow, J.A. (1963). The supervisory situation. *Journal of the American Psychoanalytic Association* 11:576–594.

Bakhtin, M. (1984) *Problems of Dostoevsky's Poetics*, transl. C. Emerson. Minneapolis: University of Minnesota Press.

Buechler, S. (1998). The analyst's experience of loneliness. *Contemporary Psychoanalysis 34*:91–113.

Cacioppo, J.T. and Patrick, B. (2008). *Loneliness: Human Nature and the Need for Social Connection.* New York: W W Norton.

Fromm-Reichmann, F. (1990). Loneliness. *Contemporary Psychoanalysis 26*:305–329.

Ingram, D. H. (1979). Time and time-keeping in psychoanalysis and psychotherapy. *American Journal of Psychoanalysis* 39:319–328.

——— (2001). Of time, narrative, and 'Cast Away'. *Journal American Academy of Psychoanalysis 29*:625-633. Also at www.psyartjournal.com/article/show/h_ingram-of_time_narrative_and_cast_away

Horney, K. (1950). *Neurosis and Human Growth.* New York: W.W. Norton

Winnicott, D. W. (1958). The capacity to be alone. *International Journal of Psychoanalysis* 39:416–420.

Chapter 12
The Loneliness of the Training Analyst
Eric Mendelsohn

Abstract:

Loneliness is a state of estrangement from self potentiated by an array of interpersonal circumstances. In this paper I consider the role and participation of the training analyst, both in the clinical setting and within the interpersonal world of the analytic institute. The conditions sponsoring loneliness as a psychic state experienced by training analysts are highlighted, and clinical challenges and opportunities for analytic engagement are described.

I begin with a memory of loss and of a subtle kind of alienation. I had been working for 10 years with a young man I had grown to love. He suffered the lingering effects of a serious childhood illness, and the work took place in the shadow of his declining health and the prospect of his early death. I saw him for the last time in the hospital, four hours before he died; and then attended his wake and funeral Mass where I briefly spoke with many of the family and friends I had heard about over the years and had come to know in that deep but once removed way that psychoanalysts do. At his partner's request he and I met some days later in my office where we sat together and spoke tentatively and awkwardly. In these circumstances, publicly and outside the analytic space, I felt constrained. While I felt a personal need for a setting in which loss could be held and shared, my commitment to the privacy of the work was an inhibiting presence, and my patient's community of mourning was one I could only engage in a marginal way. My grief felt full but its open expression was limited by my inability to speak freely and participate openly in the rituals of mourning. This paper builds on the premise that this is the kind of alienation from direct experience that lies at the center of loneliness. What I seek to highlight in this vignette is not primarily the loss of someone I cared for, as painful as this was; rather, it is the way in which I felt internally blocked and interactively constrained, unable to fully feel or give expression to my grief.

My thesis is that our loneliness, as people and in our roles as analysts, involves a particular form of blockage, a loss of connection to sustaining, nourishing internal objects and the selves we are with those objects. When we are lonely we lose an ease of access to those we love and to our loving selves. Just as loving another involves not only loving who the other is, but also loving who we are with that person, loneliness is characterized by the loss of that access and of those means of self-expression. As analysts we are lonely when we are unable, or unwilling, to be analysts; that is, when we cannot think and speak freely. At those times we lose our connection to our analytic partners and to our loving, generative analytic selves.

I believe that analysts regularly struggle with loneliness in the course of enacting their roles, and that those of us who serve as training analysts face unique and rather formidable inducements to loneliness. The task of this paper is to consider the nature and quality of loneliness as it is experienced and lived by training analysts. I will attempt to accomplish this by briefly defining loneliness, by considering the roles and relational tasks of training analysts, and by taking up aspects of the culture and social structure of analytic institutes and institute communities as they engender and hold the training analyst's loneliness. Given this project I will be highlighting an array of challenges and impediments to optimal analytic engagement in the training analysis. For the most part I will not be taking up the therapeutic possibilities of training analyses although these can be inferred from my discussion of what is problematic.

Loneliness is the companion and the close but distinct counterpart of aloneness and solitude, and each of these experiences is a manifestation of our separateness. Separateness can be thought of as irreducible while it also plays out in dialectical tension with our essential connectedness. In states of loneliness the connectivity pole of the dialectic is temporarily or more enduringly withered or blocked, and separateness threatens to deepen into isolation and alienation.

According to Sullivan (1953), the experience of loneliness takes shape over the course of time and draws upon motivational systems that emerge in successive developmental eras. These dynamic underpinnings include: the need for physical and affective contact in infancy, the needs for recognition, approval and communicative registration and response in early childhood, those for social belonging and the avoidance of ostracism in the juvenile era, and those for loving and intimate knowing in preadolescence and beyond. For Sullivan (1953) and Fromm-Reichmann (1958/1990), loneliness, at its most intense, is so unbearable that people willingly undergo anxiety in a desperate attempt to circumvent its occurrence. Indeed, both Sullivan and Fromm-Reichmann believed that the emotional fragility of many precariously integrated late adolescents expresses itself in symptomatic crises following ill-fated attempts by these interpersonally unskilled youngsters to negotiate forms of social belonging they do not comprehend and cannot manage. Loneliness is so painful an experience that people fail to notice much of what they do to manage and avoid it. As loneliness is linked to severe anxiety, people struggle unsuccessfully to learn and benefit from what they undergo when lonely.

Solitude and aloneness, the experiential counterparts of loneliness that fall within the shadow of separateness, may be chosen or even preferred states, and are not necessarily aversive (Mendelson, 1990). In its essence, loneliness involves an alienation from self, whereas aloneness and solitude combine interpersonal separateness with a receptive and open orientation to internal states. Loneliness may be thought of as an anguished, frightened rejection and avoidance of the challenges of solitude and aloneness, and an inability to

198

manage and embrace them. In states of loneliness, we are alone within ourselves, denied access to internal sources of comfort, nourishment and hopefulness. We cannot speak our hearts, and because we are blocked from self-connectedness and self-expression, we cannot deeply feel, think or know (Wilner, 1998). While loneliness may be occasioned by interpersonal loss or separation, it is essentially a form of self-alienation. That is why, as analysts, we are lonely when we are unable to be present as analysts.

This conceptualization of loneliness invites us to consider those aspects of the analyst's internal states and participation that incline toward self-alienation. If the analyst cannot be present, alive and engaged enough as analyst, she may begin to despair because, following Winnicott, she knows, "that nothing is happening when something profitable might have happened" (cited in Lavendar, 2011). Analysts are especially susceptible to loneliness when they "coast in the countertransference" (Hirsch, 2008), that is, when they eschew opportunities to engage themselves and their patients in analytically challenging ways.

In significant measure, the analyst's loneliness is an outgrowth of the asymmetrical distribution of roles in the therapy relationship. As analytic therapy is what we do, day in and day out, over the course of a professional lifetime, we inevitably bring the full array of our personal needs to the work. Beyond our often distracting and pressing needs for financial security, we need recognition, love, intimate connectedness, and reparation for harm inflicted. We need to feel powerful, effective, and competent, to mitigate and postpone inevitable losses, to cause suffering and hurt, and to feel admired and needed (Ehrenberg, 1992; Hirsch, 2008; Hoffman, 1998; Maroda, 1991; Mendelsohn, 2002; 2007). While it is increasingly recognized that these needs are unavoidably present and even, at least in some sublimated, relatively integrated forms, "legitimate" (Maroda, 2005), the analytic role requires us to subordinate our personal needs to those of the patient. Their expression is, optimally, selective, circumscribed and what is often termed "judicious." Even under the best of circumstances we work and live our professional lives in a state of considerable deprivation, prevented from fully embracing the opportunities for being known, for response, and for expressive participation that emerge in analytic work. While this may be one reason we write papers and speak with each other at conferences, we recognize the many ways that we inevitably carry and enact these needs with our patients.

Sandra Buechler (1998) has considered loneliness as it emerges in the analyst's internal experience and role relatedness. She highlights the loneliness that comes from working closely and for years on end with patients who are inclined toward self- absorption and disregard for others, patients who often do not notice us, who negate who we are and what we do, or who misconstrue us in ways that feel like assaults on our most cherished experiences of self. We also experience loneliness, according to Buechler, because we are limited in how fully and openly we can share countertransference. We regularly undergo intense experiences that, at least to some degree, we are required to hold and bracket (Slochower, 1996). Nevertheless, we are often invited, sometimes provoked, and at times simply choose to participate in ways that are not in keeping with our preferred ideals for ourselves. When that happens we may become estranged from comforting and sustaining internal presences, including those of our analysts, supervisors, teachers, and theoretical role models (Mendelsohn, 2005). When, as is inevitably the case, we find ourselves contributing to repetitious transference enactments, we suffer shame and guilt because we recognize our contribution to the patient's suffering (Mendelsohn, 2002; 2005). At these times we are at risk of suffering loneliness.

Many of us in the field are predisposed to loneliness. Indeed, some choose to become analysts because the analytic role affords, on a regular basis, seemingly safe, role defined opportunities for intense connectedness and intimacy (Schafer 1995). For those of us for whom this is the case there are both advantages and liabilities. We may be especially sensitive to the loneliness of our analysands and may readily notice and engage their emotional withdrawal. At the same time we may be prone to use the work to pursue our own needs for expressiveness and intimacy in ways that perturb and burden our analysands.

Having considered loneliness and its place in the analyst's experience, I will now turn more specifically to the loneliness of the training analyst. We begin with the language we use, specifically the term, "training analyst". If, as I have contended, loneliness is the result and expression of an alienation from self, and if the language we use sponsors a state of discomfort and self-estrangement, we will tend to feel lonely. It appears evident that "training analyst" is an awkward and vexed term.

Why is this so? Historically, most institutes had closed boundaries and their own faculty group. In this system, training analysts sat atop the hierarchy of faculty, as both the most senior and presumably the most skilled therapists and accomplished teachers of psychoanalysis. Currently, many institutes, including those with which I am affiliated, draw faculty from that institute as well as from the wider community. In most of these institutes there are no formally designated training analysts. Instead, any analyst who meets that institute's criteria may qualify as a candidate's analyst. Some who take on this role self-designate as "training analysts." Others do not, even if serving in that role. It is noteworthy that few colleagues, either among current candidates or graduate analysts, have, in my memory, made reference to their "training analyst." Instead, friends and colleagues typically say, "my analyst" or, more often, "my therapist." Not infrequently it is training analysts who use the term in a self-referential way, including times when that term has not been officially conferred.

200

In addition there is some discomfort in the field with the term "training analyst" itself. The training analyst is expected to be both a clinical analyst and, through example, if nothing else, a teacher and professional role model. The linkage of "training" and "analyst" defines a conflicted role relationship in which mentoring and personal therapy coexist in uneasy tension. In our current era, when the authoritarian and asymmetrical aspects of the analytic relationship have been increasingly recognized as shaping transference and countertransference, the tensions between the therapeutic and mentoring/teaching aspects of the training analysis have increasingly become subjects of analytic inquiry. As a result, some in the field prefer the designation "personal analyst"," a term that has some appeal while also seeming a bit ironic. Those who favor this terminological change seek to affirm that the training analysis is primarily and essentially therapeutic. While this emphasis appears to be clarifying and analytically facilitative, it potentially also serves to obscure the presence of a complex, conflicted role relationship, one that likely requires more than a terminological change to address. In sum, insofar as our language inspires intellectual confusion and participatory stumbling, it inclines us toward self-alienation.

The tensions between the mentoring/socializing and therapeutic aspects of training analyses have long been topics of concern. Over the years, attention has been paid to the complicating effects on the analysis of both the social links between candidates and their analysts and the analyst's role in the candidate's career development (Bibring, 1954; Balint, 1954; Arlow, 1982). In an earlier era, training analysts played an active part in decisions about the candidate's progression in his institute, often attending training committee meetings and reporting on the analysand's "readiness" for class work and control cases. As a result, the freedom and autonomy of the candidate were inevitably compromised, and there were difficulties establishing and maintaining a safe, exploratory analytic atmosphere. Moreover, these problems remained unnoticed because of their widespread, unquestioned acceptance. The candidate's experience of the analyst's power and prestige was not subject to analytic inquiry aside from its being seen as a neurotic manifestation in the transference. In such an atmosphere crucial material and experience often did not emerge until the candidate's second analysis, post- graduation (c.f. Greenberg 1991).

While these difficulties may strike us as self-evident from our contemporary vantage point, historically they did not emerge as subjects of analysis. Indeed, in earlier eras the candidate's professional goals and aspirations, especially those of becoming a psychoanalyst who is recognized and respected in the field, not infrequently trumped his therapeutic hopes and needs (Bibring, 1954). This state of affairs often gave training analyses a subtly false or manipulative quality. By contrast, in recent years, in most instances the training analysis is increasingly segregated from the administrative and evaluative aspects of training. Indeed, on an administrative level, there is usually a complete separation between the candidate's analysis and the rest of the educational program, other than the requirement that the candidate be in a concurrent analysis with a qualified and approved analyst. However, remnants of the earlier history can still be discerned in the background of many contemporary training analyses. This is the case because the professional goals and ambitions of both candidates and their analysts continue to find their way into the analytic relationship and are given expression there. Consider these common examples:

1.   The training analyst has just published a paper of which she is proud. In sessions, the candidate makes no mention of this even though the paper is achieving considerable attention in the analytic community. The analyst is conscious of her desire for recognition by the candidate and feels conflicted. She is unsure about inquiring into what feels like a conspicuous omission on the candidate's part, unsure whether this is also the candidate's issue in addition to it being her own. Will she refrain from taking this up, and will her awareness of her own wishes keep her from engaging an issue of importance to her patient?

2.   Another analyst has just made a controversial presentation at an institute retreat. As a result the analyst is now the object of considerable attention in the institute community, not all of it favorable. In his sessions the candidate speaks emotionally of his disappointment and anger, and states that colleagues are being narrow- minded and unfair in their response to the analyst. The analyst now feels chagrined and somewhat ashamed, for the time being, at least, questioning her decision to make the presentation in the first place. Inquiry into this proves to be awkward and constrained.

3.   Or, the candidate has written a paper and asks the analyst to read it and comment. The analyst, pleased that her analysand has taken this step, and gratified both by the writing and the request, feels inclined to say yes, but has doubts about her and her analysand's freedom to use this exchange analytically.

My sense is that situations like these are common and are most likely to become problematic in cases where one or the other participant is especially accomplished or anxious about his/her level of professional achievement. In these instances the professional aspirations and insecurities of both members of the dyad will significantly shape the course of the analysis. Moreover, in spite of meaningful changes in the culture of institutes and the theory of technique, interactions like these may prove difficult to attend to and explore.

There are other ways in which the fact that candidates and their analysts are often part of the same professional communities can lead to tensions in the analytic relationship and can engender self-alienation and loneliness. During times of heightened transference feeling, candidates sometimes talk to other candidates, or to their supervisors or advisors, about their analysts, who may become aware of this during analytic hours. These communications, which may flow through the community grapevine, may be muted or become quite audible. As an example of this sort of scenario, a memo was recently circulated to supervisory faculty at one institute reminding supervisors that it is improper to suggest to candidates that they discontinue with their current analyst and come into analysis with them. The implication of the memo was that a supervisor had responded to his supervisee's expressed negative feelings about his analysis in a way that was self-serving. There are often, in such expressions of split- off transference, undercurrents of critique, idealization or devaluation. In the context of this sort of scenario, training analysts may feel exposed and uncomfortably scrutinized and may become constricted in both their clinical and public roles. Being either admired or denigrated by candidates and colleagues, or imagining this to be the case, is not easily taken in stride, and there may be formidable resistances on the part of training analysts to opening to, and thoughtfully engaging, how the analysis is being played out in public spaces. Moreover, in the communal realm, because the public behavior and interpersonal life of both analyst and analysand often become visible and known to the other in ways that both bypass the usual boundaries and alter the pacing of the analytic process, analysts and patients may forego participation in social events or professional meetings or, alternatively, they may attend but may find that their participation is encumbered by the anticipation, observation, or fantasies about the response of the analytic partner.

These social and extra-session professional contacts between candidates and their analysts, which, in many institutes, are common and more or less inevitable, are often charged and stimulating to both. Often they stir up longings and fantasies that prove hard to address in the consulting room. For example, how able are candidates to take up unflattering reports of their analysts as teachers or supervisors, or, for that matter, to fully analyze glowing reports, and how free are analysts to pursue issues or to explore social interactions or public events they have reason to believe are of concern to the candidate? If, for example, the analyst suspects the candidate's non-attendance at an institute party is due to the candidate's discomfort with crossing paths with the analyst, and if the analyst feels reluctant to forego attending future parties, how likely is it that this situation will be openly analyzed?

One effect of this state of affairs may be that training analysts will be reluctant to analyze certain expressions of candidates' characterological difficulties. Because, as in the above examples, analysts may feel both exposed and more than usually implicated in the current manifestations of the candidate's characterological problems, they may then feel anxious and inhibited, leading to a reluctance to be active and freely inquiring. The candidate's tendencies toward idealization, envy, submissiveness, competitiveness, and so on, as they are expressed in the transference, may become difficult to explore in an atmosphere where the analyst is concerned about burdening the patient. For example, the current expression of a candidate's self-denigration may follow a meeting in which the analyst was behaving in a way that in retrospect felt to the analyst as a bit exhibitionistic. The analyst may then refrain from exploring the candidate's self-denigration, feeling implicated in the candidate's negative self-feeling. All of this supports the idea that the narcissistic issues of training analysts can become especially problematic in the analyses of candidates.

Historically the training analysis evolved from a brief, didactic introduction to clinical theory and the workings of the unconscious, to a more fully therapeutic analysis. This shift reflected the influence of Ferenczi, who, in the 1920's, voiced concern that some patients seen in analysis were having a fuller and deeper analytic experience than had their analysts, who often felt limited in exploring issues their patients needed to take up (Dupont 1988; Ferenczi 1928; 1930). I believe that one enduring challenge to the therapeutic potential of the training analysis involves the ways in which the anxieties and narcissistic issues of training analysts can lead to managing rather than deeply engaging negative transference. The analyst's vulnerability to feeling too visible, or being ill thought of within the community and by the candidate, can lead to self-estrangement, constriction of participation and feeling, and the emergence of collusively affectionate alliances with analysands that tilt analyses in the direction of supportive or mutually admiring mentoring rather than open and rigorous character analysis. The training analyst who is insecure and inhibited in these ways, which all of us are to some degree, will undergo loneliness in the sense I have described because the analyst and analysand will know on some level that something avoidant and safe is pre-empting a more challenging, lively and potentially transformational experience.

My impression, from informal conversations with colleagues, is that training analysts are vulnerable to the feeling that their status and prestige may be linked with the standing, reputation and achievements of their analysands as these are recognized within the community and the field at large. One effect of this is to become overly concerned that analysands be seen as accomplished and characterologically sound. As a result analysts may not notice when analysands refrain from revealing their more disturbing symptoms and characterological impediments. Candidates may fear sharing the depth of their unrelatedness, their more troubled ideas, their feelings of fragmentation or panic, and their sense of incompetence regarding their work as analysts. And we, as training analysts, may be reluctant to face the implications of what emerges in the analysis. How do we feel if a therapeutic outcome involves the candidate's decision not to complete analytic training? While such a decision will inevitably be painful and conflicted, to what degree do we avoid facing this option out of concern for our own prestige? How free are we, in the presence of an audience of colleagues and students, to fully consider the range of choices faced by the candidate?

The tensions between the analytic and collegial/social dimensions of the training analysis play themselves out in complex ways. As noted above, in many, perhaps most, instances, the training analyst and candidate are members of the same institute. As such, they know many people in common, often quite intimately. They attend the same conferences and social gatherings and they may hold the same, often unspoken, anticipations and fantasies about a post-analytic continuation of their relationship (Tessman, 2003). In some cases analysands have the option to take classes taught by their analysts. When they choose not to, complex and conflicted processes play out regarding who will decide not to participate in the class, teacher or student. These transactions are difficult to analyze because both members of the dyad have multiple and often competing investments in the decision. Moreover, when analyst and candidate do interact in classes and meetings the interactions are publicly observed and may become topics of communal conversation that may filter their way back to the dyad. I have had the experience, with several analysands, of feeling like I'm part of a couple observed in intimate moments. In sum, it is common for both analyst and candidate to feel far less control and protection within a boundaried analytic space than is typically and optimally the case in analytic work.

The training analyst's loneliness is held within self- states associated with impaired analytic presence. Insofar as this is the case, we must consider the analyst's struggles to tolerate and render workable experiences of vulnerability and shame. The training analyst is expected to be a role model, the exemplar of what an analyst should be. The presence and visibility of ordinary needs, flaws and weaknesses and, even more, the emergence of what might feel like disquieting needs for affirmation, companionship, and love, can become sources of shame leading to suppression and selective inattention. The analysand is an analyst in training and is likely to be a sophisticated and sensitive observer and interpreter of the analyst's participation and person. The analyst may sense that the analysand *sees* and *knows*, especially when what is discerned remains unspoken, and collusive avoidances may dominate the analysis. In this context, we are reminded of Levenson's (1995) memories of his discomfort and caution when his analyst shared his own dreams in the analysis. Levenson invariably felt that his analyst revealed far more than he was intending and was aware of, and he learned to avoid responses to the dreams that he sensed would make his analyst anxious.

Training analysts are vulnerable in other ways as well. Few of us take on this role until our late 40s, at the earliest, and the majority of us are well into middle- age, and or beyond. The awareness of both members of the dyad of the aging analyst's physical vulnerabilities, health status, and mortality are potentially poignant and meaningful aspects of the work (Harris, 2011). Too often, though, these aspects of the analyst's vulnerability are not openly addressed. Likewise avoided or overlooked may be the analyst's envy of her younger, often more energetic and hopeful, analysand (Greenberg, 1991). How openly and freely can these feelings be accessed by the analyst or expressed by the analysand? How likely is it, rather, that they will be communicated to third parties, including the analysand's next analyst? A potentially rich source of feeling, empathy and mourning may be closed off, and the analysis may become watered down and constricted (Mendelsohn, 2002).

Training analysts, as skilled, admired, but often aging and vulnerable role models, need to maintain access to their own places of pain and hurt. Without this kind of self-connectedness on the part of analysts, analysands will remain cautious and avoidant, unwilling to see, process and analyze essential aspects of their analyst's participation (Mendelsohn, 1996; 2002; 2007). In a recent paper, Deutsch (2011) recalled her analyst's illness and death during the course of her analysis. In retrospect she felt there were signs of the analyst's declining health and compromised functioning that had been collusively avoided by the dyad.

I will close with reference to a current circumstance in my practice that is rife with the potential for loneliness. Recently my wife and I separated after nearly 30 years of marriage. A significant number of my patients are in the field, and many of these, as well as most of my supervisees, are candidates in training or recent graduates of institutes I am affiliated with. I have many close friendships, some spanning decades, with colleagues in these communities. As news of my separation was shared, first personally and eventually via word of mouth, it became possible and then inevitable that patients and supervisees would learn this news. I was aware of feeling exposed and wishing for privacy. Unlike at other times of heightened preoccupation and distress (Mendelsohn 1996; 2011), I felt disinclined to share my experience with patients and I felt, in this instance, considerable self-consciousness and doubt. While I was aware of a desire for companionship and comfort, and knew I could gather in some of that sense of sustenance through my clinical relationships, I also felt that the experience of separating was new and sensitive and its implications were yet to be defined. I was aware of concerns about what my patients would think of me and my choices, and of worries about the judgments, projections, and observations of colleagues. At times I wanted to insulate myself, seeking a protective separation between my personal and professional lives.

Despite this trepidation I decided to tell patients in the institute communities that my wife and I had separated. I rationalized this by reminding myself that these patients would inevitably, and perhaps quickly, hear this from third parties and might learn of this in circumstances that would feel disruptive and exposing, including being told in an offhand way by colleagues unaware of their work with me. I call this a rationalization because, while this may have represented a good reason to share this news, I knew I wanted to talk about this for other reasons as well, including my need to assure myself that my work as an analyst would survive and thrive in the context of a wished for but nonetheless disruptive and preoccupying change in my personal life. At the same time I was aware of feeling uncharacteristically apprehensive about where the work would go.

The exploration of the revelation of my separation in the work with analytic candidates and others in the field, (as well as with some patients not in the field) is a work in process. I worry that, to date, it is going too well, which is to say that my patients sense my discomfort and are giving me a wide berth. I further worry that, my concern not withstanding, I am often content to let this be the case. One example of this that has been noteworthy to me is that not one of my patients commented when I stopped wearing an oft noticed wedding ring. The ring and my married state had figured centrally in many therapies but this change was not brought up by any of my analysands. Of course this also meant that in no instance did I raise questions about the absence of comments; to do so would have invited inquiry into an area I wished to avoid. Moreover, when I told patients about the separation, and added that it was striking to me that I hadn't worn a wedding ring for a year and neither of us had said anything about it, every patient said that he or she was stunned; no one had noticed. I had assumed that at least some patients had seen but had decided not to say anything, either wanting to respect my privacy or not wanting to provoke my anxiety. That no one had noticed suggested that patients were honoring my need for boundaried separateness. And this message was being sent and received without it emerging into awareness for either of us.

All of what I have just sketched out is, in varying ways and to varying degrees, now part of the explicit inquiry in my work with many patients, including with several candidates in training. At the same time, I suspect that elements of shared avoidance, really a mutual loneliness, still remain to be fleshed out and engaged.

In closing, I want to make clear that my effort in this paper has not been to argue that training analysts are more lonely than others who do analytic work, but rather that there are aspects of the training analyst role and relationship that engender loneliness in the analyst and, likely, in the analysand as well. While I recognize that I have highlighted an array of challenging structural and dynamic factors in the training analysis, it is my hope that identifying and thinking about these will help us address and diminish the loneliness that can shape the experience of analytic work, particularly in the culture of analytic institutes. After all, recognizing, facing and exploring realms of shared difficulty have always been at the heart of analytic work. It remains the task of a future paper to consider the opportunities for deep analytic engagement and for facilitation of the candidate's growth that can emerge in the training analysis.

References

Arlow, J. A. (1982). Psychoanalytic education: A psychoanalytic perspective. *Annual of Psychoanalysis* 10:5–20.

Balint, M. (1954). Analytic training and training analysis. *International Journal of Psycho-Analysis* 35:157–62.

Bibring, G. L. (1954). The training analysis and its place in psychoanalytic training. *International Journal of Psycho-Analysis* 35:169–73.

Buechler, S. (1998). The analyst's experience of loneliness. *Contemporary Psychoanalysis* 34 91–113.

Deutsch, R. (2011). A voice lost, a voice found: After the death of the analyst. *Psychoanalytic Inquiry* 31:526–35.

Dupont, J. (1988). *The Clinical Diary of Sandor Ferenczi.* Cambridge: Harvard University Press.

Ehrenberg, D. (1992). *The Intimate Edge.* New York: W.W. Norton.

Ferenczi, S. (1928). The elasticity of psycho-analytic technique. In: *Final Contributions to the Problems and Methods of Psycho-Analysis,* ed. M.Balint. New York: Brunner/Mazel, pp. 87–101.

———— (1930). The principles of relaxation and neocatharsis. In: *Final Contributions to the Problems and Methods of Psycho-Analysis,* ed. M Balint. New York: Brunner/Mazel, pp. 108–125.

Fromm-Reichmann, F. (1958/1990). Loneliness. *Contemporary Psychoanalysis* 26:305–29.

Greenberg, J. (1991). Countertransference and reality. *Psychoanalytic Dialogues* 1:52–73.

Harris, A. (2011). Discussion of Robin Deutcsh's, A voice lost, a voice found: After the death of the analyst. *Psychoanalytic Inquiry* 31:536–42.

Hirsch, I. (2008), *Coasting in the Countertransference.* Hillsdale, NJ: The Analytic Press.

Hoffman I, (1998). *Ritual and Spontaneity in the Psychoanalytic Process.* Hillsdale, NJ: The Analytic Press.

Lavendar, J. (2011), The phenomenology of the relational void: Probabilities and Possibilities. In: *Loneliness and Longing: Conscious and Unconscious Aspects.* eds. B. Willock, L.C. Bohm, and R.C. Curtis. New York: Routledge, pp. 121–34.

Levenson, E. A. (1995), Introduction. In: *Pioneers of Interpersonal Psychoanalysis,* eds. D.B. Stern, C.H. Mann, S. Kantor, & G. Schlesinger. Hillsdale, NJ: The Analytic Press, pp. 111–113.

Maroda, K. J. (1991). *The Power of Countertransference.* Northvale NJ: The Analytic Press.

Maroda, K. J. (2005). Legitimate gratification of the patient's needs. *Contemporary Psychoanalysis* 41:371–88.

Mendelsohn, E. (1996). More human than otherwise: Working through a time of Preoccupation and mourning. In: *The Therapist as a Person: Life Choices, Life Experiences and Their Effects on Treatment*, eds. B. Gerson, Hillsdale, NJ: The Analytic Press, pp. 21–40.

———— (2002). The analyst's bad-enough participation. *Psychoanalytic Dialogues* 12: 331–358.

———— (2005). Rules were made to be broken: Reflections on psychoanalytic education and clinical process. *Psychoanalytic Psychology* 22:261–278.

———— (2007). Analytic love: Possibilities and limitations. *Psychoanalytic Inquiry* 27:219–245.

———— (2011). The not-me and the loving self. *Psychoanalytic Perspectives* 8:62–71.

Mendelson, M. (1990). Reflections on loneliness. *Contemporary Psychoanalysis* 26:330–55.

Schafer, R. (1995). Aloneness in the countertransference. *Psychoanalytic Quarterly* 64:496–516.

Slochower, J. (1996). *Holding and Psychoanalysis: A Relational Perspective.* Hillsdale, NJ: The Analytic Press.

Sullivan, H. S. (1953). *The Interpersonal Theory of Psychiatry.* New York: W.W.Norton.

Tessman, L. (2003). *The Analyst's Analyst Within.* London: Taylor and Francis.

Wilner, W. (1998). Experience, metaphor and the crucial nature of the analyst's expressive participation. *Contemporary Psychoanalysis* 34:413–443.

Chapter 13
There Is No Place Like Home
Sandra Buechler

Abstract:

Like Dorothy in the story of *The Wonderful Wizard of Oz,* the lonely analyst yearns for home. For us, home can be an internal haven, furnished with relatively benign supervisory and other objects. This "internal chorus" can modulate our more painful and alienating clinical experiences. Along with an example of an internalized supervisory object, this paper suggests ways institutes can become more welcoming homes for candidates and graduates.

Shortly after we first meet Dorothy, whose adventure will bring her to the Wizard of Oz, she is threatened with the loss of her beloved dog, Toto. As his name implies, Toto means everything to Dorothy. His innocent mischief has evoked a mean neighbor's wrath. Dorothy pleads with her Aunty Em to no avail. Toto is banished. Her fate inextricably linked to Toto's, Dorothy, too, temporarily loses her home. I have always suspected that it isn't the first time, for why is Dorothy living with her aunt, and not her mother? Dorothy has been displaced before and is about to rediscover both the joys and terrors of being a stranger in a strange land. As Winnicott wisely emphasized, fateful experiences are often recurrences, in some sense. Dorothy's adventure teaches her valuable lessons, about faith, courage, wisdom, and compassion, about recognizing her own powers and authority, but most of all, I would say, about home. Here is how Dorothy, herself, puts it (p. 42). "No matter how dreary and gray our homes are, we people of flesh and blood would rather live there than in any other country, be it ever so beautiful. There is no place like home."

When we long for home are we really trying to recapture a state of mind, which our imagination has connected with a place? Dorothy is quick to admit that Kansas's actual charms do not account for the strength of her attachment. Similarly, I doubt that Proust would argue that the madeleine is all that special, as cookies go.

In this paper I will suggest a relationship between a state of profound loneliness and a restless yearning for a home. I will also comment on the yearning for an analytic home as I have personally experienced it, and as I believe it has played out in the professional lives of many other analysts.

I believe we have all known moments of exquisite loneliness, and yet it continues to be difficult for human beings to describe. However formulated or unformulated they may be, I think our own theories of what most counts in life shape our understanding of loneliness. Analysts are not alone in trying to penetrate the mystery of the source of its sting. Poets and portraitists have also probed it, along with Biblical scholars who study Job's abandonment by God, and fiction writers, like Dostoevsky, whose Underground Man howls with the lonely pain of feeling utterly rejected by society.

213

What, exactly, is loneliness, and how does it differ from a productive aloneness that may be sought? In previous papers (1998, 2012) I tried to name the cause of the lonely person's suffering. Frieda Fromm-Reichmann (1959) gave me the idea that the lonely person most misses faith that she will connect with others in the future. As we might expect, reading Sullivan (1953) convinced me that the problem with loneliness is its inherent insecurity. My favorite poet, Rilke, (1934) seems to me to suggest that loneliness is an inevitable part of life, made profoundly painful by setting one's will against it. Rollo May (1953) writes of loneliness as a threat to the sense of self. Because we need human relations to orient and know ourselves, loneliness endangers our sense of being ourselves. All of these ideas are useful, but it is Winnicott's (1958) understanding of loneliness that most speaks to me. In his paper on (p. 32) the capacity to be alone he tells us what is required for us to be comfortable while alone.

> The relationship of the individual to his or her internal objects, along with confidence in regard to internal relationships, provides of itself a sufficiency of living, so that temporarily he or she is able to rest contented even in the absence of external objects and stimuli.

In other words, the feel of aloneness depends on whom we are with, internally, when we are alone. A general absence of persecutory inner objects can create the relatively benign internal atmosphere, where, for a time, we can rest content. This idea led me to consider how the analyst can best live potentially lonely moments in her work. I came to believe that each of us develops a kind of internal chorus of the voices of those who have taught us. Some days I may rely on an internal conversation with my former training analyst in one session with a patient, while in another hour I may call on someone else. But this can only work if my internalized relationships with these wise elders are primarily positive and nurturing.

The internal chorus we bring to the office every day must be of comfort, and sufficiently stimulating, to encourage the creative use of aloneness. The feeling the chorus must give us is that whatever may go on today, with this patient, does not define us as analysts, for we have already defined ourselves, through our analytic identifications. We are not entirely personally and professionally at stake in each session. With this foundation we can experience aloneness with a patient as information, rather than as condemnation, either of us or of the relationship. We can turn the aloneness over in our minds, wonder what it is about, become curious about it, and see it as meaningful, as something to understand, but not as an obstacle or an indictment. An aloneness that doesn't cost us a good connection with ourselves, with our chorus, can be used creatively. A creatively used aloneness is not loneliness.

Thus, training has the potential to create, in each of us, a kind of internalized "home base," where we can refuel. For me, personally, when I feel horribly lost in a treatment I might hear my first analytic supervisor, Ralph Crowley, patiently asking me something like, "Now Sandy, let's look at what you do know about the patient." Ralph is an indelible part of my internal chorus. I am sure that, without him, the last three decades of my professional experience would have felt much lonelier.

My Kansas, then, is an internal state of mind that allows me to feel relatively at home in my work. Like Dorothy, I spend some hours in strange places, with people I hardly recognize as similar to myself. They are looking for their hearts, minds, courage, and I am trying to help them in their journeys. As I do this, I am also having my own adventure. Many years ago, in an effort to better myself as a poet, I took a course in the metaphor. I am not sure it helped me write poetry, but it has definitely informed me as an analyst. The course suggested that, in conceiving metaphors, we must look for the strange in the familiar, and the familiar in the strange. This idea has been of great use to me in my work. Entering the idiom of a patient's world, I think it is part of my job to recognize what is understandable to me, from my own experience. What seems utterly strange, at first, may become more familiar. But, at the same time, I need to understand that in some areas I may be taking it too much for granted that we are alike. It may take time for me to grasp the ways we look alike but actually think and feel differently. The seemingly familiar needs to become strange. In each session, in a way, I accompany someone in his journey to discover in himself a quality he needs, in order to fully live. At the same time, I am on my own voyage of self-discovery. But, in order to be only tolerably lonely, I must bring a few teddy bears along, to remind me of home. Dorothy never forgot Kansas. It was the home that was waiting for her. I believe that turned her loneliness in strange countries into a bearable, and sometimes enjoyable challenge.

For me, personally, a session's rote, mechanical quality is especially likely to leave me feeling painfully cut off from the warmth of the hearth. What brings me this far from home? There can be many paths. Our profession often places us in lonely positions, although we are not literally alone. We are frequently the only one who knows what we know about the patient. We can share our knowledge with no one outside the treatment, sometimes for reasons of confidentiality, sometimes out of our own self-protection. This isolation can often feel permanent. Our focus is mainly on someone else, so we have lost the centeredness that might provide ballast. At times, we don't even have ourselves to turn to, since, with certain patients, we don't feel like ourselves. Vicariously we may be experiencing trauma, but we may not be able to give ourselves any decent interval to recover, as the buzzer sounds for the next appointment and, like good Pavlovian subjects, we do what is expected of us, and go on to the next person.

215

Elsewhere (2012) I have expressed how our earliest professional experiences can have a profound impact on the whole of our careers. Here I will try to describe what I think of as the loneliest experience of my career so far, the time I felt furthest from home. When I was in my early thirties, well before my analytic training, part of my job was to consult to the nurses in a very large hospital for severely impaired children. Looking back, I would say that every hour in that setting put me close to the edge of trauma, in Freud's sense of the word. My understanding is that Freud saw as traumatic any situation that threatens to overwhelm the ego. What was overwhelming was less important in this definition than the sense of almost being overcome. Moments that stand out for me include the first time I entered a ward of hydrocephalic babies, their heads taking up much of the surface of their cribs. I don't remember this, but I imagine I had to stifle shock, prioritizing looking as though I could "handle" my feelings. Of course I am aware that this speaks to who I already was by the time I had these encounters. My own personal life experience, and my character issues, shaped my responses to these settings. But I believe the professional situations privileged certain potentials in me over others. I think my tendencies toward schizoid functioning were especially nurtured and, in a sense, rewarded. I learned to "get through" the day. I gave myself what I remember calling my "marching orders."

Each time I went out on the children's ward I told myself that I would try to make eye contact with each patient. When I entered the ward of children strapped to their chairs (ostensibly because of their self-mutilating behavior) who struggled to find a way to greet me despite being tied down, I was determined to recognize the particular human being in each child, in some way. I tried to give each a brief nod, or some kind of verbal response. Consciously, I wanted to give each a sense of still being respected as individuals, with personhood. Retrospectively I see myself as willing Sandra forward, giving her a nearly impossible (but wholly absorbing) task. Looking at each child kept me going. I was fighting my own pull to drown in misery. I was willing myself to differentiate them, bull-headedly refusing to blur them. Some of them, perhaps just as fierce as I, found a way to rock their chairs forward, to get closer to me. I was determined to meet their stubborn will with my own. They were bound to chairs. I was bound to a self-imposed resolution.

What was the short- and long-term impact of these experiences? What did I take away, about life, about myself as a person and clinician? At the time, I think what impressed me most was how close I felt to being unable to cope. My own insufficiencies were more palpable to me than my strengths. My ability to bear each hour felt tenuous. The nurses and aides seemed a lot less fragile than I felt myself to be. Most frequently, I think I felt insufficient, or, at best, barely sufficient. On good days, I could get through without crying, without retreating to the bathroom, without giving up on my goal to recognize each person. But I felt this was a "minimalist" goal, and even that was a stretch for me, most of the time. I compared myself with someone stronger, who could aim for more than I could. I don't think this more competent "other" was any particular person, but just a mythical better version of me.

Long-term I think, first of all, my schizoid tendencies to push forward, no matter what, were further etched into my character. Also fostered were some obsessive defenses. I remember dividing up the day, in my mind, and figuring ways to get through each portion. I think continuously living this close to the edge of what I could bear reinforced tendencies already well established in me. One way to see this is that, while I entered the profession already equipped with a personal schizoid/obsessive coping style, these early experiences fostered a variation on the theme. Now I had a template for "getting through" 8-hour shifts, as well as "getting through" more personal experiences.

My impression is that my sense of inadequacy in these work situations was more vivid to me than any feeling of strength. And what I felt was a profound loneliness. This Oz was just too strange, and I was too far away from any internalized Kansas. Returning to Winnicott's statement, I would say about myself in this setting that my internal objects were not sufficiently supportive to sustain me in such a harsh, bleak surround. Wherever I turned, both internally and externally, I didn't find the comforts of home.

Looking back, I think these feelings played a role in my decision to train as an analyst. I wanted to feel I could do more than just survive each day. I wanted a home base, from which I could have tolerably strange adventures. I yearned for a greater security, for a sense of professional identity, for a belief that I had a way of approaching doing treatment. Not the way, but a way. I wanted to feel more furnished. Less lonely. More at home. Some of those needs got met, at least in part.

As for the yearning for an analytic home, I have a suggestion that is especially geared toward younger analysts and candidates. You can do better than we have done, to create a community that respects, and even celebrates differences of all kinds. Particularly in this time, when our field can't afford waste, you can watch out for colleagues who may be in danger of being labeled "non-analytic" for their differences of opinion, as Bowlby, Sullivan, and many others have been. I believe that the greatest danger we face, as a field, is our own tendencies toward elitism, and its consequences.

In 2009 I edited a special issue of *Contemporary Psychoanalysis,* dedicated to exploring analysts' beliefs about training. Aware of how limited a sample I was able to survey, nevertheless I wanted to ask analysts from different countries and generations what they thought ideal training, and ideal institutes would look like. I now understand their answers to mean that institutes need to be better professional homes, where neighbors want to drop in, and family wants to return for a visit. But what changes would be necessary to create a community of professional homes? Here are just a few quotes.

(1) Peggy Crastnopol (2009, p. 361) in her paper about institute life beyond graduation, wrote that we should feel comfortable relying on our institutes for our lifelong clinical development. In her words, "If we can set this tone, our institutes will gain new meaning as potential centers for mutual nurturance, stimulation, and enrichment throughout our professional lives."

(2) Polly Young-Eisendrath (2009, p. 363) described a "resonant emotional climate, an interpersonal environment in which people are not propelled into an overwhelming fight or flight reaction as a result of emotional threat." She describes the leadership styles that curtail creativity, dialogue, inquiry, and openness. Most poignantly, for me, she writes (p. 364) of her own withdrawal from involvement in institutes. ". . . I have kept my distance from psychoanalytic politics and institutes. This distance has cost me- I am often either relatively unknown or misunderstood among my colleagues. But it has protected me from being emotionally burdened, or even destroyed, by the meanness and brutality of institute politics, flavored by the hermeneutics of suspicion."

(3) Finally, in her essay on changes she thinks need to happen in our institutes, Donna Orange (2009, p. 354) writes of being inspired by, among others, Robert Fuller, "who imagines dignitarian worlds replacing somebody-nobody hierarchies of domination, submission, bullying, and humiliation. . . ."

To close, what I want to express, particularly to those not yet in power, or just coming in to positions of influence in institutes is that you can do better than my generation has done, to create analytic homes, where colleagues feel enough security to try out new ideas, without the threat of being cast out, stigmatized, or humiliated in any way. Each of us can have a positive impact in our own institutes simply by vowing that, to borrow a phrase, if we see something, we will say something. That is, if, at a meeting, in a class, or in any context, we feel that a colleague is being treated badly, we will stand up and say something. We will not be cowed by a fear of shame or retribution. I grant that this may not be a good career move, in the short run. But in the long run it will help us become the best clinical instruments, and human beings, that we can be. I believe that to become capable analysts we need to cultivate just that kind of courage in ourselves. So I end this paper with three thoughts. First, we all yearn for a home, where we feel less lonely because we know we are fundamentally accepted and safe. Second, the next generations can do better, to create a respectful community of analytic homes. Third, there is nothing that can substitute for such an environment, in other words, there is no place like home.

References

Baum, L.F. (1900). *The Wonderful Wizard of Oz.* Chicago: George M. Hill.

Buechler, S. (1998). The analyst's experience of loneliness. *Contemporary Psychoanalysis* 34:91–115.

Buechler, S. (Ed.). (2009). Special issue on the ideal psychoanalytic institute. *Contemporary Psychoanalysis* 45.

———— . (2012*). Still Practicing: The Heartaches and Joys of a Clinical Career.* New York: Routledge.

Crastnopol, M. (2009). Institute life beyond graduation. *Contemporary Psychoanalysis 45:* :358–363.

Fromm-Reichmann, F. (1959). Loneliness. *Psychiatry* 22:1–15.

May, R. (1953). *Man's Search for Himself.* New York: W.W. Norton.

Orange, D.M. (2009). A psychoanalytic colloquium. *Contemporary Psychoanalysis* 45:353–358.

Rilke, R.M. (1934). *Letters to a Young Poet.* New York: W.W. Norton.

Sullivan, H.S. (1953). *The Interpersonal Theory of Psychiatry.* New York: W.W. Norton.

Young-Eisendrath, P. (2009). Psychoanalysis as inquiry and discovery, not suspicion. *Contemporary Psychoanalysis* 45:63–370.

Winnicott, D.W. (1958). The capacity to be alone. In: *The Maturational Process and the Facilitating Environment.* Madison, CT: International Universities Press, 1965.

Section IV—Loneliness/Solitude In life's events

Section IV—Describes loneliness as it appears in certain life circumstances: the life cycle itself, widowhood, and life in the armed service. Beginning with Chapter Fourteen, "Loneliness and the Life Cycle," Brent Willock examines the importance of loneliness with the biopsychosocial factors that progress through Erikson's conception of the life cycle. Willock wonders how this theoretical structure accounts for both the configurations of personality and psychopathology. His inquiry takes him further into the question of how emotional/relational configurations in each phase account for the ongoing state of longing and loneliness.

In Chapter Fifteen, Alma Halbert Bond captures "Marilyn Monroe, the Loneliest Person on Earth." Born to a woman suffering from schizophrenia and a father she never got to meet, Marilyn Monroe was "the most famous movie star in the world; the sex goddess whose image virtually spawned an industry" (Rangell, 2004, p. 117). On August 5, 1962 she committed suicide.

Bond asks us: Is glitter and fame ever an antidote for the tragically empty life that loneliness can bring?

The treatment approach offered by Marianne Kris in New York and Ralph Greenson in Los Angeles asks additional questions about the treatment for individuals considered to have deep disturbances that fall within the "widening scope" (Stone, 1954). Should boundaries/parameters (Eissler, 1953) be considered? How should the transference be handled?

Patsy Turrini turns our attention to the loss of a spouse in Chapter Sixteen, "The Death of the Loved Spouse, the Inner World of Grief: A Psychoanalytic   Developmental Perspective. " For Turrini, when you have an essential other, whether in development or as a partner, you are protected from the terror of loneliness. Freud (1926), she notes, showed that the essential other could be experienced as longed for but not despaired of. With desperation enters loneliness. The essential other protects the self from feeling lonely. What protection is needed depends upon what the self confronts in the early developmental years, culminating in the Oedipal phase. The early experiences of mother as a "safe haven" are part of the essential quality in the adult's object-related capacity and wishes. These cultivate later partner selection. Those cared for well-enough are prepared to seek a "good enough" partner who provides affection and security. Turrini concludes that painful normal mourning in adulthood can be partly understood in light of early painful losses and the emergence of the self, which in the loss of a loved one jeopardizes the sense of being. This section raises some interesting questions:

What is the torment of grief and what will end it?
How does one cope with the loss of a loved spouse or partner?
How does this loss differ from the loss of a sibling or close friend?
How does one's sense of identity filter loneliness?

Section IV concludes with a rare view into the world of a soldier. Goldenberg and Nathan Szajnberg present "A Soldier's Loneliness" in Chapter Seventeen. They explore how a soldier can experience loneliness, solitude and aloneness when surrounded by peers and faced with enemies. The story of three soldiers from an elite combat unit is presented. From their experiences, we learn about the continuum of loneliness and how one's pre-soldier inner life affects these critical moments which are reflected in an ambivalence even with one's firearm. Listen to the soldier's themselves in this chapter and see how Goldenberg and Szajnberg organize these stories.

How can one feel "lonely" when one is rarely alone?

Does one always feel lonely in the same way, or for the same reasons?

What strategies did these men choose to cope within the various states of loneliness, without the aid of a therapist?

What happens when loneliness combines with other unpleasant affects (e.g., sadness, boredom, anger) or conflicting affects (e.g., sense of duty or sense of desire)?

References

Eissler, K.R. (1953). The Effect of the Structure of the Ego on Psychoanalytic Technique *Journal of the American Psychoanalytic Association* 1:104–143.

Freud, S. (1926). Inhibitions, Symptoms and Anxiety. S*tandard Edition* 20:77–174, 1959.

Stone, L. (1954). The Widening Scope of Indications for Psychoanalysis. *Journal of the American Psychoanalytic Association* 2:567–594.

Chapter 14
Loneliness and the Life Cycle
Brent Willock

Abstract:

This contribution examines the importance of loneliness throughout the biopsychosocial course of life that Erik Erikson delineated. The significance of loneliness is further discussed in relation to the two primary configurations of personality and psychopathology described by Blatt (2008) in relation to that life cycle. It is argued that loneliness and longing is such a crucial emotional/relational constellation that it pervades each stage of the life cycle and even transcends the related, significant distinctions that Blatt and his coworkers have made between those whose personality and/or pathology focuses around relatedness versus self-definition.

Introduction

In previous writing (Willock, 2012 a, b) on the topic of loneliness and longing, I stated that this subject has received less attention in the psychoanalytic literature than one might have expected. I suggested that this emotional constellation merits a more prominent place in theory, clinical formulation, and practice. Those contributions demonstrated that loneliness and yearning are implicitly at the heart of the key constructs of most schools of analytic thought, implicitly. For example, their salience can readily be detected in Freud's oedipus complex, Klein's paranoid and depressive positions, and core ideas of the British Object Relations school, including Guntrip's schizoid position, Winnicott's 'incommunicado self' that is 'an isolate,' and attachment theory. In order to be able to reach our patients in their conscious and unconscious states of aloneness, I advocated for a comparative-integrative approach (Willock, 2007) that encourages clinicians to draw on the best insights from all psychoanalytic schools. This chapter extends the thinking in those contributions on the importance of loneliness by focusing on its significance throughout the life cycle.

Erikson and Beyond

When psychoanalysts contemplate the course of life, Erik Erikson's (e.g., 1950, 1959) seminal work in this area immediately comes to mind. The first few psychosocial stages he delineated correspond closely to Freud's psychosexual developmental line. In Freud's particular focus, development culminates during adolescence when, in fortunate circumstances, the genital character

227

is consolidated. Erikson, like Jung, extended Freud's contribution, devoting equal attention to challenges that arise during later phases in the life cycle.

Erikson's inaugural stage concerns the establishment of Basic Trust versus Mistrust (Freud's oral phase). This foundational era is followed by a focus on Autonomy versus Shame and Doubt (anal stage), then Initiative versus Guilt (phallic-urethral stage), Industry versus Inferiority (latency), Identity versus Role Diffusion (adolescence), Intimacy versus Isolation (young adulthood), Generativity versus Stagnation (middle age) and, finally, Integrity versus Despair (old age).

Blatt & Shichman (1983) provided a very interesting elaboration on Erikson's framework. Into his eight stages, they believed it necessary to insert one more. Their Mutuality versus Alienation (oedipal) fits nicely between Erikson's Initiative versus Guilt and his Industry versus Inferiority, that is, between the phallic-urethral stage and latency. Mutuality vs. Alienation is phase dominant from about four to six years of age. At that time, initial resolution of the oedipal crisis is underway and cooperative peer play commences. At home and in the world, a collective sense of "we" begins to compete with a more individualistic "I."

With this modification, they point out, Erikson's epigenetic model neatly illustrates a developmental process that alternates between two essential dimensions of psychic life, namely, relatedness and self-definition. Some of Erikson's stages focus on relatedness. In others, self-definition is central. These twin thrusts co-create an essential developmental dialectic throughout life. Healthy personality maturation involves the ongoing, mutually facilitating development of these two variables.

As individuals advance through life, Blatt & Shichman demonstrated that they cycle between these two foci in a recurring, one-two pattern. Infants are centered on relatedness (Trust/Mistrust). Growing toddlers emphasize self-definition (Autonomy/Shame/Doubt), followed by a second self-definitional stage (Initiative/Guilt). Oedipal children shift back to relatedness (Mutuality/Alienation). As youngsters progress through latency and adolescence, they embark on two more self-definitional stages (Industry/Inferiority, then Identity/Role Diffusion). Young adults return to relatedness (Intimacy/Isolation). Advancing through middle age to senior citizenship, we traverse two more self-definitional stages (Generativity/Stagnation and Integrity/Despair).

Evolving capacities along these two developmental lines are coordinated and mutually facilitative. For example, if one is fortunate enough to have established a solid sense of basic trust (relatedness) in life's initial stage, one is much better equipped to assert autonomy (self-definition), in opposition to primary objects, in the subsequent stage. That Autonomy and the ensuing Initiative (both self-definitional) stand one in good stead, providing self-confidence that facilitates collaborative relationships with others in the next

228

relational stage, Mutuality vs. Alienation. And so it goes, in a mutually enhancing manner, to the end of time.

Interacting throughout the life cycle, these two tracks are more independent in the beginning. Around six years of age, when children become capable of concrete operational thought (Piaget, 1955), these agendas are more easily integrated. This cognitive advance corresponds to the shift from dyadic to triadic object relations. Thinking is no longer so immediate, direct, literal, and restricted to simple contrasts that characterize dyadic relationships (such as pleasure-pain or issues of power, control, and autonomy). Youngsters can now reflect upon and contrast the types of relationship they have with each parent and that their parents have with each other. Greater blending of individuality and relatedness accompanies resolution of the oedipal crisis. Children understand themselves increasingly as both separate and part of something larger. They now have not just an ego, but also a 'wego' (Blatt & Blass, 1990).

Emergence of formal operational thought in adolescence facilitates further coordination of these developmental lines. The sense of individuality resulting from the acquisition of autonomy, initiative, and industry is now paired with growing desire to participate in social groups based upon prior establishment of trust, mutuality and cooperation. One appreciates what one has to both contribute to, and gain from, participation in the collective, unencumbered by excessive fears of losing individuality and values. Integration of self-definition and relatedness becomes ever more sophisticated as one works one's way through the challenges of later life cycle stages.

Blatt's work is congruent with Slavin & Kriegman's (1992) valuable contribution, that which showed how the adaptive design of the human psyche requires both individualistic and collectivist elements. The work of those self psychologists, and Blatt and Shichman, two ego psychologists, has much in common with Mitchell's (1988) relational-conflict model (independence vs. relationship). Blatt's double helix image graphically captures the intimate interplay between the two core, complementary motives all these theorists from such diverse schools of thought have emphasized. Their twin spiral simultaneously suggests that this dualistic design of the mind is of such fundamental importance that it has been built right into our DNA.

Loneliness and Relatedness

Although loneliness, aloneness, and longings were not the focus of either Erikson or Blatt & Shichman, or any of the above- cited authors, it is enlightening and useful to examine the life cycle in terms of those important emotions. This affective constellation's relevance is easy to discern in stages that are primarily concerned with relatedness. For example, if one's resolution of the first opposition, Trust versus Mistrust, lies closer to the mistrustful, paranoid, hypervigilant side of this dimension, one will be isolated, alone, and lonely. If one's anxieties are especially severe in this area, and one's defenses are consequently primitive and rigid, one's loneliness may be largely unconscious, masked by a guarded, aggressive, action-ready stance.

Other frequent outcomes of this first phase of life are characterized by more conscious, depressive loneliness. For example, weaning frequently gives rise to a "sense of basic loss," as Erikson (1959) notes:

> A drastic loss of accustomed mother love without proper substitution at this time can lead (under otherwise aggravating conditions) to acute infantile depression (Spitz, 1945) or to a mild but chronic state of mourning which may give a depressive undertone to the whole remainder of life. But even under more favorable circumstances, this stage seems to introduce into the psychic life a sense of division and a dim but universal nostalgia for a lost paradise. (p.60).

The salience of loneliness and yearning, though not stated in those words, is abundantly clear in Erikson's description.

Always attuned to the environment, Erikson notes that parenthood can be a desperately lonely time (p.64). Loss of previous relationships and milieus (work, social life) can contribute to this state of mind, especially for young mothers who are not blessed with good extended family support for reasons of geographical and/or emotional distance. Parents struggling with isolation and yearning, consciously or otherwise, may not provide optimally attuned caring for their offspring. Struggling with their own dysphoria, such parents may be emotionally remote and/or dismissive, fostering feelings of emptiness, loneliness, frustration and futility in their children. Other parents may try to combat their loneliness by inappropriate closeness with their children. With such caregivers, youngsters may feel smothered, guilty about their wishes for independence, longing for their parents to be more attuned to their needs.

In the second relatedness stage (oedipal), likewise, if one's resolution is toward Alienation rather than Mutuality, one may feel like an envious outsider with respect to parents and/or peers. Accompanying this loneliness and yearning, freighted with a sense of injustice and anger, can cast a lifelong shadow darkening everyday experience. One may feel like a perpetual loser, excluded from the sunshine and relational happiness everyone else seems able to locate.

In the third stage of relatedness, the young adulthood period characterized by Intimacy versus Isolation, the relevance of loneliness is again apparent. It is surely not coincidental that at this age, many individuals who at this age are having difficulties securing stable, rewarding, intimate relationships succumb to major psychiatric disorders. If one feels dangerously isolated from longed for human intimacy, one may resort to extreme measures to foster some sense of, at least, pseudo- aliveness, if not actual relatedness (e.g., addiction to por-

230

nography, promiscuity, perversion, drugs, self-cutting). These symptomatic behaviors may also entail considerable anger related to seemingly hopeless yearnings.

"A strong egoism is a protection against falling ill, but in the last resort we must begin to love in order not to fall ill, and we are bound to fall ill if, in consequence of frustration, we are unable to love" (Freud, 1914, p.85). Here Freud, like Blatt & Schichman, contrasted relatedness and self-definition (a strong egoism). At the same time, like me, he drew attention to the opposite destinies of love/health versus loneliness/illness. The polarity he Freud emphasized becomes very important during Erikson's stage of Intimacy versus Isolation. At that time, young adults try to further shift their primary thrust from family of origin, with its assets and liabilities, toward new, equally important, libidinal relationships. In this journey, they continue the weaning process (or trauma) that Erikson noted in the first stage of life. Against that possible loneliness, they hope Eros will enable them to enter a new version of the symbiotic paradise they lost long ago. (In keeping with the symbiotic spirit, Freud said of Eros that the core of his being, his purpose, is "making one out of more than one" [1930, p.108].) Many find that heavenly romantic state elusive. Their frustrated desires leave them languishing in lonely yearning. In that gap between the wished for and the real, psychiatric disorder can find fertile soil, as Freud said.

In sum, for those whose personality is primarily organized around issues pertaining to the relatedness phases of the life cycle (basic trust, mutuality, intimacy), loneliness and longing are central concerns and potential dangers. These affective themes may manifest in their lives positively or negatively, in states of health and/or dis-ease.

Yin and Yang

Blatt & Shichman believed individuals focused on relatedness encounter problems that differ from those who concentrate more on self-definition. As illustrated in the previous section, loneliness is a central issue for those whose difficulties pertain mostly to relatedness. I will now attempt to demonstrate that loneliness and longing are also very important for those whose concerns center more on self-definition.

The ancient Chinese circular symbol commonly referred to as yin and yang suggests that dichotomies are not absolute. On the black half of the paisley-shaped boundary, there is a small circle of light. Similarly, on the white side, there is a small area of darkness. This figure suggests that the binary terms in a dialectic contain elements that hint at the possibility of synthesis. I explored these ideas in my book, *Comparative-Integrative Psychoanalysis.* This dialectical understanding helps us keep in mind that even individuals highly focused on relationships will nonetheless still have some concerns

231

about self-definition, even if these may be buried under the weight of their relational focus. Likewise, personalities centered on self-definition will also have some concerns for relationships, even though these may be masked by their sometimes near addiction to matters of identity.

The first self-definitional phase, known as Autonomy versus Shame and Doubt, is highly concerned with I-dentity. Both sides of the opposition are, however, actually quite relational. The need to establish autonomy requires what self psychologists refer to as adversarial objects. For toddlers to develop a separate sense of self, they need someone to push up against, someone to whom they can say "No." The relational oppositionality of this stage is often sufficiently strong to merit the moniker, "terrible twos."

Personal anecdotes can be highly illustrative. My three-year-old grand-niece, Margot, took pride in her increasing ability to look after herself. When she would arrive at day care, her teachers typically undid her jacket, intending to hang it up, thereby facilitating her getting into the day's activities. Slightly miffed, Margot would always insist on doing up all the buttons on her coat that her teacher had just undone. She then undid each fastener by herself. Finally, she removed her outer garment. Margot's antipathy toward these uninvited adult interventions morphed into satisfaction with her own competent performance. She needed to resist anyone who interfered with her consolidating independence, no matter how well- intentioned they were. Clearly autonomy was VIP at this point in Margot's life.

One day when I was walking with Margot, she informed me that, "Small children should hold someone's hand when crossing the street." Taking her sensible statement as a not so subtle hint, I extended my hand. She was not interested. Standing about two feet tall, she informed me that, "I'm a big girl now." Here one senses an apparent conflict between trusting relatedness and independence. In this instance, the latter desire obviously gained the upper hand. My own hand was no longer wanted.

When Margot rebuffed my reaching out to her, I was surprised. I felt slightly rejected, a tad lonely. It was a pleasure to be accompanying her to the park, and I had additionally appreciated the trusting, relational overture she seemed to have been making in her initial statement about how small children should hold someone's hand when traversing roads. I was less enamored when she drew the boundary between dependent small children and independent big girls in such a way that she was ensconced in the inner circle of maturity and competence while I was on the outside, looking in at her grand developmental progression. My minor loneliness was, 'of course,' momentary. Soon I had righted my emotional balance and was enjoying Margot's assertiveness and maturation as we headed toward our destination.

Admiring Margot's spunk as she strode across the street, full of quiet confidence, determination and pride, I was momentarily in a state akin to what Winnicott (1958) described as alone in the presence of the other. His concept is very yin-yang. It grounds healthy aloneness in relationality. Margot could enjoy her autonomy (Self-definition), knowing I was in the background, keeping an eye on her safety (Relatedness). She could take my concerned presence for granted. She had satisfied herself that I (and most caregivers, especially her parents) were adequately attuned to her signals, and could withstand her minor rebuffs. It was safe for her to make space to be somewhat alone in the presence of the other. Her positive transference to me was absolutely unobjectionable and, after a few seconds, her adversarial transference (or alone-in-the-presence-of-the-other transference) was also very acceptable.

Margot's behavior (and Winnicott's concept) begs the question: Who are we with when we are alone? (c.f., Buechler, 2012). In fortunate instances, we carry with us a background sense of being with someone even when, objectively, there is no one there. In ego psychological terms, this comforting feeling reflects achievement of object constancy. In Kleinian language, we are with our internal objects (hopefully a predominance of good ones). From an Eriksonian perspective, we sustain hopeful expectations based upon the enduring, structural legacy of sufficient basic trust.

Reflecting these internalized presences, many religious people feel God is always with them. One song/hymn embodies that conviction in its title, You'll Never Walk Alone (Rodgers and Hammerstein 1945). As the most beloved Psalm puts it, "Yea, though I walk through the valley of the shadow of death, I will fear no evil: for thou art with me; thy rod and thy staff they comfort me." The valley of the shadow of death sounds like a very lonely place—one where loneliness may even assume persecutory proportions. In spite of such possibilities, the psalmist feels comforted by an invisible presence. S/he is not at all alone.

Some people relish solitude. They do not feel lonely because they are communing with their thoughts, their free associations, or with Mother Nature, music, sculpture, literature, art, etc. Less fortunate individuals cannot stand being alone for any length of time. They must distract themselves from unbearable loneliness by constant activity, stimulation, drugs, etc. Even in the presence of others, they may feel terribly alone. They carry their internal loneliness with them everywhere. For them, God (or the good internal object) is dead, or otherwise preoccupied. S/he has not been replaced by a similarly omnipresent, benevolent object or interest, be it sacred or secular.

During a psychotherapy session, a very cute little boy of early elementary school age (the self-definitional era of Industry versus Inferiority) made a slip of the tongue. He called me "Mom." Immediately, he caught his parapraxis. He proceeded to inform me how embarrassed kids feel at school when they make this mistake with their teachers.

What do such 'shameful' slips indicate? For a child who is supposedly working with issues of Industry vs. Inferiority, this embarrassment harkens back to the earliest self-definitional concerns about Autonomy vs. Shame and

Doubt. Such parapraxes cast doubts on whether one has achieved age appropriate autonomy, thereby exacerbating shame. The narcissistic wound inherent in such slips is simultaneously relational. While one hopes to come across as a big (industrious) boy, one's classmates may think one is not nearly autonomous enough. They may, instead, think one is still a mama's boy, excessively tied to her apron strings.

On the positive side, these slips suggest these children do not feel estranged from their mothers when they are away from them. Instead, they are able to unconsciously transfer good feelings from their relationship with their mothers onto their teachers (unobjectionable positive transference). They do not feel lonely and alienated at school because they are still sufficiently in contact with their home base. Unconsciously, they are still with mom even though at a more rational level they also realize they are in the academy, away from her. As well developing, industrious children, busy as beavers with all sorts of activities, these youngsters are consciously well oriented with respect to person, place, and time. Unconsciously, however, they are elsewhere, attuned to other, more fundamental, relational realities. From that important other place, embarrassing slips can arise. (For well-developed minds, it is no problem to be in two places at once, simultaneously with mother and apart from her.)

For less fortunate children, object constancy is less well achieved. At school and elsewhere, they feel lost and on their own. In attempts to dispel troubling aloneness, they may resort to hyperactivity, bullying, and other strategies for distracting themselves and engaging others. As they navigate through their daily valley of the shadow of loneliness, they must rely on their own rod. They may strike others as real 'pricks.' If they get their hands on something equivalent to a staff, they may hit others with it, rather than seeking nurturance from staff.

Being the last ones to admit to loneliness, these youngsters concoct problematic ways to create a sense of lively stimulation, to garner attention and obtain some facsimile of connection to help them get through their difficult days. They give new meaning to *attention* deficit disorder. Frequently they are given stimulant medication in attempts to dispel their deficit. If they could compose psalms or songs, their theme might be: If you're lonely (which they likely are) and you know it (which they probably do not since only losers are lonely) and you really want to show it (which they do), clap your hands (which they do in various noisy, behavioral ways).

Some of these children struggling with relational challenges pertaining to problematic object constancy have significant roots in the first self-definitional stage, Autonomy versus Shame and Doubt. They may develop counter-dependent, oppositional, defiant disorders (ODD). These children may seem to feel quite certain about their impulsive, sometimes outrageous actions, showing no shame or doubt. While narcissistic attention to self-definition and autonomy is clear in this diagnostic entity, it also has important relational roots, meanings, functions, and hopes that are extremely important and useful to know about (Willock, 1986, 1987, 1990). These youngsters may seem totally self-centered, but they are actually highly adept at engaging needed adversarial objects and auxiliary egos, even though they adamantly deny any such motivation.

With respect to the next self-definitional stage, Initiative vs. Guilt, these oppositional youngsters are famous for their often troubling initiative. Defying expectations and requirements, they insist on marching to the beat of their own drums. They seem to have no guilt about their transgressions.

Currently, Blatt and his coworkers (1983, 1990) use the everyday terms, self-definition versus relatedness, to describe the two primary configurations of personality and psychopathology they identified. Originally, they used other adjectives from the psychoanalytic lexicon, anaclitic versus introjective, to portray this same polarity. These latter labels are evocative with respect to the situation I am describing in terms of those who have or have not sufficiently internalized a background sense of the other to offset aloneness. Anaclitic personalities ward off loneliness by leaning on others. They adopt this approach in their inner worlds and everyday lives. In contrast, introjective characters are less likely to appear dependent because they relate to their ego ideal, an internalized object that they hope will provide sufficient structural support if they work hard and live up to its requirements. Both analclitic and introjective strategies can work, or fail, to varying extents.

In elucidating some of the relational issues that can be important in the primarily self-definitional phases of life, I focused mostly on the earlier stages (Autonomy vs. Shame and Doubt, Initiative vs. Guilt, Industry vs. Inferiority). One could examine the later self-definitional stages in a similar manner. For example, the role of loneliness is abundant in the adolescent self-definitional stage known as Identity vs. Identity Diffusion. Erupting sexuality thrusts teenagers from familiar wego to novel ego preoccupations. Individuating from their families exacerbates loneliness until they can establish new wegos with peers. During this transitional period, adolescents require interpersonal engagement to forge new identities. They need guidance and support from adults and acceptance and recognition from their peers. To shore up their shaky self-esteem and identity, often they huddle with similar types and hold dismissive or adversarial feelings toward different others. For example, united in their beliefs that anatomy is destiny, "jocks" may disparage "brains" and vice versa. Similar rivalries may obtain with respect to musical tastes, clothing, and various behavioral standards.

When an interviewer asked the famous singer-songwriter, Leonard Cohen, if he considered himself a poet, he replied that that judgment cannot be bestowed by oneself, only by others. That is, identity is not only self-definitional, but also relational.

In the middle age identity focused stage of Generativity vs. Stagnation, an individual may seek confirmation from others that his new sports car, career move, or lover is fantastic. These mirroring transferences involve good selfobjects.

In life's last stage, Integrity vs. Despair, senior citizens may engage in much self-reflection (life review). That introspective process may involve dialogue with internalized others and relationally derived structures such as the superego and ego ideal. It may also result in conversation with external others. Those confidants may be especially helpful with individuals who are struggling to avoid despair.

Complexities of Character

Thanks to the perspective underscored by relational psychoanalysts, we are likely to be increasingly cognizant of the relational aspects of all the main issues of the life cycle's ostensibly self-definitional stages (autonomy, shame, doubt, initiative, guilt, industry, inferiority, identity, identity diffusion, generativity, stagnation, integrity, and despair). An individual's decision to seemingly focus more on self-definition may be due to conflicts and disappointments in the relational sphere. Their loneliness and yearning may have been banished to the unconscious, sealed behind a thick defensive door. For example, people who need to strenuously resist impingement by others into their sphere of autonomy may become very isolated. They may prefer loneliness to the problems they so frequently encounter with others. In extreme cases, they may become profoundly schizoid. With their yearnings for intimacy deeply buried, they try to forge a workable, perhaps lonesome existence under circumstances that Winnicott (1965) characterized, where it is a disaster to be found, and equally disastrous not to be located by someone.

Pathological character structure may particularly suggest a specific developmental stage, but it can also draw upon issues and reflect the influence of multiple phases. I have implicitly made this point earlier but I believe it warrants being stated here explicitly. For example, those who become psychotic when faced with the stressful young adulthood issues of Intimacy versus Isolation will show signs of psychological processes related to the earliest relational phase of life when basic boundaries were just coming into being. They will manifest problems differentiating self from other, fantasy from reality, past from present, good from bad, trustworthy from untrustworthy. Similarly in the self-definitional pathologies, children with oppositional defiant disorder whose narcissistic concerns may seem primarily related to autonomy ("You're not the boss of me!") will also show difficulties with respect to relational phases, such as Mutuality versus Alienation. It can be difficult for them to interact cooperatively with anyone. They are alienated and alienating.

Summary

Throughout the life cycle, loneliness, aloneness, and longing are extremely important. These affect states are just beginning to receive the focused attention they deserve. In each of the eight developmental stages that Erikson delineated, and the ninth one added by Blatt & Shichman, issues pertaining to loneliness are prevalent. Furthermore, the construct of loneliness and longing is so powerful that it transcends the otherwise significant dialectical divide between relatedness and self-definition that Blatt and others found coursing through life in crucial, alternating ways. The omnipresence of loneliness (and its opposite, meaningful loving connection) at every phase in the life cycle speaks to the centrality of this emotional constellation in both normality and pathology. Paraphrasing Freud, we are bound to fall ill if, in consequence of developmental difficulties and other frustrations, we are unable to fulfill our longings by finding love; in order not to fall ill, we must recognize and move beyond loneliness, establishing ourselves in secure loving relationships.

References

Blatt, S.J. (2008). *Polarities of Experience: Relatedness and Self-definition in Personality Development, Psychopathology, and the Therapeutic Process.* Washington, DC: American Psychological Association.

———— & Shichman, S. (1983). Two primary configurations of psychopathology. *Psychoanalysis and Contemporary Thought* 6:187–254.

———— & Blass, R.B. (1990). Attachment and separateness—A dialectic model of the products and processes of development throughout the life cycle. *Psychoanalytic Study of the Child* 45:107–127.

Buechler, S. (2012). Someone to watch over me. In: *Loneliness and Longing: Conscious and Unconscious Aspects,* eds B.Willock, L.C. Bohm, & R.C. Curtis. London & NY: Routledge, pp. 13-28.

Erikson, E.H. (1950). *Childhood and Society.* New York: W.W. Norton.

———— (1959). *Identity and the Life Cycle.* New York: International Universities Press.

Freud, S. (1914). On Narcissism. *Standard Edition* 14:67–102.

Mitchell, S.A. (1988). *Relational Concepts in Psychoanalysis: An Integration.* Cambridge, MA .& London: Harvard University Press.

Piaget, J. (1955). *The Language and Thought of the Child,* transl, M. Gabin. New York: Meridian Books.

Rogers, R. & Hammerstein, O. (1945). You'll Never Walk Alone in: The Musical *Carousel.*

Slavin, M. & Kriegman, J. (1992). *The Adaptive Design of the Human Psyche: Psychoanalysis, Evolutionary Biology, and the Therapeutic Process.* New York: Guilford.

Spitz, R. (1945). Hospitalism. *The Psychoanalytic Study of the Child* 1:53–74.

Willock, B. (1986). Narcissistic Vulnerability in the Hyperaggressive Child: The Disregarded (Unloved Uncared-for) Self. *Psychoanalytic Psychology* 3:59–80.

———— (1987). The Devalued (Unloved, Repugnant) Self—A Second Facet of Narcissistic Vulnerability in the Aggressive, Conduct-Disordered Child. *Psychoanalytic Psychology* 4:219–240.

———— (1990). From Acting out to Interactive Play. *International Journal of Psycho-Analysis* 71:321–334.

———— (2007). *Comparative-Integrative Psychoanalysis.* Hillsdale, NJ: The Analytic Press.

———— (2012a). Loneliness, longing, and limiting theoretical frameworks. In: *Loneliness and Longing: Conscious and Unconscious Aspects*, eds. B.Willock, L.C. Bohm, & R.C. Curtis. London & NY: Routledge, pp. 295–314.

———— (2012b). Loneliness and longing: Crucial aspects of the human experience. In: *Loneliness and Longing: Conscious and Unconscious Aspects,* eds B.Willock, L.C. Bohm, & R.C. Curtis. London & NY: Routledge, pp.321–334.

Winnicott, D.W. (1958). The capacity to be alone. *International Journal of Psycho-Analysis* 39:416–420.

———— (1965). *Maturational Processes and the Facilitating Environment.* New York: International Universities Press.

Chapter 15
Marilyn Monroe, the Loneliest Person on Earth
By Alma Halbert Bond

Abstract:

The paper[1] tells of Marilyn's terribly disadvantaged child-hood, in which she was born to a psychotic mother and an absent father. She was placed in her first foster home when she was only 12 days old, and was parcelled out to twelve other foster homes during her childhood. She spent anywhere from two to four years in an orphanage. She vividly remem-bered her mother laughing and screaming as she was forcibly removed to the State Hospital in Norwalk, as the child stood there shaking and crying. Marilyn's stay in her most impor-tant foster home with the God-fearing Wayne Bolenders is discussed in greater detail.

"I was always lonely, Marilyn said, that's why I loved the movies so much. I could completely forget myself there." Later in her life, when she was already a star, All About Eve director, Joseph Mankiewicz, spoke of Marilyn as the loneliest person on earth. He said, "She was always alone. She was the most alone person I've known, and lonely."

Marilyn remained just as lonely throughout her three marriages, all of which ended in divorce. "So alone was she, yet afraid to be alone," John Gil-more wrote. "She said it was a prison and she wanted to know how to get out of it, to be set free. She said, 'I have to tell you no one in my life has ever loved me, the person inside this terrible prison.'"

Marilyn's loneliness had its advantages at times, and contributed to her becoming a great star. She said, "Talent is developed in privacy. There is a need for aloneness which I don't think most people realize for an actor. It's almost having certain kinds of secrets for yourself that you'll let the whole world in on only for a moment, when you're acting."

This poem by "Marilyn" describes the end of her life:

> Be it ever so humble
> There's no place like home,
> Unless, like Marilyn,
> You live in it alone.

---

[1] Alma Halbert Bond's paper, "Marilyn Monroe: The Loneliest Person on Earth,"[1] is largely taken from her book, *Marilyn Monroe: On the Couch,* which will be published by Bancroft Press in the fall of 2013. It is the second in Dr. Bond's On the Couch series and will be her 21st published book. The first in the series is *Jackie O: On the Couch.* More about the books can be brought up on her website, Http://alma_bond.tripod.com

Marilyn Monroe, the Loneliest Person on Earth

Norma Jeane Mortenson, later to become the great sex goddess Marilyn Monroe, was delivered by Dr. Herman M. Beerman on June 1, 1926, at Los Angeles General Hospital. When she became an adult Marilyn looked him up and asked him what the delivery was like. He said, "Marilyn, I am sorry to have to tell you that you looked like all the other babies I delivered. You were the same as all the rest." Marilyn told everybody that that was the last time she was like anybody else. Other people had families. Norma Jeane grew up alone. She said, "I knew I was different from other children because there were no kisses or promises in my life."

Her mother, Gladys Baker Mortenson, worked at the time as a lowly film cutter who pasted together spliced films at Consolidated Film Industries, a processing lab for the Hollywood studios. Norma Jeane began life with two significant strikes against her: a schizophrenic mother and no father to help raise her, to love her or to protect her from her mother's psychotic behavior. Not only was Gladys insane, but Norma Jeane never felt her mother even liked her, let alone loved her. She was always cold and unaffectionate, and Marilyn never remembered her ever holding her in her arms or kissing her. In fact, she never seemed interested in her daughter at all. "I don't believe my mother ever really wanted me," Marilyn said. "My mother said it would have been easier if I had been born dead. I believed my mother wasn't in the world anymore. The sadness I felt stayed with me all the time. . . . No one is there, the same as a shadow that is attached to your own shadow, you know, and it is not your own."

Marilyn's history of her father is an even sadder story than the one about her mother. She said, "Though my birth certificate identifies my father as Gladys's second husband, Edward Mortenson, she always said he actually was C. Stanley Gifford, a man who also worked at Consolidated Film Industries." It seems he abandoned Gladys after she told him she was pregnant. No wonder Marilyn always had trouble with the men in her life! She said, "When my own father ran away from me before he even met me, what can I expect from men who are strangers?" Her cry from the heart was always, "Alone!!!!!!! I am alone. I am always alone no matter what!"

A picture on the wall and a fantasy of Clark Gable served as the only father Marilyn ever knew. Once her mother showed her a picture thumb tacked onto the kitchen wall and said, "That's your father." Marilyn said, "I felt so excited I almost fell off the chair. It felt so good to have a father, to be able to look at his picture and know I belonged to him. And what a wonderful photograph it was! He wore a slouch hat a little gaily on the side. There was a lively smile in his eyes, and he had a thin mustache like Clark Gable. That was my first happy time, finding my father's picture. And every time I remembered how he smiled and how his hat was tipped *I felt warm and not alone."*

Norma Jeane never even got to meet her real father, C. Stanley Gifford. When she was a teenager, she got up the nerve to try to speak with him on the phone. A strange woman answered. The girl said, 'I am Norma Jeane, Gladys Baker's daughter, and would like to speak with Mr. Gifford, please." The woman said, "Feel free to call his lawyer,'" and hung up.

Twelve days after Norma Jeane was born, her mother turned her over to a foster family.

"I was a mistake," Marilyn said. "I should never have been born. My mother never wanted me. I still wish every day that she had wanted me. If she had, my whole life would have been different. When I was seven years old she was diagnosed as a paranoid schizophrenic and placed in a mental institution, where she remained for most of her life."

Marilyn added, "I guess she didn't reject me altogether. When she was out of the institution she would come and stay weekends with me at the foster home, and take me out to the beach or the movies. We both passionately loved films. Although I hate to remember it, when I was little I looked forward to her visits like nothing else. What else did a child living in an orphanage have to look forward to? I desperately waited for her visit each week. The first time she didn't show up, I stood looking out the window all day waiting for her. The nurse tried to pull me away, and said, "Norma Jean, you have to eat your dinner now.' But I held on to the curtains for dear life until I pulled them off of the rod. To add insult to injury, I was whipped on my bare buttocks for 'house wrecking."

Sooner or later, Norma Jeane was thrown out by each set of foster parents, mostly because the men in the families couldn't keep their hands off her. Before she was finished, she was placed in ten or twelve of them.

Marilyn said about living in multiple homes: "The world around me then was kind of grim. I had to learn to pretend in order to—I don't know—block the grimness. The whole world seemed sort of closed to me . . . I felt on the outside of everything, and all I could do was to dream up any kind of pretend game."

"The first and most important foster home," she continued, "was with the Wayne Bolender's, where my mother placed me for the first seven years of my life."

The child was boarded out to Ida and Wayne Bolender in Hawthorne, California twelve days after she was born. Ida and Wayne Bolender had a comfortable six-roomed bungalow which that Marilyn remembered very well. Although they didn't have a great deal of money, they increased their income by fostering children.

"I must say that life dealt a rotten set of cards to Gladys," Marilyn continued. "Her S.O.B. husband left her and kidnapped her first two children, and she never was able to recover them. That would drive me crazy, too. To be fair about it, she had no choice but to board me out, not because of psychological problems, but financial ones. She had to go back to work at Consolidated Film Industries in order to support us. She worked long hours, like from 8 a.m. to 8 p.m., and there was no one to take care of me. She paid the Bolenders five dollars a week, probably half her salary, to look after me."

"Every Saturday before she was institutionalized, Gladys would take the trolley to Hawthorne to visit me. In the early years, I desperately waited for her visit each week. One week she didn't show up, and I stood waiting by the front window until bedtime. Ida tried to pull me away, and said, 'Norma Jean, your mother is not coming today. You have to come eat your dinner.'"

"'No, no,'" I screamed. "'She will come. Just you wait and see.'"

"She kept yanking me by the shoulder. But I held on to the wall with my nails until a huge chunk fell off into my hands. 'You are a bad girl, Norma Jean,' Ida said and slapped me on the face." Marilyn raised her hand to her cheek, which was wet with tears and winced as she said, "It still hurts."

On one of her visits Gladys told Norma Jeane that when she was able to get enough money together she would come for her and they would live together in their own house. She promised the child, "I will build a lovely house for you and me to live in. It will be painted white and even have a back yard you can play in."

"After a couple of years," Norma Jeane thought, "Yeah, and the moon is made of blue cheese."

The Bolenders were a deeply religious couple who lived a comfortable lower middle class life. Ida was a rigid, conscience driven woman who forcefully pounded her beliefs into little Norma Jeane's head. Ida made the little girl promise never to smoke, drink or swear, and insisted that she attend church several times a week or she would go to Hell.

"When she lectured me about it I nodded in agreement, but kept my fingers crossed behind me," Marilyn said with a smile.

The highly intelligent child (she had a genius IQ of 169) had quickly learned to conceal from the Bolenders her desire to sing, dance, or act out a fantasy life, in order to avoid punishment. Marilyn Monroe-to-be found her own unique ways of handling boredom in church through sexual fantasies.

In the days before the term "stay at home mother" was even thought of, Ida took care of the house and several foster children, along with their natural son. Wayne was a postman who was fortunate enough to keep his job all through the Depression. He added to their low income by printing religious pamphlets for distribution to the members of their church.

"I can just see his big shoulders bulging with huge mail bags. He used to carry candy in his pocket to throw to the dogs so they wouldn't bite him. Sometimes he would give me one. . . . I miss him." Marilyn said wistfully.

"Of course he also could be terribly frightening. When I became what he considered boisterous, down came my pants and off came his leather belt, huge silver buckle and all. I will never forget the lash of his leather and the welts it caused on my bare buttocks as he pressed me against his genitals. I had to eat standing up for days. I have retained a sensitivity in my behind to the present day. But I loved him anyway. What did I know? I thought that's the way fathers were supposed to act, that they punished their children to teach them a lesson. You know the old story, 'This hurts me more than it hurts you.'"

Marilyn learned very early what turns men on. *She took a terrible trauma and converted it into a work of art.* Distorted as it is to contemplate, in a way the world has to thank Wayne Bolender for his part in giving us the sexiest behind in the history of films.

It seems, however, that in their own harsh way the Bolenders loved Norma Jeane, and they wanted to adopt her. But in a rare show of mother love, Gladys refused to allow it, as her persistent dream was that she would buy a home and take Norma Jean to live with her.

"One day, Gladys came to see me and insisted that the Bolenders turn me over to her. Ida refused, because she knew how unstable Gladys was and was frightened for my welfare. Gladys then pushed Ida into the yard and bolted into the house and locked the door. A few minutes later, she rushed back out, with one of Wayne Bolender's military duffel bags slung over her shoulder. Guess what was in it? Me!"

To Ida's everlasting horror, Gladys had stuffed a screaming Norma Jeane into the bag, zipped it up, and was lugging it away. Ida rushed at her and tried to yank the bag away from her. It split open and dumped Norma Jeane to the ground, yelling loudly, as Ida grabbed her and pulled her back into the house.

This was the first Norma Jeane learned of the craziness that plagued Gladys the rest of her life. Marilyn vividly remembered her mother laughing and screaming as she was forcibly removed to the State Hospital in Norwalk. The child stood there shaking and crying, and realized with certainty that her fantasy of living with her real mother never would come true.

"I was always lonely—that's why I loved the movies so much," Marilyn said. "I could completely forget myself. When I got home I closed the bedroom door and acted out the parts that I saw on the screen. For a twelve-year-old, it was very serious pantomime. I had a crush on every movie star. But my real heartthrob was Clark Gable."

Later in her life, when she was already a star, *All About Eve* director, Joseph Mankiewicz, spoke of Marilyn as the loneliest person on earth. He said, "She was always alone. She was the most alone person I've known, and lonely. The girl suffered from loneliness, but she wouldn't join in get-togethers and always seemed to run off by herself. She didn't make friends and she wasn't sociable. When we were on location, she'd hide in hotel rooms" (John Gilmore, p. 114).

Despite the terrible drawbacks of being raised by the God-fearing Bolenders and the traumatic beatings of her foster father, Norma Jeane had a consistent home for her first seven years, and knew some kind of parenting. It is likely that any kind of relatively normal parents are better than none at all. The Bolenders gave her what little emotional security she had, and built her a conscience, no matter how distorted. Otherwise, like so many orphans, she could have become a psychopath, or developed the family illness much sooner than she did.

"To my great surprise," Marilyn continued, "Gladys came through after all on her promise to buy a house for herself and me. In August of 1933 when I was seven years old, she signed a contract with The California Title Mortgage Company which when added to her savings gave her enough down payment to buy the small white bungalow at 6812 Arbol Drive in Hollywood."

For the first time in her short life, Norma Jeane was able to live with her mother like any normal girl.

She was happier than she had ever been. She was delighted to be living—finally—with her real mother, despite all her peculiarities. The ambience in the household was much less strict than it had been at the Bolenders, and she was allowed many more activities. Mother and daughter often went to the movies at Grauman's Egyptian Theater and Grauman's Chinese Theater, sitting side by side, gnawing Hershey Bars, and equally enchanted with the fantasies they saw on the screen.

"Some day, you will be up there," Gladys said to Norma Jeane, at a time she still was well. The child listened and believed her, and hugged the statement to her breast where she took it out every night and glowed.

Gladys also took Norma Jeane to the famous cement forecourt of Grauman's Chinese Theatre, where she proudly placed her little feet in the footprints of Clara Bow and Gloria Swanson, and dreamt that some day hers would be next to theirs.

Marilyn continued, "To my utter despair, our reunion was only too brief. As the months went by my mother became increasingly depressed until, one morning in January of 1935, she lost control of herself and lunged at Auntie Grace with a kitchen knife. My mother was pulled away from her screaming daughter and sent to Los Angeles General Hospital and later to Norwalk. Except for very brief periods, she was institutionalized for the rest of her life. Thus ended two years of the only significant amount of time I ever lived a normal life with my mother. I have always felt guilty that my love for her wasn't great enough to keep her sane."

Marilyn remained just as lonely throughout her three marriages, all of which ended in divorce. She had nothing in common with her first husband, Jim Dougherty, in what had been an arranged marriage, and they went for days without speaking to each another. Her second husband, Joe DiMaggio, was a sullen, silent man around Marilyn, who spent most of his time looking at sports on television. Speaking of that marriage, Marilyn said, "I think people need human warmth even when they are asleep and unconscious. . . . I think TV sets should be taken out of the bedroom" (p. 87, *Will Acting Spoil Marilyn Monroe?*). Her third marriage, to Arthur Miller, was no better; Miller closed himself up in his office and spent his time thinking and smoking his pipe. "If I'm going to be alone," she thought, "I want to be by myself."

In Hollywood Marilyn lived for a while at the studio club, where young would-be actresses resided. There was an important social life at the Studio Club, and the friends the actresses made were helpful in getting them jobs. But their jokes and games failed to draw Marilyn into the group. She never seemed comfortable with the other girls, who'd be chattering away, and was ill at ease with them. She shied away from get- togethers and stayed off by herself. She showed no interest in forming close friendships, and was always finding a reason to excuse herself, such as dashing off to use the phone.

It didn't help much that women were often very jealous of her. Marilyn said, "Sometimes I've been to a party where no one spoke to me a whole evening. The men, frightened by their wives or sweeties, would give me a wide berth. And the ladies would gang up in a corner to discuss my dangerous character."

"I knew I belonged to the public and to the world," she said, "not because I was talented or even beautiful, but because I never had belonged to anything or anyone else."

"So alone was she, yet afraid to be alone," John Gilmore wrote (p. 145). "She said it was a prison and she wanted to know how to get out of it, to be set free . . . She said, '. . . I have to tell you no one in my life has ever loved me. . . . the person inside this terrible prison.' "

Marilyn found little assuagement of her loneliness in her career. She said, "A career is wonderful, but you can't curl up with it on a cold night." She added, "There was something special about me," she explained, "and I knew what it was." She explained, "I was the kind of girl they found dead in a hall bedroom with an empty bottle of sleeping pills in her hand."

Marilyn once told Tom Clay, an L.A. Disk jockey, that she was lonely. "How can you be lonely?" he asked. Marilyn answered, "Have you ever been in a house with forty rooms? Well, just magnify my loneliness by forty."

Marilyn's loneliness had its advantages at times, and contributed to her becoming a great star. She said, "Talent is developed in privacy, you know. There is a need for aloneness which I don't think most people realize for an actor. It's almost having certain kinds of secrets for yourself that you'll let the whole world in on only for a moment, when you're acting."

Religion wasn't much help to Marilyn, either. She said, "The only One who loved me and watched over me was Someone I couldn't see or hear or touch. I used to draw pictures of God whenever I had time. In my pictures He looked a little like Clark Gable."

To Marilyn, Sunday was the loneliest day of the week. She said, "All the men I know are spending the day with their wives and families, and all the stores in Los Angeles are closed. You can't wander through looking at all the pretty clothes and pretending to buy something."

Sometimes she would spend Sundays at Union Station. She said wistfully, "You learned a lot watching the people there. You learned that pretty wives adored homely men and good-looking men adored homely wives. And that people in shabby clothes, carrying raggedy bundles and with three or four sticky kids clinging to them, had faces that could light up like Christmas trees when they saw each other. And you watched really homely men and women, fat ones and old ones, kiss each other as tenderly as if they were lovers in a movie."

In 1958, titled "After One Year in Analysis," Marilyn wrote in her diary, "Help help / Help / I feel life coming closer / when all I want / Is to die."

In another poem, she wrote:

> O, Time
> Be Kind
> Help this weary being
> To forget what is sad to remember
> Loose my loneliness,
> Ease my mind,
> While you eat my flesh

When astrologer Richard Ideman remarked that New York was a lonely town, she said, "Any town is lonely when you don't know who you are." Marilyn emphasized pains lingering from never-ending loneliness and a continual fear of abandonment. She said, "I am put on a tiny desert island no bigger than your kitchen. I know the tide is going to rise and the ocean will cover this little island, and I will sink."

She was alone far more than she wanted to be. She couldn't connect with anyone to be with; it didn't matter who it was. She lived in a no-man's land. A person could call across the abyss but never got closer than the reach of a voice.

According to John Gilmore (p. 27), "She lived in an invisible capsule that allowed no one to reach her. . . . She died alone, behind a closed door, with no hand to hold or voice to reach her . . . If anyone wanted to know her better, to know everything about her and make an everlasting bond, Marilyn, the bird, would fly." John Gilmore (p. 112).

The following poem, *Alone*, by Sofi Nick (www.poemhunter.com), sums up the life of Marilyn Monroe very well:

Alone

alone wherever I go
alone whatever I do
alone all the time
alone I am sad and blue.

alone I want to suicide
alone no one is by my side
alone all the time
alone I will suicide

alone I can't sleep at night
alone I am shaking from fright
alone all the time
alone I'll end my loneliness tonight

alone I cry
alone I fail when I try
alone I lived all my life
and ***now alone I will die.***

For Marilyn Monroe, as for many others, the only companion to accompany her to the grave was her loneliness.

References

Braver, A. (2012). *Misfit, a Novel.* Portland: Tin House Books.

Churchwell, S. (2004). *The Many Lives of Marilyn Monroe.* New York: Henry Holt and Co.

De La Hoz, C. (2007). *Marilyn Monroe.* Philadelphia: Platinum Fox Running Press.

Gilmore, J. (2007). *Inside Marilyn Monroe, A Memoir.* Los Angeles: Ferine Books.

Lawrence, F. (1993) *Norma Jean, The Life of Marilyn Monroe.* New York: Paragon House.

Mailer, N. (1973). *Marilyn: The Classic.* New York: Galahad Books.

Martin P. (1956). *Will Acting Spoil Marilyn Monroe?* Garden City, NY: Doubleday & Company.

Miller, A. (1964). *After the Fall.* New York: Penguin Group.

Monroe, M. & Hecht, B. (2007). *My Story.* Lanham: Taylor Trade.

Riese , R. (1987). *The Unabridged Marilyn: Her Life from A to Z* New York: Congdon & Weed, Inc.

Shevey, S. (1987). *The Marilyn Scandal.* New York: William Morrow and Co.

Steinem, G. (1996). *Marilyn.* New York: MJF Books Fine Communications, Fine Creative Media, Inc,

Taraborrelli, J. R. (2009). *The Secret Life of Marilyn Monroe.* New York: Grand Central Publishing.

Chapter 16
The Death of the Loved Spouse, the Inner World of Grief:
A Psychoanalytic Developmental Perspective
Patsy Turrini

Abstract:

In *Mourning and Melancholia* Freud (1917) provided a lens
to examine the loss of a loved one. Under normal mourning
he included "profoundly painful dejection, cessation of interest in the outside world, loss of the capacity to love, inhibition of all activity and the loss of the capacity to adopt any
new object of love (which would mean replacing him)." He
held that the infant's experiences in missing the mother were
traumatic and created "a cathexsis" called "longingful." Both
Mahler and Bowlby observed painful dejections in early infant and toddler development. Painful normal mourning in
adulthood, in part, can be understood as a remembering of
the memories and experiences of the loss of the early mother;
the symbiotic oneness, and a revival of the painful affects of
stranger anxiety, the rapprochement crisis and the agonies of
physical separation from the mother. The pain experienced at
the discovery of the separate self can elicit the sense of non-
existence. The conviction of personal existence of self is
connected to the availability of the external object (loved
one), and the death of the loved spouse can cause a 'loss of
one's sense of being' (Stolorow and Williams).
Wolf/Kohut's seven self/object functions represent necessary
elements of the viable self, lost at the death of the loved
spouse (Kohut & Wolf, 1978). Bowlby's view that "the attachment behavior in adult life is a straightforward continuation of attachment behavior in childhood is a paradigm for
understanding the death of the adult loved partner" (Bowlby,
1969, pp. 207–208). Loneliness permeates a myriad of
tortured biological, developmental or prewired experiences.
Freud formulated the idea of "a bit by bit . . . detachment of
the libido" from the object. Other theorists have offered differing views of the psychic resting place of the loved object
over time (Clewell, 2004; Rando, 1993). The goal of this paper is to expand our understanding of the inner world of grief
and its composition of loneliness.

The Loss of the Loved Spouse, Some Psychoanalytic
Developmental Observations

"Loneliness is an important feeling in which a person feels a strong sense
of emptiness, yearning, distress and solitude resulting from an inadequate

255

quantity or quality of social relationships . . . Loneliness has been described as social pain" (Wikipedia 2012). I am at ease with this definition; it fits many of my feelings, even six years after my loved husband Niel's death. I have come to learn in the aftermath of this loss that it is unexpectedly painful, debilitating and completely non-understandable. As various studies and research reports indicate, the experience of aloneness and periods of loneliness accompany the ongoingness of mourning. What is this loss of the loved other about? What causes the shattered and traumatic state? What contributes? What is its evolution? And is there a resolution? As a clinical social worker, psychoanalytic therapist and scholar of psychoanalytic observations and studies of development, not only did I seek therapeutic help, when stunned with pain at his death, I also scanned biology reports and findings from psychoanalysis to help me find my way. This paper offer descriptions of and reflections on the torment and pain of grief; expectable, normal developmental loss, separations and pain, repeating and changing over the life span; the formation and meaning of the capacity for symbiotic relatedness and oneness; internalizations, incorporations (what the self is made of), selfobjects; the sense of existence and being; the actual inputs from the external other; finding the love partner; what is lost at their death, and what is recovered after the death; and the question: Is there an end to grief, mourning and loneliness?

I begin with the torment of grief. Most observers report the first reactions to the death of the loved other is shock, resulting in a numbness and dissociative experience. Stolorow describes his reaction to his wife's death: "I seemed like a strange and alien being—not of this world. The others seemed so vitalized, engaged with one another in a lively manner. I, in contrast, felt deadened and broken, a shell of the man I had once been" (p 14). Joyce Carol Oates (2011) says, after learning of her husband's death, "You made my life possible. I owe my life to you, I can't do this alone (p 79) . . . When you are not alone, you are shielded. You are shielded from the stark implacable unspeakable indescribable terror of aloneness" (p. 110). "I am not anything now. Legally I am a 'widow' that is the box I must check. Beyond that I am not sure that I exist" (Times Book Review). Ornstein (2010) says, "acute grief is a piercing ache around the heart, a painful stabbing sensation that can be severe enough to take one's breath away. The experience makes one physically weak, making standing up, walking or even speaking difficult" (p. 643). Jacobson (1964) describes, "a feeling as if one has lost part of one's self." Bowlby (1973) writes, "the situational feature of special interest to us is being alone. Probably nothing increases the likelihood that fear will be aroused more than that. Finding oneself alone in a strange place, perhaps in darkness, and met by a sudden movement or mysterious sound, few of us would be unafraid. Were we to have with us even one stout companion, we would probably feel much braver" (p. 91). Lifton (1967) describes the "neurasthenic survivor syndrome, and psychic numbing as adaptive." He writes, "If I feel nothing, then death is not taking place; it is what we referred to as the 'identity of the dead'. We call the guilt-saturated inner sequence of this identity (I almost died); I should have died; I did die, or at least I am not really alive, or if I am alive, it is impure of me to be so; and anything I do which affirms life is also impure of me and an insult to the dead, who alone are pure; and we can see now its suggestion of psychic numbing as itself a form of symbolic death (p. 504) . . . it protects the survivor from complete helplessness. Stunned and dazed and numb hold sway (p. 501). Over time, I found myself saying, "If I had known this would be so bad, I wouldn't ever have gotten married; so bizarre the self comment when the pain was about what I wanted and had lost. For the first few months I imagined myself at night in a wood coffin where no one could hear me, and I could not hear anyone; in hindsight a clever composite impression serving the recognition of the loss, the silence of my home, the closeness to the dead, as well as a grand punishment for all that I had received—and had benefited from at his death, deprived to him; life, money, the family, air to breathe . . ." C.S. Lewis (1961) said, "No one ever told me grief felt so like fear." And last but not least, Freud said, "For the intense cathexis of longing which is concentrated on the missed or lost object (a cathexis which readily mounts up because it cannot be appeased) creates the same economic conditions as are created by the cathexis of pain which is concentrated on an injured part of the body" (1926, p. 171).

So how did we get into this predicament, we human beings? However contradictory the following descriptions, there are many in the developmental psychoanalytic world who can find the observations familiar and sensible. Hartmann (1958) brought the concept of human object seeking and capacity for object comprehension into the biology of human development. But before Hartmann helped elaborate the biological inborn ego apparatus, Freud (1926), less known for his observations of infant and child, brought attention to the mother and the stranger and wrote, "When an infant is presented with a stranger instead of the mother it will exhibit the anxiety which we have attributed to the danger of loss of object . . . that it does have anxiety there can be no doubt; but the expression of its face and its reaction of *crying indicate that it is feeling pain as well*" (p. 169). As soon as it loses sight of its mother it behaves as if it were never going to see her again; repeated consoling experiences are needed before it learns that her disappearance is usually followed by her re-appearance. The infant is not yet able to distinguish temporary absence from permanent loss . . . she encourages this knowledge of reappearance by playing with him the familiar game of covering her face and then hiding her face from it with her hands and then to its joy uncovering it again (peekaboo—by current language) by revealing it again. Thus he is enabled, as it were, to experience longing unaccompanied by despair.

Stranger reactions confront the human baby with fear of separateness and danger. The longing and awareness of aloneness in adult life, re-experienced

257

at the death of the loved spouse, have early derivatives from universal early traumatic experiential events. We are primed for the awareness of fear of loss and the pain of longing. Mahler (1979) says, "Our data indicated the phenomenological concomitants of an "unspecific craving" to the specific "object-bound" affect of "longing" (p. 172).

Stranger anxiety selected here as a first paradigm of loss, demonstrates that human beings experience pain and fear, and then joy of the connection and pleasure upon the return of the mother. This pattern is observed on the death of the loved one; loss, fear, yearning, despair, forever gone, and only after consoling does the assumption of return develop a false hope primed from the earlier experiences, as experienced in the peekaboo game; grief, sobbing, numbness (as in low-keyedness); sensations of terror and hope upon hope with expectation of return of the dead is observed. People report they see their loved one, hear them, find themselves looking for them, and have an expectation they will return, while at the same time bearing another reality, that they will not. Later I return to describe a process that provides for a return of the lost love.

Spitz (1965) further researched stranger anxiety and reactions as "indicators" of ego development observed in normal development at 6 months and understood that the infant knows the mother from the stranger (the libidinal object proper). Grotsein (1982) elaborates on stranger anxiety, and adds an important consideration, that of predator fear.

Not only does the infant feel the loss of the mother, but from an ethological perspective the stranger /predator fear, considered prewired and innate, serves as a protective mechanism to alert the person to dangerous animals, spiders, snakes and strangers. Stranger anxiety here is interpreted as an instinct for self- protection, one that is part of the armamentarium of the human being. Beyond the prewired instinct for self-protection, parents have to teach children to stay away from strangers: "don't go off with strangers, and don't get into cars with people you don't know." Parents are the safe, good people. Babies are born prepared to attach/bond and stay safe with mothers but also develop "confident expectation, wonderment, and stranger curiosity" (Mahler et al., 1979, p.123). Thus parents have the task to teach their children the difference between the friendly neighbor and the malevolent stranger.

The early image of the safe haven of mother becomes part of the object-related capacity and wishes, that then serve and direct the selection of the mate—a safe, trusted person. Lucky the people who have good care, for they are psychically equipped to seek a good mate who can care and protect. When I later describe what is lost at the death of the spouse, I will note that on my first trip out of the country, with my passport in hand, while walking the long corridors in the airport I realized that I had lost my bodyguard—my protective partner. One of Niel's important meanings for me was in his being the safety-man; he was big, tall, with a loud voice. No one would ever mess with him, nor, before him, with my mother and father of my early childhood.

If the memory of the disturbing experience and the impact of the unendurable agony of separation from the object is not enough, the Rapprochement crisis is another time that the loss of the object (mother) is experienced as monumental and terrifying. Mahler reported an "upsurge of stranger anxiety" during the rapprochement crisis. Mahler, et al. (1975), Blanck & Blanck (1975), Edward, Ruskin and Turrini (1991), describe the sharp awareness of separateness that takes place at this 18-24 month period. Having formed a "oneness" with the body of the mother in the first months of life (the symbiotic period), the child has developed a feeling of safety including feeling a part of her body. With the advancing prewired human thrust to move and explore and see the world, the toddler experiences the separate sensation of aloneness, of being separate, no longer with her and safe. The toddler is seized with the terror of separateness, and runs quickly back to the mother, refueling. Many tantrums, grief and terror reactions and emotions, can be seen at the doors of daycare centers and kindergartens as children protest leaving their parents. Parents usually experience fear at parting with their children, and are traumatized when the child is suffering at the separation. If a child is left for any length of time, physically separated from the parent, the child experiences extreme pain, despair, lethargy, and rage reactions or low-keyedness, standing near the mother's purse that she left, and feeling sick. Here again, we see an experience and event that will be repeated in the adult who has lost their loved other. There is no partner to run home to for comfort, safety and oneness. Bowlby, (1961) calls this a biological disequilibrium, "the cry of sorrow" (p. 320), "the natural pain of bodily separation" (p. 324).

The Oedipal period and the defeat of the Oedipal love/constellation, is usually not noted for its impact of separation agony, however loss is part of the resolution. Arlow (1978) describes the defeat at the loss of the partnership with the Oedipal parents, and the revenge wishes that develop. Having fallen madly in love with one's parents, by 4 and 5, there is an expectation of having a baby with each of them (the bisexual wishes of childhood) and the impression of everlasting life with them; only to have that shattered, and be told you must marry out there: Huh!? a stranger? One is inside with them, that is the "outside." Poland (2012) writes of Fear of the outside experienced as a "haunting sensation of outsiderness" throughout life. Moreover, Arlow observes a universal narcissistic mortification: the child feels unloved and unloveable, and concludes there is something wrong with them. At the death of the loved other, it is expectable and frequently reported that the newly bereaved feels abandoned, injured, unloved and unloveable. Commonly heard is the complaint, "If you had loved me you would never have died and left"—the irrational judgment alongside of the rational assessment of reality. One woman in my bereavement group told of going to the cemetery and kicking the tombstone; all of us in the group wanted to applaud. How powerful was the loved other who could reassure and vitalize our loveability every day, with comfort, conversation, smile, togetherness and the erotic, sensual life.

Symbiotic Object Related Capacity

In tracing the impact of loss, *symbiotic explanations* seem applicable. We develop the capacity for relatedness, for symbiotic relatedness, from birth (maybe before) on and wish to keep safe forever with the oneness pleasures of life. Akhtar (2009) defines "the oceanic feeling, a term employed for an expansion of the self beyond its customary temporal—spatial limits leading to a *feeling of merger with the universe at large* . . . Oneness of the self and its object world is regarded as a narcissistic illusion underneath which lurks split-off hostile destructiveness. Less comfortable to the Western world is the possibility that recapturing the infantile bliss of oneness with the universe might be a positive and transcendental occurrence" (p. 195). The oceanic feeling offers some further consideration of the universality of the extension of self-feelings into other spaces, a kind of osmosis of the body with the universe or the other.

As mentioned before, Hartmann (1958) enabled observers to consider the inborn ego apparatus, a prewired blueprint for joining and relating to an object . . . to form connection and an essential ingredient to love. Mahler, et al. (1975) and Silverman, et al. (1982) and Weinberger, & Smith (2011) have found evidence to support this pathway. Bergmann (2002) writes, "I drew attention to the point that Plato anticipated this finding when he described lovers as two people who desire nothing more than to be melted into one. I showed that the human need to fall in love is based on this wish, as well as the need to refind the symbiotic partner, symbiotic longings are awakened in the state of falling in love" (p. 42). Mahler, et al. (1975) described the essential feature of symbiosis as hallucinatory, or delusional, somatopsychic omnipotent fusion with the representation of the mother, and in particular the delusion of a common boundary of the two actually and physically separate individuals. G. Blanck (2000, p. 156) notes that developmental object relations emphasizes, beyond the term bonding, an interlocking of self and object images within the evolving representational world. "The child is taking part of the mothering person into his mental representations and making them his own as he goes on to establish his own identity. The infant who summons the mother by crying, hears her footsteps before she arrives, and organizes the pattern; cry, footsteps, being lifted out of the crib, and seizing the breast (bottle) as it is offered. . . . this is the experience of self and object in affective harmony, responding one to the other, building images of self and other that are experienced at first as united" (p.157). The adult in love does the same; the other is within and mourners report they keep listening for the sound and footsteps at the door

260

where the other would come in . . . waiting with hopeful anticipation that the other will be home. Weinberger and Smith (2011) used research with *oneness motivation* (OM) and *subliminal psychodynamic activation* (SPA) to affirm a connection between oneness and the "we" bond, and a positive therapeutic relationship." Jacobson (1964) says, "These earliest wishful fantasies of merging and being one with the mother (breast) are certainly the foundation on which all object relations as well as all future types of identification are built" (p. 39).

E. E. Cummings in a poem commented: *"i carry your heart with me (i carry it in my heart) i am never without it (anywhere i go you go, my dear; and whatever is done by only me is your doing, my darling) . . . "*

Internalizations, Incorporations and Selfobjects

If we accept that the loved other becomes part of oneself in a fused oneness, what else do we take in of the other? This section seeks to understand what becomes part of the self, and what then is lost at the death of the loved other. What do we obtain and what do we lose and long for at their death? A number of theoreticians have brought insight to the functions the adult partners provide for one another. A review of salient observations can shed light on what is the actual lived experience with the other (the external object /partner) that is internalized, often referred to as a selfobject, and then lost. Hagman (1995) in a paper, "Death of a Selfobject; Toward a Self Psychology of the Mourning Process," says, " My thesis is that mourning is essentially the transmuting internalization of the structure and function of the lost self-object" (p. 189). He cites Kohut and maintains that "the self evolves within an intersubjective context characterized by attunement and responsiveness . . . the archaic functions of the selfobject are transformed into autonomous psychic structure" (p. 193). The selfobject is the internal, affectively charged experience of the other and resides as psychic structure/part of one's being. I imagine it is located in the cells, the brain, the organs . . . in the enteroceptive, and proprioceptive systems, for that would account for the emotional/bodily pain at the death of the loved other.

For Wolf (1994), "Selfobject *experiences are needed for the emergence and maintenance of a cohesive, balanced and energetic self.* These selfobjects can be classified into various types: mirroring, idealizing, alter ego, ally-antagonist, efficacy, vitalization of affects, and perhaps others not yet discovered." He adds, from Kohut: "Throughout his life a person will experience himself as a cohesive harmonious firm unit in time and space, connected with his past and pointing meaningfully into a creative-productive future (but) only as long as, at each stage in his life, he experiences certain representatives of his human surroundings as *joyfully* responding to him, as available to him as sources of idealized strength and calmness, as being silently present but in

261

essence like him and at any rate, able to grasp his inner life more or less accurately so that their responses are attuned to his needs and allow him to grasp their inner life when his is in need of assistance" (Kohut, 1984, p. 52). Put another way, there are essential human environmental inputs required for stability of healthy positive self-esteem, self-regard and self-identity; and they are needed throughout the lifespan. And, as will be addressed later, the functions of the external object no longer exist at the partners death. Cummings poetry line, *"i like my body when it is with your body. It is so quite new a thing. Muscles better and nerves more."* The partner vitalizes the body and mind, as does the mother as she kisses the parts of the baby's body and enables them both to love the nose, mouth, toes . . . smile . . . the totality of being. If you love my body it makes me love my body. The loving spouses offer vitality to one another and affirm respectability, efficacy, respect and admiration through thick and thin, illness and aging, till death do they part. Niel once said to me, "When I see you I always feel happy."—and this from a man who could remain passive in face at many times. For my part, I always felt happy seeing him. Fortunately, I can experience the Niel in abstensia, the Niel within, the fun, smart, good, loving Niel. I can see the angry, demanding guy too . . . but I enjoy the good dancer, historian, and funny jokester Niel, the man that picked me for love, marriage, to meet his family, and to chart the future with children in mind. These inner rewards temper the aloneness and loneliness, and the loss of him. (More on these vitalizing inner experiences, later.)

Further Thoughts on the Stability of Self; Existence of Being

Akhtar (2006) has posed the following problem: 'If your spouse (significant other) does not talk to you for two days you begin to feel you do not exist'. If this is so, we get another look at how powerful the withdrawal of connection truly is. There are lonely and isolating times in a loving marriage; perhaps when someone is 'not talking,' or is away, or ill, or has failed to call on time, or been forgetful of something important to the other. Akhtar's thought on non-existence flags how delicate our psychic inner life can be.

Freud (1895) coined the term Sensation of Identity and described it as nmemic images, experienced early in life, with one's "first satisfying object and . . . first hostile object, as well as . . . sole helping power. For this reason it is in relation to a fellow human-being that a human-being learns to cognize . . . visual perceptions (of the other) will coincide in the subject with memories of visual impressions . . . of his own body . . . (thus) if, for instance, he (the other) screams (it) will awaken the memory of his own screaming and at the same time of his own experiences of pain . . . the activity of memory . . . can be traced back to information from the subject's own body" (p. 330-31). White (1972) built a case for the lifelong wish for repetition of the original need satisfaction, she called this cathexis of the familiar. We perceive, take in, connect, in unconscious perceptions, with the loved other. Freud wrote in the Project, "While one is perceiving the perception, one copies the movement oneself—that is, one innervates so strongly that the motor image of one's own is aroused to coincide with the other" (p. 333).

Does this help explain to me why I—and so many others—go, over and over again, the moments of life with the other, and replay the causes and occurrence of the death. We need to illuminate the inner perception of the other in order to fulfill the feeling of self-aliveness. His existence is my existence. Thus I don't exist? How foolish . . . here I sit, alive, well, writing and looking forward to the day this effort will come out in a book, and imagining that some will understand, learn and like what I am saying (and bearing up with the idea that others will not). I am here. I exist, with the vitality of the recollections and connection to the inner presence of the loved other. Niel's pink roses are blooming, in October, outside the window as I write at my computer. He is here in his roses. I thank him for this ongoing gift.

Williams, who in his article *The Pain of Exclusion* (February, 2011) presents research that adds serious data describing the impact of disruptions, writes, "Even trivial episodes of ostracism can shatter your sense of self . . . no matter how people are left out, their response is swift and powerful, inducing a social agony that the brain registers as physical pain . . . even brief episodes (of shunning) involving strangers or people we dislike activate pain centers . . . " (pp. 30–37). Death too often catalyzes the fantasy of the deceased as the perpetrator of deliberate exclusion. Williams' important research demonstrates pain in loss and underscores aloneness and loneliness set off by exclusions, and yes, definitely by the death of the loved other.

For Stolorow, "Ontology is the study of being; hence I use the phrase ontological unconsciousness to denote a loss of one's sense of being. When my traumatized states (his wife had suddenly died) could not find a relational home, I became deadened, and my world became dull. When such a home became once again present, I came alive and the vividness of my world returned" (p. 26).

Through incorporation, identification, merging wishes, and selective identification the loved spouse becomes internalized as part of self; their functions, values and attitudes are integral parts of the self and the marriage bond.

Falling in Love and the Found Loved Spouse

With internalized, reasonable developmental psychic health, a safe trusted admired and exciting person is found who offers love, magnetism, pleasure, trustworthiness, is capable of building a relationship and planning for the future, and has the capacity to bring joy and fun to life. A oneness forms (being on the same page, in tune). There is pleasure in the oneness; the two cleaving together, as many marriage ceremonies say. There is a plan for the future that carries with it the unconscious meaning of immortality and foreverness. Having children adds to the feeling of immortality; our children can be our immortality objects (Mendell & Turrini, 2001). The marriage bond may carry more power than the earlier safe places did, because of its special form of recognition and the assumption of its permanence—the future is now secured. The attributions of ideal states and perceptions to and from the other and the WE can contribute to the powerful meaning of the love affair, with its mission, commitment, loyalty and foreverness. Love and life are timeless in primary process thinking.

What Is Lost At The Death Of The Loved One?

What is lost at the death of the loved other? Lost is the real presence, voice, sounds, and body of the person who could usually provide pleasure; lost is the safety of the caring partner; lost are all the plans for the future—the sunlight on the future is gone, blank and black prevail. Lost are the happy endings after being apart (separations in time and space always ended in the return of the loved other); lost is the dependable person with knowledge of the household and legal papers—or whatever was essential in practical or domestic matters. Lost is the internal joy of looking forward (the joy of anticipation), the "can't wait to get home to see you and tell you what happened." Lost is the person who could always make you feel loved. Lost is the protection against abandonment fears, and stranger and predator fears; lost is the precious friend; lost is the satisfying feeling of carrying forth the mission of loving and caring and uplifting the other, the self-satisfaction of connection internally experienced in the course of a day. Lost is the laughing over old jokes; and mulling and reviewing family and world history; lost is putting arms around one another, and soothing the head, and finding the lost eyeglasses.

Florence (2002) says, "When someone you love dies, a part of yourself dies too." Lost is the ability to control pain. Rando (1993) describes grief spasms, "grief attacks": "an acute upsurge of grief that occurs suddenly and often when least expected after the death. It interrupts ongoing activities and temporarily leaves a person feeling out of control . . . sometimes felt as waves or pangs that produce painful emotional and physical sensations (p. 44) . . . Physical effects are manifest in the body; anorexia, apathy, feelings of emptiness, heaviness, feeling something is stuck in the throat, smothering sensations, trembling, et al." (p. 46).

Some friends or those who never experienced the loss of the intimate/love partner are unable to understand; they are impatient and judgmental about grief feelings. Lost is the camaraderie of certain others, adding more isolation and aloneness. Emery (1998) explains, "unfortunately, our society provides little support for the normal process of remembering and exploring the complicated feelings related to loss . . . our culture's values, such as the emphasis on being optimistic and taking control of one's life, are antithetical to the mourning process . . . the contemporary family and friends of the grieving person may not recognize that they are witnessing a normal process. They may be frightened by the mourner's open expression of sadness, pain, anger and fear that he is on the verge of a psychological breakdown . . . one clergy-man has commented, 'there is an epidemic of unhealed grief in our society.'" Thus the griever is alone, hides their feelings, feels isolated, not understood, set aside, excluded, definitely an outsider and clearly feeling lonely; not only for the lost love, but for a community of others who can understand grief. In the eight-session bereavement group I attended, for the over 60's, with a won-derful clinical social worker, we begged her to stay with us after the 8 ses-sions. Tom, who sat next to me, said to her, "but we can't end, you know I don't *have* a mother!" All 10 of us in the group were in agreement. It makes sense that the death of the loved spouse feels like the death of one's mother; how powerful and multidimensional the loved other becomes.

Hagman (1995) notes, "the loss is of the specific, unique and distinct na-ture of the selfobject—one of the core issues in bereavement has caused the irreplaceable rupture that leads to affective turmoil, and dramatic psychic change" (p.199).

In letters to her friends, Oates said: "Losing a spouse of 47 years is like losing a part of yourself—*the most valuable part.* What is left behind seems so depleted, broken" (p. 84). "There are bouts of *utter loneliness* and a sense of purposelessness" (p. 5). "There does not seem to be much purpose to my life now, except these meaningless but necessary tasks (like speaking with a fu-neral director), buying a cemetery plot and looking for the Last Will & Testa-ment" (p. 84).

The Assumptive World theory explains that a large swath of internal in-formation is shaken and lost at the death of the loved other. Lost, for openers, is the sense of victory over death. We feel immortal in the unconscious—or, let us say, we live a dual reality: foreverness/(immortality) as one belief alongside the awareness of the reality of death. Rando (1993) defines the as-sumptive world "as an organized schema containing everything a person assumes to be true about the world and the self on the basis of previous ex-periences . . . the death of a loved one always violates the mourner's specific assumptions about the loved one's continued interactive presence and violates the countless expectations the mourner held for that person's forming a sig-nificant part of the world" (p. 51). Freud (1915), wrote, "To anyone who lis-tened to us we were of course prepared to maintain that death was the neces-sary outcome of life, that everyone owes nature a death and must expect to pay the death. In short, that death was natural, undeniable and unavoidable. In reality, however we were accustomed to behave as it were otherwise. . . . It is indeed impossible to imagine our own death; and whenever we attempt to do so we are in fact still present as spectators. . . . (How many times I have imagined my funeral and considered what I would like said) . . . the psychoanalytic school could venture on the assertion that at bottom no one believes in his own death, or to put the same thing in another way, that in the unconscious every one of us is convinced of his own immortality" (p. 289).

In, Capacity to Cure: Inevitable Failure, Guilt and Symptoms, a chapter in the book *The Inner World of the Mother,* Turrini (2003) observes that the belief in the invincible capacity to cure begins to develop in the first year of life; we can cure anyone from anything (p. 149). Despite higher-level awareness, the original grandiose belief remains as a substrate in the inner world of the adult (mother/spouse). Primary process magical cures develop that serve to support this inner erroneous conviction (pp. 149-168). Death of the other demonstrates failure and helplessness over life and curing. Death, of course, brings an end to "keeping the other person alive"—or does it? Let us look at the resting place of the loved spouse.

The Object Is Not Lost

Clewell (2004) discusses Freud's "Late Theory of Endless Mourning." In this paper she points out that in "On Transience," Freud (1916) repeats and begins to challenge his early account of mourning. His work substantially revises our understanding of what it means to work through a loss. Working through no longer entails abandoning the object and reinvesting the free libido in a new one: it no longer entails accepting consolation in the form of an external substitute for the loss . . . rather, working through depends on taking the lost other into the structure of one's own identity, a form of preserving the lost object in and as the self" (p. 60). Freud confirms the persistence of mourning when he generalizes from the experience of his daughter's death nine years earlier: "Although we know that after such a loss the acute state of mourning will subside, we also know we shall remain inconsolable and will never find a substitute. . . . It is the way it should be. It is the only way of perpetuating the love which we do not want to relinquish" (p. 61).

Ornstein (2010) describes it as follows: "A significant change in his (Freud's) theory occurred when the emphasis shifted from the overriding importance he accorded detachment (decathexis), to an increasing emphasis on the internalization of the lost object" (p. 632). In her article, *The Missing Tombstone, Reflections on Mourning and Creativity* she refers to analytic authors who consider that "successful mourning involves a demand that we make on ourselves to create something—whether it be a memory, a dream, a story a poem, a response to a poem—that begins to meet, to be equal to, the full complexity of our relationship to what has been lost and to the experience of loss itself" (p. 636). This is an optimistic view, that loss and loneliness can be eliminated.

Rando (1993) views mourning through the process of enabling the mourner to recognize the loss, react, and recollect and re-experience the deceased and the relationship: "Before mourners are able to relinquish old attachments and subsequently readjust to move adaptively into the new world without forgetting the old, they must first (a) review and remember realistically and (b) revive and re-experience the feelings associated with the deceased and the relationship. The loved spouse becomes alive in inner recollection and representation; he/she resides in the inner world, and vitalizing memories and sensations that bring forth pleasure, fond remembrance, joy and the experience of loving, and lovability." In 1988, Rando said, " I have found that most have an insufficient understanding of what is necessary to successfully resolve grief. For example, they don't help you develop a new type of relationship with your deceased loved one or talk about how to keep that person 'alive' appropriately. . ." (p. 4). One of the times I felt so stuck in loss, a clinical social work therapist who had studied with Rando suggested I write letters to Niel, and tell him what he had done for me and describe what was lost. As odd as that first sounded, it was a delightful experience. . . . I was directed to communicate with Niel, to enliven him in my mind's eye, which is in my body, and I was to learn how much he had done for me; giving breath and words to past experiences that probably were resting in the preconscious. I was freed for the foreground vitalization of the Niel in me—to have a lively, personified inner Niel with meanings and emotions . . . my opened eyes. This is the opposite of decathexis, and a valuable treatment option for those helping the mourner, a new construction of life within. I recalled our academic commitments and support of each other; our running the world while reading the *New York Times* in bed each morning for 50 years; the joy of holding hands in the movies, among other lovely ongoing vivid memories. I moved from a conviction of decathecting the object to the alive object. When, recently, a fifty-year-old patient with three young children told me her husband had died suddenly of a heart attack, she also said she knew he was really in California playing baseball—trips that he often had taken. We both nodded. Even her trip to a medium at our local theater seemed reasonable. Another woman visits the gravesite and has a conversation. So be it. These folks are moving along with their lives, these are inner relationships that serve them well.

I end with a few lines from May Sarton's poem "All Souls" Here we get a glimpse of the powerful enduring bonds we all share with our lost loved ones:

Did someone say that there would be,
An end, an end, Oh, an end to love and mourning?
What has been once so interwoven cannot be raveled,
Not the gift ungiven,

References

Akhtar, S. (2006). Seminar Lecture, Cape Cod. Massachusetts.

───── (2009). *Comprehensive Dictionary of Psychoanalysis.* London: Karnac Books, p. 195.

Arlow, J.A. (1978). Pyromania and the primal scene: A psychoanalytic comment on the work of Yukio Mishima. *Psychoanalytic Quarterly* 47:24-51.

Bergmann, M. (2002), *The Hartmann Era.* New York: Other Press, p.42.

Blanck, G. (2000). *Primer of Psychotherapy; A Developmental Perspective.* Northvale , NJ: Jason Aronson.

───── & Blanck, R. (1974). *Ego Psychology; Theory and Practice.* New York Columbia University Press.

Bowlby, J. (1961). Process of Mourning, *International Journal of Psychoanalysis* 42:317–340.

───── (1969). Attachment and Loss: Vol. 1: Attachment. *International Psychoanalytic Library.* London: Hogarth Press, pp. 1–401.

───── (1973). Attachment and Loss Vol 11. Separation Anxiety. *International Psychoanalytic Library.* London: Hogarth Press, p. 91.

Breuer, J. & Freud, S. (1895). Studies on hysteria. *Standard Edition* 2:1–321.

Clewell, T. (2004). Mourning beyond melancholia: Freud's psychoanalysis of loss, *Journal of the American Psychoanalytic Association* 52:43–67.

Emery, P. (1998), Nassau Newsnotes. *Clinical Social Work Newsletter,* Spring, p 8.

Edward, J., & Ruskin, N., & Turrini, P, (1991). *Separation Individuation, Theory and Application,* 2nd ed. New York: Brunner/Mazel.

Florence, S.S. (2002). *When You Lose Someone You Love. . . .a journey through the heart of grief,* A Helen Exley Giftbook, in the Journeys Series.

Freud, S. (1915). Thoughts for the Times on War and Death, 11, Our Attitudes Towards Death. *Standard Edition* X1V:289–300.

───── (1917). Mourning and Melancholia. *Standard Edition* 14:237–260.

───── (1926). Inhibitions, Symptoms and Anxiety. *Standard Edition.* 20:75–175.

───── (1950). Project for a Scientific Psychology (1950 [1895]). *Standard Edition* I: 281–391

Grotstein, J. (1982), The Spectrum of Aggression, *Psychoanalytic Inquiry* 2:193–211.

Hagman, G. (1995). The death of the selfobject: Toward a self psychology of the mourning process. *Progress in Self Psychology* 11:189–205.

Hartmann, H. (1939–1958). *Ego Psychology and the Problem of Adaptation.* New York: International Universities Press.

Jacobson, E. (1964). *Self and the Object World.* New York: International Universities Press .

Kohut, H., & Wolf, E.S. (1978). The Disorders of the Self and their Treatment: An Outline. *International Journal of Psycho-Analysis* 59:413-425.

——— (1984). *How Does Analysis Cure?* eds. A. Goldberg & P.E. Stepansky. Chicago, IL: University of Chicago Press.

Lewis. C.S. (1961). *A Grief Observed.* New York: Harper Collins.

Lifton J. (1967). *Death in Life. Survivors of Hiroshima.* New York: Random House.

Mahler, M., Bergman, A., & Pine, F. (1975). *Separation Individuation.* New York: Jason Aronson.

Mahler, M. (1979). *The Selected Papers of Margaret Mahler.* New York: Jason Aronson.

Mendell, D., & Turrini, P. (2003). *Inner World of the Mother.* Madison, CT: Psychosocial Press.

Oates, J. (2011), *A Widows's Story, A Memoir,* New York: Harper Collins.

Ornstein, A. (2010). The missing tombstone: Reflections on mourning and creativity. *Journal of the American Psychoanalytic Association* 58:631–648.

Poland, W. (2012). "Outsiderness", lecture, Sando Rado Lecture, Columbia University, & Association for Psychoanalytic Medicine, Academy of Medicine, New York City.

Rando, T. (1993). *Treatment of Complicated Mourning,* Champaign, IL: Research Press. www.researchpress.com

——— (1988) *How to Go On Living When Someone You Love Dies.* New York: Bantam Books.

Silverman, H., Lachmann, F., & Milich, R. (1982) *The Search for Oneness.* New York: International Universities Press, New York.

Spitz, R. (1965). *The First Year of Life: A Psychoanalytic Study of Normal and Deviant Development of Object Relations.* New York: International Universities Press.

Stolorow, R. (2007). *Trauma and Human Existence, Autobiographical, Psychoanalytic and Philosophical Reflections,* New York: Routledge.

Turrini, P. (2003). Capacity to Cure: Inevitable Failure, Guilt and Symptoms. In: The Inner World of the Mother. Madison:, CT: International Universities Press.

Weinberger J. & Smith, B. (2011). Investigating merger: Subliminal psychodynamic activation and oneness in motivation research. *Journal of the American Psychoanalytic Association* 59:557–570.

Wikipedia, (2012a). Broken Heart, http://wikipedia.org/wiki/Broken Heart

——— (2012b), Loneliness, http://en.wikipedia.org/wiki/loneliness

Williams, K. (2011). The Pain of Exclusion. *Scientific American Mind* January/February, 21:30–37.

Wolf, E. (1994). Selfobject Experiences: Development, psychopathology, Treatment. In: *Mahler and Kohut,* eds. S. Kramer & S. Akhtar. London: Jason Aronson.

Chapter 17
A Soldier's Loneliness
Amit Goldenberg and Nathan Szajnberg

Abstract:

Loneliness, solitude, aloneness—how can a soldier experience these feelings when they are surrounded by buddies and faced with enemies? We will listen to the experiences of three soldiers in elite combat units who can teach us about the continuum of loneliness, about how one's pre-soldier inner life colors these experiences, even how one's weapon—never parted from—serves as an ambivalent companion. Much of this chapter will be the words of the soldiers; then we will initiate some thoughts.

First, background. All these young men are citizen-soldiers from elite units in the Israel Defense Forces. That is, enlisted at seventeen or eighteen, they served the required three years and then, for those promoted to officer, an additional year or more; afterwards, all returned to civilian life. But, civilian life in Israel is unique for its young men and women. At least for men, they are required to serve in the reserves up to one month annually until they are forty; when there is war, they are called up for additional time. All the battles are within a few kilometers, or at most a six-hour drive from their homes; unlike the U.S. Army, they serve close to home.

Second, more background on what makes one "elite." Each recruit is given an overall rating for army, the Kaba score. It is empirically derived and involves not only academic excellence, IQ, physical health and stamina, but also factors such as ethnic and family backgrounds: empirically, for instance, those from Yemenite or Druze or Kibbutz backgrounds make better soldiers.

But, how can one feel 'lonely' in the army, other than homesick, when one is surrounded by body masses of so many other people, and rarely is alone? Here is a vignette about how one retired general describes driving his son to the Bakum, the recruitment center. This was his only son, and father and mother agreed that for his seventeenth year before recruitment, they would treat him as a prince; give him whatever he desired. On the day of recruitment, the father drove his "prince" to the Bakum. When he arrived, he saw thousands of other fathers and their princes—thousands. What, he thought, makes his son more a prince than the others? (The boy went on to become a pilot and flew the first Ethiopian refugees to Israel in Operation Solomon. Of this act by his son, the father—a retired general who developed the Israel helicopter attack force and the first IDF orchestra—is proudest. [Szajnberg, 2011]).

One soldier described his tactic to keep from getting picked on by officers in the Bakum: always look like you are going someplace, about to do something. Then, among the thousands surrounding, you are less likely to get picked out for some unsavory task.

273

When we listen to these soldiers, we hear multiple flavors of loneliness, from early in their service, to when they are "veterans," all of age twenty-one. We hear how their buddies help or don't. We hear how context, such as the hand-to-hand combat in Gaza, affects loneliness. And we hear how one's weapon, which must always be in one's possession, serves various functions around loneliness: The Hebrew for gun, "Neshek," has the same root as "kiss," (Nishika), just as the word for bullet, Kadoor, is a homonym with "ball," Kadoor. There is even a verbal intimacy with the weapon in Hebrew. How much must one be with one's weapon? A favorite officer tactic is to wait for a green recruit to take a piss, leaving his weapon behind: the officer nabs the gun and the recruit returns empty-handed and is then punished for not guarding his weapon.

Another vignette. When I drove back from a small town in Israel to return to Jerusalem, I (NS) offered a ride to some young soldiers. Five piled in, threw their rucksacks into the baggage, but sat with their M16's, muzzle upwards at attention, between their knees; my Toyota Prius was bristling with arms, possibly, just possibly, the best armed Prius in the Middle East.

Let's listen to Ori, a member of Sayeret Matkal, the Israeli equivalent of Delta Force,[1] Green Berets or Navy Seals. Here, Ori Speaks:

---

[1] Haney's Inside Delta Force described the selection course and its inception in detail. Haney writes, the selection course began with standard tests including push-ups, sit-ups, a 2-mile (3.2 km) run, an inverted crawl and a 100 meter swim while fully dressed. The selection candidates were then put through a series of land navigation courses, including an 18-mile (29 km), all-night land navigation course while carrying a 40-pound (18 kg) rucksack. With every march, the rucksack's weight and the distance of the courses are increased, and the time standards to complete the task are shortened. The physical testing ended with a 40-mile (64 km) march with a 45-pound (20 kg) rucksack over very rough terrain, which had to be completed in an unknown amount of time. Haney wrote that only the senior officers and NCO in charge of Selection are allowed to see the set time limits, but all assessment and selection tasks and conditions were set by Delta training cadre [14][15]. The mental portion of the testing began with numerous psychological exams. The men then went in front of a board of Delta instructors, unit psychologists and the Delta commander, who each ask the candidate a barrage of questions and then dissect every response and mannerism of the candidate with the purpose to mentally exhaust the candidate. The unit commander then approaches the candidate and tells him if he has been selected. If an individual is selected for Delta, he undergoes an intense 6-month Operator Training Course (OTC), to learn counter-terrorism and counter-intelligence techniques. This includes ?re-arm accuracy and various other munitions training
Training: Operator Training Course: According to the book Inside Delta Force, by Eric Haney, OTC consisted of the following events. Although OTC has probably changed since then, it remains around 6 months long.

274

Marksmanship: The students shoot stationary targets at close range until they are able to achieve almost complete accuracy. They will then move on to moving targets. Once shooting skills are perfected, they will move to a shooting house where they will clear rooms of "enemy" targets. At first it will be done by one student, then two at a time, three at a time, and finally four. After the students learn techniques to clear a room, "hostages" are added to the room and mixed with the enemies.

Demolitions; Combined skills: The FBI, FAA, and other agencies were used to advise the training of this portion of OTC. Sometimes commercial airliners such as Delta Air Lines would allow Delta to train on their aircraft.

Students learn how to break into many different locks, such as a car's, and safes. Demolition and how to build bombs out of various commonly found materials. The new Delta operators use both demolition and marksmanship skills at the shoothouse and other training facilities to train for hostage and counter-terrorist operations with both assault and sniper troops working together. They practice terrorist or hostage situations in buildings, aircraft, and other settings.

All trainees learn how to set sniper positions around a building with hostages in it. They learn the proper ways to set up a OTC and communicate in an organized manner. Although Delta has specialized sniper troops, all members go through this training.

* The students then go back to the shoothouse and the "hostages" are replaced with other students and Delta Force members. It is known that live ammunition has been used in these exercises, to test the students and build trust among them.

* Trade Craft – During the first OTC's and creation of Delta, CIA personnel were used to teach this portion.

* Students learn different espionage-related skills such as dead drops, brief encounters, pickups, load and unload signals, danger and safe signals, surveillance and countersurveillance.

* Executive Protection—During the first OTC's and creation of Delta, the U.S. State Department's Diplomatic Security Service and the United States Secret Service would advise Delta in this portion of training.

Culmination Exercise

* Although these are the main skills taught in every OTC, no OTC classes are ever exactly the same.

Delta Force has occasionally cross-trained with similar units from allied countries. Students take an advanced driving course learning how to use a vehicle or many vehicles as defensive and offensive weapons. They then learn techniques developed by the Secret Service and DSS on how to cover a VIP and diplomatic protection missions.

A final test that requires the students to apply and dynamically adapt all of the skills that they have learned.

275

"The first memory I have about loneliness and the army is during my first guard duty at the second day of my service. We were guarding our small campsite with no clear purpose inside a huge base, as the base itself was guarded from the outside. This was the beginning of my disciplinary education. I realized there is no real purpose in the duty, but accepted it anyhow. It was right after I got my gun; (on the one hand) I was very excited that I have it with me. On the other hand, I remember realizing how heavy and annoying it is; I thought to myself that in the last few days, more and more things were put on my body (heavy shoes, uniform, gun, a clip, the ammunition vest, helmet) and made movement much less fun. I was assigned for my guard duty between 16:00 and 17:00, a full hour. I specifically remember the hour as I saw the sun sinking down. I wore my helmet, vest and held my gun and went to the position to start the shift. Five minutes after beginning, I became bored and terrified: this is how my life will look in the next three years. I looked at the people in the distance and did not feel connected to them. I remember the feeling of loneliness together with the realization that this is what I will experience in the future. I decided to start singing to myself, see if I can remember all the words of a song. There was a Radiohead song that I loved called "Exit music." These are the words:

> Wake . . . from your sleep
> The drying of your tears
> Today we escape, we escape.
> Pack . . . and get dressed
> Before your father hears us
> Before all hell breaks loose
> Breathe, keep breathing
> Don't lose your nerve
> Breathe, keep breathing
> I can't do this alone.
> Sing . . . us a song
> A song to keep us warm
> There's such a chill, such a chill
> You can laugh
> A spineless laugh
> We hope your rules and wisdom choke you
> Now we are one in everlasting peace
> We hope that you choke, that you choke
> We hope that you choke, that you choke
> We hope that you choke, that you choke

I sang the song repeatedly and it calmed me down. I said to myself, from now on, I will sing every time that I have a duty and this way I will feel better, this is how I will survive. I looked at my watch; time did not pass. I looked, and looked, and looked, and walked a little more and tried to think of things, my friends at home, my parents. Tried to imagine how it would feel to come back home. Finally the hour passed. I remember thinking to myself that this is what the army really is. How did I not know it before? Why did nobody tell me about this?"

Why didn't anybody tell me about this? Ori's father was a senior officer in the reserves, looked forward to his monthly reunion with his buddies. Ori knew a lot about the army, just not this, the moments of loneliness and boredom and terror, and even feeling unconnected to the humankind around him. He had been recruited and trained as a pilot, but when he was assigned to fly cargo planes, as opposed to jets, he chose to "demote" himself to Sayeret Matkal, and became a sniper in his unit. At one point, he was stationed outside Ramallah, he trained his gun on Yasir Arafat, waiting for an order to shoot him, an order, that obviously never came. He recalls using his high-powered site to read the hand written notes that Arafat got from visitors: he was struck at what an old man Arafat appeared to be. He recalled pissing in a bottle on the days that he was alone, behind a berm, waiting for that order that never came.

Here, Ori describes the imaginary character, Shmeuly, he created in basic training, about whom he wrote over the next few years.

"In a diary that I wrote during basic training, I wrote in one of the pages, under the headline 'alone'": "How many friends does Shmeuly have? A million, but he is all alone. Shmuely sometimes feels that his destiny in this world is just to walk and not stop. Everybody talks, all day long, everyone is sad, happy, hugging each other, crying on others' shoulders and never stops. Shmuely stands all alone. Sometimes he cries, sometimes he is happy, but usually it's the same feeling. Do you understand me?"

Ori brings us a few months later, after basic training, mobilized in the territories.

"We were sent right after basic training for a week of "field work." The officers claimed this was so we will know more about the army life in the Palestinian territories. We got assigned with a group of older soldiers from another unit. They took advantage of the motivated soldiers who came to redeem them for the week, and put us right in the toughest guarding stands. The shifts were 4:8 shifts. 4 hours of guard duty and 8 hours of "rest," in which we had to do other stuff, such as cleaning and cooking. The rest of the time, we were sent on special operations, such as arrests and ambushes. My stand was a tower at the North West end of the base. This was a very big base; much too large for the amount of soldiers who were there at the time. It was also in the middle of the West Bank and I (felt) scared. I despised my 4 hours of duty. I did not know what the hell could I do not to die from boredom. . . . the first few days I tried Zen meditation . . . calm and unaware of time and boredom and the loneliness I felt all through that week. After a week I started taking books to the guard booth. I read Jorge Luis Borges and The Victim, by Saul Bellow. I loved his descriptions of New York. It was the most remote and different place I could imagine, compared to where I was . . . . Reading while guarding was completely forbidden, I felt I had no other choice to . . . keep my sanity. One night, while reading with a flashlight, an officer came to give me coffee and check up on me; he caught me with the book. I begged him to not tell anyone; punishment was staying up in the base during the weekend and I felt I had to go home. He nodded and left. He spoke to no one."

Part of advanced training is to be left alone to navigate the desert without a map. Let us follow him.

"In advanced training, we had weeks of one person navigation sessions (Nivut badad). This meant navigating to different points without a map; we memorized the map. We walked 30-40 Kilometers every night. Some weeks included food deprivation, and some included only 1 hour of sleep. While nights were very lonely, I already felt I could cope better with the time alone. It was almost like I have a break from everything that was going on and I could be me again. I mostly fantasized: about women. I would meet at home, things I would do, how one day I would be a great scientist or a writer. Sometimes, I imagined a girl as some kind of a background picture in the night skies, like the mother of the universe. She had long hair and was smiling at me with her beautiful eyes. She was between a mother and a lover. I also sang a lot to myself; told stories from my childhood. To deal with the sadness of loneliness, I imagined I had super powers and could fly elsewhere. This way I could escape and return and nobody could notice.

As training advanced, we spend more time alone. For one week, we studied the navigation path; the second week, we hiked alone. We sought shelter during the day, waited for the sunset, then hiked again. I remember lying down on the ground, looking at insects or playing with my finger with the dust for hours. I got much better at coping with being alone for longer periods of time, but also felt melancholic for long hours. I kept trying not to give up on life, and would pack a book with me or a pen and a notebook so I could write and read. In one of the weeks, someone from an older team met me at a water point and gave me a letter from a girl I dated back then. I read it during that week, maybe 100 times, and during the nights, I imagined the meetings with her at the end of the week. This was one of the more easy weeks for me. When I came back home I realized I created a completely different person in my head, and that the real girl was a pale version of the one I remembered. Since I imagined full intimate conversations with this girl, I didn't know how to start and talk about regular stuff. At the end, I just left her in the middle of the night on Friday and came back home.

I remember before the long navigation weeks started, I would get this thick sadness and stop to communicate with other people. Our team had a person following us and taking care of the administration. He was a very quiet guy, and I always preferred riding with him to the field or back to the base. He was always giving me a cigarette and we would smoke in silence. This was much better for me to start the weeks like this.

Another strong feeling I recall well, was while spending time with my teammates. I suddenly felt that I am very different, that they could never understand me. A burden I carried all the time, was the feeling that I could not give up the appearance of being strong. Once you start being weak, I felt, you are done.

Then, I became sad, quiet and look at everyone from the outside. I felt lonely and detached; I wanted to go home."

Note the flavors of loneliness that evolved with training and service: at times mixed with fear or boredom, at times, feeling disconnected, detached even when with buddies.

Note also the ways in which Ori copes with these states of loneliness. Fantasies: of the night sky as mother/lover; of the smile in the sky's face; of a future greatness as scientist or writer; he imagined himself in New York; he developed the superpower of flying (a form of regression in the service of the ego); His early song of Exit involves escaping with another and a sense of anger at the ones with rules and "wisdom" (such as his officers, his government); he recruited childhood stories and created an imaginary friend about whom he wrote throughout his service. Meditation did not work, but later, a cigarette with a buddy in silence did. Note the predominance of high level defenses but detachment may also be used.

Let's turn to our second soldier. Boaz felt lonely in the crowd of soldiers on his first day:

"We had a show about Golani (Brigade, his unit) and everybody got up and danced to the songs. I set sat in my chair and felt I am different and lonely. I felt like this a lot during the start but then I met a group of people I connected with."

This feeling recurred. Yet, paradoxically, he realizes one precipitant for loneliness is loss of his cohort. Because he was a medic, he had to stay back when most of his unit was sent for commander course. That is, he felt alone in the crowd and alone when they left him. When his group left, this precipitated a crisis:

"I remember going to Hebron and meeting this guy I knew from home who just got off the army due to psychological reasons. He looked so happy to me, so relieved. He told me this is the right thing to do and I appreciated this man. I remember (returning) to a guard duty by myself, feeling like I do not want to be there, that I am not going to make it during the duty. I think that as a kid I could not be alone. I always needed more people next to me. After the service, I changed and started to prefer (solitude) sometimes. But at this time, I remember great sadness.

Shvizut. You have to do things and you cannot choose not to do them. You are always harassed and there is no rest. Coming back to the army from home is very connected to me with the feeling of detachment and loneliness. I was a good soldier, I wanted to be a good soldier but I felt that my loneliness and sadness are taking over me. Guard duty, in general, is strongly connected to me with being lonely. The feeling is so strong. It is boredom combined with loneliness."

Shvizut is an acronym that refers to a specific feeling that a soldier has of sadness that he has when he needs to return to his duty on Sunday morning after a Shabbat leave. In Israel, one becomes accustomed to the Sunday morning sights of young men in green khakis, loaded down with backpacks, bristling with M-16's, crowded into public buses.

Listen to what Daniel did to overcome the loneliness and boredom of guard duty:

"I played games, for example: I had a timer in my watch and I tried repeatedly to start and pause it directly at 10 seconds exactly. I would try to remember the 92 clubs in the English soccer leagues, who played in which team, anything that could distract me. I remember planning on not looking at the clock for a while and then hoping that time passed up faster. Trying to count the seconds in my head and then see if I am right. All these games to keep me distracted."

Boaz returns to the personal crisis when his unit left for three months commander training: during this time, guard duty was a respite, not a burden:

"Now when I think about it, when my friends left, it was a big crisis for me. I started to see an army psychologist and asked him to get me out of the army. I did not feel close to anyone. I remember missing my friends and not knowing what to do. I was almost out of the army and then my friends came back from the commander's course and I felt okay again. It was the hardest 3 months of my service.

During that time I remember coming back home and feeling so bad and angry. I did not talk to anyone and wanted to be alone all weekend.

I remember once during that time I decided to escape from the base with another guy. This was a way for us to stop feeling lonely, by planning it together. We planned to leave back home and to stay there for two weeks until the military police will come and take us to prison. This way they would kick us from the operating unit. At the day of the escape, I folded and he left and came back after half an hour. We spent more than two weeks on planning, just for the hope, so we would feel connected. I realized back then I do not want to sit in prison.

I remember that a weekend after, I came back home and told my mother I cannot go back, that I was done. My mom said to me, you can do whatever you want; I will support you no matter what you will do. At the end I came back. I kept doing it for a while, trying to get her approval and then staying. I felt that staying is the proper thing to do.

At that time it wasn't like during basic training. I wanted to guard, guarding meant being undisturbed. It was not a burden. I wanted to be alone. Sometime guarding with just one person was the best. In Hebron I had a friend who loved soccer, we would play a game of trying to remember names of players. We played it for hours."

His buddies, upon return, became a tonic for his loneliness:

"I remember being supported by the friends I started the army with. I feel like they know me. I would sit in my bed and my friend would come and say, Boaz is depressed again, let's make him happy, and make me laugh. If it were not for them, I would have lost my mind. They were the best people, I still feel very connected with them.

The more the army progressed; I remember being very sad all the time but also feeling very motivated to do. I coped with the sadness and loneliness with doing stuff. The more I progressed in the army the more I realized I had to do in order to feel better. Being active and closer to my old friends, that's what saved me."

What was his relationship with his gun?

"I personally was not playing a lot with my weapon, but there were others who were using it a lot to play. When I was in Lebanon, there was a guy who was guarding at nights and he kept claiming that he recognized something just so he could shoot. We would sometimes do this, a few people were guarding the base at different points and we were lonely and bored, so someone would start shooting at the air and all the rest would follow. After a while, the officers realized that he was fucked up and sent him out of Lebanon to stop the shootings. We would do so many things to pass the time, to laugh together. Just shoot at thin air to feel better.

Note that guard duty carried different valences at different periods in the army: early, there was loneliness and boredom; later, when he was angry, felt abandoned by his buddies, and wanted to escape, guard duty offered him time to be alone.

Also, we learn that he thought seriously of going AWOL, as did Ori. Thinking this is not unusual. What is remarkable is the self-restraint to not do this. Another young man, one who had profound rebelliousness against his father (who was so soft-spoken, not militant, so this made rebellion all the more difficult for this boy), decided to go AWOL when the army did not give him placement in one of the most elite units. When he told his father and wanted his father to shelter him and lie to the army, his father quietly refused. When the boy returned and was in the slammer for three months, he returned to duty as a charges-d'affaires of an officer who recognized the young man's intelligence and ability and thought he could redirect his energies, as he did.

Let's listen to one more soldier who speaks of being alone versus loneliness.

Uri:

"Being alone (solitude) was typical for me (before the army); I was not . . . popular kid at school; I was used to being alone. The constant socialization in the army, was the most threatening feeling to me.

I remember the first night off we got in Jerusalem. It was basically just an evening to spend at the city before you go back to base. It was very weird, you suddenly find yourself in a city with your uniforms. The minute they released us, people got together in groups; (in contrast), right away I left to be alone. It was automatic and I did not look at it as if it was anything out of the ordinary. Today at work I can be very aware of being alone, but then I felt like I did not have a choice. The possibility of being alone for a few hours from the social interaction was so intuitive that I just left. I remember going up the hill on Ben Yehuda street, just walking to get detached from everyone like a bomb shot from a cannon. Only now, I understand how irregular this was.

A few hours later, when we returned, I had a guard duty, which was right outside of my friend's room. I heard them talking in the room, 'Did you see Uri? What an idiot! How he was walking alone.' Only then I realized how weird this must have looked. The guy who said it, I thought of him as my friend and I got so offended I couldn't forgive him until today.

I felt back then that there was always a demand to do things in a certain way, to be a certain someone. I felt that I was tested for very narrow things and that I was very bad at them. I felt that I was the worst soldier."

In fact, this boy is placed in an excellent tank unit and served admirably.

Then, after his Gaza experience, he rethinks the nature of loneliness. He is "leftist" politically, doesn't support the settlements, but politics gets thin when rockets keep flying on your compatriots.

"I remember when the second intifada started, they took us and told us that we are going to Gaza. Everyone seemed happy about this; only I and another guy were revolted by the idea. I think that happiness is the army material that I did not have; the fact that I did not have it made me more vulnerable to loneliness

In Gaza I had to be close to my fellow soldiers, because I felt danger. My dependence was comforting and served as a shield. The feeling of loneliness (in Gaza) was completely opposite to before; I kept looking to be near people, hoping they will save me."

Uri comes to a new understanding of his loneliness.

"Loneliness is a matter of understanding. The minute someone understands you, you are not lonely anymore. Only rarely, I felt that I was understood, and I always felt that I am more complex than what the reality is. Maybe I am idealizing this, and of course I had good experiences with other people, but only when they were responsible for me. For me, the opposite of loneliness was dependence.

Back then I was a lost person. I did not have a strong identity; for me that means loneliness. The more you define yourself easily, the less you are lonely."

And his gun?

"The weapon for me was always a comfort. As I was always terrified, this helped me a lot to define who I was and gave me power. On the other hand, I did not feel full control over my weapon; it gives me false sense of control."

Discussion

When we listen to these young men, we hear recurrent themes of loneliness, which can combine with boredom, and terror; loneliness evolves over the course of service and even varies from soldier to soldier: while most agree that the loneliness of guard duty consistently haunts the soldier, one felt lonely in the crowd of his fellow soldiers at first, to value them dearly over time and in the terror of war. Note also how carefully Ori first notices how his body feels different, now weighted down with equipment, armor, weapon. Such embodied body-foreignness can foster a sense of alienation.

In contrast, listen to the panoply of defenses awakened by loneliness. The range of defenses recalls that of Vallaint, et al. (1986) and later Cramer's (2006) hierarchy of defenses. Many of these helped the soldier restore himself. Ori early on created his alter ego, his imaginary character who had a million friends but felt alone. He used a song of escape (and disdain to the rulers and wise men) to become a consoling tune for his service. He recalled childhood stories. Two men read on guard duty, against regulations. On long night hikes, the night sky became a beautiful woman mother/lover who smiled and accompanied him.

One consoled himself with an ex-girlfriend's letter, as well as toying with sand or ants when he had to lay prone for hours. One played time games and mind games with the 92 teams in the English soccer league. And they were benefited from doing and being with their buddies. They thought of escaping, but also imagined flying or feeling detached from those around them: the latter two feelings may be more internally regressed, but also protect the soldier from the external exigencies of going AWOL.

There is another profound difference binding army to democracy: "we serve close to home . . . . We serve and defend our homes, . . . we are involved in politics, but . . . our politics have a direct and harsh affect on our lives. If Israel's prime minister . . . negotiates with the PLO, this will probably affect life in the next reserve. If he decides to keep a settlement . . . we . . . must guard it."

We may not be surprised at the creative range of measures these soldiers use, when we recall that this is a select group: those judged chosen to serve in the better units. But these men, referred to as "reluctant warriors," (Szajnberg, 2011) are not the macho, militaristic jarheads of Hollywood lore; while in action they may be Rio Bravo John Waynes, in attitude they are more Bogart's Marlowe, not flashy, sardonic, effective, quietly self-assured. They are deeply human, they serve because they feel they must, and they will serve as best as they can and are expected to be. And when they are done, they are ready to leave. And they leave us with, we hope, further thoughts about the range of loneliness, and how to cope with this feeling of void.

References

Cramer P. (2006). *Protecting the Self: Defense Mechanisms in Action.* New York: Guilford.

Haney, E.L. (2002). *Inside Delta Force: the story of America's elite counter-terrorist unit.* New York: Dell Publishing.

Szajnberg, N.M. (2011). *Reluctant Warriors: Israelis Suspended Between Rome and Jerusalem.* New York: IPBooks.

Vaillant, G.E., Bond, M., & Vaillant, C. O. (1986). An empirically validated hierarchy of defense mechanisms. *Archives of General Psychiatry* 73:786–794.

Chapter 18
Conclusion
Death is the God of Loneliness
Richard Gottlieb

> *Virgil understood that death begins and never ends,*
> *that it's the god of loneliness.*
> —Philip Schultz[18]

Loneliness is not a psychiatric diagnosis. It makes no appearance in the *Diagnostic and Statistical Manual* of the American Psychiatric Association. Nor is it what analysts call a "signal affect"—like anxiety, depressive affect, and shame—one that, in keeping with Freud's view of anxiety, provides the motive force for defense. Loneliness is a painful complex emotional state that spares none of us. The feeling of loneliness takes hold in states of alienation from ourselves, in which we feel we are not ourselves, not wholly ourselves, or when we feel that a part of ourselves has been torn away. Loneliness has a *forever* aspect. This is why the poet, Schultz, writes that death is "the god of loneliness": it begins and never ends. During their first seventeen days, thirty-three miners thought their ordeal would never end, trapped more than two thousand feet under a Chilean mountain. Their private thoughts turned to cannibalism. "Who will be the first to die? Who will I eat?" There were group discussions of self-asphyxiation as a way to end their suffering. "We can run the generator and seal ourselves into the chamber." Following day seventeen, when the sounds of a probe from the surface signaled that they would be rescued, they suffered seven and one half more weeks under the same conditions but their loneliness lifted. Géricault's painting *The Raft of the Medusa*[19] (1818-1819) depicts the hopelessness of men holding on to life on a raft as a ship, oblivious of their situation, passes in the distance. Despair is a part of loneliness. Schultz—and Virgil—are correct in recognizing that a sense of hopelessness is essential to the experience of loneliness.

It is this aspect of loneliness, its *forever* quality that is its source of horror and its link with death that helps us distinguish it from other states of aloneness such as solitude and withdrawal into creative activity. While not an illness or "disorder," relief from loneliness is very commonly what analytic patients are seeking when they first consult us. A young man who had been rejected by his girlfriend, his first love, told me tearfully that he had sought my help because he had exhausted his friends' patience. He felt they no longer wanted to hear about his misery. Patients with problems forming and sustaining intimate relationships commonly carry a chronic burden of loneliness born of the hopelessness they feel about their futures. Grief—a frequent initial presentation of even more complex problems—brings fear and loneliness in its wide wake.

In his poem Schultz evokes loneliness by creating a group of images. He writes of waiting for hours shivering in the predawn cold; of his being differ-

---

[18] Schultz, Philip (2008). *The God of Loneliness, The New Yorker,* May 5, 2008, page 64. The poem appears in full at the end of this chapter.
[19] The painting is in the Louvre.

ent and alienated from the other men; and of his feeling he has to hide his interest in poetry from them. He evokes an image of the solitary madness of a soldier returned from Iraq who never leaves his room, playing video games night and day. He conjures bodily injury, describing the boy who has lost his teeth. Dying soldiers, rivers of blood, the unavoidable yet mad absurdity of war—he tells of all of these in thirty-three brief lines, culminating in the terror of losing loved ones, his own sons, and finally closes with the terrifying, ironic "it's what men do for their sons." What do men do for their sons, we ask? Stand on line outside the Target store to buy the latest video game? No, not that, says the poet. "I know exactly when my boys will be old enough for war," he writes. Men send their sons to war, that's what they do.

The contributors to this volume have identified an exquisitely painful yet complex emotional state, loneliness. Taken together, this assemblage of essays embodies a kaleidoscope of contemporary psychoanalytic views on this most important subject. To investigate loneliness is analogous to investigating pain. While, like pain, loneliness accompanies so many of the conditions for which we analysts are consulted, it can appear in different guises, sometimes gaping and obvious like a wound, sometimes invisible, lurking beneath the surface like a silent cancer. Also, like pain, a certain degree of loneliness is the unavoidable common fate of all humans. And it can occur in anyone.

In what follows I will ever so briefly summarize what I take to be the salient points of each contribution and add some observations of my own. These are rich essays, full of revealing clinical detail, theoretical subtlety, and acute observations. I urge the reader not to take my few meager paragraphs on each chapter to be thoroughgoing explications. They are intended, rather as intriguing aftertastes of the feast upon which we have indulged.

Section I—Loneliness, Creativity, and the Artists

1. Lois Oppenheim on Samuel Beckett

Professor Oppenheim brings to her very brief essay on the life and work of Samuel Beckett a long immersion in that artist's work and a deep familiarity with his biography. While abjuring naive efforts to reduce an artist's production to his life story, she is able to illustrate how Beckett was pulled toward experimenting with (she calls it "playing with") the human need to oscillate between the pain of loneliness that draws us to seek intimacy with others and the fear of loss of ourselves that causes us to flee such intimacies and seek solitude. Oppenheim shows us that although this oscillation is a universal human condition, it was especially powerful for Samuel Beckett. It—that is, the oscillation—is everywhere in evidence in his work, from the indelibly memorable visual staging of his plays to his frantic manipulation of language to his individual characterizations and finally to his portrayals of relationships.

Oppenheim's criticism opens a window onto Beckett's *oeuvre* that allows us to grasp what is sometimes otherwise latent, perplexing, or obscure. She is able to guide us through his more bizarre landscapes without oversimplification or resorting to reductionist accounts, common errors committed in much so-called psychoanalytic criticism or psychobiography. At the same time Professor Oppenheim is psychoanalytically sensitive, so that it strikes her that Beckett's portraits of human oscillation (from isolation to loneliness to going-in-search-of the other to the terror of confused or lost identity to flight from intimacy back to isolation, loneliness, and so forth) are suggestive of some of what has been written about the oscillation of the psychoanalytic situation itself. In particular, Oppenheim realizes that Leo Stone was groping for words to describe a similar tension, one deliberately realized by the psychoanalytic treatment setup, when he wrote of the latter being a setting of "deprivation in intimacy" (1977). In a sense it is this very deprivation in intimacy that can move the psychoanalytic work forward, and it is this same dimension that tends to make analytic work possible. It is that deprivation in intimacy, in Stone's meaning of these words, that is violated and collapsed by the many and varied means by which analysts may abandon their task and trample necessary therapeutic boundaries (Gabbard and Lester, 1995). To imagine such a travesty, imagine a Sistine Chapel ceiling in which God and Adam are holding hands rather than being in their state of separated-yet-intimate tension.

Beckett is an extreme case, both because of his creative brilliance and the depth of his psychopathology. But Oppenheim has made clear that the issue of oscillation around intimacy and solitude that he portrays, "plays with," and seems to have endured is neither extreme nor unusual. It seems instead to be universal, and so one of the reasons for this artist's wide appeal.

2. Danielle Knafo on the solitude of artists and the creative process

Like Oppenheim examining Beckett, Knafo focuses on the solitude of artistic endeavor and creation. Knafo's interest is not so much in the artist's conflict that results in the kind of moth-flame oscillation described by Oppenheim. What engages Knafo is the artist's need for solitude as a condition necessary for creative processes to emerge. Sometimes, radical solitude may be an unwanted visitation, as was the case for Jean-Dominique Bauby who, because of a massive stroke, was trapped inside his body able to move only his eyelid. But Bauby was able to salvage from his horrendous fate the solitude necessary to produce a memoir, his *The Diving Bell and the Butterfly*.

While claiming that "artistic creation is, in essence, a solitary vocation," Knafo acknowledges that even while one—or, in particular, an artist—is alone, he or she may be relating to one or more important internal objects. I recall listening to Hannah Arendt once say, "When I am by myself I am never alone." I understood her to mean that when by herself (solitude) she was in communication with the others, in her scholarly philosophic world, with whom she communed about the issues of concern to her. This must be true of all of us, in the same sense that Winnicott intended when he said, famously, that there is no such thing as a baby. Speaking to this truth, Knafo tells us that solitude and relationship are interrelated and layered states that exist in dynamic interaction.

And yet Knafo recognizes that ultimately, there is some sense in which we are each of us utterly and absolutely alone. This experience can be the most unsettling, awful human experience of all, an indescribable and impenetrable burden that "drives us . . . to connect with others . . . This movement itself is an act of creativity, for each individual must find a way to deal with his or her own solitude. Therefore, creativity too is not an option; *it is a necessary condition of being radically alone*." (Italics in Knafo's original.)

Knafo concludes her investigation of aloneness, solitude, and creativity with an examination of gendered solitude. "Solitude for women is different," Knafo avers, "than it is for men." Much of her argument here is sociological, deriving the differences she finds primarily from the differing social roles of men and women in our culture.

Ultimately Knafo tells us that we humans are burdened by a "ground" (in the sense of in the background, a *basso continuo*, always present) experience of our utter aloneness in the universe. She writes that "Indeed, we all have . . . within us a state of dreaded isolation that exists just beneath the surface of our consciousness . . . That this terror-filled emptiness quickly makes itself known . . . when one encounters the loss of a significant other or when one is faced with a terminal illness . . . It underlies all human dread." Creativity, that of the artist or of us ordinary mortals, comprises our efforts to reach toward relatedness from within that state of dreaded isolation.

3. Arlene Kramer Richards: *The Skin I Live In* (A film by Almodovar)

Dr. Richards organizes her discussion of loneliness around the 2011 Pedro Almodovar film *The Skin I Live In* (*La Piel Que Habito*). The film's plot is a bizarre story of a beautiful woman—the prisoner of a doctor who performs experiments on her—who, it turns out, is not a woman after all. "She" had previously been a man whom the doctor had forced to undergo a sex change operation. Watching this film literally makes the viewer's skin crawl, yet we can recognize in Almodovar's script concrete representations of essential aspects of loneliness. Later in this volume several other authors (Mendelsohn, Buechler, Turrini) stress the idea that loneliness is undergirded by experiences of alienation from one's self, of loss of or distance from our usually confident sense of identity, of who we are. This alienation is represented in the film as eerily concrete: the "woman" had been a man; "her" skin is not in fact her skin.

Richards exploits this bizarre story to examine the many connections between our bodies—especially our skin and genitalia—our sense of self, and our identities because the film explores the possibilities implicit in our experience when these are lost or alienated from us. This alienation, Richards notes, can happen not only when imposed upon us by an insane doctor (as in the film), it happens regularly in development throughout our lives. We are not snakes that shed their skins periodically, but inevitably and inexorably our bodies undergo changes that alienate us from who we used to be. This process is especially evident and powerful at certain of development's nodal points, puberty and menopause or climacteric. These changes can create a state of "loneliness for one's self," a state that Richards says leaves a person lonely "in the most radical way imaginable." Attempts to avoid this extremely painful state are known to clinicians and include the, sometimes frantic, pursuit of cosmetic surgery by the aging and the, sometimes tragic, ways in which adolescents alter their bodies.

Richards is proposing that the state of longing for oneself, illustrated by *The Skin I Live In*, is "a form of loneliness that no one has ever seen before." Almodovar's novelty was made possible in part because of the advent of sex reassignment surgery: it is now possible for someone to long for their former sexual and gender identity.

4. Jeffrey Stern on Forms and Transformations of Loneliness

Jeffrey Stern makes the unusual claim that to be able to experience loneliness reflects an earlier developmental achievement. It is this idea that sets apart his meditation on our subject. "Our loneliness," he writes, "—defined as our ability to love in the face of loss, privation, and impossibility—is what makes us human."

Loneliness is our ability to love in the face of loss, privation, and impossibility. I find his idea intriguing, although it would be difficult to demonstrate whether he is correct in all cases. In making this claim Stern relies primarily on the developmental ideas of Winnicott and, to a lesser extent, Kohut. For Stern, "good enough" mothering is a precondition of that experience we call loneliness. In Kohut's terms he would say that without early adequately empathic mirroring, experiences of true loneliness would not be possible. Extending this logic through the views of a wide swath of relational thinkers, we might add that processes of early structure formation that rely on positive interactions with caretakers are necessary preconditions of loneliness. The idea is that the lonely individual must have been able to form and sustain a loving bond with the Other in order to experience the longing for reunion that is at the center of experiences of loneliness. One senses here an allusion to Winnicott's "The use of an object" (1969): where—in early development—there has been too much absence the (internal) bond is severed. Odysseus, writes Stern, was capable of feeling lonely (on Calypso's Island) because he "holds the memory of Penelope and his kingdom and child within him from the moment he leaves Ithaca . . . [His] loneliness functions like a radio signal that guides him home." Emphasizing his central point, Stern muses, "One wonders if his

293

men—all of whom perish during the ten-year voyage—do so because they lack the sort of inner bonds Odysseus has to those they leave behind."

While for Stern loneliness is a capacity, it is also a painful feeling state. Art, he writes, "is a response to loneliness and loss." He does not add that art is also frequently a response that is colored by the experience of loneliness itself, sometimes deeply colored by it. Thus it is true that some of our best and most enduring works of art are at one and the same time responses to and portraits of loneliness. And with this principle in mind, Stern leads us on a brief journey through the worlds of film and literature, lighting upon moments of exquisite loneliness as developed by our best artists. Stern becomes a kind of tour guide, pointing out the portrayals of loneliness in a host of works, including Scorcese's *Hugo*, Homer's *Odyssey*, Disney's version of *Pinocchio*, the *Genesis* stories of the creation of Adam and Eve and the expulsion from the Garden, Spielberg's *A. I.*, a collection of literary monsters (curiously not including Frankenstein's very lonely monster or Dracula), an assortment of fairy tales, and ending up with a survey of some of Shakespeare's lonely characters and the loneliness of Shakespeare himself.

At one point Stern becomes much more personal, musing upon "the opaque and formal psychoanalysts I was trained by, who sat unseen and largely unknown behind their couches saying almost nothing." These reflections cause him to wonder if for him, and others so treated, the relational turn in contemporary psychoanalytic technique did not at least in part evolve out of our loneliness engendered by having to assume the opaque and formal roles of our teachers. Although Stern does not develop this perspective any further than to raise this question, we shall return to a fuller consideration of the loneliness of psychoanalytic training in Section III.

Section II—The Clinical Dimensions of Loneliness

5. Lucille Spira on Shades of Loneliness: Psychological and Social Perspectives

Dr. Spira's focus is clinical. She is interested in the lonely person in the room with us. Why is she suffering? Why can she not help herself? How can we help her? Dr. Spira ends on a note of therapeutic caution. She writes, "As an interim step, some people may be helped to feel pleasure in their solitude." Loneliness is not a psychiatric diagnosis; it "transcends diagnostic categories." Forced to assign loneliness to a category, we have to say it is a symptom comprised of painful affects, a longing for companionship or intimacy, a sense of involuntary isolation, mixed together with feelings of rejection, inadequacy, a measure of despair or hopelessness, and at times a painful nostalgia for an idealized past.

Refreshingly, Dr. Spira includes in her analysis a survey of the biological and socio-demographic factors (*e.g.*, widowhood, age, gender, educational status) that can be considered "risk factors" for loneliness. Wisely, she insists "the psychological, biological, and social intertwine in determining a person's loneliness." These multiple determinants are too often overlooked by psychoanalysts whose focus may be on the deepest unconscious psychological layers. I thank Dr. Spira for this important reminder.

While emphasizing the complexity of experiences of loneliness, Dr. Spira is able to convey a bit of the poignancy of her patients' stories. Especially moving is the clinical narrative of an ill obese woman who is coaxed out of her self-imposed and lonely social isolation by an invitation from two younger women to join them for coffee. In the excitement of her newfound social engagement, she attempts to bound over a bench, injures her arm, and has to burden the group with a trip to the emergency room. More than anything, she feels she has humiliated herself and withdraws once again into lonely isolation. Dr. Spira shows us a sensitive response to this woman's mishap, a response that is at once therapeutically ambitious, mindful of the patient's vulnerabilities, and rather insightful.

6. Jerome S. Blackman on "Object Clarification" in the Treatment of Lonely Heterosexual Men

Dr. Blackman presents three memorable psychotherapy cases, one lasting eleven years and the others considerably briefer, in which his patient's most manifest suffering was the pain of longing for an intimate female companion. Analysts will easily recognize a central therapeutic dilemma in these treatments: What is the therapist to do—if anything—when it becomes clear that their patient has crippling limitations in their capacity to understand the "other"? In Blackman's first case his patient was unaware of aspects of his own behavior that guaranteed that any woman he approached would reject him. Although the ultimate outcome of this treatment is unknown, Blackman decided to coach his patient about how to behave differently, first explaining to him how his dates might be misinterpreting his behavior. In the second and third cases, where the patients were less disturbed, the technique was similar, a technique Blackman calls "object clarification." In object clarification, the therapist sets about to explain the other, her psychology, motivations, fears, and so on to the patient. Blackman says he undertakes this strategy because he sees the patient's problem as caused by a limited area of faulty reality testing.

Can "mentalizing" be taught? This might be one way of stating the question implicit in Blackman's technique and argument. Especially in recent years, the capacity to understand that the other has a mind, that that mind causes the other to behave in certain ways, and that that mind is a function of that person's individual wishes, history, fears, hatreds and so on, has been studied extensively. These very complex functions have been grouped together into an umbrella capacity called "mentalization," or "theory of mind," among other terms. The capacity for mentalization has been viewed as an enormously important developmental achievement, dependent for its success upon the nature of our earliest object relationships. Blackman's technique of "object clarification," as well as its possibilities for success and failure, must raise for us some intriguing questions because it is a form of replacement therapy: the therapist will instruct or model or replace crucial steps in his patient's development that were absent, unavailable, or went awry during an early critical period.

One of Blackman's patients seems to have done reasonably well with this technique. But there are so many likely "confounds" in the eleven year long once-weekly psychotherapy that it would be hard to know for sure the effects of "object clarification." The other two cases did not seem to improve much.

I believe there is potentially a rich theoretical exploration here should Blackman wish to expand upon his ideas. Since mentalization is such a complex process early in development, can it be studied or theorized in the adult therapeutic situation? How much of the improvement we see in successful psychotherapies or analyses is attributable to our patients' improved mentalization? Does "object clarification" have always to be as direct as Blackman describes, or can the improvement (if it occurs) in the ability to mentalize instead be attributable to the effects of ordinary pick-and-shovel psychoanalytic work?

7. Anita Weinreb Katz on Exploring the Emergent Experience of Loneliness in Two Men During Their Psychoanalytic Journey.

Following a brief introduction highlighting the work of Ogden, Katz narrates the histories of two treatments. Unlike most other clinical presentations in this volume (Lynch's patient is another exception), neither of Katz' two male heterosexual patients complained of loneliness at the outset of their treatments. In fact, neither was aware that they were lonely. Following Ogden (and Stern in an earlier chapter of this volume), Katz believes that the capacity to consciously experience loneliness is a developmental achievement. Her two male patients were, at the beginning of the therapeutic work, unaware of feeling lonely. Not only is the awareness of loneliness a developmental achievement, according to Katz, she illustrates her view that its emergence during analysis is similarly an achievement—in this case a therapeutic one. She writes that "the analytic work [that Katz narrates in this chapter] enabled [her patients'] underlying loneliness to emerge and be experienced."

The two cases are sensitively drawn; Katz' emotional involvement is highlighted, as are some of her revelations to her patients of her involvement, especially to the second, "Dan." "I told him I had been thinking about him over the weekend," she writes. To which Dan responded: "That's bullshit," a comment that hurt her, discouraged her and made her feel lonely herself. A bit later Dr. Katz herself became "sad and tearful . . . I said 'I'm feeling the sadness you are unable to let yourself feel . . . It's OK. I'm feeling what's hard for you to feel with me.'" Katz reports that these intimate interactions had profound effects on both the near-term future of the therapy and Dan's experience outside the therapy. It is interesting to contemplate the impact of Dan on Katz, how she felt moved to tears and deep sadness, and the impact of Katz on Dan, how he was capable of further therapeutic movement as a result. These considerations seem to be part of the larger contemporary psychoanalytic conversation about the therapist's self-revelations and their value.

8. Arthur A. Lynch on The Complex Nature of Loneliness

Dr. Lynch reminds us that loneliness is a "complex affect state" and not "a single phenomenon." He illustrates that complexity through the presentation of engaging aspects of a lengthy psychoanalytic treatment that include his patient's history, associations, and therapeutic change as well as the analyst's interventions, thoughts, and surprises. In the course of the narration of his case Lynch makes an important clinical point clear: loneliness, when it exists and is an important aspect of an analysand's mental functioning, may not always be manifest, let alone conscious. Like all painful affect states (and pleasurable ones as well) loneliness may be so defended against that there is little if any conscious awareness of it. This important point reminded me of a case, recently described by D. B. Stern (2009) and summarized by me (Gottlieb, 2010), in which an isolated narcissistic woman was moved to tears by Stern's comment, "I think you feel lonely . . . I think you've always felt lonely." Prior to these comments Stern's patient had never described herself to him as lonely nor had he consciously thought of her as such—she seemed "perfect" to him, so well put-together and self-sufficient.

Similarly, Lynch observed that "by analyzing the narcissistic character defense we were able to make room for a more painful affect of loneliness that lay at its base." I am tempted to think of this as *latent loneliness*, latent in the sense that Lansky (*e.g.*, 2005) and his colleagues have developed in their concept of latent shame.

There is much else to recommend Lynch's detailed description of his work with "James," especially his attention to the elements of James' particular compromise formations as these emerged piecemeal in the analysis.

9. Jenny Kahn Kaufmann and Peter Kaufmann on Witnessing: its Essentialness in Psychoanalytic Treatment.

The Kaufmanns present an analytic case that they feel illustrates the importance of the analyst's *witnessing* of the analysand's experience. They use the concept of analytic witnessing following the example of Poland's fine paper (2000). When the analyst's witnessing is missing from treatment the effects can be disastrous, especially in the ways that its absence can induce an unbearable sense of aloneness and loneliness in the analysand. Witnessing, they argue, is an essential element in ordinary individual development as well, and its absence can have similarly disastrous results. Their idea of the absence of witnessing and the consequences of this absence comes very close in my view to the way Léon Wurmser (*e.g.*, Chapter Two and pp. 152 *ff.*) has used the term *soul blindness*. In both cases we are trying to describe the effects of a parent (or later an analyst) who is unable—or unwilling—to grasp and understand the child's (and later the adult analysand's) experience. I have occasionally treated patients where soul blindness—or the absence of witnessing during their formative period—figured prominently, and the results have been very serious psychopathology. The Kauffmans have usefully extended the concept of witnessing (and the failures of witnessing) into adult life and in particular into analytic treatments.

Section III - Loneliness/Solitude in The Psychoanalytic Training Process

10. Jamieson Webster: on The Loneliness of the Candidate: Solitude and Solicited Identifications

Dr. Webster's discussion of the loneliness of the psychoanalytic candidate deserves to be widely read by psychoanalytic candidates and their "trainers." Early in her essay she recalls "I don't think that I've ever felt as lonely as I have felt in analytic training." These are strong words, but they are true and they draw attention not only to the intense loneliness and solitude that are the regular experience of candidates in training, but they cause us to question as well whether such experiences are in fact necessary to the experience of becoming a psychoanalyst. It is to this latter, most intriguing question that Webster addresses the larger part of her elegant and thoughtful essay. In so doing she relies heavily on the fascinating but little known story of Rosine Lefort, a young analyst-in-training and analysand of Lacan's. Briefly, after 18 months of analysis with Lacan Lefort tells him that because of the work she is doing in a foundling home she cannot remain in analysis with him. "She felt she needed to leave her analysis for a period of time and work in almost complete solitude." At the time of her decision to leave Lacan she was working with a thirteen-month-old girl, Nadia. Lacan evidently "allowed" her to leave without putting pressure on her to examine her decision. She returned to analysis with Lacan thirteen months later. The thirteen month interval was a remarkable period for Rosine Lefort, one during which—alone and lonely—she began to learn to become a psychoanalyst and to some extent became one. One assumes, from the way Webster tells the story, that it was this accomplishment that allowed Lefort to return to Lacan.

There are nested stories here. The outermost is Webster's own story that includes her own intense loneliness and her temptations to reduce this painful affect state through empty identifications with teachers, analyst, supervisors, and institutional dogma. These are all distractions from what Webster sees as the crucial task, "the transformation of loneliness in the creation of the psychoanalytic listener." She continues, "the kind of creativity and capacity for pleasure that psychoanalysis must constantly reinvent in order to move forward is an idea . . . that has supported me in the darkest moments of training." The next innermost story is that of Rosine Lefort who had to leave analytic training and her training analysis in order to discover or invent psychoanalysis for herself. Only then could she return to her official "training." The final, innermost story is that of "Nadia," first seen by Lefort at a mere thirteen months of age, a psychotic or pre-psychotic child, who is able to acquire her subjectivity, separateness, and desire through her psychoanalytic work with Rosine.

These convergent nested stories convey many messages, including Webster's insistence upon the inherent necessity of solitude and loneliness required for one to become a psychoanalyst. This is no easy task. Many obstacles stand ready to interfere with the process. Implicit also is Webster's message to the trainers, who are cautioned against providing or enforcing impediments to processes leading to a true acquisition of the skill of psychoanalytic listening.

Webster's is a very rich essay.

11. Douglas H. Ingram on Loneliness and Solitude in the Psychoanalytic Training Process—From the Chair of the Supervising Analyst.

Dr. Ingram's focus is on the supervisory (or the term he prefers, consultative) process and the experiences within it for both the therapist and consultant (and often, the patient). He offers the useful distinction of the therapist's experience of loneliness *from* the patient and his experience of loneliness *with* the patient. In the first of these the therapist may feel lonely even though he is sitting with the patient. Ingram's examples are taken from everyday clinical experience. The therapist may feel left out, excluded, alone, and lonely when—in a session or series of sessions—his patient is preoccupied with another important "object" in his life such as a lover, spouse, child or parent. The self-preoccupation of a narcissistic patient may leave a vulnerable therapist feeling lonely. Similarly, the character structure of a therapist will determine in which clinical situations he may feel loneliness.

Ingram coins the term loneliness *with* the patient to describe those situations in which the therapist experiences himself together with his patient but cut off, isolated, or in need of a connection with others. An extreme example of this might occur when a patient is involved in criminal, perverse, or suicidal behavior and the therapist is alone with this information and has a sense of responsibility for the behavior of his patient. In all of these cases consultation can be ameliorative of the experiences of loneliness and, of course, potentially helpful to the therapeutic process.

12. Eric Mendelsohn on The Loneliness of the Training Analyst

Mendelsohn emphasizes a sense of being alienated or separated from one's self as a key component of the experience of loneliness. He writes that "loneliness is a state of estrangement from self. . . ." It follows from a definition that emphasizes self-alienation that the training analyst—one who analyzes candidates within a closed institutional setting—will have an uncommon if not unique set of difficulties involving loneliness. The community jointly shared by candidate and training analyst is at the root of many of these situations. One such, according to Mendelsohn, may occur when the professional goals and ambitions of candidate and analyst "find their way" into the analytic relationship. The result may be that the analyst may avoid his otherwise usual approach to analyzing the candidate's professional competition with him. The analyst is in this way alienated from his (analyzing) self as the avoidant collusion develops. Similar collusions or avoidances on the part of the training analyst may develop when, for example, the candidate behaves in a way that the analyst feels reflects badly on him (on the training analyst, that is).

Although Mendelsohn correctly describes situations like these as unique to the training analyst's situation, it is clear that very similar situations regularly arise in *any* analysis. Their structures are actually commonplace but the details are different since they do not involve the professional world of psychoanalysis.

13. Sandra Buechler on Encounters with Loneliness

Buechler says that she took a course on metaphor in order to improve her work as a poet. She is not sure it helped her as poet, she writes, but it definitely informed her as an analyst. I would add that it seemed to have helped her as an analytic writer. Her psychoanalytic discussion of loneliness is brief, simply stated, and delicately articulate. We feel the "sting" of loneliness, she argues, when we are far from our homes. Our homes, fundamentally, are our world of internal objects that—optimally—can provide us with a sense of security, of being ourselves even when the going gets rough. She calls this community of our internal objects our internal chorus and, like Winnicott, she feels that when this internal chorus is "good enough" we can rely on its support in times of trouble, aloneness, abandonment, or at those times when we are under assault.

Buechler's idea that loneliness involves a sense of alienation from one's chorus of internal objects is not very different from that expressed by Mendelsohn. Also like Mendelsohn, Buechler is interested in experiences in the psychoanalytic training situation. Correctly, Buechler observes that our institutes are—for better or worse—our (professional and to a great extent personal) homes. We can feel close to home or far from these homes (the sting of loneliness). These analytic homes are not always optimal, with their politics, power struggles, demands for orthodoxy, and discouragement of difference. With her eye toward a better future Buechler pleads for the newer generation of institute leadership to be mindful of the issues that can make for a better—

or worse—home environment. Analysts that come from better homes will be better analysts and happier, less lonely, individuals.

Section IV—Life Events

14. Brent Willock: on Loneliness and the Life Cycle

Willock takes as his framework Erikson's 8 stages of man plus a ninth developed by Blatt and Schichman and sketches a developmental sequence of loneliness by discussing its place in each stage. While one could in theory do this for any affect, Willock justifies his focus on loneliness by asserting that "loneliness and longing is such a crucial emotional/relational constellation that it pervades each stage of the life cycle." Moreover, although Blatt et al. divide personality configurations along the dimension "relatedness versus self-definition," Willock contends that the loneliness/longing constellation needs to be considered crucial to conflict in both arenas, those centered around self-definition as well as those centered around relatedness.

15. Alma Halbert Bond on Marilyn Monroe, the Loneliest Person on Earth.

Bond's discussion of Marilyn Monroe is comprised mostly of Monroe's own words about her near-constant and unbearable loneliness. Undoubtedly there have been many others as lonely as Monroe, others rejected by their mothers and fathers, others exiled to foster homes, others surely as unloved as she was, but Monroe's case is interesting to us because she was the object of so much public attention. We ask ourselves: How could *she* have been so very lonely when she had so much of the kind of attention that so many of us aspire to? Yet her beauty, wealth, and considerable intelligence (it is a remarkable feature of Bond's essay how astonishingly articulate Monroe is) could not spare her the misery of profound loneliness and longing.

16. Patsy Turrini on The Death of the Loved Spouse, the Inner World of Grief: A Psychoanalytic Developmental Perspective

Patsy Turrini's remarkable chapter combines her deeply personal account of her emotional state following the sudden and unexpected death of her husband of 47 years with an exploratory review of the literature on the psychodynamics of loss. Shattered by the emotional pain she felt, she turned to the literature on loss, grief, and mourning, studying the biology of grief as well as the efforts of psychoanalytic theorists. We are the fortunate beneficiaries of her efforts. Turrini brings substantial narrative skills and erudition to her task, a task she did not seek but which was thrust upon her by her agonized state. She wished to understand what was happening to her.

Turrini makes the connection between death and loneliness more explicit than our other contributors. In this sense she is in accord with the poet

Schultz: "death begins and never ends." But whereas Schultz understands this from the perspective of the dead, Turrini creates psychoanalytic poetry out of the experience of the survivor.

In other ways her treatment of states of loneliness is in keeping with that of some other authors of this collection insofar as she starts from the position that a major aspect of what is lost in loneliness is the self—or put another way, there is an alienation from aspects of the self or one is not able to be one's self. How can it be that the death of a loved other can have this result? Here Turrini endorses a two person psychology and its presumed developmental architecture. Since the Other is so deeply involved in the early formation of the self (as well as in maintaining and stabilizing the adult self and self esteem), the loss of a loved other must of necessity imply a degree of amputation of parts of the self as well. Naturally, Turrini turns to self-psychology here and in particular to the role of selfobjects in development and maturity. Developmental studies and theories such as those of Kohut, Mahler, and Beebe and Lachman complement selections from Joyce Carol Oates (who wrote about her reactions to her husband's death), C. S. Lewis, and E. E. Cummings (whose love poem "I like my body" speaks of the loved other being part of the self), among others.

It seems that we are on the verge of recognizing a neural basis of the entanglement of self and other about which Turrini writes so movingly. We know that the mirror neuron system exists, but we are still in the exploratory stages of understanding how it functions and interacts with other neuronal collections. Astonishingly (to me at least) Turrini excerpts a quotation from Freud's *Project* that suggests his awareness of the effects of such a system. There Freud wrote, "While one is perceiving the perception, one copies the movement oneself—that is, one innervates so strongly, that the motor image of one's own is aroused to coincide with the other."

17. Nathan Szajnberg and Amit Goldenberg: on A Soldier's Loneliness

Szajnberg and Goldenberg present a small series of excerpts from interviews he conducted with Israeli soldiers, all young men. Not surprisingly these men, separated from their homes and at times in situations of mortal danger, described feeling alone and lonely. They were reliant on companionship to manage these feelings. The range of companionship Szajnberg's soldiers described is of interest, especially because these companions were not always fellow humans or even animate beings. Of singular importance were these soldiers' buddies, fellow members of their military unit or team. But the rest were either imaginary or inanimate. One man developed an imaginary friend, Shmuely. Another imagined a "girl back home" who turned out to be so different from his imagining when he met her on leave he picked up and walked out on her on their first date—this after longing for "her" for weeks. Another soldier imagined a chimerical mother/lover who lived in the night sky above him. Others related to their M16s as their companions.

Final Comments

In closing I wish to draw additional attention to the three essays that include cries for action, cries that I did not highlight in my introductory paragraphs. These are the chapters written by Webster, Beuchler, and Stern. Webster suggests that a degree of painful loneliness may be a necessary form of suffering along the path towards acquiring the capacity for psychoanalytic listening. She moreover suggests that the need for such a degree of loneliness ought not to be pathologized by training institutions, even when it might mean discontinuation or withdrawal from the training analysis. Such loneliness could perhaps be a necessity for those who seek and can tolerate it. Webster argues that indentifications with senior authority figures or with doctrine are very poor substitutes. Institutes would do well to recognize this.

Buechler correctly identifies the psychoanalytic institute as an analyst's *home* in the most powerful sense of that term. She asserts that there is much yet to be done for these training institutes to fashion themselves into the kinds of supportive homes that produce less lonely analysts. In the end she exhorts the younger generation of analysts to do better than we have done with this project.

Stern remembers the distant figures who were his training analysts and the ways in which these figures left him feeling alone and abandoned on their couches. Stern too feels that these were not the best of role models and speculates that the relational turn in psychoanalysis may represent in part the younger generation of analysts' efforts to avoid the loneliness experienced by their own trainers. Implied is Stern's view that the relational turn has improved the lives of its trainees, although much may remain to be done.

How can we not feel grateful to this group of nineteen analytic scholars and clinicians for their focused work on this all-important subject?

References

Gabbard, G. O., and Lester, E. P. (1995).. *Boundaries and Boundary Violations in Psychoanalysis*, American Psychiatric Publishing, Washington, D. C.

Gottlieb, R. M. (2010). Coke or Pepsi?—Reflections on Freudian and Relational Psychoanalysis in Dialogue. *Contemporary Psychoanalyssi* 46:87–100.

Lansky, M.R. (2005). The Impossibility of Forgiveness: Shame Fantasies as Instigators of Vengefulness in Euripides' *Medea.*. *Journal of the American Psychoanalytic Association* 53:437–464.

Poland, W.S. (2000). The analyst's witnessing and otherness. *Journal of the American Psychoanalytic Association* 38:17–34.

Stern, D.B. (2009). Panel presentation at "Minding the Gap: Freudian and Relational/Interpersonal Psychoanalysis in Dialogue," held at the New York Psychoanalytic Institute. Panelists: E. Samberg, P. Bromberg, D. B. Stern, P. B. Dunn; R. M. Gottlieb, Panel Chair. Held on February 28, 2009.

Stone, L. (1977). *The Psychoanalytic Situation*. New York: International Universities Press.

Winnicott, D. W. (1969). The use of an object. *International Journal of Psychoanalysis,* 50:711–716.

Wurmser, L. (2007). *Torment Me, but Don't Abandon Me:Psychoanalysis of the Severe Neuroses in a New Key* (1st Edition), Northvale, NJ: Jason Aronson.

THE GOD OF LONELINESS

It's a cold Sunday February morning
and I'm one of eight men waiting
for the doors of Toys R Us to open
in a mall on the eastern tip of Long Island.
We've come for the Japanese electronic game
that's so hard to find. Last week, I waited
three hours for a store in Manhattan
to disappoint me. The first today, bundled
in six layers, I stood shivering in the dawn light
reading the new Aeneid translation, which I hid
when the others came, stamping boots
and rubbing gloveless hands, joking about
sacrificing sleep for ungrateful sons. "My boy broke
two front teeth playing hockey," a man wearing
shorts laughs. "This is his reward." My sons
will leap into my arms, remember this morning
all their lives. "The game is for my oldest boy,
just back from Iraq," a man in overalls says
from the back of the line. "He plays these games
in his room all day. I'm not worried, he'll snap out of it,
he's earned his rest." These men fix leaks, lay
foundations for other men's dreams without complaint.
They've been waiting in the cold since Aeneas
founded Rome on rivers of blood. Virgil understood that
death begins and never ends, that it's the god of loneliness.
Through the window, a clerk shouts, "We've only five."
The others seem not to know what to do with their hands,
tuck them under their arms, or let them hang,
naked and useless. Is it because our hands remember
what they held, the promises they made? I know
exactly when my boys will be old enough for war.
Soon three of us will wait across the street at Target,
because it's what men do for their sons.

—Philip Schultz

Cumulative References

Adler, G. & Buie, D.H. (1979). Aloneness and borderline psychopathology: The possible relevance of child development issues. *International Journal of Psycho-Analysis* 60:83–96.

Akhtar, S. (1996). "Someday . . ." and "If only . . ." fantasies: pathological optimism and inordinate nostalgia as related forms of idealization. *Journal of the American Psychoanalytic Association* 44:723–53.

——— (1999). *Inner Torment, Living Between Conflict and Fragmentation.* Jason Aronson.

——— (2006). Seminar Lecture. Cape Cod, Massachusetts.

——— (2009). *Comprehensive Dictionary of Psychoanalysis.* London: Karnac Books.

Anisfeld, L. & Richards, A. (2000). The Replacement Child: Variations on a Theme In History and Psychoanalysis. *Psychoanalytic Study of the Child*, 41:299–308.

Anzieu, D. (1989). *The Skin Ego.* New Haven: Yale University Press.

Arlow, J.A. (1963). The supervisory situation. *Journal of the American Psychoanalytic Association* 11:576–594.

——— (1969). Unconscious fantasy and disturbances of conscious experience. *Psychoanalytic Quarterly* 38:1–27.

——— (1982). Psychoanalytic education: A psychoanalytic perspective. *Annual of Psychoanalysis* 10:5–20.

——— & Brenner, C. (1990). The Psychoanalytic Process. *Psychoanalytic Quarterly* 59:678–692.

Auster, P. (1982). *The Invention of Solitude.* New York: Penguin Books.

Bach, S. (1985) *Narcissistic States and the Therapeutic Process.* New York and London: Jason Aronson.

Bacharach, B. (1953). *"Wishin' and Hopin'."* http://www.onlinesheetmusic.com/wishin-and-hopin-p120860.aspx

Bakhtin, M. (1984). *Problems of Dostoevsky's Poetics,* transl. C. Emerson. Minneapolis: University of Minnesota Press.

Balint, M. (1968). *The Basic Fault.* NY: Brunner Mazel, 1979.

Bauby, J-D. (1997). *The Diving Bell and the Butterfly: A Memoir of Life in Death,* transl. Jeremy Leggart. New York: Vintage Books.

Baum, L.F. (1900). *The Wonderful Wizard of Oz.* Chicago: George M. Hill.

Becker, E. (1973). The Denial of Death. New York: Free Press.

Bergmann, M. (2002), *The Hartmann Era.* New York: Other Press, p. 42.

Bevington, D., ed. (1992). *The Complete Works of Shakespeare.* New York. Harper.

Bibring, G.L. (1954). The training analysis and its place in psychoanalytic training. *International Journal of Psycho-Analysis* 35:169–73.

Bion, W.R. (1959). Attacks on linking. In: *Second Thoughts: Selected Papers on Psycho-Analysis*. New York: Aronson, pp. 93–109, 1967.

Blackman, J. (2003). *101 Defenses: How the Mind Shields Itself*. New York: Routledge.

———— (2010). *Get the Diagnosis Right: Assessment and Treatment Selection for Mental Disorders*. New York: Routledge.

———— (2012). The Therapist's Answer Book. Solutions to 101 Tricky Problems in Psychotherapy. New York: Routledge.

Blanck, G. (2000). *Primer Of Psychotherapy; A Developmental Perspective*, Northvale, NJ: Jason Aronson.

———— & Blanck, R. (1974). *Ego Psychology: Theory and Practice*. New York: Columbia University Press.

Blatt, S.J. (2008). *Polarities of Experience: Relatedness and Self-definition in Personality Development, Psychopathology, and the Therapeutic Process*. Washington, DC: American Psychological Association.

———— & Shichman, S. (1983). Two primary configurations of psychopathology. *Psychoanalysis and Contemporary Thought* 6:187–254.

———— & Blass, R.B. (1990). Attachment and separateness—A dialectic model of the products and processes of development throughout the life cycle. *Psychoanalytic Study of the Child* 45:107–127.

Blechner, M. (2009). *Sex Changes*. New York: Routledge.

Bollas, C. (1983). The Expressive Uses of the Counter-Transference—Notes to the Patient from Oneself. *Contemporary Psychoanalysis* 19:1–33.

———— (1989). *Forces of Destiny: Psychoanalysis and the Human Idiom*. London: Free Association.

Bowlby, J. (1961). Process of Mourning. *International Journal of Psycho-Analysis* 42:317–340.

———— (1969). *Attachment*. New York: Basic Books.

———— (1969). Attachment and Loss: Vol. 1: Attachment. *International Psycho-analytical Library* (79): London: Hogarth Press.

———— (1973). Attachment and Loss Vol 11. Separation Anxiety. *The International Psycho-analytical Library* (95). London: Hogarth Press.

Braver, A. (2012). *Misfit, a Novel*. Portland: Tin House Books.

Brenner, C. (1974).. On the Nature and Development of Affects: A Unified Theory. *Psychoanalytic Quarterly* 43:532–556.

———— Reporter (1975). *Alterations in Defenses during Psychoanalysis*. The Kris Study Group of the New York Psychoanalytic Institute, Monograph VI, ed. B. Fine & H. Waldhorn. New York: International Universities Press.

———— (1979). Depressive Affect, Anxiety, and Psychic Conflict in the Phallic-Oedipal Phase. *Psychoanalytic Quarterly* 48:177–197.

———— (1982). *The Mind in Conflict*. Madison, CT: International Universities Press.

———— (2006). *Psychoanalysis: Or Mind and Meaning*. New York: Psychoanalytic Quarterly Press.

Breuer, J. & Freud, S. (1895). Studies on Hysteria. *Standard Edition* 2:1–321.

Bruch, H. (1958). Developmental obesity and schizophrenia. *Psychiatry* 21:65-70.

Buchholz, E. (1997). *The Call of Solitude: Alonetime in a World of Attachment*. New York: Simon & Schuster.

Buechler, S. (1998). The analyst's experience of loneliness. *Contemporary Psychoanalysis* 34:91–115.

———— (Ed.). (2009). Special issue on the ideal psychoanalytic institute. *Contemporary Psychoanalysis* 45.

———— (2012). *Still Practicing: The Heartaches and Joys of a Clinical Career*. New York: Routledge.

———— (2012). Someone to watch over me. In: *Loneliness and Longing: Conscious and Unconscious Aspects,* eds B.Willock, L.C. Bohm, & R.C. Curtis. London & NY: Routledge, pp. 13–28.

Buie, D (1981). Empathy: Its nature and limitations. *Journal of the American Psychoanalytic Association* 29:281–307.

———— (2012). *Core Issues in the Treatment of Personality Disordered Patients*. American Psychoanalytic Association Plenary Address.

Burke, N. (1997). InVisible Worlds: On Women and Solitude. *Gender and Psychoanalysis*, 2:327–341.

Cacioppo, John T. & Patrick, W. (2008). *Loneliness: Human Nature and the Need for Social Connection*. New York: W.W. Norton.

Churchwell, S. (2004). *The Many Lives of Marilyn Monroe*. New York: Henry Holt.

Clewell, T. (2004). Mourning beyond melancholia: Freud's psychoanalysis of loss, *Journal of the American Psychoanalytic Association* 52:43–67.

Cohen, N.A. (1982). On loneliness and the ageing process. *International Journal of Psychoanalysis* 63:149–155.

Crastnopol, M. (2009). Institute life beyond graduation. *Contemporary Psychoanalysis* 45:358–363.

Cramer P. (2006). *Protecting the Self: Defense Mechanisms in Action*. New York Guilford.

Dawson, J. (1997). *Logical dilemmas: The life and work of Kurt Gödel*. Wellesley, MA: AK Peters.

De La Hoz , C. (2007). *Marilyn Monroe*. Philadelphia: Platinum Fox Running Press.

Deutsch, R. (2011). A voice lost, a voice found: After the death of the analyst. *Psychoanalytic Inquiry* 31:526–35.

Dillard, A. (1974). *Pilgrim at Tinker Creek*. New York: Harper Collins.

Dimen, M. (2005) Sexuality and suffering or the Eew! factor. *Studies in Gender and Sexuality* 6:1–8.

Dobisz, J. (2004). *The Wisdom of Solitude: A Zen Retreat in the Woods*. New York: HarperCollins.

Dupont, J. (1988). *The Clinical Diary of Sandor Ferenczi*. Cambridge: Harvard University Press.

Eco, U. ed. (2010). *On Beauty.* New York: Rizzoli.

——— (2011) *On Ugliness.* New York: Rizzoli.

Edward, J, & Ruskin, N. & Turrini, P. (1991). *Separation Individuation, Theory and Application*, 2nd ed. New York: Brunner/Mazel,

Ehrenberg, D. (1992). *The Intimate Edge.* New York: Norton.

Eigen, M. (2009). *Flames from the Unconscious: Trauma, Madness, and Faith.* London: Karnac Books.

Eisenstadt, M., Haynal, A., Rentchnick, P, De Senarclens, P. (1989). *Parental Loss and Achievement.* Madison, CT: International Universities Press.

Emery, P. (1998). Nassau Newsnotes. *Clinical Social Work Newsletter* Spring, p 8.

Erikson, E. H. (1965). Inner and outer space: Reflections on womanhood. In: *The Women in America,* ed. Robert Jay Lifton. Boston: Houghton.

——— (1950). *Childhood and Society.* New York: Norton.

——— (1959). *Identity and the Life Cycle.* New York: International Universities Press.

Erlich, S, (1998) On Loneliness, Narcissism and Intimacy. *American Journal of Psychoanalysis* 58:35–162.

Fairbairn, W.R.D. (1943). The repression and the return of the bad objects (with special reference to war neurosis). *In Psychoanalytic Studies of Personality.* London: Routledge & Kegan Paul, p. 59–81.

——— (1954) *An Object-Relations Theory of Personality.* New York: Basic Books.

——— (1963). An object relations theory of the personality. In: *From Instinct to Self: The Selected Papers of W.R.D. Fairbairn. Vol. I. Clinical and Theoretical Papers,* eds. E. Fairbairn, Birtle & E.D. Scharff,. Northvale, NJ: Jason Aronson, 1994, pp. 155–156.

Fenichel, O. (1940). The study of defense mechanisms and its importance for psychoanalytic technique. In *The Collected Papers of Otto Fenichel.* Second series, pp 183—197. New York: W.W. Norton.

Ferenczi, S. (1928). The elasticity of psycho-analytic technique. In: *Final Contributions to the Problems and Methods of Psycho-Analysis,* ed. M.Balint. New York: Brunner/Mazel, pp. 87–101.

——— (1930). The principles of relaxation and neocatharsis. In: *Final Contributions to the Problems and Methods of Psycho-Analysis,* M Balint, Ed. New York: Brunner/Mazel, 108–125.

Florence, S. (2002). *When You Lose Someone You Love. . . a journey through the heart of grief,* A Helen Exley Giftbook, in the Journeys Series.

310

Freud, S. (1905). On Psychotherapy. *Standard Edition* 7: 255–268.

——— (1914). On Narcissism. *Standard Edition* 14:67–102

——— (1915). "Thoughts for the Times on War and Death, 11, Our Attitudes Towards Death, *Standard Edition* 14 289–300.

——— (1916–1917). Introductory Lectures on Psycho-Analysis. *Standard Edition* 16:392–411.

——— (1917). Mourning and Melancholia. *Standard Edition* 14:237–260.

——— (1919) *The Uncanny*. *Standard Edition* 17: 219–256.

——— (1920). Beyond the Pleasure Principle. *Standard Edition* 18.

——— (1926). Inhibitions, Symptoms and Anxiety. *Standard Edition*. 20:75–175.

——— (1950). Project for a Scientific Psychology (1950 [1895]). *Standard Edition* 1: 281–391.

Freud, A. (1958). Adolescence. *Psychoanalytic Study of the Child* 13:255–278.

Friedan, B. (1963). *The Feminine Mystique*. New York: Norton.

Fromm, E. (1941). *Escape from Freedom*. New York: Holt, Rineheart & Winston.

Fromm-Reichmann, F. (1959). Loneliness. *Psychiatry* 22 1–15.

——— (1990). Loneliness. *Contemporary Psychoanalysis* 26:305–329.

Frosch, J. (1988). Psychotic character versus borderline. *International Journal of Psychoanalysis* 69:347–357.

Gabbard, G.O., and Lester, E.P. (1995). *Boundaries and Boundary Violations in Psychoanalysis*, Washington, D. C American Psychiatric Publishing.

Gerson, S. (2009). When the Third is Dead: Memory, Mourning and Witnessing in the Aftermath of the Holocaust. *International Journal of Psychoanalysis*. 90:1341–1357.

Gilbert, S. & Gubar, S. (1979). *The Madwoman in the Attic: The Woman Writer and the Nineteenth-Century Literary Imagination*. New Haven: Yale University Press.

Gil, H. (1987). Effects of Oedipal triumph caused by collapse or death of the parent. *International Journal of Psychoanalysis*. 68:251–260.

Gilligan, C. (1982). *In a Different Voice: Psychological Theory and Women's Development*. Cambridge: Harvard University Press.

Gilmore, J. (2007). *Inside Marilyn Monroe, A Memoir*. Los Angeles: Ferine Books.

Gilot, F. (2001). A Painter's Perspective. In *The Origins of Creativity*. ed. K. H. Pfenninger & V. Shubik. New York: Oxford University Press.

Goldstein, E.G. & Horowitz, L. (2003). *Contemporary Psychotherapy and Lesbian Identity*. Hillsdale, NJ: Analytic Press.

Gottlieb, R.M. (2010). Coke or Pepsi?—Reflections on Freudian and Relational Psychoanalysis in Dialogue. *Contemporary Psychoanalysis*

311

46:87–100.

Gray, P. (1973). Psychoanalytic Technique and the Ego's Capacity for Viewing. Intrapsychic Activity. *Journal of the American Psychoanalytic Association* 21:474–494.

——— (1996). Undoing the Lag in the Technique of Conflict and Defense Analysis. *Psychoanalytic Study of the Child* 51:87–101.

Green, A. (2001). The dead mother. In: *Life Narcissism, Death Narcissism,* transl, Andrew Weller. London, New York: Free Associations Books.

Greenberg, J. (1991). Countertransference and reality. *Psychoanalytic Dialogues* 1:52–73.

Grotstein, J. (1982). The Spectrum of Aggression. *Psychoanalytic Inquiry* 2:193–211.

Grumbach, D. (1995). *Fifty Days of Solitude.* Boston: Beacon Press.

Hagman, G. (1995). The death of the selfobject: Toward a self psychology of the mourning process. *Progress in Self Psychology* 11:189–205.

Halberstadt-Freud, H.C. (1991). *Freud, Proust, Perversion and Love.* Berwyn, PA: Swets & Zeitlinger.

Haney, E.L. (2002). *Inside Delta Force: The Story of America's Elite Counterterrorist Unit.* New York: Dell Publishing.

Harris, A. (2011). Discussion of Robin Deutcsh's, A Voice Lost, a Voice Found: After The Death of the Analyst. *Psychoanalytic Inquiry* 31:536–542.

Hartmann, H. (1939–1958). *Ego Psychology and the Problem of Adaptation.* New York: International Universities Press.

Herrera, H. (1983). *Frida: A Biography of Frida Kahlo.* New York: Harper Colophon Books.

Heilburn, C. (1997). *The Last Gift of Time: Life Beyond Sixty.* New York: Ballantine.

Herzog, J. (1980). Sleep disturbance and father hunger in 18- to 28-month old boys—the Erlkönig syndrome. *Psychoanalytic Study of the Child* 35:219–233.

——— (2001). *Father Hunger: Explorations with Adults and Children.* New York: Routledge.

Hirsch, I. (2008), *Coasting in the Countertransference.* Hillsdale, NJ: The Analytic Press.

Hirschmann, J.R. & Munter, C.H. (1988). *Overcoming Overeating.* New York: Addison-Wesley.

Hoffman, I. (1998). *Ritual and Spontaneity in the Psychoanalytic Process.* Hillsdale, NJ: The Analytic Press

Horney, K. (1950). *Neurosis and Human Growth.* New York: W.W. Norton.

Ingram, D.H. (1979). Time and time-keeping in psychoanalysis and psychotherapy. *American Journal of Psychoanalysis* 39:319–328.

————— (2001). Of time, narrative, and *Cast Away*. *Journal American Academy of Psychoanalysis* 29:625–633. Also at:
www.psyartjournal.com/article/show/h_ingram-of_time_narrative_and_cast_away

Irigaray, L. (1977). *This Sex Which Is Not One*. transl. Catherine Porter. Ithaca: Cornell University Press.

Izard, C.E., (1971). *The Face of Emotion*. New York: Appleton-Century-Crofts.

Jacobson, E. (1961). Adolescent moods and the remodeling of psychic structures in adolescence. *Psychoanalytic Study of the Child* 16:164–183.

————— (1964). *Self and the Object World*. New York: International Universities Press.

Jarvis, V. (1965). Loneliness and compulsion. *Journal of the American Psychoanalytic Association* 13:122–58.

Kafka, F. (1973). *Letters to Felice*. ed. E, Heller & H. Born, transl. J. Stern & E. Duckworth. New York: Shocken Bookes, pp. 155–156.

Kanzer, M. (1953). Past and present in the transference. *Journal of the American Psychoanalytic Association* 1:144–154.

Kaplan, H. A. (1987). The psychopathology of nostalgia. *Psychoanalytic Review* 74:465–486.

Karper, K. (1994). *Where God Begins to Be: A Woman's Journey into Solitude*. Grand Rapids, MI: Eerdmans.

Kernberg, O.F. (1970). Factors in the Psychoanalytic Treatment of Narcissistic Personalities. *Journal of the American Psychoanalytic Association* 18:51–85.

————— (1974). Further Contributions to the Treatment of Narcissistic Personalities. *International Journal of Psycho-Analysis* 55:215–240

————— Yeomans, F.E., Clarkin, J.F. and Levy, K.N., (2008). Transference Focused Psychotherapy: Overview and Update. *International Journal of Psycho-Analysis* 89:601–620.

Klein, M. (1963). On the sense of loneliness. In: *Writings of Melanie Klein 1946–1963*. New York: New Library of Psychoanalysis, 1984, pp. 300–313.

Knafo, D. (1993). *Egon Schiele: A Self in Creation: A Psychoanalytic Study of the Artist's Self-Portraits*. Cranbury, NJ: Associated Universities Press.

————— (2002). Revisiting Ernst Kris' concept of regression in the service of the ego in art. *Psychoanalytic Psychology* 19:24–49.

————— (2009). *In her Own Image: Women's Self-Representation in Twentieth-Century Art*. Cranbury, NJ: Associated Universities Press

Koch, P. (1994). *Solitude: A Philosophical Encounter*. Chicago, IL: Open Court.

Kohut, H. (1959). Introspection, Empathy, and Psychoanalysis: An Examination of the Relationship Between Mode of Observation and Theory. *Journal of the American Psychoanalytic Association* 7:459–483.

————— (1971). *The Analysis of the Self.* New York: International Universities Press.

————— (1977). *The Restoration of the Self.* Madison. International Universities Press.

————— (1984). *How Does Analysis Cure?* ed. A. Goldberg & P.E. Stepansky. Chicago, IL: University of Chicago Press.

————— & Wolf, E.S. (1978). The Disorders of the Self and their Treatment: An Outline. *International Journal of Psycho-Analysis* 59:413–425.

Koller, A. (1990). *The Stations of Solitude.* New York: William Morrow & Co.

Koontz, D. (2003–2012). *Odd Thomas series* (novels). New York: Bantam Books.

Lacan, J. (1949). 'Le Stade du miroir comme formateur de la fonction de Je, telle qu'elle nous est revelee dans l'expérience psychanalytique', Revue français de psychanalyse 1949:13:4.

————— (2006). *Écrit,* transl. B. Fink. New York: W. W. Norton.

Lansky, Melvin R. (2005): "The Impossibility of Forgiveness: Shame Fantasies as Instigators of Vengefulness in Euripides' *Medea.*"*Journal of the American Psychoanalytic Association* 53:437–464.

Laplanche, J. (2011). *Freud and the Sexual.* New York: IPBooks.

Lasky, R. (1984). Dynamics and problems in the treatment of the Oedipal winner. *Psychoanalytic Review* 71:351–374.

Lavendar, J. (2011). The phenomenology of the relational void: Probabilities and Possibilities. In: *Loneliness and Longing: Conscious and Unconscious Aspects.* eds. B. Willock, L.C. Bohm, & R.C. Curtis. New York: Routledge, pp. 121–134.

Lewis. C.S. (1961). *A Grief Observed.* New York: Harper Collins.

Lawrence , F. (1993) *Norma Jean, The Life of Marilyn Monroe.* New York: Paragon House.

Lefort, R. (1994). *Birth of the Other,* transl. M. Du Ry, L. Watson, & L. Rodriguez. Chicago: University of Illinois Press.

Lemma, A. (2010). *Under the Skin.* London: Routledge.

Levenson, E.A. (1995), Introduction. In: *Pioneers of Interpersonal Psychoanalysis,* eds. D.B. Stern, C.H. Mann, S. Kantor, G. Schlesinger. Hillsdale, NJ: The Analytic Press, pp. 111–113.

Lieberman, J.S. (1991). Issues in the psychoanalytic treatment of single females over thirty. *Psychoanalytic Review* 78:176–198.

Lifton R. J. (1967). *Death in Life, Survivors of Hiroshima.* New York: Random House.

Lotterman, A. (2011). Psychotherapy can benefit schizophrenic patients. *The American Psychoanalyst* .45:12–16.

Mahler, M. (1979). *The Selected Papers of Margaret Mahler*. New York: Jason Aronson.

——— Bergman, A. & Pine, F. (1975). *Separation Individuation*. New York: Jason Aronson.

——— Pine, F & Bergman, A. (2000). *The Psychological Birth of the Human Infant: Symbiosis and Individuation*. New York: Basic Books.

Mailer, N. (1973). *Marilyn: The Classic*. New York: Galahad Books.

Malin, J. & Boynton, V. (2003). *Herspace: Women, Writing, and Solitude*. New York: The Haworth Press.

Maroda, K. J. (1991). *The Power of Countertransference*. Northvale NJ: The Analytic Press.

——— (2005). Legitimate gratification of the patient's needs. *Contemporary Psychoanalysis* 41:371–88.

Martin, A. (2005). *Agnes Martin Writings, ed. Dieter Schwarz*. Berlin: Hatje Cantz

Martin, P. (1956). *Will Acting Spoil Marilyn Monroe?* Garden City, NY: Doubleday & Company.

May, R. (1953). *Man's Search for Himself*. New York: W.W. Norton.

Mendelsohn, E. (1996). More human than otherwise: Working through a time of preoccupation and mourning. In: *The Therapist as a Person: Life Choices, Life Experiences and Their Effects on Treatment*, ed. B. Gerson, Hillsdale, NJ: The Analytic Press, pp. 21–40.

——— (2002). The analyst's bad-enough participation. *Psychoanalytic Dialogues* 12: 331–358.

——— (2005). Rules were made to be broken: Reflections on psychoanalytic education and clinical process. *Psychoanalytic Psychology* 22:261–278.

——— (2007). Analytic love: Possibilities and limitations. *Psychoanalytic Inquiry* 27:219–245.

——— (2011). The not-me and the loving self. *Psychoanalytic Perspectives* 8:62–71.

Mendelson, M. (1990). Reflections on loneliness. *Contemporary Psychoanalysis* 26:330–355.

Mendell, D., & Turrini, P. (2003). *Inner World of the Mother*. Madison, CT: Psychosocial Press.

Miller, A. (1964). *After the Fall*. New York: Penguin Group.

Miller, L. (1992–1993). Alone in the temple: A personal essay on solitude and the woman poet. *Kansas Quarterly* 24/25:200–214.

Mills, S. (2002). *Epicurean Simplicity*. Washington, DC: Island Press.

Mitchell, S.A. (1988). *Relational Concepts in Psychoanalysis: An Integration*. Cambridge, MA /London: Harvard University Press

315

———— (2000). You've got to suffer if you want to sing the blues. *Psychoanalytic Dialogues* 10:713–733.

Modell, A. (1993). *The Private Self.* Cambridge: Harvard University Press.

Moffat, M.J. & Paynter, C. (1974). *Revelations: Diaries of Women.* New York: Random House.

Monroe, M. & Hecht, B. (2007). *My Story.* Lanham: Taylor Trade.

Nochlin, L. (1971). Why have there been no great women artists? In: *Women, Art, and Power and Other Essays.* New York: Harper and Row, 1988, pp. 145–178.

Oates, J. (2011). *A Widow's Story: A Memoir.* New York: Harper Collins.

Ogden, T.H., (1992). *The Primitive Edge of Experience.* Northvale, NJ : Jason Aronson.

———— (1994). Projective identification and the subjugating third. In: *Subjects of Analysis.* Northvale, NJ: Aronson, pp. 97–106.

Olds, J. & R.S. Schwartz (2009). *The Lonely American: Drifting Apart in the Twenty-First Century.* Boston: Beacon Press.

Olsen, T. (1965). *Silences.* New York: Delacorte Press.

Orange, D.M. (2009). A psychoanalytic colloquium. *Contemporary Psychoanalysis* 45:353–358.

———— (2010). Recognition as: Intersubjective Vulnerability in the Psychoanalytic Dialogue. *International Journal of Psychoanalytic Self Psychology* 5:227–243.

Ornstein, A. (2010). The Missing Tombstone: Reflections on Mourning and Creativity. *Journal of the American Psychoanalytic Association* 58:631–648.

Paniagua, C. (2011). Psychotherapy and Close-Process Technique. *International Journal of Psycho-Analysis* 92:43–56.

Parker, I. (2012) The story of a suicide. *The New Yorker*, Feb 6, 2012.

Parkes, C (1987). *Bereavement: Studies of Grief in Adult Life*, 2nd ed. Madison, CT: International Universities Press.

Phillips, A. (1993). On risk and solitude. In *On Kissing, Tickling and Being Bored: Psychoanalytic Essays on the Unexamined Life.* Cambridge: Harvard University Press.

Phillips, S. (2001). The overstimulation of everyday life: New Aspects of male homosexuality. *Journal of the American Psychoanalytic Association* 49:1235–267.

Piaget, J. (1955). *The Language and Thought of the Child,* transl, M. Gabain. New York: Meridian Books.

Poland,W. (2000). The analyst's witnessing and otherness. *Journal of the American Psychoanalytic Association* 48:17–34.

———— (2012). Outsiderness, Sandor Rado Lecture, Columbia University, & Association for Psychoanalytic Medicine, Academy of Medicine, New York City.

Pray, M. (1996). Two Different Methods of Analyzing Defense. In *Danger and Defense: The Technique of Close Process Attention,* ed. M. Goldberger, Northvale, NJ: Jason Aronson.

Proust, Marcel. (1896–1919). A race accursed. In: *On Art and Literature* transl. S.T. Warner, introduction T. Kilmartin. New York: Carroll & Graf Publishers, Inc. pp.210–229, 1997.

———— (1913–1927). In *Search of Lost Time.* (6 volumes), transl. C.K. Scott Moncrieff & Terence Kilmartin, rev. D. J. Enright, introduction Richard Howard. New York: Modern Library Edition, 2003.

———— (1956). *Letters to His Mother,* transl. & ed. G.D. Painter with an essay by P.H. Johnson. New York: The Citadel Press.

Quinodoz, J-M. (1993). *The Taming of Solitude. Separation Anxiety in Psychoanalysis,* trans. P. Slotkin. London and New York: Routledge.

———— (1996).The sense of solitude in the psychoanalytic encounter. International Journal of Psycho-Analysis, 77:481–496.

Racker, H. (1953). A contribution to the problem of countertransference. *International Journal of Psycho-Analysis* 34:313–324.

Rando, T. (1988) *How to Go on Living When Someone You Love Dies.* New York: Bantam Books.

———— (1993).*Treatment of Complicated Mourning,* Champaign, IL: Research Press

Riese , R. (1987). *The Unabridged Marilyn: Her Life from A to Z,* New York: Congdon & Weed, Inc.

Renik, O. (1999). Playing one's cards face up in analysis: an approach to the problem of self-disclosure. *Psychoanalytic Quarterly* 68:521–539.

Richards, A.D. (1981). Self Theory, Conflict Theory, and the Problem of Hypochondriasis. *Psychoanalytic Study of the Child* 36:319–33.

Richards, A.K. and Spira, L.(2003). On being lonely: fear of one's own aggression as an impediment to intimacy. *Psychoanalytic Quarterly* 72:357–374.

———— (2012). Proust and the lonely pleasure of longing. In: *Loneliness and Longing: Conscious and Unconscious Aspects,* eds. B, Willock, L.C.Bohm, & R.C. Curtis. London & New York: Routledge.

Rilke, R.M. 1934. *Letters to a Young Poet.* transl. M.D. Herter Norton. New York: W.W. Norton.

Roudinesco, E. (1997). *Jacques Lacan,* transl. B. Bray. New York: Columbia University Press.

Salomon, D. (1997). *Utopia Parkway: The Life and Work of Joseph Cornell.* New York: Farrar, Straus & Giroux.

Sander, F. (2010). *Created in Our Own Images.com.* New York: IPBooks.

Sarton, M. (1973). *Journal of a Solitude.* New York: W.W. Norton.

Satran, G. (1978). Notes on Loneliness. *Journal of the American Academy Psychoanalysis* 6:281–300.

317

Schafer, R. (1983). *The Analytic Attitude*. London: Hogarth Books.
————— (1995). Aloneness in the countertransference. *Psychoanalytic Quarterly* 64:496–516.
Seiden, H. M. (2012). On the Longing for Home. In: *Loneliness and Longing: Conscious and Unconscious Aspects,* ed. B. Willock, L.C. Bohm, & R.C. Curtis. London: Routledge.
Settlage, C. (1996). Transcending old age: Creativity, development and psychoanalysis. In: The life of a centenarian. *International Journal of Psycho-Analysis* 77:549–564.
Shevey , S. (1987). *The Marilyn Scandal.* New York: William Morrow and Co.
Silverman, H., Lachmann, F., Milich, R. (1982). *The Search for Oneness.* New York: International Universities Press.
Sinkman, E. (2012). *The Psychology of Beauty.* New York: Rowan, Littlefield.
Skelton, R. (Ed.). (2006). The Edinburgh International Encyclopaedia of Psychoanalysis. In: Tuckett, D. & Levinson, N.A., eds. (2010). *PEP Consolidated Psychoanalytic Glossary.* London: Psychoanalytic Electronic Publishing.
Slavin, M. & Kriegman, J. (1992). *The Adaptive Design of the Human Psyche: Psychoanalysis, Evolutionary Biology, and the Therapeutic Process.* New York: Guilford.
Slochower, J. (1996). *Holding and Psychoanalysis: A Relational Perspective.* Hillsdale, NJ: The Analytic Press.
Spence, D.P. (1982). *Narrative Truth and Historical Truth: Meaning and Interpretation in Psychoanalysis.* London and New York: W.W. Norton.
Spira, L. & Richards, A.K. (2003a). The "sweet and sour" of being lonely and alone. *The Psychoanalytic Study of the Child* 58:214–227.
————— (2003b). On Being Lonely, Socially isolated and Single: Multiple Perspectives. *Psychoanalysis and Psychotherapy* 20:3–21.
Spitz, R. (1945). Hospitalism. *The Psychoanalytic Study of the Child* 1:53–74.
————— (1965). *The First Year of Life: A Psychoanalytic Study of Normal and Deviant Development of Object Relations.* New York: International Universities Press.
Steinem , G. (1996). *Marilyn.* New York: MJF Books Fine Communications, Fine Creative Media, Inc.
Stern, D.B. (2009). Panel presentation at "Minding the Gap: Freudian and Relational/Interpersonal Psychoanalysis in Dialogue," held at the New York Psychoanalytic Institute. Panelists: E. Samberg, P. Bromberg, D.B. Stern, P.B. Dunn; R.M. Gottlieb, Panel Chair. Held on February 28, 2009.
Stern, D.N. (1985). *The Interpersonal World of the Infant: A view from psychoanalysis and developmental psychology.* New York: W.W. Norton.

Stern, J. (1990). King Lear: The Transference of the Kingdom. *Shakespeare Quarterly* 41:299–308.

Stierlin, H. (1965–66). The Dialectic of Related Loneliness. *Psychoanalytic Review* 52:26–40.

Stolorow, R. (2007). *Trauma and Human Existence, Autobiographical, Psychoanalytic and Philosophical Reflections,* New York: Routledge.

Stone, L (1954). The Widening Scope of Indications for Psychoanalysis. *Journal of the American Psychoanalytic Association* 2:567–594.

——— (1977). *The Psychoanalytic Situation.* New York: International Universities Press.

Storr, A. (1988). *Solitude: A Return to the Self.* New York: Ballantine.

Strauss, N. (2005). The *Game: Penetrating the Secret Society of Pickup Artists* .New York: It Books. http://www.stylelife.com/.

Sullivan, H.S. (1953). *The Interpersonal Theory of Psychiatry,* ed. H.S. Perry & M.L. Gawel. New York: W.W. Norton.

Szajnberg, N.M. (2011). *Reluctant Warriors: Israelis Suspended Between Rome and Jerusalem.* New York: IPBooks.

Taraborrelli , J.R. (2009). *The Secret Life of Marilyn Monroe.* New York: Grand Central Publishing.

Tessman, L. (2003). *The Analyst's Analyst Within.* London: Taylor and Francis.

Turrini, P. (2003). Capacity to Cure: Inevitable Failure, Guilt and Symptoms. In: The Inner World of the Mother. Madison:, CT: International Universities Press.

Vaillant, G.E., Bond, M., & Vaillant, C.O. (1986). An empirically validated hierarchy of defense mechanisms. *Archives of General Psychiatry* 73:786–794.

Volkan, V. (2009). *Searching for the Perfect Woman: The Story of a Complete Psychoanalysis.* Northvale, NJ: Aronson.

Weiss, R. S. (1973). *Loneliness: The Experience of Social and Emotional Isolation.* Cambridge, MA: MIT Press.

Weinberger , J. & Smith, B. (2011). Investigating merger: Subliminal psychodynamic activation and oneness in motivation research. *Journal of the American Psychoanalytic Association* 59:557–570.

Wikipedia, (2012a). Broken Heart, http://wikipedia.org/wiki/Broken-Heart

Wikipedia, (2012b). Loneliness, http://en.wikipedia.org/wiki/loneliness

Williams, K. (2011). The pain of exclusion. *Scientific American Mind* January/February, 21:30–37.

Willock, B. (1986). Narcissistic Vulnerability in the Hyperaggressive Child: The Disregarded (Unloved Uncared-for) Self. *Psychoanalytic Psychology* 3:59–80.

——— (1987). The Devalued (Unloved, Repugnant) Self—A Second Facet of Narcissistic Vulnerability in the Aggressive, Conduct-Disordered Child. *Psychoanalytic Psychology* 4:219–240.

319

———— (1990). From acting out to interactive play. *International Journal of Psycho-Analysis* 71:321–334.

———— (2007). *Comparative-Integrative Psychoanalysis.* Hillsdale, NJ: The Analytic Press.

———— (2012a). Loneliness, longing, and limiting theoretical frameworks. In: *Loneliness and Longing: Conscious and Unconscious Aspects,* eds. B.Willock, L.C. Bohm, & R.C. Curtis. London & NY: Routledge, pp. 295–314.

———— (2012b). Loneliness and longing: Crucial aspects of the human experience. In: *Loneliness and Longing: Conscious and Unconscious Aspects,* eds. B. Willock, L.C. Bohm, & R.C. Curtis. London & NY: Routledge , pp. 21–334.

———— (2012c) *Loneliness and Longing: Conscious and Unconscious Aspects.,* eds. B. Willock, L.C. Bohm, & R.C. Curtis. London & New York: Routledge Press.

Wilner, W. (1998). Experience, metaphor and the crucial nature of the analyst's expressive participation. *Contemporary Psychoanalysis* 34: 413–443.

Winnicott, D. W. (1958). The capacity to be alone. *International Journal of Psycho-Analysis* 39:416–420.

———— (1965); *The Maturational Processes and the Facilitating Environment.* New York: International Universities Press.

———— (1969). The use of an object. *International Journal of Psychoanalysis* 50: 711–716.

———— (1988). *Human Nature.* London: Free Association Books.

———— (1971). *Playing and Reality.* London: Tavistock Publications.

———— (1973). *The Child, the Family, and the Outside World.* Middlesex, Da Capo.

———— (1974). Fear of Breakdown. *International Review of Psycho-Analysis.* 1:103–07.

Wolf, E. (1994). Selfobject Experiences: Development, psychopathology, treatment. In: *Mahler and Kohut,* eds. S. Kramer & S. Akhtar. London: Jason Aronson.

Wurmser, L. (2007). *Torment Me, but Don't Abandon Me: Psychoanalysis of the Severe Neuroses in a New Key,* First Edition. New York: Jason Aronson.

Young-Eisendrath, P. (2009). Psychoanalysis as inquiry and discovery, not suspicion. *Contemporary Psychoanalysis* 45:63–370.

Zilboorg, G. (1938), Loneliness. *Atlantic Monthly* 161:45–54.

Contributors

Jerome S. Blackman, M.D., D.F.A.P.A., F.A.C.Psa. is a Professor of Clinical Psychiatry, Eastern Virginia Medical School, Norfolk. Author of *101 Defenses*, *Get the Diagnosis Right*, and *The Therapist's Answer Book* (all printed by Routledge, NY). He is also a member of the Civilian Psychiatry Faculty, Naval Medical Center, Portsmouth, VA.

Alma Halbert Bond received her Ph.D. from Columbia University, and became a highly successful psychoanalyst for 37 years in New York City. *Jackie O: On the Couch*, the first of her On the Couch series to be published by Bancroft Press, received a Pinnacle Book Achievement Award, Indie award for Best Historical fiction, and Finalist International Book Awards. *Margaret Mahler, a Biography of the Psychoanalyst* was published by McFarland Press in 2008, and received two awards. Dr. Bond has had 18 other books published, including *Michelle Obama, a Biography*, which was an International Books Award Finalist. She is currently working on a biography of Marilyn Monroe, to be published by Bancroft Press in the fall of 2013. Her website is Http://alma_bond.tripod.com.

Sandra Buechler, Ph.D. is a Training and Supervising Analyst at the William Alanson White Institute. She is also a supervisor at Columbia Presbyterian Hospital's internship and postdoctoral programs, and a supervisor at the Institute for Contemporary Psychotherapy. A graduate of the William Alanson White Institute, Dr. Buechler has written extensively on emotions in psychoanalysis, including papers on hope, joy, loneliness, and mourning in the analyst and patient. *Clinical Values: Emotions that Guide Psychoanalytic Treatment,* published by Analytic Press, July, 2004, examines the role of hope, courage, the capacity to bear loss, the ability to achieve emotional balance, and other factors in treatment. Her second book, *Making a Difference in Patients' Lives: Emotional Experience in the Therapeutic Setting* (Routledge, 2008), describes her personal view of the process of therapeutic change. *Still Practicing: The Heartaches and Joys of a Clinical Career* (Routledge, 2012) looks at some sources of shame, sorrow, and resilience at various stages of a clinical career.

Amit Goldenberg is currently a graduate student at Hebrew University in Israel, and the Manager of Dr. Eran Halperin's Emotions in Conflict Laboratory at the interdisciplinary school in Herzeliya. This research is focused on group-based guilt, informational self-censorship and militarization processes.

Richard M. Gottlieb, M.D. is Associate Editor for Clinical Studies of the *Journal of the, American Psychoanalytic Association.* He was the founding President of the Berkshire Psychoanalytic Institute and served as the first Chairman of its Education Committee. A recipient of prizes and awards for his writing and teaching, he lectures widely in the U.S. and abroad.

Douglas Ingram, M.D. is a Training & Supervising Analyst, A.I.P. and N.Y. Medical College Psychoanalytic Institute; Clinical Professor of Psychiatry, and former Dean, A.I.P.; Medical Director, Karen Horney Clinic. He received an Award for Excellence from the American College of Psychoanalysts (2008) for his editorship of the *Journal of the American Academy of Psychoanalysis and Dynamic Psychiatry,* and is a past President of the Academy. Editor, Karen Horney's *Final Lectures on Psychoanalytic Technique* (Norton 1987); recent publications include "When Long Term Therapy is Not Long Enough" (*J.A.A.D.P,* Spring, 2011).

Anita Katz, Ph.D., Faculty of N.Y.U. Postdoctoral Program in Psychotherapy and Psychoanalysis, the Object Relations Institute, and the Metropolitan Institute of Psychoanalytic Psychotherapy; Member of I.P.T.A.R. and fellow of I.P.A.; Clinical supervisor at N.Y.U. Postdoctoral Program and C.U.N.Y. Published on Masochism, Fathers and Daughters and many movie reviews, including: *The Vanishing, A Woman Under the Influence, Proof, American Beauty* and *Utz.* Pending publication: *Rupture and Repair.* Various committee work, including the colloquium committee and the Admissions Committee at N.Y.U. Post Doc. Clinical supervisor at N.Y.U. Postdoctoral Program and C.U.N.Y. Published journal articles on oedipal issues encountered throughout the life cycle, a book chapter on Parents Revisiting Adolescent Issues, and a chapter on psychosomatic issues.

Jenny Kahn Kaufmann, Ph.D. is a Supervising Analyst and a faculty member at the William Alanson White Institute. She is a supervisor at Beth Israel Hospital and The Psychological Center at C.U.N.Y. She is interested in trauma and early loss. Jenny works in private practice in New York City.

Peter Kaufmann, Ph.D. is an instructor and supervisor at the Stephen Mitchell Center, the National Institute for the Psychotherapies and the Institute for the Psychoanalytic Study of Subjectivity. He teaches courses on Comparative Psychoanalysis, and is particularly interested in trauma and mourning. Peter is in private practice in New York City.

Danielle Knafo, Ph.D. is a Professor in the Clinical Psychology Doctoral Program at L.I.U. and a faculty member and supervisor at N.Y.U.'s Postdoctoral Program for Psychoanalysis and Psychotherapy. She has written and lectured extensively on psychoanalysis and creativity, gender and trauma. Her most recent book is *Dancing with the Unconscious: The Art of Psychoanalysis and the Psychoanalysis of Art.* She is a clinical psychologist and psychoanalyst and she maintains a private practice in Manhattan and Great Neck, NY.

Arthur A. Lynch, Ph.D. is President of the Board of Directors, a senior faculty member, and a Training and Supervising Analyst at the American Institute for Psychoanalysis. He is an Adjunct Professor at Columbia University School of Social Work, where he has taught for the past 30 years. He is Board Certified in Psychoanalysis and has co-authored numerous articles on comparative and historical psychoanalysis. He is in private practice in New York City.

Eric Mendelsohn, Ph.D. is on the teaching and supervisory faculties at the National Institute for the Psychotherapies, Training Institute and National Training Program; the Westchester Center for the Study of Psychoanalysis and Psychotherapy, and the Postgraduate Program in Psychoanalysis and Psychotherapy at Adelphi University. Dr. Mendelsohn has served in the role of Training Analyst at these institutes. He has also been on the visiting faculty at the Michigan Psychoanalytic Institute. He has written about clinical process and the therapist-patient relationship in analytic therapy.

Lois Oppenheim, Ph.D. is Distinguished Scholar, Professor of French, and Chair of the Department of Modern Languages and Literatures at Montclair State University, where she teaches courses in both literature and applied psychoanalysis. She is also Scholar Associate Member of the New York Psychoanalytic Society and Institute, and Honorary Member of the William Alanson White Society. Dr. Oppenheim has authored or edited eleven books, the most recent being *Imagination from Fantasy to Delusion* (Routledge, 2012), *A Curious Intimacy: Art and Neuro-Psychoanalysis* (Routledge, 2005), and *The Painted Word: Samuel Beckett's Dialogue With Art* (Univ. of Michigan Press, 2000). Dr. Oppenheim continues as host of N.Y.P.S.I.'s popular "Conversations with. . . ." series of discussions on creativity, and is co-creator of the documentary film on mental health stigma (currently in production) called *The Madness Project.*

Arlene Kramer Richards, Ed.D., Fellow, Training and Supervising Analyst, I.P.T.A.R.; Training Analyst, New York Freudian Society & I.P.A.; Faculty, Tongji Medical College of Huazhong University of Science and Technology at Wuhan, China. Former President, Div. 39, A.P.A: Co-Chair APsaA Discussion Group: Towards an Understanding of Loneliness and Aloneness. Coauthor of *Dream Portrait* (IUP 1992); coeditor of*Fantasy, Myth and Reality* [for J. Arlow] (I.U.P. 1988), *The Spectrum of Psychoanalysis* [for M.S. Bergmann] (I.U.P. 1994), and *The Perverse Transference* [for H. Etchegoyen] (Jason Aronson 1997).

Lucille Spira, Ph.D., L.C.S.W., Member, New York School for Psychoanalytic Psychotherapy and Psychoanalysis (N.Y.S.P.P.); Facilitator, N.Y.S.P.P. literary group. Presentations on loneliness at N.Y.S.P.P., N.P.A.P., A.Psa.A.and A.P.A. (Div. 39). Former Adjunct Faculty, N.Y. U. Silver School of Social Work (Doctoral Program) and Hunter College School of Social Work (PostMasters' Program) and NYSPP; Co-Chair APsaA Discussion Group: Towards an Understanding of Loneliness and Aloneness. She has published articles in various psychoanalytic and social work journals on loneliness and other areas of interest.

Jeffrey Stern, Ph.D., core teaching faculty the Chicago Institute for Psychoanalysis; lecturer in Psychiatry, Pritzker School of Medicine, The University of Chicago; Professor of Psychoanalysis, Wuhan University, Wuhan, China. Associate Editor, The Annual of Psychoanalysis. Articles: *Shakespeare Quarterly, The Journal of the American Psychoanalytic Association, Psychoanalytic Review, Psychoanalytic Psychology, The International Journal of the Psychology of the Self.*

Nathan Szajnberg, M.D., Wallerstein Research Fellow in Psychoanalysis; Lecturer, Columbia University.Training Analyst, Israel Psa. Society; Faculty and Chair of Scientific Committee at N.Y.P.S.I.; Member, Assoc. for Psa. Medicine; Former Sigmund Freud Prof. of Psa., Hebrew University. Author of: *Educating the Emotions: Bruno Bettelheim and Psychoanalytic Development* (Springer 1992), *Reluctant Warriors: Israelis Suspended Between Rome and Jerusalem* (IPBooks, 2011); coauthor of *Lives Across Time / Growing Up: Paths to Emotional Health and Emotional Illness* (Karnac 2008). His latest project is a book on Ethiopian/Israeli 6-yr.-olds and their families (in progress).

Patsy Turrini, M.S.W., L.C.S.W., Coauthor of *Separation/Individuation: Theory and Application,* and *Inner World of the Mother.* Has written numerous papers. Faculty, New York School for the Study of Psychotherapy and Psychoanalysis, and Adjunct Faculty, Derner Institute, Adelphi University, Advanced program in Psychoanalysis and Psychotherapy; Originator of the Mothers Center Model, Motherscenters.org.

Jamieson Webster, Ph.D., teaches at Eugene Lang College, is on the faculty at the Institute for Psychoanalytic Training and Research, and supervises in the clinical psychology doctoral program of City University of New York. She is the author of *The Life and Death of Psychoanalysis: On Unconscious Desire and its Sublimation* with Karnac (2011).

Brent Willock, Ph.D. President, Toronto Institute and Society for Contemporary Psychoanalysis. Faculty and member of the Board of Directors, Toronto Child Psychoanalytic Program. Faculty, Institute for the Advancement of Self Psychology. Author, *Comparative-Integrative Psychoanalysis* (Routledge, 2007). First editor, *Loneliness and Longing: Conscious and Unconscious Aspects* (Routledge, 2012).